THE COMPLETE BOOK
OF PREGNANCY
AND CHILDBIRTH

THE COMPLETE BOOK OF PREGNANCY AND CHILDBIRTH

Sheila Kitzinger

Photography by Camilla Jessel

Alfred A. Knopf   New York   1983

The Complete Book of Pregnancy and Childbirth was conceived, edited and designed by Dorling Kindersley Limited, 9 Henrietta Street, London WC2 8PS

Project editor	**Sybil del Strother**
Art editor	**Ginger Weatherley**
Editor	**Lindy Newton**
Designer	**Bob Gordon**
Assistant designer	**Julia Harris**
Consultants for American edition	**Janice Presser Greene Toinette Lippe**
Managing editor	**Jackie Douglas**
Editorial director	**Christopher Davis**
Art director	**Roger Bristow**

This is a Borzoi Book published by Alfred A. Knopf. Inc.

Copyright © 1980 by Dorling Kindersley Ltd, London
Text copyright © 1980 by Sheila Kitzinger

Library of Congress Cataloging in Publication Data

Kitzinger, Sheila.
  The complete book of pregnancy and childbirth.

  Includes index.
  1. Pregnancy. 2. Childbirth. I. Title.
[DNLM: 1. Pregnancy—Popular works. 2. Labor—
Popular works. WQ150 K62c]
RG525.K518   1980   618.2   80–7650
ISBN 0–394–51349–5

Printed in the United States by R. R. Donnelley & Sons
Published December 8, 1980
Reprinted five times
Seventh printing, October 1983

Contents

Introduction

Having a baby has become so complicated in the Western world today that not many women have the chance of simply doing what comes naturally. It has become increasingly difficult for a woman to find a doctor or midwife who will assure her of continuing support and service throughout her pregnancy and labor. These natural events can then sometimes turn into a distressing ordeal.

The modern technology of obstetrics, with its blinking lights and humming machinery, is reassuring for some women but alarms many others. There has been a technological takeover of childbirth in recent years and women's bodies are now often regulated by space age technology and monitoring systems. As a result many mothers feel that it is not they, but the doctors, who are having the baby. Some obstetricians are convinced that their patients should not know more than is "good" for them and should simply give them their trust. It is a concept which this book implicitly questions.

More and more women are deciding that they want to be active birthgivers rather than submit passively to delivery. To do this you need to prepare yourself well in advance with an understanding of how to adapt to the work being done by your uterus, using breathing, relaxation, change of position, massage and focused concentration to "get in tune with" the contractions. So there is a good deal of practical material in the book on how to do this. It is not just a matter of learning exercises. There is a harmony and rhythm about a natural labor; with each contraction wave you are swept on toward the birth of the baby, in a pattern which makes of labor a process greater than all its separate parts and in which all techniques are submerged by the total satisfying experience.

This book describes the choices which are available so that you can decide how you would like to have your baby, the kind of setting and care you prefer, how you see your own role and how you wish your baby to be welcomed into the world. I include suggestions on talking with your doctor, how to present what you want, ask about all the things which worry you and share in making the important decisions about yourself and your baby. The book also sets out to give a kind of map of the route through pregnancy and labor and out the other side, explaining who does what to you and why, what they are looking for and what happens when things are not straightforward. In doing this I have tried to use some of the words and phrases that you may hear used or see written on your chart so that you will understand them when you meet them.

Since an increasing number of couples want to be together during the important time of birth, and share in it fully, the book is threaded through with recognition of the father's importance for his partner and baby and suggestions as to how he can help most effectively during pregnancy, labor and the time after the birth. A baby is bound to change a couple's life style, their feelings about each other and the kind of partnership they have. The man, as well as the woman, often faces emotional challenges, and this is rarely acknowledged in our society. So another thing that I have done in this book is to focus on the experience of childbirth for him.

The powerful emotions which exist between a mother and her newborn baby have a biological survival value for the human species. The minutes, hours and days immediately following birth are among the most important for the baby and the new mother. They are literally "getting in touch" with each other. This is an important time for the new father, too, and for any other children of the family, since "bonding" occurs not only between the mother and the baby but also between the father and baby and the siblings as well.

Most new parents gain in confidence and find it easiest to have "conversations" with their baby when they are in an environment where they feel safe and among friends, when they can explore their baby, take it into bed with them and stroke, hold and cuddle it as much as they wish, and when there are no rules to be obeyed or standards to live up to. In this book I hope to show how a couple can create the kind of setting and atmosphere for birth, whether at home or in the hospital, which nourishes relationships in the family. The way in which a baby is greeted is a matter not only of plans, methods and systems, but of human emotions, and the spark which gives life and color to the interaction between a couple and their child is the spontaneous emotion experienced by both parents. I believe that we need to give much more thought to the environment in which the powerful emotions connected with birth can have free expression and in which both partners in the relationship can really be *themselves*.

Caring for the emotional aspects of birth is not a question of pampering or indulgent treatment of women. It is absolutely basic to the welding of the ties which bind human beings together in a family and families into the larger society. This is why I write not only about medical events, but about the quality of relationships important between people and the kind of society we want to create.

Pregnancy and childbirth are normal life processes, not illnesses. You feel the incredible surge of life moving inside you, the ripening of your body heavy with fruit deep inside it, and then at last the flood of vitality as labor starts and your uterus contracts in wave after wave bringing your baby into your arms. It is exciting, awe inspiring and deeply satisfying. At the same time you grow up a bit, learn more about yourself and your partner, develop in understanding and awareness. I hope that this book will help you to savor the intense reality of the experience of childbearing and enjoy it to the full.

Notes to the reader It is always difficult when writing about babies to know whether to use "he" or "she". By convention they are usually called "he", and this is often easiest in practice as it distinguishes the baby from the mother. Although I sometimes call the baby "it", I have mainly used a mixture of "he" and "she", since babies are people with their own budding personalities right from the start. I hope that the reader will not find this too awkward and if there is a bias towards "she", note that my five babies were all girls, so it comes naturally to me.

Throughout the text references to research are marked with an asterisk (*); this indicates that the works in which the research findings have been published are given in Appendix 2, page 333, under the appropriate page number.

Author's acknowledgments I should like to thank all those women who have helped me understand more about the experience of childbirth and how it was for them. From every couple I have taught I have learned something new or seen things in a different light. I have learned far more than I have ever taught.

My husband, Uwe, and our five daughters, Celia, Nell, Tess, Polly and Jenny are generous in their acceptance of my work, the time I give to couples having babies and the inevitable phone calls punctuating family get togethers and meals. Knowing that Uwe values what I am doing and gives me his full emotional support generates fresh strength in me to carry on when the going gets rough.

Sybil del Strother of Dorling Kindersley has been a skilled and understanding editor; she and her team really soaked themselves in the subject of birth. I know readers will enjoy the photographs by Camilla Jessel who also studied very carefully my approach to birth so that she could express this in the photographs. And my special thanks go to Eleanor Enkin whose gorgeous photographs of mothers and families and babies in her husband's obstetric unit at McMaster University Hospital, Hamilton, Ontario, formed the basis for the drawings which focus on family centered care. Murray Enkin, Associate Professor of Obstetrics at McMaster, read every single word of the text and looked at it from a medical point of view, but often commented too as a warm and caring human being. I have learned a great deal about human relations in the hospital from both Murray and Eleanor.

The main part of the book was typed by Audrey Macefield, a marvelous secretary, and the final portion by Margaret Pearson, my present secretary, whose help and lively interest and commitment I value deeply.

Giving birth

*One birth...not especially difficult,
nor especially easy...not a
formula, not a blueprint...just some
moments during a labor and the
beginnings of a new life.*

…in the first stage the contractions of the uterus dilate the cervix…

…in the second stage the head is being pressed down through the birth canal…

*...then baby's head crowns
slides out face down...*

...the head rotates...

...the mother reaches down to touch her baby before it is born...

...the moment of birth...gently, quietly, the baby is lifted and placed in close, warm contact with her skin...

...she takes his hand to tell him that all is well in this world of new sensations...

*...now both parents are absorbed in the
reality of their newborn, caressing him
with their hands...*

...when the baby is ready he will fasten on to his mother's breast...

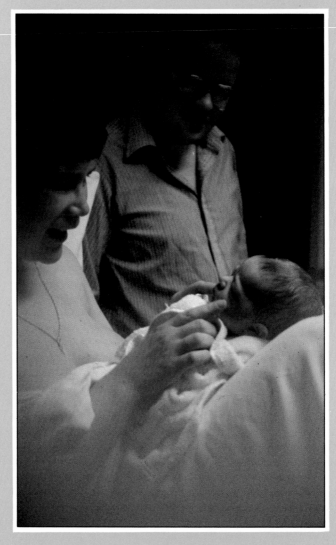

...not only a new baby is born,
but a new family too.

PREGNANCY: THE EARLY WEEKS

Finding out you are pregnant
Planning & preparation

Finding out
you are pregnant

Some women are convinced that they are pregnant from the moment of conception, while others have such irregular periods that a long gap in between does not alert them to the possibility of pregnancy. But for most women the first sign of pregnancy is a missed period.

Perhaps it is five days since the day when you expected it, but then you start wondering if your dates were wrong. Perhaps you usually make a note on your calendar, but last time you forgot. You lie in bed, unable to sleep, trying to fix the dates firmly in your mind by finding some useful landmark, like your mother's visit or the end of a particular work assignment. Still another three days go by and the reality gradually dawns: you might be pregnant. You might not be, but it does seem quite possible that you are. When should you go to the doctor and how early can you know if you are really pregnant?

When to diagnose   Until recently it was usual to visit the doctor after missing two periods. Nowadays there is a strong case for finding out if you are pregnant before two periods have been missed. It is during these few weeks, before the pregnancy is confirmed and while the embryo is still no larger than a grape, that the major organs of the body and the brain itself are being formed; the sooner you know that you are pregnant the sooner you can start caring for yourself and for the baby.

An early confirmation of pregnancy is also important if you take any medicines, including tranquilizers, sleeping pills and over-the-counter preparations. You will want to avoid taking drugs which could harm the developing baby (see page 90). It is also useful to know early for social reasons—you may want to take a trip or redecorate at the time the baby is due.

If there is a possibility that you may want an abortion it is essential to diagnose pregnancy early: an abortion at eight weeks is much safer and less upsetting than one after ten weeks. The sooner you discover that you are pregnant, the earlier the challenge of parenthood becomes a reality to you, and you can start to plan for how life is bound to change after the birth.

How to diagnose   Pregnancy can be diagnosed a week or ten days after you miss your first period. An embryo releases large quantities of a hormone called human chorionic gonadotrophin (HCG) into your bloodstream from around eight days after your period has been missed—about 20 days after conception. The presence or absence of this hormone can be detected in your urine by means of a simple test. You can either take a urine sample into your local physician, or to a clinic that does pregnancy testing, or you can use one of the do-it-yourself kits. Whichever method you choose, you should test the first urine passed, on a day when you have not drunk anything during the previous night or first thing in the morning. Drinking dilutes the urine, which contains a higher concentration of hormones at this time than at any other point of the day. Store the urine in an absolutely clean jar or bottle, free from any traces of soap or detergent. You then either take it in, send it off to be tested, or test it yourself.

Do-it-yourself test To carry out a urine pregnancy test yourself, you mix a drop of urine with the chemicals provided in the kit. If you are pregnant, the presence of HCG in your urine will prevent the mixture from coagulating. It is important to follow

A do-it-yourself pregnancy test
After collecting the first urine of the day and following the instructions below, you must wait exactly two hours for the result. If you are pregnant, the chemicals in the test will react with a hormone (HCG) in your urine to form a dark ring, which is a positive result. If you are not pregnant, no ring will form and the result is negative. These results can be seen in the mirror.

Test tube
Plastic tube
Mirror
Lid

Positive   Negative

1 *Remove the stopper from the test tube, and empty the contents of the plastic tube into it.*

2 *Draw up some of the urine passed first thing in the morning into the (now empty) plastic tube.*

3 *Squeeze exactly three drops of urine into the test tube, and replace the stopper.*

4 *Shake the test tube well for 10 seconds; then replace it in the box and leave it for 2 hours.*

the instructions enclosed with do-it-yourself pregnancy tests very carefully, and best to wait for two weeks after you have missed a period (six weeks from the first day of your last period if your cycle is average) before carrying out a test. By then there is less chance of a false result than there is earlier on, and if the result is positive you are almost certainly pregnant. If the result is negative, but your period has still not come a few days later, do the test again. It is possible that you conceived later than you thought likely and that at the time of the first test there was not enough pregnancy hormone in your urine to indicate pregnancy. If your periods are irregular or far apart the chances of a false result are increased. The result may also be falsely negative if you are taking anti-depressants or if you are near the menopause. Wait a few more days before doing the test again.

Going to the doctor If you take a specimen of urine with you, the doctor can have it tested, and you will also be given an internal examination. He or she introduces two gloved fingers into your vagina as far as they will go, while pressing with the other hand into your abdomen where the top of the uterus lies. If it is more than six weeks since the first day of your last period the doctor can feel the already softened lower part of the uterus, which is also slightly enlarged. The neck of the uterus, or cervix, which protrudes into the vagina, is felt as firmer than the lower part of the uterus, and is about the same consistency as the tip of your nose. This internal change is known as "Hegar's sign".

The examination may be uncomfortable but will not be painful. As the examining fingers are introduced, give a long, slow breath out through your mouth and continue breathing as slowly as you can.

HAVING A VAGINAL EXAMINATION
You may be examined vaginally early on in your pregnancy. If you are more than 6 weeks pregnant the doctor can detect a slight softening and enlargement of the uterus. The developing embryo is well protected and cannot be dislodged by the examination.

Dating Once the pregnancy is confirmed by your doctor it will be dated from the first day of your last menstrual period. If you cannot recollect this date with accuracy the doctor will probably ask you to make a guess at it. This means that from then on the length of your pregnancy is calculated in terms of so many weeks, including the weeks from the beginning of your last period to the time when conception occurred. Since ovulation is most common midway between two periods, the usual medical way of dating pregnancy adds an extra two weeks to its length. The length of the average pregnancy is approximately 266 days from the date of conception: your doctor will therefore arrive at your expected date of delivery (the EDD) by adding 280 days, or 40 weeks, to the first day of your last period (the chart below is

When is your baby due?
Look down the columns of the chart at the figures set in bold type to find the first day of your last period. The date next to it is 280 days later, and is therefore your estimated date of delivery (EDD).

Jan Oct	Feb Nov	Mar Dec	Apr Jan	May Feb	June Mar	July Apr	Aug May	Sept June	Oct July	Nov Aug	Dec Sept
1 8	1 8	1 6	1 6	1 5	1 8	1 7	1 8	1 8	1 8	1 8	1 7
2 9	2 9	2 7	2 7	2 6	2 9	2 8	2 9	2 9	2 9	2 9	2 8
3 10	3 10	3 8	3 8	3 7	3 10	3 9	3 10	3 10	3 10	3 10	3 9
4 11	4 11	4 9	4 9	4 8	4 11	4 10	4 11	4 11	4 11	4 11	4 10
5 12	5 12	5 10	5 10	5 9	5 12	5 11	5 12	5 12	5 12	5 12	5 11
6 13	6 13	6 11	6 11	6 10	6 13	6 12	6 13	6 13	6 13	6 13	6 12
7 14	7 14	7 12	7 12	7 11	7 14	7 13	7 14	7 14	7 14	7 14	7 13
8 15	8 15	8 13	8 13	8 12	8 15	8 14	8 15	8 15	8 15	8 15	8 14
9 16	9 16	9 14	9 14	9 13	9 16	9 15	9 16	9 16	9 16	9 16	9 15
10 17	10 17	10 15	10 15	10 14	10 17	10 16	10 17	10 17	10 17	10 17	10 16
11 18	11 18	11 16	11 16	11 15	11 18	11 17	11 18	11 18	11 18	11 18	11 17
12 19	12 19	12 17	12 17	12 16	12 19	12 18	12 19	12 19	12 19	12 19	12 18
13 20	13 20	13 18	13 18	13 17	13 20	13 19	13 20	13 20	13 20	13 20	13 19
14 21	14 21	14 19	14 19	14 18	14 21	14 20	14 21	14 21	14 21	14 21	14 20
15 22	15 22	15 20	15 20	15 19	15 22	15 21	15 22	15 22	15 22	15 22	15 21
16 23	16 23	16 21	16 21	16 20	16 23	16 22	16 23	16 23	16 23	16 23	16 22
17 24	17 24	17 22	17 22	17 21	17 24	17 23	17 24	17 24	17 24	17 24	17 23
18 25	18 25	18 23	18 23	18 22	18 25	18 24	18 25	18 25	18 25	18 25	18 24
19 26	19 26	19 24	19 24	19 23	19 26	19 25	19 26	19 26	19 26	19 26	19 25
20 27	20 27	20 25	20 25	20 24	20 27	20 26	20 27	20 27	20 27	20 27	20 26
21 28	21 28	21 26	21 26	21 25	21 28	21 27	21 28	21 28	21 28	21 28	21 27
22 29	22 29	22 27	22 27	22 26	22 29	22 28	22 29	22 29	22 29	22 29	22 28
23 30	23 30	23 28	23 28	23 27	23 30	23 29	23 30	23 30	23 30	23 30	23 29
24 31	24 1	24 29	24 29	24 28	24 31	24 30	24 31	24 1	24 31	24 31	24 30
25 1	25 2	25 30	25 30	25 1	25 1	25 1	25 1	25 2	25 1	25 1	25 1
26 2	26 3	26 31	26 31	26 2	26 2	26 2	26 2	26 3	26 2	26 2	26 2
27 3	27 4	27 1	27 1	27 3	27 3	27 3	27 3	27 4	27 3	27 3	27 3
28 4	28 5	28 2	28 2	28 4	28 4	28 4	28 4	28 5	28 4	28 4	28 4
29 5		29 3	29 3	29 5	29 5	29 5	29 5	29 6	29 5	29 5	29 5
30 6		30 4	30 4	30 6	30 6	30 6	30 6	30 7	30 6	30 6	30 6
31 7		31 5		31 7		31 7	31 7		31 7		31 7
Jan Nov	Feb Dec	Mar Jan	Apr Feb	May Mar	June Apr	July May	Aug June	Sept July	Oct Aug	Nov Sept	Dec Oct

calculated according to this convention). You may find that you pay your first visit to the clinic knowing that it is ten weeks since you conceived, but emerge three months pregnant!

But since not all women ovulate halfway between two periods, the medical convention of adding on an extra two weeks is an artificial one, and an inaccurate method of working out when a baby is due. It is wise to think of the EDD as an approximate estimation rather than the day when you expect to go into labor.

If you have just stopped taking the birth-control pill your dates may be completely wrong. The period which immediately follows your last pill may not be followed by ovulation or you may have a slight spotting of blood which is not really a period. It may take several months to reestablish your natural cycle, and until then you cannot predict with any certainty when, or whether, you are going to ovulate. You might be a month or more out in your dates. This is obviously very important in estimating when the baby is due, especially since it could mean labor being induced unnecessarily (see page 252). It is advisable to wait for at least three months after stopping the pill before trying to conceive; during this time you should use some other method of contraception.

Conceiving while using contraception If you conceive with an IUD (intrauterine device or coil) still inside you, your chances of miscarrying increase. It is important to see your doctor quickly, as the IUD should be removed if possible and this can only be done early in pregnancy. Sometimes doctors advise abortion. This is certainly not necessary if you want the baby: even if it is too late to remove the IUD, many women deliver the IUD with the placenta after an uneventful pregnancy and birth.

It is possible to conceive while taking the pill, if you miss one or more days when you should have been taking it or if you have a stomach upset with vomiting so that you fail to absorb the hormones. If you do conceive but continue to take the pill for several months while pregnant, there is a slightly increased risk to the baby of congenital abnormalities. But the vast majority of women who have taken the pill while pregnant give birth to babies who appear healthy and normal.

Sometimes a doctor prescribes pills containing the hormones estrogen and progesterone to discover whether or not a woman is pregnant, the idea being that you take them and if you are not pregnant your period starts. These hormone pills carry the same slight risk to the baby as the pill does: do not take them.

Early signs **Breast changes** Even before your pregnancy is confirmed there may be early indications other than a missed period. Breast changes, in preparation for milk production, occur in the first weeks. The brownish circles round the nipples (the areolae) become darker and the little bumps on them (Montgomery's tubercles) more prominent. If you are pink-skinned, you may notice that the lacy network of blood vessels in your breasts has

You may notice changes in your breasts early in pregnancy, including an increase in size, a darkening of the nipples and the areolae, and extra prominence of the little bumps on the areolae known as Montgomery's tubercles.

become much more obvious. Blue veins run over the breasts like rivers on a map. Your breasts also feel tender and heavy. Women with small breasts may note an obvious increase in size very early on, and are often delighted. If you have large breasts already, you may not notice any size change at this stage.

Tiredness Enormous metabolic changes take place in pregnancy and your whole body has to adjust to the process of growing a baby. It is not surprising that you may feel tired and that you cannot carry on just as before. Many women complain of extreme tiredness in the first eight or ten weeks. But as your body adjusts to the pregnancy the fatigue vanishes and the middle months are often easy. If you are feeling tired, it is only sensible to take the message from your body and go to bed early or have an early evening nap when you get in from work.

If it is your second (or third) pregnancy, you may find that you are constantly tired. Women who thoroughly enjoyed their first pregnancy say that the second one is much harder to cope with because they are exhausted by the non-stop pace of their first child's daily life. The only solution is to organize your life as well as you can; try to have at least a short time every day when you are completely free from domestic responsibilities. Even half an hour every evening when your partner attends to the child and the dishes can be relaxing if you enjoy it to the full. (See page 152 for more information about second and later pregnancies.)

Nausea Another common sign of pregnancy is nausea. These waves of sickness often happen early in the morning, but they may also occur in the early evening, or even—more rarely—at other times of the day. Some women just feel very sick, others actually vomit. Tiredness contributes to nausea, but so does an empty stomach: small frequent snacks of high protein foods may relieve the feeling. If you suffer from morning sickness, a cup of tea and a few crackers or dry toast immediately on waking may prevent the nausea—keep the crackers beside your bed. As a general rule cut out all greasy fried foods, tobacco, and alcohol. Some women become really ill with vomiting (see page 118), although most stop feeling sick during the fourth month of pregnancy.

There is some evidence that women who experience pregnancy nausea are less likely than others to have miscarriages. This can be a cheering thought. But nausea does not exist in all cultures; many societies have other illnesses and disabilities or special dreams which they connect with pregnancy. Margaret Mead points out that in some societies of New Guinea boils are considered to be a typical symptom of pregnancy. Some Jamaicans do not acknowledge pregnancy until they have had a special fertility dream of ripe fruit bursting with seed. Dreams of this kind are characteristic of early pregnancy. It is as if all women need definite signs with which to link pregnancy so that they can say, "I feel this, therefore I must be expecting a baby."

66 The first 3 months were wretched because I had continual nausea. I worried about what this might be doing to our baby—but here she is, chubby and beautiful. It doesn't seem to have affected her at all. **99**

You may suffer from nausea for the first time in your second or third pregnancy. This is almost certainly as a result of tiredness, and you may not relieve the nausea within three months unless you can somehow arrange to have more rest.

Emotional reactions to pregnancy

66 We're over the moon! I never believed it could happen to me. I feel so pleased with myself. I know it's ridiculous, but it's as if I was the first human being ever to have a baby! 99

However much you want a baby, finding out that you really are pregnant can produce a flood of conflicting emotions: triumph ("We've done it!"), a sense of being trapped ("There's no going back—now what?"), fear ("Mother had an awful time having me—shall I be able to stand the pain?"), apprehension ("Will we still love each other in the same way?") and doubt ("Will he still want me once my waist starts getting thicker?"). It is surprising how many women respond to their first pregnancy with shock and feel that it has happened "too soon", even though they very much want a baby and have considered the matter carefully before stopping contraception. Confronted with the reality and the physical changes of pregnancy, they want to say: "Stop! I haven't prepared myself for this. Let's go back and start again."

If you discover that you are pregnant when you did not plan to be, you may also feel unfairly trapped. Yet, perversely, many women (for whom pregnancy is not a disaster) are aware of an odd pleasure that their fertility has triumphed over their conscious wish. Your partner may suspect that you wanted a baby all along and have not been "playing fair". Starting a baby under such circumstances can lead to conflict between you, because he may feel that you have not been open with him. Try not to go off and discuss the matter with other people as if your man were the enemy. Talk about it together: you need to understand each other.

Feelings about motherhood You may have a crisis of self-confidence, feeling that you will be no good as a mother because you have no maternal instincts. But mothering is a learned activity and very little of it purely instinctive. Moreover for the first-time mother in our society, who may never have handled a newborn baby before, most of the learning goes on after the baby is born. The teacher is the baby. You may not start off as an expert, but your baby soon turns you into one.

Feelings about being on show You may feel suddenly that your most intimate relationship with the man you love is publicly displayed, not just because you are pregnant and everybody knows, but because of the physical examinations and exposure at the prenatal clinic, and the advice that people keep giving you. This sense of becoming public property may be intensified by the obvious pleasure of parents who have been wanting you to get pregnant for a long time.

Yet your body holds life. The wonder of that cannot really be understood by anyone else. You stand naked in front of the mirror and look for changes. You rest your hand on your tummy and wonder if you can feel the tiny seed of a baby beginning to grow inside you. You think back to when you made love, wonder which time it was and if, perhaps, you really knew then that you had conceived.

Feelings about your body If you feel on bad terms with your body as it starts out on the work of early pregnancy, arrange to attend some pregnancy exercise or dance classes if these are available in your area. A list of organizations which can help you is on page 337. If these classes are not specially for pregnant women, let your teacher know that you are pregnant. Get out in the fresh air and walk. Start doing the movements suggested on pages 104–105 a few times each day to pep up your circulation and increase vitality. In some countries massage is an anticipated and very pleasant part of being pregnant, so you could go to a masseuse or your partner could learn how to massage you (see page 165). This can be particularly useful if you are tense and find it difficult to relax.

Feelings of your partner You are not the only person who has to adjust emotionally in pregnancy. Your partner needs to as well. He does not have to cope with physical changes, but the emotional impact of a first pregnancy is no less real, and the passage into fatherhood constitutes a major transition in his life. For a man this process is often delayed until several things have happened: the pregnancy has been officially confirmed; your figure has obviously changed; the baby has moved and he has felt it fluttering.

Emotions of joy, pride and wonder may war with others which are disturbing. There may be financial problems which can cause a man to feel a sense of deep and burdensome responsibility for the woman bearing his child and for the new life that is coming. A man, too, may feel trapped by pregnancy. Perhaps his relationship with the woman was intended to remain free and untrammeled by babies (especially if the couple have not discussed pregnancy and planned for it together). His job may now assume importance not only in its own right, but because he feels an urgent need to be successful before the baby comes, as if it threatens his own powers of achievement. A man, too, may be frightened of birth and even of his partner's pregnant body, which can seem dangerous and not to be touched in case the baby is dislodged. He may feel, quite wrongly, that his own sexual desires are a terrible threat to the baby. For some men the whole of pregnancy is a time of stress.

Discussing your emotions together It does not help to bottle up these emotions. Talk about them together. If you pretend they are not there, they become destructive. What you are feeling is normal and thousands of other couples experience it too. It may be possible to work out together a sensible strategy so that some parts of your lives are left free from responsibility: you could avoid relatives until you feel better able to cope with them, or you may be able to arrange to visit the prenatal clinic together, so that your partner can

Finding that your clothes don't fit any more may be the first time that you really believe you are pregnant. . . .

meet the doctor and be present during the physical examination. Reading together about birth helps to replace ignorance with knowledge about the role a man can actively play in childbirth.

Lying together in bed, cuddling, and exploring each other's bodies is a way of communicating through loving touch and tenderness. It is a way of nourishing your partnership, making it ready for the new person who is entering it. Since words often disguise your real feelings and complicate matters, find opportunities to meet each other through touch.

Pregnancy is not merely a waiting time. It is a time for working out together what you value in your relationship and what kind of world you both want to create for your child. This is not a question of furnishing a nursery and making things ready for the baby, but of helping each other to change from people who are responsible just for themselves into a mother and a father, with the new responsibility that parenthood brings. A man and a woman need to grow into parents. Then not only a baby, but a new family is born.

The woman alone

66 I've always had irregular periods so I didn't notice. The doctor said "Do you realize you're pregnant?" I was stunned! Alan's married you know. It was too late for an abortion. 99

Pregnancy and childbirth are not easy when you do not have a partner to give you love and care. It is even more difficult once the baby is born to take complete responsibility for a new life. Yet many women have done this successfully and have reared happy, healthy children.

Talking about the single mother and the challenges she faces is in a way misleading, because women on their own bearing babies do not fall into one category any more than women with partners do. The reasons why single women embark on pregnancy, and decide to go on with it, vary widely. Some women continue with a pregnancy only because they are unwilling or unable to face up to it, and drift on hoping that it might go away. Others are bearing a much-wanted child "before it is too late". Others again loved the father of the child and hoped that the relationship would continue, but then found themselves rejected and bearing a child alone. Then there are women whose men die while they are pregnant, leaving them to face the future alone.

Whatever your reasons for having a child on your own, financial problems may loom large. Trying to combine a job with rearing a child, while knowing that there is no one else to take over in time of need, can be difficult. It is important to anticipate and share the problems, and a good idea to seek counseling from people who understand them and who may be able to put you in touch with other sources of help. Contact the organizations listed on page 337 before you have your baby and see what they have to offer. These organizations are also designed to help you cope with all the practical difficulties that can crop up, such as housing, finding day care for the baby and sorting out which benefits you are entitled to.

Register for childbirth education classes (see page 158) early. Many women delay and then find that the classes are full. The International Childbirth Education Association and the American

35

Society for Psychoprophylaxis in Obstetrics (addresses on page 337) can tell you about classes, postnatal support and breast-feeding counseling in your locality.

Sometimes a man who is not your permanent partner is still willing to accept some of the responsibilities of fatherhood. It is quite common in a prenatal class to have couples who do not plan to marry or even to stay together. Be frank with your childbirth educator so that she has a chance to get to know you, and perhaps both of you, as people and not just as students. It may be possible to arrange to see her privately for a session.

Emotional support in labor

66 I was so pleased to see Ann come through the door. I coped with a difficult labor only because of her, and think without her I might have gone under. 99

Think ahead to the birth and decide whether you would like to have a companion with you. Childbirth can feel very solitary if you do not have someone with you to encourage you and provide continuous emotional support. This person could be a good woman friend, a childbirth educator, your sister or mother, or a man friend who understands what birth is about and can give the right kind of help. Most hospitals nowadays allow a companion in labor, although they often restrict you to one person, and sometimes they state that it must be the father of the baby. Discuss the matter with your doctor and with your childbirth educator, and if necessary state your request in writing to the Medical Director of the hospital or in person to the Director of Nursing.

If there is no one who can be with you in labor, discuss the subject in advance with your obstetrician. Say that you would particularly value someone as a companion to be with you throughout labor, and that you do not know anyone who can come with you; ask whether there is anyone in the hospital—preferably someone you could meet beforehand—who could be with you. The doctor may say that you will have the nurses and will not be left alone. But a labor companion is different and is simply there as a friend, to give you emotional support and to remind you of your relaxation and breathing. If you are in a teaching hospital there will almost certainly be a student nurse who can do this. If it is a midwifery training school there is usually a student midwife who can fill the same role.

But suppose that you have to be without a companion in labor. Make the nurse your friend and ask her for help. Unfortunately there is not much continuity of care in hospitals, and you may have to get to know two or three nurses, one after another, which is asking a lot of someone in active labor. On the other hand, sometimes a midwife will stay on duty so that she can be with you until after the delivery.

Managing alone

If your man has been unwilling to accept responsibility or perhaps even acknowledge your pregnancy, you probably feel angry and resentful. One woman, who had been told she could never have a baby but who found herself pregnant, said, "I hadn't realized just how much his marriage was a going concern.

Just when I most needed him I had to come to terms with the fact that he didn't want to break up his marriage and was devoted to his kids. In fact, my pregnancy was terribly embarrassing for him! I suddenly felt dreadfully on my own. I didn't hear from him through a large part of the pregnancy because it was the summer holidays and he went abroad with his family."

Another woman's husband left her when she was four months pregnant because he said he could not stand the idea of a third child. He had left her several times before for short periods and the baby was conceived during a reconciliation. Her great fear was that she would find him on the doorstep again, since she had been through so much emotional turmoil that she did not feel she could cope mentally with any more scenes and upheavals. This led to a strained and difficult pregnancy, followed by a prolonged labor and forceps delivery because of incoordinate uterine action.

A university lecturer who had decided in advance that she wanted a baby but not a man said that her colleagues accepted this but that she found it hard to tell her family: "Mother thought I was mad and said how could she ever let her friends know. I thought about them all at their coffee mornings and thought, 'Oh my God, I don't suppose she can.' I thought it would be hardest explaining to my 80-year-old grandmother but she was the one who understood best." This woman could not go home when her pregnancy became obvious because of the effect on her parents' neighbors and friends, although her parents did adjust to the idea after the baby was born and became proud grandparents.

Some women are rejected by parents, although one girl said: "In a way I rejected *them* and their values, by going ahead and having the baby." Even so, however "free" of your parents you feel and however you delight in being independent of them, cutting roots like this can be extremely painful. You may feel guilty, even if you do not accept the social conventions which thrust the feelings of guilt upon you. You may worry about imposing your views on your child, who will learn that in friends' houses there is a father as well as a mother.

Yet single mothers all stress that you do need help and must have the grace to accept it, for your child's sake as well as yours. There are the all-important questions of where you are going to live, what you are going to live on, whether you should and can go back to work, and if so when. You must also consider how you are going to retain any sort of mobility with a baby, how you will deal with the relationship between sex, motherhood, the other things you want to do and the needs you want to fulfil, and how you are going to feel when things are difficult or impossible because of the baby. Many of the difficulties confronted by single women are the same as those faced by women with partners, but intensified because the women are alone and unsupported. As one girl said, in order to go through with having a baby on your own, "You need to *really want* that child!"

Planning & preparation

Throughout history most babies were born at home. Maternity hospitals were first started for homeless women and were really extensions of the poor-houses. Many of the babies born in these hospitals were then put in foundling institutions. These first maternity hospitals were convenient centers for medical students to learn and practice obstetrics, but infection was rampant, as doctors conveyed bacteria on their hands from one patient to another, and many babies and mothers died. They were the most dangerous places in which women could possibly give birth.

The twentieth century saw a revolution in hospital obstetrics so that, instead of being the most dangerous places to have a baby, most modern hospitals are now the safest. Yet, despite these extremely rapid advances, and the tendency for most doctors to recommend a hospital birth, many women still feel that a home birth would be the most appropriate for their particular requirements.

Where would you like to have your baby?

66 My husband is a very nervous man. I've decided on hospital. 99

66 Home! I want to do it *my* way. 99

Even before you become pregnant, it is worth thinking about whether you would like to have your baby at home or in hospital and discussing it with your doctor. You may have decided, for example, that you would prefer to have your baby at home, yet discover that your doctor is unwilling or unable to attend you. If there are no specific medical reasons for this, you might want to change your doctor before you start a pregnancy. Whether you want to have a home birth or a hospital birth, it is important to inform your doctor as early in your pregnancy as possible, as it is often difficult to change your mind once wheels have been set in motion. It is a good idea to make a list of the things that are really important to you about the birth and the time immediately after and to decide which environment best meets your requirements, home or hospital.

Hospital birth

Most women who decide to have babies in the hospital do so primarily because they are convinced it is the safest place. They want to be sure that all the skills and equipment of modern obstetrics are at hand for their babies' sake. For some women, especially those having their first child, giving birth is a frightening experience, a step in the dark, and they feel more secure in the knowledge that they are in the hands of people who have been specially trained to cope with any possible emergency. Often a woman who fears that the labor will be painful opts for a hospital delivery, knowing that certain painkillers are available only in hospital and not wanting to take the chance of finding herself without necessary relief from pain when it is too late to change her mind.

Once you know you are pregnant find out all you can about childbirth so that you know what to ask for and who can help. . . .

Sometimes a woman may know and trust a particular obstetrician and want to be cared for by this person, while another wants to go to hospital because she feels she would benefit from a period of release from the pressures of home and family. Occasionally a woman's husband wants her to go to hospital because he is very worried about birth at home. He may just be frightened of being involved, but more often he is afraid he might have to deliver the baby himself.

Medical
reasons for
hospital birth

As well as those women who would prefer the security of a hospital birth, there are those for whom it is advisable to give birth in hospital whatever their personal preferences. It is wise to consider hospital care if you have diabetes, a heart or kidney condition, or if you smoke cigarettes regularly (see page 91). Your doctor will also send you to hospital if you develop pre-eclampsia (see page 121) or if you go into labor three weeks or more before the baby is due; you will probably be advised against home delivery if your baby is breech, since it may need help with breathing immediately after birth (see page 286). There are really no absolutes, but there are certain things which make childbirth a little more risky.

If you are to be a first-time mother over 30, for instance, labor *may* be longer than if you were younger and many doctors would advise you to be in hospital so that you can have labor speeded up or help with the delivery. Many doctors believe that all first-time mothers (primigravidas) should give birth in the hospital because, they say, a labor is only normal in retrospect and there is always a small chance that even after a perfectly normal pregnancy you may have complications which will entail you being moved to hospital at the last minute.

If you have had a hemorrhage with a previous labor, either before or after the delivery, it is wise to choose a hospital birth because you may need a quick blood transfusion if it happens again. The same goes for a retained placenta or a delayed third stage in a previous labor. If you are very short, under 5ft 2in (1·55m), or take a size 5 shoe or less, your pelvis may be a tight fit for the baby to get through, though many short women do give birth easily. Any other indications of disproportion, because of the way the baby is lying, for example, should also make you plan for a hospital birth.

Three or more miscarriages are another reason for having the baby in hospital, because previous problems of this kind *may* mean that labor will present problems (though often everything is straightforward). Obviously, if you have lost a baby because of a difficult birth, you are unlikely to take the small but real additional risk of a home birth and will want to know that, if the baby should need it, intensive care is available at the hospital where you are giving birth. Doctors also advise mothers of twins to give birth in hospital, partly because they are very likely to come early and to be of low birthweight and partly because the second twin can get stuck (see pages 78–83).

Choices in hospital care

There are two main kinds of hospital obstetrical care: private and service (clinic). In addition, many hospitals are beginning to offer a certified nurse midwife program. If you have decided that a hospital birth is right for you, you will need to think about the alternatives available to you within the hospital system.

The private obstetrician Most women choose a private obstetrician who is affiliated with a hospital near their home. This may be convenient, but it is even more important to find an obstetrician whom you like and who understands the kind of birth for which you hope and is prepared to help you have it.

Finding a private obstetrician with whom you have a good relationship can be difficult. Most obstetricians in the United States are men and may not see your point of view about birth. Go to the first visit with a list of questions so that you can make your decision on a practical basis. Some questions you might want answered include:

What is your policy on induction?
When do you recommend induction?
What percentage of your patients had a natural unmedicated birth last year?
Do you routinely order medications, intravenous drips (IV), enemas, monitors, or do you judge each situation individually?
What position do most of the women you deliver adopt for the second stage?
Are they encouraged to try different positions?
Do these include kneeling, being on all fours and squatting?
Do you usually hand the naked baby straight to the mother?
Can the mother lift the baby out herself if she wishes?
Are you willing to wait for the cord to stop pulsating before clamping it?
How much time do the mother and baby normally have skin contact following delivery?
Can the baby be put to the breast on the delivery table?
Are you willing to dim the lights when the baby is born?
Do you routinely suction the baby at delivery?
If the baby is breathing well would you be willing to wait and see whether this is needed?
If the baby requires special care can both parents visit the intensive care unit and touch and hold their baby if it is well enough?
Can the mother breastfeed the baby in special care if it is well enough?
What percentage of your patients breastfed last year?
Do you encourage family centered care?
If yes: How do you see this working in practical terms?

Obviously, the higher the proportion of women who have had the type of birth experience you hope for, the greater the probability that the doctor will help you realize your hopes. Remember that the private obstetrician can write orders for anything you agree together, whether or not it is considered to be routine practice in that particular hospital.

The obstetrical clinic Most obstetrical clinics are located within large metropolitan teaching hospitals. As the name suggests, in exchange for the low cost or free care, the patient serves as "teaching material" for the medical students and resident physicians. Thus there is a higher risk of having unnecessary procedures performed on your body. Teaching hospitals tend to have a great deal of technologically advanced machinery and may be justified for the mother and baby "at risk", when there is a higher than average chance of something going wrong. These hospitals also have neonatal intensive care units where sophisticated technology and a specially skilled staff will be available to treat the high risk baby immediately after birth.

Certified nurse midwife care This type of maternity care is not yet widely available throughout the United States. For information on the availability in your area, contact the American College of Nurse Midwives (see page 337).

The typical hospital nurse midwife practices in a group, backed by one or more obstetricians. The certified nurse midwife has been specifically trained to deal with normal pregnancy, normal birth, and normal post partum. She cares for the well woman at all stages but if any abnormality develops must refer the patient to an obstetrician. Even if this happens, the nurse midwife usually stays with the patient, offering her emotional support.

No matter what type of hospital care you choose, be sure to tour the hospital before you make a definite decision. If this is not the usual practice in the hospital, contact the Head Nurse of Obstetrics and ask for the name of the childbirth educator. Another source of information about the hospital, obstetricians, midwives, clinics and such is your local childbirth education association. (See page 337 for a list of organizations to contact). If there is no childbirth education association near you, contact your local women's organization.

Home birth

66 I had a traumatic experience in the hospital last time, so we've decided to have it at home. 99

At the same time that hospital birth becomes more and more the standard way to have a baby there is a small but steady increase in the number of women who decide to have their babies at home. There are a variety of reasons which may lead a woman to make this choice.

Most women who have a baby at home after a previous hospital birth say that they enjoyed it much more and feel that it must have been pleasanter for the baby. Some opt for home births because they want to give birth in a familiar, comfortable, nonmedical environment, surrounded by their own things, in the home they have created with their partner. They want to be able to make their own decisions, to give birth in their own way and behave spontaneously, without being forced into the role of patient and having to conform to hospital rules and regulations. They also want to avoid having to change rooms and move from a bed to a delivery room, and to be able to adopt any position they find comfortable. At home you are in charge and the doctor or midwife is a familiar and welcome guest in your home. For some, this relationship and cooperation with just a few helpers is important.

Some women say that since birth is an act of love, personal and intimate, it should ideally take place in one's own bed, without unnecessary observers, among friends in a loving atmosphere. They want to know that the father of the baby or a close friend can be present throughout, can take an active part, and can give emotional support through the labor. Some would like the father to "catch" the baby himself. Most hospitals allow fathers to be present for labor and delivery nowadays, but they are still sent out for a wide range of minor procedures and examinations, often just when the laboring woman feels she needs her partner most. Often a woman would like to insure that her baby has a "gentle birth" and is welcomed into the world tenderly, without the machinery and bright lights that are almost inevitable in hospitals.

The importance of bonding

Evidence of recent research on bonding between mother, father and baby points to the importance of the time immediately following birth for the couple to get to know their baby and feel it belongs to them and they to it. In many hospitals separation is still arbitrarily imposed on new parents, time for cuddling is either restricted or denied and routines take precedence over the emotional unfolding which heralds the birth of a family. Many women suspect that medical intervention is often unnecessary and that they will have a better chance of giving birth naturally and without drugs at home. They believe that full awareness of what is happening to them is a valuable experience and that drugs can harm their unborn babies. After a previous difficult hospital birth, one pregnant woman said: "I was determined to have a natural birth this time. Last time I had the whole works, and finished up with an epidural and a forceps delivery. I can't help thinking that if I let things take their own time and keep walking round and can relax and use my breathing and feel comfortable in my own home, with the people I love around me, my body will know what to do. Of course, I'll go to hospital if it looks as if the baby is at risk, and I'm quite prepared to move there in strong labor if need be, because then I'll know things haven't worked out, and it would be silly to take unnecessary risks. But I want the chance to have a natural birth. And I don't think I'll get it in hospital."

If you already have other children, you may be concerned that they should see birth as a normal, happy part of life and not, instead, as a surgical operation that entails you going off to a hospital. Birth is a family affair and the baby should belong to the whole family. Some women hope that the other child or

As your toddler helps you to sort out clothes for the new baby, it may be hard to believe that he ever wore them himself . . .

children can be involved in the labor and some would like them present at the birth. This is impossible to arrange in most hospitals. Mothers of toddlers often worry that separation from them will lead to emotional and behavioral problems in the older child, and this just at a time when the new baby puts in an appearance. And there are those mothers who just find it impossible to get someone to look after their family while they are away in hospital. It is sometimes stated that women having their fourth or subsequent babies should always give birth in hospital, but if all your previous pregnancies and labors have been straightforward, there is no additional risk with a fourth or fifth birth and some definite advantage.

Some doctors are reluctant to give their approval to a home birth once you are actually pregnant, even though they have seemed flexible earlier. For example, one woman said that her doctor had agreed to a home birth for her third child "in principle" before the pregnancy but then "did her best to change our minds. She did not really understand that there was absolutely no one who could come to look after the other children, and that I would not have my husband with me if the baby was not born at home. . . . There were many occasions when I was reduced to tears on my arrival home. Had I been less determined, or without my husband's support, I should have given in."

If you would like to give birth at home and your doctor is unsympathetic, contact the organizations listed on page 337.

Responsibilities of parents choosing home birth

Since home birth is not the standard in the United States, a pregnant woman takes on additional responsibilities when she chooses to deliver at home. It is vital to consider whether or not you are willing to meet them. They include:

The selection of a competent birth attendant This may be a physician, Certified Nurse Midwife or well-trained lay midwife. Be sure to ask for and check references carefully.

Starting prenatal care early in the pregnancy Screening for maternal and fetal abnormalities must continue throughout.

Particular attention to nutrition There is a significant relationship between the mother's diet in pregnancy and the health of her baby at birth and after.

Preparation for childbirth Mothers planning a home birth need an especially clear understanding of how their bodies function in labor and delivery.

Education for breastfeeding Breastfeeding after birth helps the uterus contract, making use of oxytoxic drugs less necessary.

Attendance at home birth classes, if available.

Obtaining supplies, as requested by the birth attendant.

Preparing for postpartum needs of mother and baby Planning ahead for the household simplifies life after birth.

Even if a visit to the doctor means a long wait you do have the opportunity of meeting other expectant mothers, knowing all the while that you are doing the very best for yourself and your baby.

Childbirth education

One ingredient of a happy birth is good prenatal care, so that you are confident that you are healthy and the baby starts life under the best possible conditions. It is only because prenatal care has become so much more efficient that there is justification in stressing the emotional aspects of having a baby. Good childbirth education means regular visits to a prenatal class (see page 158). You do not need to attend classes until you are about five months pregnant, but it is worth thinking about the different classes available and perhaps beginning a few exercises earlier than this. Classes in preparation for birth cannot be expected to take the place of preventive medicine during pregnancy, however, and no woman should think it is safe to go it alone, hoping that everything will turn out all right if she simply eats wisely, does her exercises and learns all that she can about labor. Of course she might be lucky, but it is an unnecessary risk to take. It is no part of the philosophy of prepared childbirth that women should squat in the woods to have their babies without help, for sometimes medical care during pregnancy can make all the difference between life and death for the baby—and even, very occasionally, for you too. Women who do not have regular prenatal care are more likely to have problems in childbirth.*

Unfortunately, whether you choose private or clinic care, waiting for appointments is usually a fact of life. Take a good book or needlework or make friends with another expectant mother going to the same doctor or clinic and you can keep each other company.

Some couples come together (a few doctors and clinics actually encourage fathers to be there) but usually this is not expected and fathers may be asked to remain in the waiting room. If, however, it is important to you that you both talk to the doctor and that your partner is involved in the pregnancy, not only

66 I like being with all the other pregnant women. I thought "We're all growing babies!" And everyone is so friendly and they explain everything. I revel in it. 99

66 On one occasion I waited 3 hours before being seen. I felt sorry for moms with toddlers. No provision was made for them except a broken rocking horse. 99

the birth, it is worthwhile being quietly but firmly persistent to get what you want. Think through beforehand any questions or worries you may have. Many women find it easier to write down their questions so that they will not forget to ask in the rush. If there is anything you particularly hope for about the way in which you have your baby, tell the obstetrician or nurse midwife and ask if it can be noted down on your record.

Routine tests   Most women see their doctor or nurse midwife once a month until they are 32 weeks pregnant. At this stage you will be seen every two weeks and in your final month will be given weekly appointments.

During a typical visit you may be weighed before you see the doctor. While the baby is growing, you will probably be putting on weight fairly steadily. Your blood pressure will be taken at each visit, and this is especially important toward the end of pregnancy, when it is more likely to rise (see page 121). Your blood group is determined and a test is done to check whether

---

Understanding your medical record

Para 0	The mother has had no previous birth.
Para 1 (or 2)	The mother has had one (or two) previous births.
Para 2 1	The mother has had two previous births plus a miscarriage (or termination) before 28 weeks.
LMP	Last menstrual period.
EDD/EDC	Expected date of delivery or expected date of confinement.
Alb	Albumin in urine. Your urine is analyzed for the presence of sugar, which is a sign of diabetes, and albumin (protein), which can be a sign of toxemia. When sugar is present, it is noted as a percentage. Two per cent is a large amount. Ideally albumin should not be present at all.
Hb	Hemoglobin, an oxygen-carrying substance present in red blood cells. If your hemoglobin level is lower than 10·5 per cent, you are considered to be anemic and will be prescribed iron. Because of the greater quantity of circulating blood, most pregnant women have reduced hemoglobin, and this is normal.
Fe	Iron. This means that you have been prescribed iron.
BP	Blood pressure. This is the pressure inside the arteries as the blood is pumped from the heart. The pressure built up every time the heart beats is called *systolic* pressure. Between beats the heart muscle relaxes and the pressure drops. This lower level is called *diastolic* pressure. The systolic pressure is the upper figure on your card, the diastolic pressure is the lower one. The lower figure is more significant than the upper one. A woman is considered to have high blood pressure, hypertension, if it exceeds 140/90 when measured on more than one occasion (see page 121).
FH	Fetal heart.
H/NH	Heard or not heard, usually referring to the fetal heart. In the last weeks of pregnancy the actual heart rate is often written in.
Edema	Swelling. Part of your weight gain is due to water retention, causing puffiness in the feet and ankles, face and vulva. A great deal of fluid retention may indicate impending toxemia, but it can be perfectly normal.

the baby might develop rhesus disease (see page 99). Your blood sample is automatically tested for syphilis. Regular finger prick tests may be done for anemia.

At the first prenatal clinic visit you will probably have an internal examination (see page 28). At most subsequent visits the uterus and baby will be felt by abdominal palpation. As this is done, you should let a long breath out and release your tummy completely, then go on breathing slowly, releasing more on each breath out. This makes it easier for the doctor to feel how the baby is lying and is much more comfortable for you than if you are tense.

The examining hands feel first for the distance between your pubic bone and the baby and then the top of the uterus. This is called fundal palpation. The hands move down the sides of the baby so that the back and limbs are discovered. The part of the baby that is over the cervix is said to be presenting. The doctor or midwife turns to face your feet and presses the hands downwards and from side to side to determine whether the baby's

Fundus	The top of the uterus. As the baby grows, the fundus is pushed up to just above your navel at 22 weeks and under your ribs at 36 weeks. But when the baby drops down into the bony pelvis ready for birth the fundus is lower again (see page 67). You can find your own fundus and chart its position week by week through your pregnancy. Lie on your back, tummy bare and, with the sides and palms of your hands, feel round the hard top of your uterus, pressing against what feels like a wall of muscle.
PP	The presenting part of the baby. This is the part which is down at the bottom of the uterus and likely to be the first to press through the opening cervix if you are at the end of pregnancy. In the last few weeks the doctor may note the presentation more precisely, so that you can get an idea of exactly what part of the baby is in the cervix.
Vx/Vtx	Vertex. This indicates that the baby's position is head down, as it should be.
Ceph	Cephalic. This also indicates that the baby's position is head down.
Brim	The inlet of your pelvis.
Long L	Longitudinal lie. The baby is lying parallel to your spine.
LOA	Left occipito anterior.
LOP	Left occipito posterior.
ROA	Right occipito anterior.
ROP	Right occipito posterior.

These terms all refer to the position (anterior or posterior) of the crown of the baby's head (occiput) in relation to your body (right or left). Therefore ROP means that the back of the baby's head is to your right and back and LOA means that the back of the baby's head is to your left and front.

RSA	Right sacrum anterior. This is the most common breech presentation.
Trans	Transverse lie. The baby is lying across your abdomen rather than head up or down.
Eng/E	Engaged. This is written on your card when the baby's head has dropped down into your pelvis, which can happen any time from about six weeks before you go into labor until after you have actually started.
T	Term. The doctor writes this on your card when it is estimated that you are right at the end of your pregnancy and the baby is ready to be born.

A visit to the clinic

When you arrive, a nurse takes your urine sample . . .

. . . then you are weighed.

Your blood pressure is recorded . . .

. . . and sometimes a blood sample is taken from your arm or your fingertip.

Then a doctor examines your abdomen to check the baby's position and assess its growth.

head, buttocks or any other part, is presenting. The next maneuver tends to be uncomfortable but is not always done and is quickly performed. Facing you again, the doctor spreads one hand wide and presses in above your pubic bone to feel the exact position of the presenting part in relation to the pelvis.

Take the opportunity to find out how your baby is lying and discuss it with your doctor or nurse midwife if there is anything that worries you. Notice fetal movements and report if there is any pronounced change in their frequency or type. The best way of monitoring a pregnancy is for the obstetrician or nurse midwife and the expectant mother to work together.

Talking to doctors

Some people have doctors with whom they quickly feel at ease. They experience little difficulty in finding out the medical alternatives open to them in pregnancy and discuss their requirements with their doctors. However, the expectant mother and her doctor are likely to meet in a system where time is at a premium and sometimes one or both of them finds it difficult to break out from a formal doctor-patient relationship.

Being pregnant is a physiological process. It also involves a kind of emotional journey into being a patient. And as if all this were not enough, it propels you into new kinds of social relationships. Some of these are with the professionals you encounter during your pregnancy. So, as well as having to understand the changes taking place in your body and your emotions, you may have to develop new social skills which help you to create a satisfactory dialogue with those who care for you and your baby. This is especially the case where you meet different doctors at each clinic visit and others again when you are in labor. The lack of continuity in care is one of the main criticisms that women make about childbirth in a hospital today.*

Some women also feel very emotionally vulnerable when pregnant and cannot help crying under stress, even though (or perhaps because) it is the last thing they *want* to do. You are in no way abnormal if you feel surges of emotion which are difficult or impossible to control, but it means that you may feel at a disadvantage in an interview with a doctor.

This possibility is a good reason for having your partner or a close friend or relative with you on such occasions. It is important, of course, that you discuss your wishes thoroughly with this person first. You may find it useful for him or her to play "the devil's advocate" and act out an imagined encounter so that you have some practice in discussing the subject and develop a strategy. Do not make the mistake of anticipating opposition from the hospital staff; you will probably be pleasantly surprised, but do be prepared to present your wishes cogently and to give carefully thought out reasons for what you want.

See that you are well briefed about the matters you want to discuss. There is now a good deal of published research on

66 The obstetrician was very pleasant. He told me they'd just had a baby 3 months ago. That made a lot of difference. 99

66 I had to sit in a little cubicle for ages feeling cut off from the world. 99

emotional and sociological aspects of maternity care, for example, and many papers on the technology of modern obstetrics and the active management of labor (see page 246) which are published in medical journals. It will help if you have the correct references and a clear idea of some of the most important statements. If you are attending childbirth education classes, ask your prenatal teacher to help you. The International Childbirth Education Association produces booklets and sells books which may be relevant, and there are other organizations which may be able to give advice (see page 337).

Preparing your questions Since questions may go out of your head when you actually have a chance to ask them (pregnancy amnesia is a well known phenomenon), and because some doctors seem to concentrate exclusively on the lower end of your body to the exclusion of interest in you as a person, it is a good idea to jot down subjects you want to discuss. Different treatments are done routinely in different hospitals. You may not want some or all of these, and it is best to state your preferences as early as possible. On the other hand, you may want a treatment which would not usually be given in your hospital but is probably available if you make a special request. Your list could include questions about the doctor's attitude toward shaving your pubic hair, routinely giving enemas or suppositories, the use of intravenous drips (IVs), toward electronic monitoring, episiotomy and the use of forceps (see pages 246–261). You could also ask about the availability of epidurals (see page 242) and whether or not you will be able to keep your baby with you day and night. It may also be important for you to know whether there will be much help with breastfeeding. Be specific in your requests, to avoid misunderstandings later on.

If you have not made an appointment with a discussion in mind, sometimes the office or clinic is so crowded that you feel reluctant to take up anybody's time. Even so, it is probably worth saying that you have made a note of things you would like to discuss and ask whether it is convenient that day or, if not, whether you can arrange to have some time to talk at the next visit. There is no need to be apologetic about wanting further information or asking for the doctor's help to achieve the kind of birth you would like. After all, you are not just a baby-producing machine!

During the interview sit in a relaxed way, check that fingers and toes are unclenched, and breathe out just before speaking for the first time. Make eye contact and address the doctor by his or her name.

When a woman is nervous, she tends to pitch her voice too high. Modulate it so that it does not sound too demanding. You might smile nervously without realizing it. This can be confusing for the doctor, who may think that you are happy about something when you are not. Or the doctor unconsciously smiles because he or she is concerned to get you to accept another

Regular medical check ups will help you keep track of your baby's growth and development . . .

point of view and is sugaring the pill; your spontaneous reaction may then be to smile back, perhaps giving the doctor the idea that you are content when in fact you are not. Be conscious of when and why you are smiling.

Avoid aggression and state your requests clearly and concisely. If you lose your temper, you may be classified as a difficult patient or be considered neurotic and are bound to find this upsetting. If you encounter opposition or are made to feel that you cannot know what is in your best interests, don't throw in the sponge but restate your wishes firmly and give the reasons for them. It is a good idea to include requests that are not top priority, so that there is a possibility of compromise on some matters. Belligerence only provokes further opposition. Tell the doctor instead how unhappy or disappointed his or her decision makes you feel.

You may want to take notes of the conversation. You can always say: "I'd like to think more about that; may I just make a note of it?" Be careful not to imply that you are cross-examining the doctor and writing down any answers in preparation for a later attack. Listen to the doctor with concentration and make it clear that you are listening by "playing back" the important statements: "Do you mean . . . ?" "So you are saying that . . . ?" and rephrase whatever has been said as accurately as you can. You can sometimes add to your remark the *implications* that you think such a statement entails. By clarifying a point in this way you may be working towards modifying it. For example, if the doctor says, "I never allow husbands to remain if I have to give the patient a vaginal examination or do a forceps delivery because they only get in the way", you might ask: "Are you saying that it is dangerous for a husband to stay because he might affect your judgment?" Not many experienced obstetricians would say that the presence of a husband could affect their professional judgment, and the doctor might reply: "Well, I've known some fathers who . . ." and tell you a story about men who have fainted. You might then choose to say: "I take it you feel happier about a man who stays calm and who gives emotional support to his wife?"

If your interview has gone badly, you can consider changing your doctor or, if there is more than one maternity hospital in your area, the hospital where you give birth. But give yourself a few days to simmer down and think the whole subject over calmly. You can write a letter to the doctor politely explaining your reasons for seeking other care and at the same time it is a good idea to send copies also to the Medical Director if it concerns a hospital.

But such drastic measures are often unnecessary and you should find that you have opened up the possibility of getting the kind of childbirth you want. Good communication with your doctor means that, if for medical reasons you do not get all you had hoped for, you will understand why and can at least take an active part in the decision-making.

PREGNANCY: PHYSICAL AND EMOTIONAL CHANGES

Life in the uterus

66 I don't really
know I'm pregnant. I
mean, it's as if nothing
has happened. I see
women who look
about 12 months
pregnant and I think
"Will I ever look like
you?" I can't believe
there is a baby
there. **99**

In the first days of pregnancy life is budding in cells far smaller
than a pin-head. Because everything is happening on such a
minute scale, it can be difficult to accept the reality of a baby
growing deep inside you. Even when you begin to believe in
your pregnancy, other people remain unaware of it. It can seem
as if an explosion has taken place without anybody noticing, or
as if all the colors have become more brilliant but everyone
else is carrying on as usual. The chance meeting of one out of
four hundred million sperm with a ripe and waiting egg has
resulted in a dramatic series of events, conducted on a scale so
miniature that you cannot feel the astonishing life process
unfolding inside you, even though you know it is happening.

Fertilization

At birth the ovaries of every baby girl contain almost 500,000
potential single-cell eggs, but they do not ripen until the menstrual periods begin. Each cell that ripens into an egg is nourished
by nearly 5000 others that will never themselves ripen. From
your first period until the menopause, when your periods stop,
you may carry up to 4000 ripe eggs; each month between 100
and 150 begin to ripen, but usually only one a month reaches full
maturity and is capable of being fertilized. The frequency with
which eggs are produced and released is determined by hormones, which interact regularly in a system known as the
menstrual cycle.

This cycle lasts for about a month and begins when a hormone released by the pituitary gland stimulates an ovary to
start ripening an egg. As the egg matures, the ovary releases
estrogen into the bloodstream. The estrogen stops the pituitary
gland from continuing to produce its hormone, so no more
eggs are stimulated into ripening. It also makes the uterine
lining change and thicken in anticipation of the egg, which
bursts out of the follicle (a capsule bulging on the surface of the
ovary), about midway through each menstrual cycle. It is then
drawn by the fingered tentacles of the fallopian tube into its long
canal, which is about the thickness of a ballpoint refill.

The egg itself is a minute speck. It is barely visible to the naked
eye, yet when it meets with a still more minuscule sperm it has
the potential to develop into a human being. The follicle (also
known as the corpus luteum) that held the egg begins to produce progesterone, which carries on the work that the estrogen
has been doing. If the egg is not fertilized within a few days,
the follicle dries up and the progesterone level falls dramatically.
As a result the uterine lining proceeds to decompose, and a
menstrual period occurs.

Even while bleeding is going on the menstrual cycle renews
itself: the pituitary gland is stimulating the ovary into ripening
a new egg. But if the egg is fertilized the follicle does not shrivel

Sperm meets egg and dissolves . . .
the two nuclei will then fuse. . . .

The menstrual cycle

While a follicle is developing in the ovary, the uterus is building up a lining composed mainly of coiled arteries and glands. If the ripe egg released from the ovary is not fertilized, the uterus sheds the top layer of this lining (menstruation) and the process begins again.

This diagram shows an external view of the ovary of a fully grown woman.

This diagram of a section through an ovary shows the stages of development of the follicle during any one menstrual cycle.

OVULATION CYCLE

| Growth of follicle | Ovulation | Corpus luteum | New follicle |

Days 1 2 3 4 5 6 7 8 9 10 11 12 13 14 15 16 17 18 19 20 21 22 23 24 25 26 27 28 1 2 3 4 5

UTERINE CYCLE

In pregnancy the lining continues to thicken

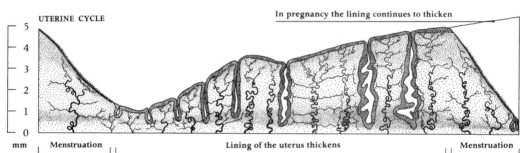

5 · 4 · 3 · 2 · 1 · 0

mm

| Menstruation | Lining of the uterus thickens | Menstruation |

up, the progesterone level does not drop and the uterine lining continues to thicken, so that you do not have a period.

The usual pattern is that the ovary on one side releases an egg one month, the one on the other side the next. Sometimes one ovary becomes especially active for a few months. Occasionally only one ovary is functioning: if part of a fallopian tube or an ovary has been surgically removed the other one usually takes on the work of both, with no loss of fertility.

Sperms are so tiny that 30,000 of them placed side by side would only just stretch across a beer bottle top. A man ejaculates hundreds of millions of sperms every time he has an orgasm. After intercourse, a mere 2000 of these survive the arduous journey up the vagina, through the uterus to the fallopian tubes, and only one sperm can eventually fertilize a ripe egg, which immediately puts up a chemical barrier to keep all others out.

Each sperm is shaped like a tadpole with a long, lashing tail which makes it highly mobile. The head is rounded and holds the gene-carrying nucleus. When a sperm meets the egg it burrows deep into it and its nucleus fuses with the nucleus of the egg. It is at this moment that the genes, or the units of inheritance, of the two parents first meet.

Genetics

Inside the nucleus of every body cell—with two exceptions—there are 46 chromosomes, making 23 pairs. The two exceptions are the egg cell and the sperm cell, which have 23 chromosomes each instead of 46. Chromosomes are rodlike structures shaped like Egyptian hieroglyphs, each containing thousands of genes.

When the nucleus of the sperm cell fuses with the nucleus of the egg, each chromosome—and each gene inside each chromosome—unites with its opposite number. The newly fertilized cell now contains 46 chromosomes, like every other human cell. The physical characteristics of the future person are determined, and the cell can start to develop into a human being.

Boy or girl? Out of the 23 pairs of chromosomes in every human cell one pair determines the person's sex. The two sex chromosomes in a female cell are known as XX, and the two in a male cell as XY. Since the egg and the sperm cell contain half the usual number of chromosomes, every egg cell contains 22 chromosomes plus one sex chromosome, which is an X. Every sperm cell contains 22 chromosomes plus one sex chromosome, which can be either an X or a Y. The sex of the baby depends on these differences between sperm cells. If the egg is fertilized by a sperm with an X chromosome, the union of the two sex chromosomes will result in XX, a girl. If the egg is fertilized by a sperm with a Y chromosome, the union of the two sex chromosomes will result in XY, a boy. There is usually about a 50/50 chance that a boy or a girl will be conceived; statistically it appears that as women grow older and also as they bear more children, the chance of having a girl is slightly increased.

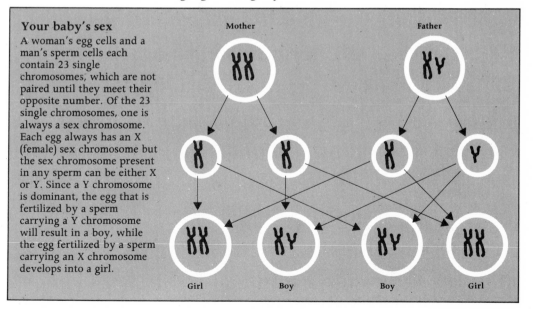

Your baby's sex
A woman's egg cells and a man's sperm cells each contain 23 single chromosomes, which are not paired until they meet their opposite number. Of the 23 single chromosomes, one is always a sex chromosome. Each egg always has an X (female) sex chromosome but the sex chromosome present in any sperm can be either X or Y. Since a Y chromosome is dominant, the egg that is fertilized by a sperm carrying a Y chromosome will result in a boy, while the egg fertilized by a sperm carrying an X chromosome develops into a girl.

Mother

Father

Girl

Boy

Boy

Girl

The female reproductive organs

When a woman ovulates, the released egg from one of the two ovaries is immediately drawn into a fallopian tube where, if intercourse has taken place, it may be fertilized by a sperm. The fertilized egg embeds itself in the lining of the uterus. If the egg is not fertilized, it is shed, along with the lining of the uterus, down through the opening in the cervix and out of the vagina: this is menstruation.

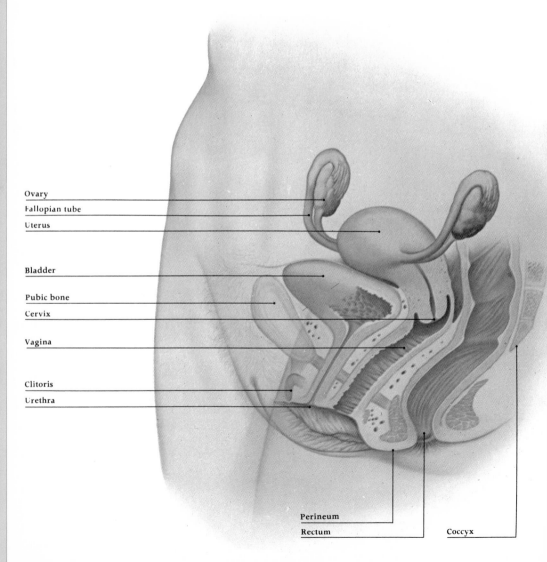

Ovary
Fallopian tube
Uterus

Bladder
Pubic bone
Cervix

Vagina

Clitoris
Urethra

Perineum
Rectum
Coccyx

The male reproductive organs

Sperms mature in both testes, which are enclosed within the scrotum. They travel up through each vas deferens, where they are stored temporarily. When a man is sexually aroused, his penis becomes erect and the outlet from the bladder into the ejaculatory duct is closed, leaving it free for the sperms. The sperms entering the ejaculatory duct are accompanied by secretions from the seminal vesicles, Cowper's glands and the prostate gland. About a teaspoonful of the fluid (semen), containing millions of sperms, is ejaculated from the urethra at orgasm.

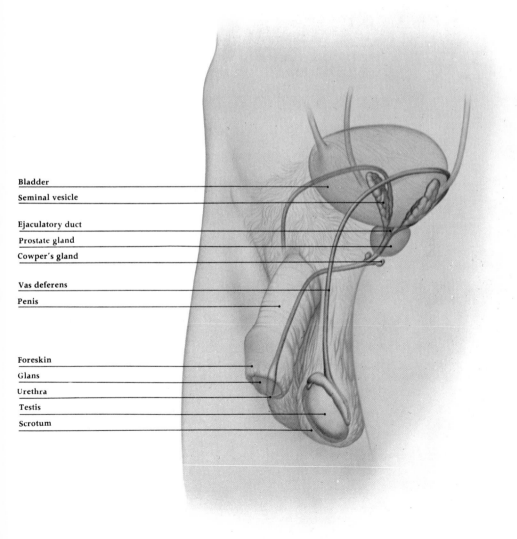

Bladder

Seminal vesicle

Ejaculatory duct

Prostate gland

Cowper's gland

Vas deferens

Penis

Foreskin

Glans

Urethra

Testis

Scrotum

Although the baby's sex is determined by the sex chromosome carried by the sperm, it is also partly a consequence of the environment into which that sperm is received. Natural alkalinity or acidity of the secretions in your reproductive tract make it easier for some sperms to survive their long journey than for others. Traditionally an acid medium has been thought to increase the chances of having a male child, and an alkaline medium a female child; because of this people have douched with acid or alkaline solutions before intercourse, but there is little evidence that this significantly affects your chances of producing one sex or the other.

Dominant and recessive genes

When a Y chromosome meets an X chromosome, the Y chromosome dominates to produce a boy. Similarly, when a gene encounters its opposite number one always takes precedence. A baby receives half of its genes from each parent. If a gene from one parent for brown eyes meets a gene from the other for blue eyes, the gene for brown eyes will always prevail. This does not mean that a child of one brown-eyed and one blue-eyed parent will always have brown eyes. But the gene for brown eyes is known as *dominant*, the one for blue eyes as

Dominant and recessive genes

Since the gene for blond hair is recessive, the blond haired grandparents in this family group must possess two blond haired genes, one of which has to be passed on to each of

their children. This means that the dark haired mother and father in the group must each have a recessive gene for blond hair, giving them a one-in-four chance of producing a blond child.

Grandparents

Grandparents

Mother Father

Children

recessive. So someone with brown eyes who has received a gene for blue eyes from one parent retains the blue-eye gene as a recessive gene. If he or she should have a child by another brown-eyed person also with a recessive gene for blue eyes, there is a one in four chance that both parents will pass on their recessive genes for blue eyes to produce a blue-eyed child. This ability of two brown-eyed parents to have a blue-eyed child is a simple example of the way in which heredity introduces diversification with each generation.

Defective genes Occasionally genes are defective, but since healthy genes are usually dominant over faulty ones, your baby's normal development is almost always assured. Some defective genes are carried by the sex chromosomes, and then the children of one sex only are affected. Color-blindness, for instance, is carried by some women in one of their two X chromosomes; since the normal gene in their other X chromosome is dominant over the faulty one they do not suffer from color-blindness. But if a boy inherits an X chromosome with a faulty gene he has no other X chromosome with a healthy gene to dominate it, so he is color-blind. Thus color-blindness is transmitted through alternating generations of affected boys and carrier mothers. Hemophilia is passed on in the same way.

If you are anxious about the possibility of your children inheriting any diseases or handicaps from your family or your partner's, tell your doctor before you become pregnant if possible. Failing that, as soon as your pregnancy is confirmed ask to talk to a genetic counselor. There is a skilled genetic counselor in every teaching hospital who can tell you the mathematical chances of your bearing a defective child and about the tests that can be carried out (see page 183). If it is discovered that you are carrying an abnormal child, your pregnancy can be terminated *if you wish*. Nobody has to agree to termination of pregnancy even if bearing a handicapped child.

The beginnings of pregnancy

The genetic make-up of the future child is decided at the moment of fertilization. But conception is a process, not a split-second event. Immediately after it has been penetrated, the egg starts to divide. It divides repeatedly as it is swept along the fallopian tubes to the uterus, which it reaches seven days after leaving the ovary. By this time it is a clustered ball of cells, called a blastocyst, like a tiny blackberry but hollow in the center. The blastocyst floats in the cavity of the uterus until about the tenth day, when it embeds itself into the uterine lining.

Some blastocysts, perhaps as many as one in three, do not manage to root themselves into the wall of the uterus, and are swept out with the next menstrual period. Conception is only complete when the blastocyst has successfully nested into the wall of the uterus: you have not yet missed a period.

Implantation The cells now number several hundred. The blastocyst releases enzymes which penetrate the lining of the uterus, causing the tissues to disintegrate and the blood and cells—on which the blastocyst can feed—to seep out. They make a kind of nourishing soup, whose quality depends on the preparatory state of the uterine lining. Sometimes this is not rich enough to maintain the pregnancy and there is a miscarriage, which just resembles a late and rather heavy period, without your ever realizing that you have been pregnant. An inadequately nourishing uterine lining is one cause of infertility.

Early development During the second week of the fertilized egg's life, the cells become differentiated. One set becomes the amniotic sac, or the envelope of salty water in which the baby will later grow. Another cluster develops into the yolk sac out of which the embryo can make blood corpuscles. Yet another group becomes the placenta (see page 64). In between these structures are other rapidly developing cells which will form the baby. These cells are at first just an embryonic disc, but they grow lengthways during the third week until there is clearly a head and a tail end, with the yolk sac attached by a stalk to the middle of the embryonic disc.

At this point you are about one week past the date when you expected your period to come. Although you are not sure, perhaps you suspect that you might be pregnant.

Six weeks pregnant It is three or four weeks after the meeting of sperm and egg, and about two weeks since you missed your period. According to the medical method of dating pregnancy (see page 29), you are about five or six weeks pregnant. The

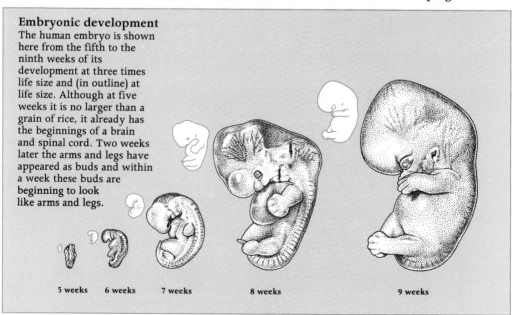

Embryonic development
The human embryo is shown here from the fifth to the ninth weeks of its development at three times life size and (in outline) at life size. Although at five weeks it is no larger than a grain of rice, it already has the beginnings of a brain and spinal cord. Two weeks later the arms and legs have appeared as buds and within a week these buds are beginning to look like arms and legs.

5 weeks   6 weeks   7 weeks   8 weeks   9 weeks

HANDS AND FEET
These develop at a slightly different rate, the feet being about a week behind the hands until the 13th week.

7 weeks

8 weeks

13 weeks

7 weeks

8 weeks

13 weeks

cluster of living cells has now developed into an embryo: there is a head and a neck with rudimentary eyes and ears, a brain, and a heart which is already beating, although it has only two chambers instead of the four which will develop shortly. There is a bloodstream and a digestive system, kidneys and a liver, and tiny buds which will later become arms and legs.

A rod of cells develops called the notochord, which later becomes the spine and is the first indication of the skeleton to come. The embryo develops from the head end down, so that at this stage the lower part of its back is as yet barely formed and looks more like a tail. In fact, while now the size of a coffee bean, the embryo closely resembles a miniature sea horse.

Seven weeks pregnant A week later the embryo is about the size of a lima bean, and recognizably human. Its body has plumped out into a baby shape, even though the head is at a strange angle in relation to the body. It has visible nostrils, lips and tongue, and even the buds of its first teeth. Four chambers have developed in the heart. The limb buds have grown into arms and legs, although as yet the hands and feet are no more than ridges.

Eight weeks pregnant The baby is still smaller than your little toe. It floats in the amniotic sac like an astronaut in space, attached to its life-support system. The heart has started the vigorous pumping of blood which will continue for a lifetime. The brain glimmers through skin as thin as waxed paper, revealing every tiny branching blood vessel beneath. The jaw is not yet fully formed, but the face is recognizably human. The ears are slung low and have not yet been molded into their correct position. The eyes are covered by an intact skin, which will eventually split to become the eyelids. The head of the embryo is huge in relation to its body. The limbs elongate and elbows and knees appear. Even now the baby is trying out some gentle kicking, though you cannot feel any movement.

All the organs and features of the embryo are completed in the course of the next month. The face grows from the top, and as the lower parts form the neck is elongated and a chin develops. The nose and outer ear are completely formed. Fingers and toes are visible, though webbing stretches between them.

By the time you are 12 weeks pregnant all the basic physical equipment of the embryo is in working order. The head is still big for the body and the limbs small; few muscles are working yet. All the internal organs have formed and some of them are functioning. The genitals have developed, but it is not yet easy to tell what sex the baby is. The umbilical cord has started to circulate blood between the embryo and the group of membranes attached to the wall of the uterus. It is at this stage that the embryo begins to rely on these membranes for nourishment and the placenta starts to function. From now on the baby is known as a fetus and the rest of its time in the uterus is spent on growth and maturation.

The placenta

In the early weeks of pregnancy one cluster of cells begins to develop into the placenta, which is an organ grown especially to nourish the baby and to excrete its waste products. The outside layer of this cell cluster develops into a membrane with hundreds of tiny roots which penetrate the uterine tissues.

Your blood does not flow directly into the baby at any stage of pregnancy. It passes across the tissues on the maternal side of the placenta and the baby's blood passes back across the tissues on the other side. The two bloodstreams are separated by the membrane; chemical substances can be diffused from one bloodstream to the other through the membrane, but the bloodstreams themselves never mix. The baby can thus have a different blood group from yours, while still taking its nourishment from your blood. In the same way its waste products are passed back through the placenta into your bloodstream, to be excreted by your kidneys.

Although the baby makes breathing movements, it does not breathe inside you: it takes its oxygen from your blood and passes back carbon dioxide. The oxygen diffuses through the membrane into its blood in the same way that oxygen from the air passes through the lining of your lungs. The placenta therefore works rather like a coffee filter: the coffee grains never enter the jug, but substances from them filter into it. Changes in your blood as a result of stress, illness, or toxic substances that you inhale, swallow or smoke (see pages 90–99) will affect the quality of the substances which flow through what used to be thought of as a placental barrier, but is now recognized as being more like a fine sieve.

Blood takes only half a minute to flow from the baby's heart to the placenta and back again to the baby's heart. The flow of blood through the placenta in the fourth month of pregnancy is about 8 gallons or 27·5 liters a day, and by the end of pregnancy 100 gallons or 330 liters of blood are passing through each day. (See page 193 for more about the placenta at the end of pregnancy.)

As the placenta starts to function, it gradually takes over responsibility for production of a range of hormones, including estrogen and progesterone, from the glands which normally secrete these hormones. Estrogen and progesterone control most of the changes in your body during pregnancy. The estrogen stimulates the growth of the uterus and the development of new uterine blood vessels, and also causes the milk glands in your breasts to develop so that you can feed the baby. The progesterone prevents the uterus from contracting strongly and endangering the baby during pregnancy, and thus holds off the start of labor until term. When the baby is ready to be born, the progesterone level drops. By this time the uterus has become exquisitely sensitive to the level of estrogen in the blood, so that when the placenta reduces its output of progesterone, the

Fetal circulation

This simplified diagram shows how blood circulates around the fetus. The blood that travels along the umbilical cord toward the fetus has received oxygen from its mother through the placenta. Before traveling to the fetal heart, it mixes with some of the deoxygenated blood that has already circulated through the fetus. This mixture travels through the heart and is pumped up into the head and around the body, becoming, as it does so, less oxygenated. To obtain more oxygen, it returns to the placenta via the heart again, most of it bypassing the lungs. At birth the blood vessels around the baby's navel are automatically sealed off and the baby's circulation rapidly adapts to self survival, with the lungs taking over the function of oxygenating the blood.

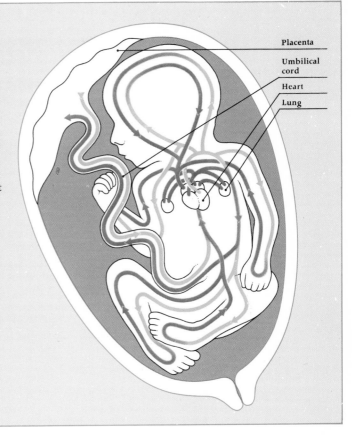

Placenta
Umbilical cord
Heart
Lung

KEY

Oxygenated blood

Deoxygenated blood

estrogen stimulant takes over: it initiates labor and then it insures that the uterus continues to contract strongly right through to the end of the third stage.

The growing baby

At 12 weeks   The fetus is quite recognizably a human baby, with a large head and a small, rounded rump; the sex organs are distinguishable though as yet incomplete; the eyes are closed, with the retina showing dark and round through the translucent skin. The toes and fingers are formed; the arms are the right length in proportion to the body and the nails are beginning to grow. The ribs and spine are just starting to harden into bone and the baby is moving vigorously. You cannot yet feel these movements, but it is kicking, curling its toes up and down, rotating its feet and wrists, clenching and unclenching its fists, pressing its lips together, frowning and making other facial expressions. The baby is also swallowing the amniotic fluid, gurgling it from its mouth or passing it out through its bladder.

There is still plenty of room in the uterus, so the fetus can swoop and undulate in its own enclosed sea.

At 16 weeks Although the baby is growing rapidly, it could still nestle easily into a teacup. Its face is developing specifically human features, though the chin is still small and the mouth wide in comparison. The eyes are huge, closed and spaced far apart. The baby is covered with a fine down, called lanugo. This is the earliest stage at which you may first become aware of its movements. At first these feel like butterflies or little fish zigzagging about in bursts of activity, but soon they are unmistakably the kicking and lunging movements of a live being deep inside your body.

At 20 weeks The baby is half as long as it will be at delivery and about as heavy as a medium-sized Spanish onion (8 oz or 250 grams). You could still hold it in the palm of your hand. The closed eyes are bulbous, because the face has not yet plumped out round them. Hair on the head is starting to grow and there are delicate eyebrows. The baby's movements are becoming more complex and it may even be sucking its thumb.

You will probably notice that there are times when your baby seems to be asleep and times when it moves very actively (often when you have just settled down to go to sleep yourself). This seems to be partly because when you lie down it is easier for the baby to move. When moving around you also automatically rock the baby in your pelvis (see page 110), so when you are busiest the baby is often asleep.

At 24 weeks The baby is about the length of your telephone receiver (13 in or 32 cm). It is covered with vernix, a creamy substance which protects its skin inside the uterus and prevents it from becoming waterlogged. This vernix sticks to hairy parts and many babies are born still coated with it. You may notice that your baby responds to loud noises and to music, especially to the brass section of an orchestra. If you are practicing relaxation and slow breathing, you may feel the baby become remarkably active and begin to leap around energetically.

At 28 weeks The fetus is now legally viable: if it is born it must be registered as a birth. If it dies it is considered to be a stillbirth rather than a miscarriage. With modern intensive care a baby at this stage has a 60–70 per cent chance of survival—even higher in some units. The main problem encountered is usually that the baby's lungs have not yet developed bubbles of surfactant, the substance which prevents the complete collapse of the lungs between each breath. There is also still very little fat under the baby's skin, so its temperature control mechanisms could not yet work efficiently.

The baby has virtually filled all the available space in the uterus. Most babies turn upside down at some point during the seventh month and then seem to fit more comfortably. By now you may be able to distinguish the baby's bottom from a foot or a knee. When you lie in the bath you can enjoy watching the baby swivel from one side of your abdomen to the other. Foot

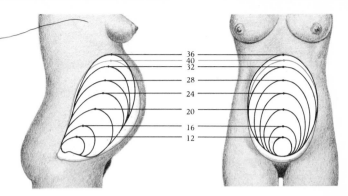

THE CHANGING UTERUS
Although the uterus is expanding throughout pregnancy, this increase in size is not usually visible until the fourth month, when it is too large to stay hidden in the pelvis. From the 12th week the uterus enlarges at a regular rate until the 36th week, when the fundus reaches to just below the breastbone. In women having their first child, the baby sometimes engages in the pelvis at about this date, so that the fundus descends slightly, even though the uterus has not shrunk.

and knee movements are more jerky than whole-body movements and hands produce soft flutters like sea anemones moving. It is now possible for other people to feel the baby kicking.

Throughout later pregnancy you can often anticipate the periods of most hectic movement; many babies are at their most energetic between eight and eleven pm.

At 32 weeks By the time the eighth month has come the baby lacks only some lung surfactant and a good layer of insulating fat before it is ready to be born. Movements are vigorous: the prods coming from the feet are so energetic that they may make you catch your breath. Every now and again the baby may jerk spasmodically in what can be a rather alarming manner; some women wonder whether their babies are having epileptic fits. But such jerking is usually an attack of hiccups, brought on perhaps because the baby has been gulping amniotic fluid.

At 36 weeks At some point between 36 weeks and term (which is 40 weeks from the first day of your last menstrual period) the baby will probably descend into the pelvis with its head firmly fixed like an egg in an eggcup. It is then said to be "engaged"; this is a good sign and one indication that the baby can pass through the pelvic cavity without difficulty. Once your baby has engaged you are slung lower and can often feel the head like a coconut hanging between your legs. It is uncomfortable to sit down fast on a hard chair and you may also experience peculiar sensations in your vagina like mild electric shocks (see page 188).

After the baby has engaged, its larger body movements tend to be limited; you will probably feel only the kicking of legs and feet, the action of the head as it uses the pelvic floor as a trampoline and the fainter movements of the arms. But although the movements change in type no day should pass without some lively indications from the baby of its presence (see page 195).

The last weeks may be tiring and involve tedious inaction. The baby is three times heavier at delivery than it was at 28 weeks, weighs anything from $5\frac{1}{2}$ to 11 lbs (2·5–5 kg) and is between 18 and 22 in long (44–55 cm). It is now ready for its extraordinary journey to life.

Forty weeks of life

The next ten pages show, life size, different stages of the development of a baby from the moment of conception to its last week in the uterus. The illustration below shows the journey of the egg along the fallopian tube, where it is fertilized, to the uterus. During this five day journey, the single cell egg divides into over a hundred cells.

One of the sperms that have arrived in the fallopian tube penetrates the ripe egg.

The head of the sperm separates from the tail and approaches the egg's nucleus.

The chromosomes of the two nuclei pair off to create a two cell egg.

The two cells divide as the egg continues its journey along the fallopian tube.

As the cells continue to divide they gradually get smaller and smaller.

On about the fifth day the egg reaches the uterus and loses its jellylike coating.

Six or seven days after fertilization the egg embeds itself in the uterine lining.

Eight weeks pregnant

The baby is just under 1 in (2·5 cm) long. The bones of its arms and legs start to harden and the baby makes slight movements, still too featherlight for the mother to notice. The baby's face is developing. Some time during this week the baby starts to open its mouth and the upper palate forms. The jaw is taking shape, with muscles which will enable the baby to suck and chew. The sound perceiving mechanism of the ear has now developed.

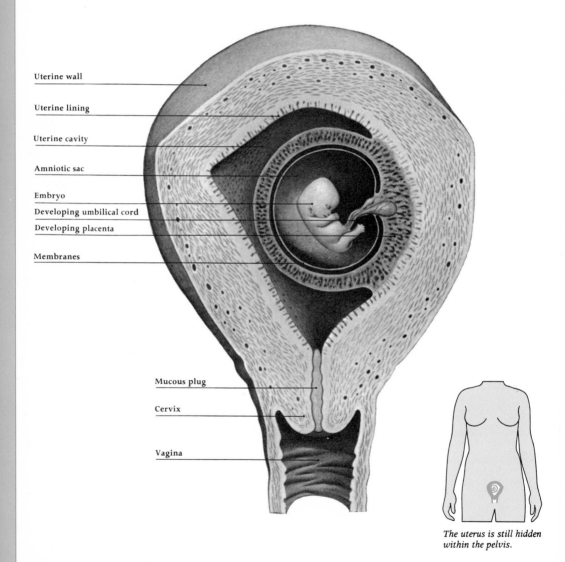

Uterine wall

Uterine lining

Uterine cavity

Amniotic sac

Embryo

Developing umbilical cord

Developing placenta

Membranes

Mucous plug

Cervix

Vagina

The uterus is still hidden within the pelvis.

Twelve weeks pregnant
The baby is now just over 2 in (5 cm) long. Its head is more rounded and is no longer so top heavy: it is about two-thirds the size of the body. The eyes are widely separated in a broad face. The jaws have 32 permanent tooth buds and the baby is starting to suck. It is already exercising the muscles that will be used in breathing after birth.

The growing uterus can now be felt through the abdominal wall.

71

Twenty weeks pregnant

The baby's rate of growth, which has been very rapid, slows down a little at this stage. It is about 10 in (25 cm) long. Legs are now the right length in proportion to the body and there are miniature nails on the toes. The mother feels movement, at first faint then growing stronger. Hair on the baby's head and delicately etched eyebrows have appeared and there is a fine downy hair called lanugo over much of the body.

The top of the uterus reaches to just below the navel.

Twenty-four weeks pregnant
The baby is thin and the skin is wrinkled. The face is now fully formed and the eyes are rather prominent because fat pads have not yet built up in the cheeks.

The fundus is in line with the top of the hips.

73

Thirty-six weeks pregnant

There is no longer enough room in the uterus for the baby to move around freely. It has settled into one position and the main movements the mother feels are jabs from the arms and legs. By now the skin is smooth and peachlike and the body has plumped out. When the baby is awake, the eyes are open and it is aware of strong light flowing through the tissues of its mother's abdominal wall. If it is born at this time, the baby has an excellent chance of survival.

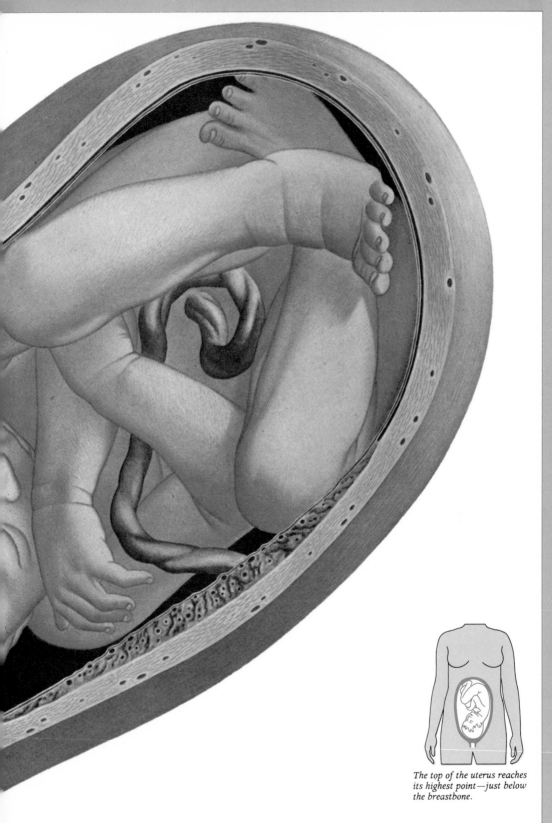

The top of the uterus reaches its highest point—just below the breastbone.

Forty weeks pregnant

The baby is now about eight times bigger than it was at three months, when all its vital organs were formed, and has increased in weight approximately 600 times. Most of the lanugo has dropped off, though there may still be some down the center of the back, in front of the ears and low on the forehead. The fingernails extend beyond the fingers and may need cutting at birth so that the baby does not scratch its face.

The uterus has moved down a
little into the pelvis, so that
the fundus drops slightly from
its highest point.

Expecting twins

Finding out that you are going to have twins usually comes as a shock. Some women suspect quite early in their pregnancy that this will be the case, especially if they have already had a singleton pregnancy with which they can compare this one. If you are a fraternal twin (see below), you are about twice as likely to give birth to twins yourself as are other women, so you may be on the lookout for any confirmation of your suspicions. The likelihood of your having fraternal twins depends on heredity, your age, race and the number of children you have already had. Although fraternal twins often skip a generation, the chances of them occurring in successive generations are high. The frequency of identical twins seems independent of these variables.

Mixed feelings   However, if nothing has led you to suspect that you are carrying more than one baby, it can be very upsetting to be told, after a prenatal visit or an ultrasound scan (see page 46), that suddenly all your expectations of birth and afterward need readjusting.

How twins are conceived

Normally conception occurs when one egg released from a woman's ovary is fertilized by one male sperm. Seven out of ten pairs of twins result from the woman releasing two eggs, which are then fertilized quite independently by two sperm (fraternal twins). Usually the two eggs then implant and develop separately in the uterus. Less commonly one egg fertilized by one sperm divides, resulting in two developing babies with the same inherited characteristics (identical twins). Often this division occurs after implantation in the uterus.

IDENTICAL TWINS
Identical twinning occurs after, rather than at, fertilization, and often after implantation in the uterus. As a result the twins almost always share a placenta although each has its own cord and bag of water.

FRATERNAL TWINS
Fraternal twins have separate water bags and cords, and separate placentas too. Occasionally the two eggs implant close together in the uterus, so that the placentas become fused and it looks as though the twins are sharing the same one.

**Monozygotic (one egg)
or identical twins**

**Dizygotic (two egg)
or fraternal twins**

> **❝** I heard that I was expecting twins when I was about 29 weeks pregnant, spent two days weeping intermittently, and didn't really whip up much enthusiasm about the idea right to the end of the pregnancy. **❞**

If you are to be a mother for the first time, the natural apprehension you originally felt about the labor and how you would cope with a new baby is greatly increased. Added to this you wonder how you will manage two babies at the same time in all their noisy reality—two mouths to feed, two diapers to change each time, two babies to bathe, two loads of clothes to wash, two budding personalities who will need your love and attention.

One woman, who was dismayed on hearing that she was expecting twins, said that she never really veered from this attitude throughout the rest of her pregnancy. During a hospital stay in her eighth month of pregnancy, she took the opportunity of watching mothers who had recently given birth to twins, and felt that all her worries were justified, since they seemed to have such trouble in managing two babies. However, shortly after her twins were born, she was able to comment on the "totally unexpected delight of being .able to breastfeed both, often simultaneously". She did admit, though, that it was hard work at first and that "the intense joy and delight the babies now give has only come gradually as we have gotten to know them".

Sometimes a woman is unhappy to discover that she is expecting twins because she has been planning for a home birth and

Positions of twins in the uterus

Twins fill the available space in the uterus more quickly than a single baby, so they may adopt the positions in which they will be born at an earlier stage.

The pictures below show fraternal twins (with two placentas), but the same positions apply to identical twins (with a single placenta).

This presentation, with both twins in the cephalic or head down position, is the most common. It is also the most straightforward: birth should present no special complication.

When one twin is head down and the other head up the breech baby is often born second. The first baby opens up the birth canal so that the breech baby can usually be born vaginally without difficulty.

If both babies are breech the risk of complications will be evaluated in advance. A Cesarean section may be performed in preference to a vaginal delivery.

When one baby is lying transversely and the babies are large for your pelvis, a Cesarean section will be carried out. If the babies are not large, it is usually possible to turn the second baby after delivery of the first.

The prospect of twins may come as a shock, but the reality may more than compensate. . . .

this may no longer be possible. Doctors usually advise hospital birth for twins, since the chances of a complicated delivery, especially for the second twin, are increased and it is more likely that they will be premature and underweight.

Alternatively a woman may be overjoyed to find that she is going to have twins. Perhaps she had wanted more than one child, but was not particularly enjoying her pregnancy and certainly not looking forward to another. Suddenly she discovers that she can have two children for the price of one pregnancy and labor!

Rest The first thing to accept is that a pregnancy with two babies tumbling about inside can be more of a strain than an ordinary pregnancy. The risk of developing preeclampsia (see page 121) is higher; as the babies are more likely to be born prematurely, they may not be so strong. Because they have to share the space in the uterus and the nutrition available through the placenta, twins are often of low birthweight. To help avoid extra strain, you need regular rest times and frequent early nights. If you already have other children, it is worth making an effort to find some motherly person who can look after them for an hour or so each day so that you can really relax without feeling that you will be needed in a minute.

In late pregnancy a baby who has not been growing well in the uterus invariably grows better if the mother has more rest and actually stays in bed. (Lying down in a darkened room for three hours every afternoon is ideal.) This is why many obstetricians move you into hospital for a compulsory rest. But if you are able to plan ahead and make other arrangements, you may avoid any anxiety about the babies' growth and be able to convince your doctor that you can reorganize your life well enough to have adequate rest at home.

There is no need to be an invalid. But if you think about the extra demands made on your body by a multiple pregnancy you will realize that your whole system has to adjust to the babies' needs. Such an adjustment involves widespread metabolic changes; there is also extra pressure put on your digestive organs and on your diaphragm and lungs, as well as stress on bones (on your lower ribs, which tend to splay out, and on your spine, for example). Your muscles too cope with much of the extra stress of a twin pregnancy, especially your tummy muscles, your pelvic floor, and the muscles of legs, feet, arms, shoulders and back, which have to support the extra weight and do the work of lifting and coping with your body mechanics. Over and above all this a general crowding out may make you feel very full and heavy.

So rest is good for you and will help your body adjust to the increased demands made on it by a multiple pregnancy. And the rest that helps most is rest taken *before* you become exhausted and irritable and *before* you feel that you cannot carry on a minute longer.

Comfort You may find it very uncomfortable to lie flat. The heavy uterus is pressing on major blood vessels in that position too, so, both for your own comfort and for the blood supply to the babies, lie either well propped up or in a three-quarters-over position (see page 114). Prop your breasts with one pillow and put two under your upper knee if this feels good. Even more so than with a singleton pregnancy, special back supports may be needed in the last few weeks. A small bean bag may be comfortable; so might a contour pillow with other pillows, two foam wedges, or the kind of cushion that is sold for reading in bed. Whatever you choose, make sure that your support relieves the strain caused by extra pressure in the small of your back.

BACK SUPPORT
If you are carrying twins you are most likely to feel the strain caused by the extra weight in the small of your back. A special contour pillow (below and right) or a bean bag (far right) will give the support you need.

Exercise Sensible body mechanics are also more important when you are expecting more than one baby (see pages 111–114). Learn how to counteract the effect of the enlarged and heavy uterus by standing straight and tall, with tail tucked in. Aim to balance on the balls of your feet rather than being flatfooted and waddling like a duck, which is only too easy to do when you are overtired. Above all learn how to get up from a lying-down position by rolling over, if necessary kicking off with your foot and hand against solid objects, and then rising on to all fours (see page 109).

Pelvic floor exercises (see page 106) are important throughout, whether you are carrying one baby or two; with twins they will be especially vital after the birth, as the muscles around the vagina have been stretched by the extra weight of two babies. It is a good idea in any case to do these exercises from early pregnancy, before there is any appreciable change in weight, as muscle tone is really best built up before there is any particular stress on the muscles. If your pelvic floor muscles are under a great deal of strain, you should do these exercises while lying on the floor with your lower legs raised on a chair. In this position weight is not pressing on the pelvic muscles, and it is easier to feel what is happening there, even in advanced pregnancy when the babies may be very low down.

You will probably be aware of the babies moving a great deal inside you. Your abdomen feels like a basket full of puppies. It can be difficult to sleep, and you are often woken by all the internal activity. Practicing release from tension and deliberately letting muscles relax all over your body can help enormously by giving you complete rest (see page 167).

Some mothers worry in case the babies are harming each other. They can certainly shuffle each other up a bit, but each one is sealed off in its own bag of waters, and this also means that each baby bobs around like a cork in a tumbler of water. The water cushions them from shock and allows free movement until the very last weeks of pregnancy when the pelvic girdle cradles the babies so closely that you may feel hardly any movement.

Diet   For a detailed discussion of diet in pregnancy see page 84. The demands made on your body by a twin pregnancy require an even more careful attention to diet than is necessary in a singleton pregnancy. So aim to have a diet high in protein with plenty of salads and fruit and only those foods which are of value to you and the babies. Cut out the ice cream, flabby slices of bread, sickly doughnuts and cookies. The easiest way to do this is to convince yourself how awful they are and to think instead of rich golden hunks of cheese, glowing fruit salad, a peach that melts in the mouth, jade green watercress, crisp celery, rosy apples and a luscious, long glass of creamy milk.

To save laboring over a hot stove, have at least one raw food meal a day, which will give you a good supply of vitamins. You might like to buy some new cook books that concentrate on salads and fruit and stimulate your imagination. If you normally eat white bread and cereals, now is the time to switch to whole-wheat bread, brown rice and whole grains. Eating like this will help you not only while you are pregnant but after the babies come, as you cannot feel full of vitality if you are poorly nourished and weighed down with "junk" foods that give you nothing but calories.

The more tired you become the more you may feel that you cannot be bothered about arranging meals and shopping for food. But your health depends on your having a good diet and not skimping on protein, vitamins and minerals. Is there any chance of getting help with shopping? Could someone else shop for you? Or could you and your partner or a friend do it together in bulk, loading up a car? (But do not lift boxes and bags into the trunk yourself or attempt to unload them!) If you have to shop unaided, use a wheeled shopping cart and avoid carrying bags. There is probably a store in your area which will deliver goods provided that you order enough at one time. If you live in the country, a village store may do this when they know you are expecting twins. Or could you come to an agreement, such as your partner taking a neighbor who has no car to the supermarket, so that she can help him shop for you?

Your baby's wellbeing

Looking after yourself in pregnancy, from the very first weeks, is probably more important for the welfare of your baby than anything else you can do. It is your responsibility to provide the best possible environment for the developing baby and to care for yourself so that you have the best chance of reaching the end of pregnancy healthy and full of vitality.

Nutrition

Your baby depends on what you eat and drink for adequate nourishment in the uterus. Until recently it was thought that provided the expectant mother had a "sensible" diet there was no need to give her any advice about what she should eat, because the fetus would always take whatever it needed. There were certain "do nots", the most important of which was "do *not* eat for two". But such a vague instruction led to large numbers of women going through pregnancy on inadequate diets. Recent research on nutrition in pregnancy suggests that when diets are inadequate the result is that some babies die or are in poor condition, and some mothers have difficult pregnancies, labors and subsequent illness.*

If you half starve yourself or eat low quality food you deprive your baby too: you are more likely to have a miscarriage and, if the pregnancy is maintained, your baby is more likely either to be born prematurely or to be inadequately nourished in the uterus and therefore of low birthweight. Inadequate nutrition in the later part of pregnancy can also affect the child's brain development.*

Weight gain in pregnancy		
Your total weight gain in pregnancy is made up as follows:		However much weight you gain during your pregnancy, you will gain it at approximately the following rate:

Weight of baby	38%	
Weight of placenta	9%	
Weight of amniotic fluid	11%	
Increase in weight of uterus and breasts	20%	
Increase in weight of blood	22%	
Total weight gain	100%	

0–12 weeks	0%
12–20 weeks	25%
20–30 weeks	50%
30–36 weeks	25%
36–40 weeks	0%

So, as a rough guide, you can assume that if—for instance—you are 30 weeks pregnant, the weight you have gained since the beginning of your pregnancy will be about 75% of your total weight gain.

Weight gain

It is normal to put on between 25 and 35 lbs in pregnancy (11–16 kg). Some women put on more, with no ill effects. It is wrong to assume that because your baby will probably weigh 6¼ to 8½ lbs (3–4 kg) at birth, all the rest of the weight that you put on is fat. You must consider the weight of the placenta, the membranes and the amniotic fluid, as well as the increase in size of the uterus and breasts, and the increase in volume of your blood. Fluid retention also accounts for a substantial weight gain in some women (see page 89). All these things return to normal after the birth.

Since different women gain weight at different rates it is impossible to be dogmatic about how much weight you should put on. Responsible medical opinion now is that "arbitrary weight restriction is potentially harmful to both mother and baby"*. If you start off your pregnancy underweight you and your baby may benefit from a bigger weight gain than the woman who begins pregnancy already overweight. It is certainly most unwise for any woman to try to remain slim during pregnancy, and an attempt to keep your figure might result in the eventual loss of your baby.

One way of checking to see whether you are putting on superfluous fat, which you will be left with after the birth, is to measure your upper thighs each week, keeping a record of the measurement. This is a way of recording the increase in your own body fat as distinct from the weight you gain as a result of the pregnancy. The measurement should stay about the same, although fluid retention may increase it slightly in the last weeks of pregnancy.

Protein

Women who are not pregnant are recommended to have 2 oz (56 g) of protein a day for optimum health. When you are pregnant you need nearly twice as much. The foods rich in protein are lean meat, fish, beans, nuts, brewer's yeast, eggs, milk, cheese and the other dairy products.

All proteins are made up of chemical substances—called amino acids—in different combinations. Animal or "first class" proteins contain all the amino acids necessary for the protein to be effective; vegetable proteins, which used to be called "second class", only contain some of these amino acids, and therefore they should be eaten either with a small quantity of animal protein or in different combinations. If you are a vegetarian who eats no animal products, combine beans with a wheat product at the same meal—say, beans with brown flour pastry, or lentils with wholewheat bread*.

You will obtain adequate protein if you make sure that every day you have the following: two eggs; one quart of milk or the equivalent in cheese or yoghurt; two servings of meat, fish, poultry or a vegetarian combination dish; four servings of whole grains or wholewheat bread. (If you are a vegetarian be sure to use high protein substitutes for meat such as tofu, beans and nuts.)

85

Protein becomes particularly important if you are ill or fighting an infection, or if you feel overtaxed and exhausted. If you cannot face proper meals, protein and other essential foods can be obtained in the form of a drink. Try the following high energy cocktail:*

Nine-month cocktail

This makes one milkshake containing 50 grams of high quality protein, plus vitamins and minerals.

1 cup of whole milk   1 banana
$\frac{1}{3}$ cup of instant nonfat dry milk powder   1 tablespoon of honey
4 tablespoons of soy powder
   (obtainable from health food
   stores)

Blend all the ingredients together until smooth.

Carbohydrates

You need carbohydrates for energy. They are found in sugar, and in the foods you eat in bulk, such as bread, flour, cereals and root vegetables. Most foods containing carbohydrates contain other valuable nutrients too; potatoes—especially if you eat them in their jackets—can contribute protein and vitamin C as well as carbohydrate, and wholewheat bread provides B vitamins, iron and the fiber which helps to prevent constipation. If you eat small quantities of these foods daily, you should need no other carbohydrates. But if foods rich in carbohydrates are the foods you enjoy most, you may put on unnecessary weight.

If you are overweight before starting pregnancy, or if you are putting on a lot of superfluous fat (see page 85 for a method of checking this), it is a good idea to cut out all white flour and sugar, and all products containing them. Cakes, puddings and cookies do not do much to help your unborn baby's health. If you like sugar in tea and coffee, train yourself to enjoy both of these without it.

Fats

Your body's need for fat increases in pregnancy, but if you are eating a nutritious diet, you are taking in enough fat. You can deliberately reduce your intake by trimming fat off meat, by using less butter, by boiling or steaming foods rather than frying or sautéeing them, and by cutting out rich sauces. You will find that cottage or pot cheese and yoghurt are both useful ingredients for low fat sauces.

Milk and dairy products

Milk is usually recommended for the pregnant woman, but unless your diet is grossly inadequate in protein you do not need more than one quart a day. If you fill yourself up with milk drinks you may dampen your appetite for other foods you and your baby need. Some women do not like milk or are allergic to it. You can have skim milk or eat cheese or yoghurt instead; if it is simply a matter of taste, disguise the milk in sauces or dishes where you are not aware of it. One ounce of hard cheese substitutes for one glass of milk.

Vitamins It is important that most of your vitamin intake should come from food. Trying to get the right dosage of vitamins, and the right balance between different vitamins, from supplements rather than from food is unwise. The chart on page 88 tells you which vitamins are in which foods, what they are for and whether it is ever advisable to take a supplement.

Minerals Minerals and trace elements are a vital part of your diet, but if you are eating plenty of the foods rich in protein and vitamins you are unlikely to suffer from a mineral deficiency. Iron and calcium are probably the only minerals about which you need to be especially concerned.

Iron is necessary for the formation of red blood cells. Red blood cells contain a substance known as hemoglobin; if your blood contains insufficient hemoglobin not enough oxygen is carried to your baby and you become very tired. Vitamin C helps your body to absorb iron, whereas antacid medicines stop you from benefiting fully from it. Liver is a good source of iron, as is dark molasses, egg yolk, whole grains, legumes, all dark green leafy vegetables such as watercress, raisins, prunes, brewer's yeast and nuts.

Extra iron is often prescribed in pregnancy. If you eat plenty of foods rich in iron, you should have good reserves stored in your liver, and not need to take extra. The fetus draws on these reserves, so that it can store enough in its own liver to last for several months after birth—a vital need, since milk contains almost no iron. But if, like many women, you are, without realizing it, iron deficient (slightly anemic) before embarking on pregnancy, a supplement is probably advisable.

You probably need about twice as much iron when you are pregnant as you do before conception.

Calcium is necessary for the formation of strong bones and teeth. It enables blood to clot and your muscles to work smoothly. The oxalic acid in spinach and cocoa reduces the absorption of calcium: do not depend on a chocolate milk drink for your chief calcium intake.

Your baby's teeth start to bud very early on in pregnancy, so your calcium intake in the first four months matters a great deal. Milk is a useful source, as are other dairy foods. Calcium is also contained in leafy vegetables, whole grains, legumes and nuts. You need almost twice as much when you are pregnant.

Women at risk Certain women are at "nutritional risk" and need to pay special attention to diet; for them vitamin and mineral supplements may be useful. The ones particularly at risk are those pregnant during adolescence (while they are still growing themselves), women who are underweight when they become pregnant, women who are overweight because of excess consumption of carbohydrates and fats, those living on a very restricted range of foods like a macrobiotic diet, women who have lost a baby

Vitamins in pregnancy

Vitamin	What it does	Foods it is in	Increase needed in pregnancy	Supplement needed in pregnancy
Vitamin A	*Maintains skin, body tissues, vision; helps your body to resist infection.*	*Mainly green and orange vegetables, liver. Also dairy foods.*	*None.*	*None.*
B VITAMINS **B₁** **Thiamine**	*Maintains brain, heart and nerves. Enables your body to make use of carbohydrate.*	*Most foods, but especially whole grains and yeast products. Lost in over-cooking.*	*None.*	*None.*
B₂ **Riboflavin**	*Helps tissue growth and regeneration, especially skin and eyes. Allows your body to use carbo-hydrate, fat and protein.*	*Mainly yeast, legumes and green vegetables. Also milk, eggs, brains, kidneys and liver. Often lost if exposed to light.*	*None.*	*None.*
B₃ **Niacin**	*Helps to keep tissues healthy and allows your body to use protein.*	*Meat, fish, peanuts, legumes, eggs, milk.*	*None.*	*None.*
B₆ **Pyridoxine**	*Allows your body to make use of protein. Insures cell division.*	*Most foods, but especially meat, fish, dried vegetables, whole grains, potatoes, bananas.*	*None.*	*None. In fact it is wise to avoid a supplement as large amounts can suppress lactation and some cases of "rebound" deficiency have been reported in babies whose mothers took enormous doses during pregnancy.*
B₁₂ **Cyano-cobalamin**	*Helps to form hemo-globin and the baby's central nervous system. Allows your body to make use of protein, folic acid and fatty acids.*	*Meat and fish, especially liver.*	*None.*	*A capsule might be advisable for vegetarians.*
Pantothenic acid	*Maintains nerves and red blood cells. Essential for breakdown of fat and carbohydrate.*	*Most foods, especially meat, eggs, cheese, whole grains, peanuts and some green vegetables.*	*90%—nearly double the normal intake.*	*None.*
Folic acid	*Aids cell division and the development of the baby's central nervous system.*	*Liver, green leafy vegetables.*	*100%—double the normal intake.*	*Often prescribed at the same time as iron.*
Vitamin C	*Helps form the body's connective tissue, collagen, and assists the absorption of iron. Therefore main-tains blood vessel walls, helping to prevent hemorrhage; assists healing and the formation of strong bones.*	*Fresh vegetables and fresh fruit, especially citrus fruit.*	*None.*	*Occasionally prescribed to help the absorption of iron.*
Vitamin D	*Helps form and maintain bones.*	*Liver and fish liver oils. Also butter, egg yolk, milk.*	*None.*	*None.*
Vitamin E	*Helps to protect cells from damage and degeneration.*	*Most foods, especially wheatgerm.*	*None.*	*None.*
Vitamin K	*Plays vital part in process leading to blood coagulation.*	*Manufactured in human colon. Also in green leafy vegetables.*	*None.*	*None.*

from miscarriage or stillbirth before, and women who have had three pregnancies within two years. Also included in this high risk category are women suffering from some chronic diseases involving the regular use of drugs, women who smoke, heavy drinkers and those with multiple pregnancies*.

Recent research* has demonstrated that taking a multivitamin preparation for at least one month *before conception* and up to the second missed period helps to prevent spina bifida and anencephaly (both known as neural tube defects). The woman is then well nourished both at the time of conception and during the crucial early stages, when the baby's spinal cord is being formed and a neural tube defect could occur. The research was carried out with mothers who already had one baby with a neural tube defect and whose chances of producing a second child with a similar handicap were therefore much higher than average. Only one such baby was born to 178 women who took the vitamins. 13 handicapped babies were born to 260 women who did not take the vitamins.

Salt and fluid retention

It used to be thought that salt was dangerous in pregnancy and was one cause of preeclampsia (see page 121). It has now been established that salt is necessary for a normal pregnancy. When a group of expectant mothers had no salt diets they had *more* preeclampsia than a control group of women who had as much salt as they wished*. Cutting out salt can also cause cramps in hot weather. Since you tend to retain more fluid when you are pregnant, you will only maintain the usual level of saltiness in all your body fluids by having as much salt as your appetite dictates*.

Occasionally special diets are prescribed for pregnant women in order to reduce fluid retention, which used to be thought dangerous in itself. But these special diets can harm the unborn baby. Women with mild fluid retention (edema) usually produce babies in just as good a condition as those who have no signs of it at all. Ankle, foot and leg swelling on very hot days, when you have been on a plane trip or after you have been standing for a long time, is therefore nothing to worry about. If your skin is looking very puffy, take more rest and look at your diet to see how you can increase your protein intake (see page 85); if your fingers and face become swollen you should mention it to the doctor, as it is a sign that your kidneys are not coping well with the excretion of waste products from your body. This in turn may mean that your placenta is not working efficiently.

You cannot prevent edema by cutting down on fluids, so drink as much as you want. Drinking to thirst and salting to taste will help your kidneys to work well through pregnancy.

Eating a balanced diet

Throughout pregnancy bear in mind that you are providing nutrition for three distinct but interdependent biological entities: your own body, the developing baby and the placenta*. This triple nutritional task demands a really good, high protein diet rich in vitamins and minerals.

A salad a day is a must, but remember that you can use finely chopped cabbage when lettuce and other salad greens are hard to find—and it makes a nice change. Experiment with salads and try mixing fruit and vegetables. Apples go well with most savory things. A baked potato with cheese and a cabbage based salad are a good source of protein, vitamin C and calcium. If you can spare time to bake your own whole grain bread, add extra wheat germ or soy flour to it and this way you have added to your diet another valuable source of protein, iron, B vitamins and fiber.

Eating well does not always mean eating expensively. You revise your diet to save money by cutting out unnecessary foods such as carbonated drinks, coffee, packaged desserts and soups, bakery and candy store items, and starchy sugary puddings. Milk, eggs and cheese are relatively cheap, and a main course can be made out of any vegetables in season topped with a white sauce and a crusty layer of cheese browned under the grill.

> 66 I'm taking the opportunity of reforming Chris's eating habits. It's all salads and wholewheat bread and food that's good for you. 99

Drugs

The full range of substances to which the embryo and fetus may be vulnerable is not yet known. It is wise to take the fewest possible medicines of any kind during pregnancy, especially in the first few weeks when the embryo is forming and when the placenta is only just starting to be active. (You should therefore take care during the second half of the menstrual cycle if there is any chance that you might be pregnant.) It used to be thought that the placenta (see page 64) acted as an effective barrier to all poisons in the maternal bloodstream. But it is now known that many drugs—including nicotine and alcohol—can cross the placenta and might affect the baby*.

> 66 Everything you read in the papers about drugs in early pregnancy, it's so terrifying! I can't remember what I took in those 8 weeks and it's haunting me. 99

If you think of how the fertilized egg has to divide, travel along the fallopian tube, embed itself into the lining of the uterus and develop into a baby, you can imagine how such delicate and complex processes can be interfered with by chemicals which have been introduced into your bloodstream.

The liver and the kidneys are the organs of your body which deal with drugs and turn them into material which can be excreted in the urine. In an unborn—and even a newborn—baby these organs are still immature. The fetus is therefore not able to excrete many of the drugs which may reach it through the placenta. Instead, such drugs can accumulate in its body in toxic quantities. It is vital to remember, when taking any drug, that a dosage which may be right for you is far in excess of that which is suitable for your tiny baby.

Everyone remembers the thalidomide disaster*, when a sedative which was thought to be mild and safe was prescribed for women in early pregnancy. As a result of this sedative more than five thousand babies were born with badly deformed limbs, or none at all. Thalidomide is an extreme example of the effect that a drug can have on the development of an unborn baby. But all drugs are potentially harmful if misused. You should think carefully before taking any drug when pregnant, especially in the early weeks. The word *drug* in this context includes not only drugs prescribed for specific conditions, but also nicotine, alcohol, and medicines bought over the counter such as laxatives or aspirin.

Drugs which are known to cause abnormalities of any kind are said to be "teratogenic". In the very early stages of a pregnancy any toxic or teratogenic drugs would probably prevent the egg from ever settling firmly in the uterus, so that you would not even realize that you were pregnant but would just have a delayed period; if you were to take the same drug slightly later, you would probably miscarry. At a later stage still, the pregnancy might continue, but there would be a risk of the baby being damaged by the drug.

Weighing the different risks Clearly some pregnant women need drugs, and may be very ill without them. Illness in the mother can also affect the developing baby. For instance running a very high temperature (see page 98) seems to be teratogenic at certain phases of pregnancy, so it may be safer to take aspirin to get your temperature down than to try and cope without any medicines. It is always a question of balancing the risks to the baby against your need and the stress which may be caused to you by not having drug treatment.

Since the thalidomide disaster there has been acute awareness of the need to screen all new drugs before they are prescribed to pregnant women, and doctors are being increasingly careful. But drugs which have been in use a long time remain on the market without being tested. And it is difficult to be certain about any drugs, because animal experiments may produce damage in one species, yet not in another. This can work either way: rats may be affected, but not human babies, or babies may be affected when rats are not.

People are often ignorant about the chemical substances they introduce into their bodies. Antacids for the relief of indigestion, cough medicines, sleeping pills (barbiturates), antihistamines used in the treatment of hay fever and antibiotics are just some commonly used drugs which alter the body's chemical balance. A great many pregnant women take over the counter as well as prescribed drugs of one kind or another in the first weeks of pregnancy, and no one has much idea of the possible risks. There are other harmful substances which you may not even think of as being drugs, including cigarettes and alcohol. Even tea and coffee have been investigated as causing possible damage to the growing baby*.

Smoking There are positive steps you can take to give your baby the best start in life and other things which you should avoid since they are known to be detrimental. First and foremost among the dangers is smoking. Whether or not you inhale, nicotine passes into your bloodstream and from there into the baby's. It makes the fetal heart speed up and interrupts the baby's respiratory movements, which are a rehearsal for breathing. In effect the baby coughs and splutters.

Smoking interferes with the efficiency of the placenta and is the most widespread and effective way of pumping a powerful poison into an unborn baby's bloodstream. Nicotine makes the blood vessels in the placenta constrict so that less oxygen and fewer nutritional substances reach the baby.

Mothers who smoke bear babies who weigh less than babies of mothers who do not smoke and the baby's weight drops in direct relation to the number of cigarettes consumed*. This does not mean that some smokers do not have good sized babies but that statistically babies of smokers can be shown to be deprived of the best possible nutrition in the uterus. The reason for this is not just that a woman who smokes tends to eat less. Cigarettes have a direct effect on the growth of the baby*. It could be that some women make the mistake of thinking that labor will be easier if their babies are lighter in weight. Labor with a tiny, underweight baby is no easier or shorter than labor with a good sized baby, and your baby is much more likely to be healthy and easy to care for if you have not smoked.

Smoking after the fourth month of pregnancy is a major cause of prematurity and the birth of underweight babies who, although they have had the full time in the uterus, are stunted in development and may have to be cared for in a special care baby unit. Smoking also increases the chances of bleeding during pregnancy, miscarriage (women who smoke are twice as likely to miscarry as those who do not), premature rupture of the membranes, hemorrhage before or early in labor, hemorrhage after delivery, congenital abnormality, stillbirth, and death of the baby in the week following delivery*. The more a woman smokes, the more likely these things are to happen.

How to give up If you are a heavy smoker and dependent on cigarettes to get through the day it may be very difficult to give them up, even for the sake of your baby. Fortunately the nausea of early pregnancy or just a sudden dislike of cigarettes prompts many women to cut them out. Even if this does not happen spontaneously you can use the techniques of aversion therapy to condition yourself to break the habit. Every time you feel queasy or vomit make yourself think "cigarette" and use the association between vividly picturing the act of smoking and the overwhelming sensations of nausea to train yourself to develop a dislike of cigarettes.

How to cut down If you are past the nauseous stage of pregnancy or feel perfectly fit throughout, as many women do, you should still try to reduce your cigarettes to at least half of the usual number. Ask your partner to help by cutting down his consumption in the same way; if the two of you are making the same effort, your determination is strengthened. Also, recent studies suggest that even being in a smoky room for a long time—

6 6 I really get scared when someone lights up. I think, "Why should my baby have that poison in its bloodstream?" I can get quite rude about it! 9 9

known as being a "passive" smoker—should be avoided whenever possible. The more you can both cut down the better for all three of you.

You may be feeling terribly guilty about smoking while still unable to give it up. You might feel like a murderer, but the guiltier you become the more you want a cigarette to help you calm down. It is certain that guilt and emotional stress can also affect your metabolism adversely, including your heart rate, blood pressure, breathing, muscle tone and the adrenalin in your bloodstream. The question then arises as to how much stress you should tolerate in trying to give up smoking. If you know how to release tension you may be able to cope by smoking each cigarette only halfway down and still find that it helps you enough to "unwind".

This is where your own judgment of the relative importance to you of smoking or not smoking in pregnancy is essential. Every pregnant woman has the right to be fully informed of the risks of smoking and also to make her own decision on the subject. No one can *make* you stop smoking, however many dire warnings they give: you decide.

Your baby cannot choose whether or not to smoke. A mother chooses for her child.

Alcohol Alcohol is as much a drug as anything you may take in the form of a pill. The safe minimal dose in pregnancy is not yet known, but because alcohol is socially accepted it is easy to forget that its use should be restricted. Fortunately many women develop an aversion to it in any form.

Some women's metabolisms are unable to break alcohol down into harmless substances and it passes straight through the placenta to the fetus in its poisonous form. If you are one of these women, you should not drink at all. You can have a blood test after drinking to discover how well you are able to metabolize alcohol, but this is not done routinely. There is no reason why you should not ask your doctor to do this simple test before you even start a pregnancy.

The less well you metabolize alcohol the more careful you should be. Even if you metabolize it normally, there is evidence that a single "binge" during pregnancy may affect some babies, depending on the stage of development they have reached. So although common sense would indicate that you can drink in moderation and still have a perfect baby, unfortunately you cannot assume that this is the case. Limit your intake of alcohol to an occasional glass of wine.

Being careful about drugs Think about any drugs you may be taking when you intend to conceive, and ask your doctor's advice. Do not wait until your first prenatal visit or even—if possible—until you are sure you are pregnant. If there is any chance that you might be pregnant, avoid taking any drugs which are not absolutely essential to your health.

If a doctor other than your obstetrician is treating you, especially in the early months of pregnancy before it is obvious that you are having a baby, make sure that he or she realizes that you are pregnant before prescribing. This may be particularly relevant if you are ill when away from home.

Go through your medicine chest when you stop using contraception. Make a list of the contents and ask your doctor whether there are any which are likely to be unsafe during pregnancy. Throw away, by flushing down the toilet, or return to the druggist, any drugs which were not prescribed for you, which are out of date, or which your doctor advises you to get rid of.

Mood changing drugs

Because so little is known about the effect of mood changing drugs it is wise to limit their use or cut them out altogether. Marijuana or Valium may help you to relax on an occasion when you cannot easily "switch off". But explore other ways of releasing tension. The effects of disciplined relaxation (see page 165) are likely to help your unborn baby more than anything you can take in through your mouth. They are positive things you can do for yourself and your baby, ways of tuning in to your body rather than making an attempt to escape from it or deaden its sensations.

Marijuana Little is known of the effects of marijuana on the baby. Its strength varies widely, and its immediate effects on the user vary with expectation, the company in which it is taken, and previous experience of it. Claims have been made that it can be teratogenic, but they have not been proved.

LSD This extremely powerful drug can damage the chromosomes in the embryo if taken in the first 12 weeks of pregnancy; later on in the pregnancy it may interfere with the growth of the baby. Do not take it.

Mild tranquilizers are often prescribed during pregnancy but may still be harmful. Diazepam (Valium) is sometimes used in treating preeclampsia (see page 121) to bring blood pressure down. But it is best to stop taking even a mild tranquilizer as you approach the time when you expect to go into labor. Valium taken just before labor starts or during the course of labor can result in the baby having a low Apgar score (see page 280) at birth and breathing difficulties. The baby may also take a long time to start feeding properly, as well as becoming chilled more easily than usual*.

Powerful tranquilizers such as chlorpromazine (Thorazine) and haloperidol (Haldol) should not be used in pregnancy. If you think you might have conceived, you may be prescribed a milder tranquilizer. This is important because the strong tranquilizers can affect the development of the baby's nervous system. Thorazine taken over a prolonged period can damage the baby's eyes*.

Sleeping pills These include tranquilizers, antihistamines (see below) and hypnotics. Hypnotics are of two different kinds. Some are barbiturates, which are highly addictive even over a short period and are now almost never prescribed: phenobarbital (Luminal), amobarbital (Amytal), pentobarbital (Nembutal), and secobarbital (Seconal). Others are not barbiturates: chloral hydrate, flurazepam (Dalmane) and glutethimide (Doriden). Non barbiturates also seem to be addictive if taken over a long period. Not enough is known about the effect of hypnotics on the unborn baby; certainly large doses of barbiturates can cause respiratory depression at birth. The baby is doped along with the mother. The best solution is to do without sleeping pills if you can; try and overcome insomnia by altering the pattern of your daily life so as to allow for more conscious relaxation both during the day and at night.

Painkillers **Aspirin** The most widely used painkiller is aspirin (salicylate) and its derivatives. If you have a headache or other pain, try to get rid of it by resting in a quiet, darkened room before resorting to aspirin. If rest is not an effective remedy, a few aspirin are unlikely to be harmful. But never dose yourself repeatedly: a recurring headache should be discussed with your doctor. If taken regularly (say every four to six hours) during the few days before you go into labor, aspirin can produce difficulties in blood clotting in the newborn baby and it has been known to cause neonatal jaundice; sometimes it can damage the baby's central nervous system.

Codeine is addictive: the baby of the mother who has been taking several pills daily throughout pregnancy may be born dependent, produce severe withdrawal symptoms, and in some cases even die.

Acetaminophen (Tylenol) can cause liver and kidney damage in the person taking large doses. It should be used with caution in pregnancy, since the baby's liver and kidneys can suffer from relatively small doses.

Some migraine drugs can cause the uterus to contract during pregnancy, thus endangering the fetus. Discuss alternative ways of treating migraine with your doctor before undertaking a pregnancy.

Antinausea drugs Drugs for nausea and vomiting are of three different kinds: anticholinergenic drugs, antihistamine drugs and phenothiazine drugs*. They can all have side effects.

The first category treats nausea by acting on your nervous system; it reduces secretions, including stomach acid, and relieves muscle spasm. No one can be sure whether these drugs are completely safe for the fetus. Antihistamines, which include Benadryl, Dramamine, and Chlor-Trimeton block the action of histamine (a substance to which some people are allergic) and may cause drowsiness. They are best not used in pregnancy as high dosage may cause fetal abnormalities. Early pregnancy nausea may best be controlled by eating small portions of protein foods frequently throughout the day.

It seems then that drugs to control pregnancy sickness should not be used unless specifically prescribed by a doctor who knows you are pregnant. Do not take any pills for travel sickness if you think you may be pregnant.

Antibiotics

Antibiotics may be prescribed in pregnancy; obviously their use is sometimes necessary and any disadvantages to the baby are outweighed. Never use antibiotics left in a bottle which were prescribed for a previous infection, even if you have exactly the same kind of infection as before. Tell your doctor that you think you may be pregnant, or remind him or her that you are pregnant, when you ask for a prescription.

Penicillin appears to be the safest antibiotic to take during the period of pregnancy, when one is essential.

Sulphonamides (which are not really antibiotics but effective antibacterials) are used to treat urinary infections. If you need to have sulphonamide treatment you may be advised to stop a week or so before the baby is due, to let it out of your system before you go into labor. Otherwise the newborn baby's kidneys may not be able to cope with excreting the drug and the baby may develop neonatal jaundice which can damage its central nervous system.

Tetracycline, a wide spectrum antibiotic, is deposited in the unborn baby's teeth and may cause yellow mottling and staining. It can also stop the growth of the baby's bones during the period when it is taken, so should not be used during pregnancy.

Streptomycin, another wide spectrum antibiotic, should never be taken in pregnancy. One of the drugs used to treat tuberculosis, it can cause deafness in the baby.

Drugs to treat constipation

Stool softeners, such as Colace, probably do no harm, used in moderation.

Stimulant laxatives, which include senna-based aperients such as Senokot, cascara, Dorbane and Dulcolax, seem to be safe for the fetus, but they may cause you to lose excessive amounts of fluid. Make sure that you drink plenty of liquids if you are taking any of these preparations.

Saline laxatives, including milk of magnesia and magnesium sulfate (Epsom salts), can also cause dehydration if you do not drink plenty of fluids, but otherwise they do not appear to be harmful to the fetus when used infrequently.

Various types of oil lubricate the bowels. But avoid liquid paraffin which reduces the absorption of vitamins A, D and K. A lack of vitamin K may lead to disorders of blood clotting in the baby. Extra fluids alone may cure your constipation, especially if you adjust your diet to include bran. (See page 117 for more about constipation.)

Drugs to reduce fluid retention
Diuretics increase the excretion of salt and water from the body, and in so doing make your kidneys work very hard. They are used in the prevention and treatment of preeclampsia (see page 121). They diminish blood flow through the placenta, reducing the oxygen and nutritional factors available to the baby. Since there is no proof that taking diuretics avoids preeclampsia, it is best to avoid them*. Discuss the matter with your doctor.

Steroids
Steroids are used for the treatment of asthma or hay fever, for eczema and other skin disorders, and for rheumatism and arthritis. They affect the salt and water balance of the body, as well as sugar, carbohydrate, protein, fat and calcium metabolism. Steroids may cause fetal abnormalities with prolonged use through pregnancy (although this is by no means always the case). But some women cannot avoid using them—women, for example, with severe asthma. If you are on steroids and plan to become pregnant, let your doctor know. It may be possible for you to change to a milder drug before starting the pregnancy.

Since steroids are often used in the form of skin ointments, do not use any cream prescribed for skin irritation in pregnancy unless there is real need for it.

Drugs to treat thyroid conditions
You may need to take drugs for an under or over active thyroid, but be aware that such drugs can have an effect on the baby's thyroid. Propylthiouracil should be used only in low doses during pregnancy. You may be advised to stop using it four or five weeks before the expected date of delivery, to allow the baby time to produce an adequate number of its own thyroid hormones, which the drug destroys. Discuss the drugs you are taking with your doctor, if possible before embarking on a pregnancy in the first place.

Anticoagulants
These drugs are prescribed for deep vein thrombosis or for a pulmonary embolism—both serious conditions caused by blood clots. Anticoagulants can cause hemorrhage in the baby and some, such as warfarin sodium (Coumadin) should not be taken in the last three months of pregnancy. If an anticoagulant needs to be given towards the end of pregnancy, Heparin by injection is the safest. Any adverse effects on the fetus can be reversed by small doses of vitamin K given to the baby after delivery*.

Drugs to treat diabetes
Drugs which are taken by mouth to reduce blood sugar should not be used during pregnancy*. They can cause miscarriage or fetal abnormalities. Injections of insulin are safer. If you are diabetic and want to get pregnant, let your doctor know and discuss in advance how the pregnancy will be managed (see page 122).

Anti-convulsants If you normally take anticonvulsants or antiepileptic drugs, discuss the possibility with your doctor of modifying your treatment before you become pregnant. These drugs may cause cleft palate in the baby.

General anesthetics There are times when a general anesthetic may be necessary during pregnancy; but if possible such anesthetics should be avoided because the baby becomes anesthetized too. Make sure that if your doctor or dentist recommends general anesthesia for anything he or she knows you are pregnant.

Other harmful influences

X rays In pregnancy it is wise to cut down the use of X rays to the minimum, because there is no safe threshold for radiation, and hence no minimum level at which you can be assured that X rays are safe for your unborn child. So avoid X rays during pregnancy if possible, or in the second half of the menstrual cycle if there is a chance that you might be pregnant.

Radiation can partially destroy the genetic material which acts as the blueprint for the normal development of each cell of the body. A damaged cell is called a mutation. Radiation can have the greatest effects on an embryo which is in the initial stages of development, and a badly affected embryo is likely to be aborted spontaneously. But X-rays taken in pregnancy can also have an effect after birth*: there is evidence that X rays are associated with a higher than usual chance of developing diseases of the respiratory system, blood disorders and infectious illnesses in childhood.

There are some cases in which diagnostic X rays are important and the only means of discovering certain disorders. If a doctor or a dentist advises X rays, take professional advice, but check whether they really are essential.

High temperature If you find you are running a temperature, go to bed, drink plenty of fluids and sponge yourself down with cold water, or have cool baths or showers to lower your body temperature. Do not just let your temperature rise. There is a slight chance that a very high temperature—say, over 102°F (39°C)—in the first four months of pregnancy can damage a baby*. The most crucial time is during the third and fourth weeks after conception. This is a horrifying thing to learn in late pregnancy if you know you had flu earlier on, but most babies are born whole and healthy even when the mother has run a high temperature. Nevertheless, it is sensible to avoid becoming run down, and so more susceptible to infection, if you think you may be pregnant. Keep up a high intake of protein and vitamin C in your diet so that you reduce the risk of contracting an infection. As far as we know, there does not seem to be any risk of serious damage to the fetus from a high temperature at any time after the 16th week of pregnancy.

6 6 I had some sort of virus, with a high temperature, sore throat and everything. And I was scared stiff. In fact, it haunted me right through the pregnancy, wondering if the baby was normal. And she's gorgeous. 9 9

Hot saunas and hot baths lasting for a long time can also produce a temperature high enough to harm a developing baby, so keep the temperatures down in pregnancy. Your own comfort is probably the best guide.

Vaccination Vaccinations are not recommended during the first four months of pregnancy, during which time there is a small risk of damage to the fetus. In the later months, most vaccinations (apart from rubella; see below) are considered harmless, although you should avoid smallpox vaccination throughout pregnancy, especially if you have never been vaccinated against smallpox before. If you are traveling to a country which still insists on smallpox vaccination, you can obtain exemption with a certificate of pregnancy from your doctor.

Rubella (German measles) is such a mild disease that many people have it in childhood without knowing it. Unfortunately, if you contract rubella when you are pregnant, the germs may cross the placenta and in the first 20 weeks of pregnancy they can have a serious effect on the baby. It is therefore sensible to have a blood test before you even become pregnant: if the test shows that you have never had rubella you can be vaccinated against it. Alternatively, if you are already pregnant you can be vaccinated immediately after the birth of your baby.

The protection afforded by rubella vaccination lasts at least seven years, and probably much longer. After you have been vaccinated, be very careful about contraception for the next three months, since you should not conceive until you have had time to build up immunity to the virus in your system. Never have a rubella vaccination if you think you might be pregnant.

If you did not have a rubella vaccination before you started your pregnancy and have never had the disease, avoid all contact with children who might possibly have it. If you think you have been in contact with rubella, get in touch with your doctor immediately. He or she may offer you an injection of gamma globulin, but the chances of the baby being damaged by rubella in the first three months of pregnancy are high, especially in the first eight weeks; if you contract the disease you may want to consider an abortion.

The Rhesus negative woman All blood is either Rhesus positive or Rhesus negative. 86% of people are Rhesus positive, which means that their blood contains something known as the Rhesus factor. This factor is tested for early on in your pregnancy as part of your routine blood test. Its presence or absence is noted, but is only important in one combination of circumstances: if you are Rhesus negative and the baby's father is Rhesus positive. There is no problem if the baby is Rhesus negative, but 40% of all Rhesus positive babies in these circumstances are affected by a specific condition.

If you are a Rhesus negative mother bearing a Rhesus positive baby, some of the baby's red blood cells may leak into your circulation. This is particularly likely in late pregnancy and at delivery. Your body then responds to the Rhesus factor present in the baby's cells as if to an invader, and begins to manufacture antibodies against it. The danger arises when some of these antibodies leak back from your circulation into the baby's, where they proceed to destroy large numbers of the baby's own red blood cells.

The flow of red blood cells each way across the placenta is not usually substantial enough during a first pregnancy to cause your body to develop such antibodies. But when your first baby is born, some of its blood may flow from the placenta into your circulation. This triggers the creation of antibodies to the Rhesus factor in your blood. From then on you produce antibodies to the Rhesus factor, and the next time you are pregnant with a Rhesus

The Rhesus factor
A Rhesus negative woman rarely has problems with her first baby, because in a normal pregnancy the maternal and fetal bloodstreams never mix. At delivery, however, some of the baby's blood cells can enter the mother's bloodstream. If the baby is Rhesus positive the mother's blood develops antibodies to the baby's blood cells. The danger is that in a subsequent pregnancy the antibodies will cross the placenta and attack another Rhesus positive baby's blood.

EACH SUBSEQUENT PREGNANCY

THE FIRST PREGNANCY

In a second pregnancy, these antibodies cross the placenta. If the new baby is also Rhesus positive its blood is damaged (in severe cases destroyed) by the mother's antibodies.

The Rhesus factor is only important when a Rhesus negative woman is carrying a Rhesus positive baby. At delivery some of the baby's positive blood cells may leak into the maternal bloodstream. As a result the woman develops antibodies which destroy any Rhesus positive blood cells.

KEY

⊟	Rhesus negative blood
⊞	Rhesus positive blood
▲	Rhesus antibodies

THE SOLUTION

Doctors now routinely inject a serum into Rhesus negative women within 48 hours of the birth of each baby. The serum prevents antibodies to Rhesus positive blood developing in the maternal bloodstream.

positive baby your antibodies may attack the baby's blood vigorously. It may get jaundice, its brain can be damaged, severe anemia may develop and it may not survive.

There are several things that can be done about this. The first and simplest is an injection, given to the Rhesus negative mother immediately after the birth of a Rhesus positive baby. It is a serum which stops her biological defense mechanisms acting against foreign Rhesus substances. A fresh injection of this serum is given after each subsequent delivery. The same routine is followed after a miscarriage or a termination of pregnancy too, since it is possible that the aborted fetus was Rhesus positive and that some of its blood entered the mother's bloodstream.

It is no good giving this serum *after* a woman's body has already produced antibodies. If a high proportion of antibodies is detected in your blood during a second or subsequent pregnancy, and your baby is known to be at risk, amniocentesis may be performed (see page 186) and the amniotic fluid analyzed for the presence of bilirubin (bile pigment). An anemic fetus excretes into the fluid large amounts of bilirubin from destroyed red blood cells.

If this is the case and if the baby is sufficiently mature to face life outside you, the labor may be induced early. If necessary the baby can be treated immediately after delivery and given a complete blood transfusion to eradicate all the antibodies from its bloodstream.

Such a transfusion is only possible when antibodies build up at the end of pregnancy. It does not help the baby who is still too tiny to be born. Fortunately as more and more Rhesus negative women are routinely immunized after delivery this situation is increasingly rare. If it does occur, a blood transfusion can be given to the fetus any time from the 22nd week of pregnancy. This operation can be done using fiber optics, where the light is attached to a long needle inserted through the abdominal wall (see page 187).

An incompetent cervix Occasionally a woman's cervix may be torn from a previous difficult labor or from a midpregnancy termination. You would not find this out until your next pregnancy, when you might lose your baby after the fourth month as a result of cervical incompetence (see page 292).

An obstetrician would probably recommend sewing the cervix closed for the duration of any subsequent pregnancy. This is a relatively simple procedure: once the pregnancy is established, a suture is inserted under anesthesia and is threaded through and around the cervix like the drawstring of a purse. The suture is removed when you are 36 weeks pregnant or later. Some obstetricians like to induce labor at this point because they say it is simpler, since contractions often start shortly after the removal of the suture anyway. You are not compelled to have labor induced, however, and should decide whether this is what you want in such circumstances.

Your physical wellbeing

To get the most out of the experience of being pregnant, you should insure that your body is in good condition. Remember that healthy activity can be pleasurable in itself as well as being an excellent preparation for labor. Sometimes books on pregnancy and even childbirth educators give the impression that childbirth is an athletic event for which you have to train like a marathon runner, a kind of examination for which you must study assiduously, or even an ordeal with which you are unlikely to cope but which will be quickly forgotten afterwards. No wonder expectant mothers become anxious! No mention is made of the excitement, joy and sheer pleasure that many women experience in childbirth.

Most women look forward to childbirth with excited anticipation. They know that there is a slight chance of something going wrong but that the better they have prepared themselves by doing bodytoning movements and exercises, the more likely they are to be able to handle any emergencies.

Getting to know your body

Before beginning exercises, it is useful to gain an awareness early in pregnancy of how your body works and what is taking place in your reproductive organs. One way of doing this is to have a closer look at your genitals. For a clear view, you can kneel or squat over a mirror. A flashlight might help you to see the area better.

The perineum The perineum is the tissue around your vagina and between your vagina and anus. Just before delivery it begins to bulge and its tissues fan out and open up as the ball of the baby's head presses through it.

The vagina Your vagina is the soft, cushioned canal which holds the penis during sexual intercourse; it is also the passage through which the baby is delivered. The outer part of the vagina is the vulva, consisting of layers of outer and inner lips (labia) constructed like the overlapping petals of a rose. During pregnancy they change in color from red to purple, the effect of the pregnancy hormones which have also darkened your nipples, maybe your face and other parts of your skin.

Insert one or two fingers into your vagina and feel around the stretchy folds inside. Though the sides of the vagina are normally touching each other and there is no hollow space, notice how readily they spread apart. They open like an accordion when the baby is pressing down through them to be born, and hormones flowing in your bloodstream will make them even softer and more flexible in later pregnancy.

The clitoris

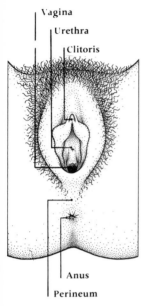

Vagina
Urethra
Clitoris

Anus
Perineum

Your clitoris is like a bud rising from the inner lips at the upper (front) end of your vagina. Its base and the inner lips around it are very sensitive, and pressure or stroking of these parts produces sexual excitement. As you touch its root, you may notice that it swells up. You will see that there is a hood or fold of skin surrounding the clitoris and that this connects up with the inner lips. So anything in your vagina which stretches the inner lips apart will also pull on this hood and the clitoris will be stimulated in this way as well as by direct manipulation.

A woman's genitals vary as much as a man's. Just as penises are different sizes, for example, the clitoris may be the size and shape of a small pea or more like the curved center of an orchid. Women's labia vary too. Some are firm, some soft, some large and fleshy, others smaller. A woman may worry that masturbation might have changed the shape of her labia or clitoris, but these· organs are so flexible that pulling, pressing or rubbing them does not produce permanent structural changes. Doctors and midwives cannot tell your sex life by examining your vulva, though many women harbor a secret fear that they can.

At delivery the baby presses against this whole area that you are examining, easing forward the tissues so that they open up like elastic, and then slides out with a rush of liquid. After the baby is born these flexible tissues spring back again; at first they will not be as firm as they were before, but during the weeks after childbirth they gain in tone.

The cervix

Now introduce your longest finger deep inside your vagina and you meet the rounded, firm cervix (the neck of the womb), the part of the uterus that will open (dilate) when you are in labor. Early in pregnancy it will feel like the tip of your nose. You may notice a little dip in the middle, like the dimple in the center of a buttoned cushion. This is where the mucous plug is situated, and this plug, like the cork in a bottle, seals off the uterus from the outside. At the end of pregnancy the cervix will have softened and, when you touch it with your finger, it will feel more like your mouth when it is soft and relaxed than like your nose. This is one of the signs that you are ready to go into labor. The cervix is "ripe".

The pelvic floor

The muscles which support everything inside the pelvic cavity (including the uterus, the bladder and the rectum) are called the pelvic floor. They have special significance for your health and vitality, whatever age you are and whether or not you are pregnant. The upright position that human beings have adopted in preference to the all fours stance puts an extra stress on these muscle layers in pregnancy.

Though these muscles form a coordinated working structure, they are not really a "floor" at all. They are slanted at different angles and levels and can be held with varying degrees of firmness. The easiest way to find these muscles, of which some women are not aware, is to interrupt a stream of urine, since you bring

Keeping fit during pregnancy

While you are pregnant it is easy to allow muscles that were previously firm and elastic to sag. You are putting on weight, your figure is changing and you may assume that sagging muscles are an inevitable accompaniment to these changes. However, gentle, toning exercises, aimed at firming up your abdominal muscles and avoiding back strain, can do you and your baby nothing but good.

Pelvic rocking

Lie on a flat surface, your head and shoulders supported by pillows and your knees bent with the feet flat. Experiment with pressing the small of your back against the floor or bed and then releasing it so that you produce a gentle, rhythmic, rocking movement. Then roll your hips round in a very slow, circular, hula-hoop movement.

1 Keeping your upper back pressed firmly down, slightly raise your hips and buttocks and rock them gently to and fro.

2 Roll your pelvis around—as if you were doing a slow languorous belly dance while lying down.

Wrong

Although double-leg raising and sit-ups are exercises often recommended for pregnant women, they do not in fact strengthen the abdominal muscles. These muscles do not work to lift the legs but to stabilize the lower back. If they are not strong to start with, they cannot cope with the effort involved when the legs or trunk are raised, and the result is back strain or torn abdominal muscles.

Double-leg raising is rarely effective in toning abdominal muscles and should never be done in pregnancy or in the 4 weeks following birth.

Sit-ups can cause harm in pregnancy. They should never be done with the knees and back held straight if you are pregnant or in the first 6 weeks after childbirth.

Leg sliding

Leg sliding is a gentle exercise that allows you to tone up your tummy muscles efficiently without straining them. Do it five or six times at first and gradually build up until you can do it comfortably 10 or 15 times. If at any point you feel your back aching, stop. Leg sliding is best done lying on your back on a firm surface with a pillow under your head and shoulders.

1 *Keeping the small of your back pressed down, bend your knees so that your feet are flat on the floor.*

2 *Slowly extend both legs until they are straight.*

3 *Draw one knee back up, then the other, without lifting the small of your back off the floor.*

Testing for separation of the rectus muscle

If you are starting exercises in the last three months of pregnancy, find out whether you have already damaged your rectus muscle. You will need to be careful when doing exercises for toning up your abdomen if this muscle has separated (see page 107).

1 *Lying on your back with your knees bent, slowly raise your head and shoulders about 8 in (20 cm), stretching your arms out in front of you.*

2 *Place your hands on your tummy. A small soft bulge like a marshmallow in the middle below your navel means the rectus muscle has probably separated.*

The pelvic floor muscles form a figure 8 around the vagina and anus. Learning to contract and release these muscles efficiently during pregnancy will help you both during labor and after your baby is born.

all of the pelvic floor muscles into play when you do this. Or you can think of them as forming a figure eight round the front and back passages. In the middle of the eight is a horizontal bar, the transverse perineal muscle. When the muscles of the pelvic floor are contracted, the circular shapes of the eight change to almond shapes and the transverse perineal muscle is pulled up and over towards the pubic bone (the firm ridge of bone just above your clitoris) like the opening lid of a roll-top desk. You can feel this happening from both inside and outside if you put one finger inside the vagina and a thumb over the pubis.

Your pelvic floor muscles contract spontaneously during love-making, increasing your sensations of pleasure and those of your partner. Awareness and control of these muscles are important in labor too, when you will need to be able to release them as you press the baby down the birth canal.

Some people can hold their pelvic muscles contracted much longer than others, and you may notice, when you first try to contract these muscles, that they tire and tremble. To exercise your pelvic floor muscles gradually, you can pretend that this area is an elevator which you are taking to the first floor. You hold it there, then move on to the second floor, and so on until the muscles are fully contracted. Then release them gradually to the ground floor. Finally finish with a toning movement by drawing the muscles up to the first floor again. If you do this between 20 and 30 times a day you will be able to hold them firm for longer periods, building up to a count of eight or nine without holding your breath or tightening up your shoulders. But always alternate tightening movements with resting spaces to allow the muscles to be reoxygenated in the intervals between activity.

Toning your abdominal muscles

The human backbone is curved, not straight as in many four legged animals. In some people it is almost S-shaped. Because of the forward load produced by pregnancy, strain is put on the spine, especially in the small of the back, and the upper spine may be pushed into the wrong position to compensate.

The abdominal muscles

Four legged mammals take the extra weight of pregnancy on their abdominal muscles slung evenly between the front and back limbs. Despite their upright stance, human beings also need well toned abdominal muscles for comfortable pregnancy because, if these are flabby, the back muscles are forced to take on too much work to support the spine. When this happens, the vertebrae of the lower spine are forced into an unnatural position and the discs between them are subjected to great pressure. They may slide and become displaced. This leads to exhausting back-ache. Girdles cannot help much; they just take over some of the work that healthy muscles should be doing. The best girdle is composed of your own tummy and buttock muscles, and both sets need to be toned to provide mutual support.

To understand what will benefit your abdominal muscles and what might be harmful to them, it is useful to know how this girdle of muscles is constructed and how it works.

The muscle running from top to bottom down the front is called the rectus muscle and it bears much of the load of late pregnancy. It is separated into two halves by a line down the center which is like a seam. When you are about halfway through your pregnancy, this may show as a dark line in your skin from your navel down to your pubic hair line, although it does not occur in all women. You can see the same line as an indentation about the width of a pencil in photographs of Mr Universe flexing his muscles and caving in his abdomen. The two sides of the rectus muscle can be pulled apart if the muscle is subjected to too great a stress and then the muscle "unzips". Constipation and straining on the toilet can sometimes cause this muscle to separate.

You can test yourself to find out if there is any separation of the rectus muscle. Lying on your back with a pillow under your head, knees bent, rest your hands on your tummy and *very slowly* lift your head and shoulders with your chin tucked in. If you can feel a soft bulging area the width of a finger or more, the muscle has separated. If this is the case, you can rehabilitate the muscle after the baby is born (see page 303). Meanwhile concentrate on leg sliding (see page 105).

Some exercises that are intended to strengthen the abdominal muscles can also cause the rectus muscle to separate. You should never try double-leg raising exercises while you are pregnant, or even single-leg raising unless the muscles are already in very good condition. Nor should you do exercises that entail putting your feet under a heavy piece of furniture and then raising the upper parts of your body or any kind of sit-ups without using your hands to help. Not only can these exercises damage the abdominal muscles, they can also strain the back.

Exploring pelvic movement

The bones that form the pelvis are like a cradle for the baby growing inside you, a cradle that can rock in all directions. Feel your pelvic bones with your fingers. Start with your hip bones. Press in over their upper ridges and then walk your fingers around and down into the small of your back where your hip girdle joins your spine. The point at which it does so is the sacrum, the bone which forms the back of the pelvis and the outlet through which the baby descends to be born.

Now walk the fingers around again to the big bones at the side, then down into the groin and around the front till they meet at your pubic bone. This forms the front of the pelvis and the baby dips down under this bridge of bone just before delivery. Notice that your pubis is much lower than your sacrum. The human pelvis is tilted. Once you have found exactly where these bones are and have a clear picture of them, get your partner to feel them too. Guide his hands so that he is able to track your pelvis accurately.

Sacrum

Pubis

Posture and balance

*Good posture is essential to your physical wellbeing during
pregnancy. This means not only learning to stand and walk in the
best way, so that your baby is cradled in the pelvis in a position
that is comfortable for both of you, but also performing other
everyday movements, such as getting out of bed, in a way
calculated to avoid unnecessary strain. To achieve good posture
you need to improve the tone of your muscles and to learn how to
use only those muscles necessary for whatever you are doing.
If you are looking good and walking with a spring in your step,
you will probably also feel much better.*

Maintaining good posture

Make a point of tucking
in your buttock muscles,
and feel your tummy
muscles working to
straighten out your spine.
Keep your shoulders
dropped. Now imagine a
string is pulling your
head straight up, and
notice the back of your
neck lengthening.

Wrong
*If the weight of
your uterus makes
you stand back on
your heels, with
your bottom stuck
out and your
shoulders flung
back, your spine
becomes hollowed
and you get low
backache.*

Tailor sitting

Tailor sitting is an
ideal way of rounding
out the lower back.
As long as you take
care not to slouch
over, it can be
one of the most
comfortable
positions for
sitting during
pregnancy.

Bridging

In late pregnancy your tummy muscles can feel so
stretched that it might be difficult to exercise them
consciously. If this is the case, it helps to tighten your
buttock muscles, since this means that you pull in your
tummy muscles too. Bridging improves the tone of your
buttock muscles and helps the circulation in your legs.

*1 Lie on the floor with your
heels raised on a low table
or stool.*

*2 Tighten your buttock and
abdominal muscles and lift
your bottom up off the floor,
keeping your back straight.*

*3 Hold this position for
several seconds, then slowly
lower your hips.*

The rocking-chair exercise

This exercise encourages good posture by allowing you to press out the small of your back while keeping the rest of your body aligned. You become the rocking chair that rocks to and fro, and you need a partner to set you in motion and provide the firm surface against which you press your lower back. Avoid hollowing your back at any time.

Getting up from lying down

If you sit up suddenly after you have been lying on your back, you put great pressure on your tummy muscles, especially in advanced pregnancy. The method below is a way of avoiding undue strain on these muscles, and, since it involves changing from a horizontal to an upright position in gentle stages, it is also good for the circulation.

1 *Your partner stands in front of you with his hands on your hips.*

2 *You rock your pelvis gently backwards and forwards between his hands several times.*

1 *Roll over on to one side, swinging your shoulders round and drawing up your knees.*

2 *Push yourself up with your upper arm while swiveling your legs from the hips over to the edge of the bed.*

3 *Now he stands at your side and puts one hand on the small of your back and the other hand over your lower tummy.*

4 *You continue the rocking movement, pushing against his hand with the small of your back and then moving away from it.*

3 *Tighten your buttocks and swing your legs over the side of the bed in a smooth and coordinated movement.*

Pelvic rocking Lie on any flat surface (it can be a firm bed), with your head and shoulders supported by two pillows and your knees bent with the feet flat. Explore the capacity for movement in your pelvis. Experiment with gentle, rhythmic rocking, then try rolling the cradle round as if you were doing a very slow hula hoop movement. This is a kind of belly dancing while lying down, in which you tighten your tummy muscles while pressing your buttocks together. As you do so, notice how the muscles are alternately tightened and released and the way in which tummy and buttock muscles work in a coordinated way.

Now combine this movement with controlled breathing. Each time you pull your tummy muscles *in* and press your buttocks together, give a strong breath *out* through your mouth. Then, as you release the muscles and rock your pelvis gently forward (it is a very slight movement), allow your lungs to fill up with air, breathing in through your nose. Do it at your own pace, emphasizing the breath out and letting the breath in take care of itself. This movement done in early pregnancy is a good way of toning abdominal muscles for the work they must do later.

Now rest your fingers on the big bones at the front of the pelvis on either side. Continue the movement with the breathing and notice the swing up and down of these bones. This is the distance the bony cradle rocks as you walk and move around in pregnancy. The baby is accustomed to these movements during its intrauterine existence, and it is not surprising that rocking a newborn baby quietens and soothes it. Research shows that a baby being rocked is most likely to be comforted by a swing of 3 in (7.5 cm) to either side*. This corresponds exactly with the arc of the pelvic rock.

A position with firm support for your spine is best for practicing this pelvic rocking. Other positions allow you to hollow your back in an exaggerated way, which can be harmful, especially in advanced pregnancy, because it puts stress on the sacroiliac joint, which is situated at the top of your buttocks. Such strain is particularly bad for you when you are pregnant because your ligaments are already softened by hormones released into the blood during pregnancy to make the vagina and cervix more flexible in preparation for the birth. Once these ligaments have softened, any form of pelvic rocking which involves back *hollowing* can cause more backache.

Exercises in pregnancy

Exercises to help you cope with the stresses of pregnancy should be matched by others designed to help your adjustment after childbirth, since this is the time when the speediest and most dramatic physical changes are happening to you. Postnatal exercises are simply a modification of the ones you learn in pregnancy, so there is no need for you to learn completely new ones after the birth. In this book postnatal exercises are described on pages 302–303.

Posture and balance

Good posture maintained every day is more important than pregnancy gymnastics. As the weight load changes you should give conscious thought to balance and body mechanics, something that is usually taken for granted. It is not just a matter of "standing straight, head up" like the girl who walks with a book on her head, but of understanding how to economize on muscle work and use only those muscles that are needed for any task. This always results in more graceful and comfortable movement without straining and effort.

Standing To achieve good posture, you should stand with your back to a wall, heels far enough away from it for your seat and shoulders just to touch it. Press the small of your back towards the wall and you will feel your seat tucking under and your tummy muscles working to straighten out your spine. Make sure that you do not tighten your shoulders. Keep them dropped. Now imagine that a string is pulling your head up from the center at the top and notice the back of your neck lengthening. Relax your jaw. (Your jaw muscles cannot force your head up!) Walk a few steps away from the wall. You will find that you are in a stiff, exaggerated stance like a soldier on duty. Let the muscles settle into a more comfortable state. The rocking chair exercise (see page 109) encourages good posture, and can be done with the help of your partner.

Walking Whenever possible, walk rather than stand. The healthiest, most rhythmic and natural all around exercise is walking. If you have to stand around, exercise your feet while you do so, even if only by screwing up and extending your toes, going up onto the ball of the foot and down again and shifting weight from one foot to the other. Muscles in the feet and legs pump blood back to the heart, so movement is important to maintain good circulation in the legs.

You can also increase the tone of your buttock muscles and help the circulation in your legs by bridging (see page 108).*

Sitting Sit back on your chair and see that your spine is well supported. If necessary, put a small cushion in the small of the back. In the last few weeks of your pregnancy you may need more support than this, especially if you are carrying twins (see page 82). If you have to write or type at a desk for any length of time, occasionally rest your head down on it and stretch the back of your neck.

Bending and lifting Use your legs, not your back, when you reach down for anything. This means that, whenever possible, you should bend your knees and get right down to the load. Kneel or squat when you are working low down, cleaning the tub or making a low bed, for example. Avoid misusing your spine as if it were a crane. For some jobs, such as wiping or polishing a floor, it is most comfortable to get onto all fours. This takes the weight of the baby off your spine and is surprisingly comfortable, especially if you do have backache.

Aches and pains

In late pregnancy you are carrying more weight which, instead of being evenly distributed, is centered in one area and so affects your balance. This extra weight alone can cause aches and pains by straining muscles and causing you to adopt an unnatural stance, leading to further strain. The way the baby is lying can also cause discomfort and occasionally sharp shooting pain when the baby is pressing against a nerve.

Foot exercises

Foot exercises discourage varicose veins in the legs by stimulating the blood flow back to the heart. When you are sitting down or having a rest, practice drawing the letters of the alphabet with your feet, one foot at a time, keeping your legs still. You will find that you can easily read or do some work at the same time.

At any time when you are sitting comfortably, draw letters or even whole words, moving only your feet and ankles.

The angry cat

However many exercises you do with your back well supported, it feels good to get the weight of the baby off your spine occasionally. You can do this by going on to all fours and rocking your pelvis, an exercise sometimes known as "the angry cat". This is a kind of pelvic rocking reversed.

1 *Get on to all fours, keeping the small of your back flat, not hollowed.*

2 *Without moving your elbows or knees, tighten your tummy muscles and hump up your lower back. Relax back to the flat position after a few seconds.*

Wrong

Never under any circumstances allow the lower back to cave in.

The wheelbarrow

Towards the end of pregnancy many women have pain in the groin. This usually occurs as a result of pressure from the baby on the joints of the pelvis. To relieve the discomfort, try this exercise, your partner kneeling very close to you.

2 Your partner slowly lifts your hips. He holds them up for a moment, then gently lowers them.

1 Lie on your back with your knees bent. Your partner holds your hips at either side.

Wall stretching

A good way to lift your ribs off your expanding uterus is simply to stretch high with first one arm then the other, until you are comfortable. A similar exercise may be done by sitting with your back pressed against a wall to help alignment.

The shoulder roll

Upper backache, which is caused by poor posture or heavy breasts, can be relieved by doing the shoulder-roll exercise.

1 Sit with your back pressed against a wall and your legs stretched out in front of you.

2 Swing your arms out to the sides at shoulder level and, with your hands pressed against the wall, walk your fingers up it.

3 Turn your palms outward when your hands have reached as high as they can go.

Rest your fingertips on your shoulders and rotate your elbows back.

Lying down and getting up The front-lateral or "three-quarters-over" position is often the most comfortable when you are lying in bed. It may help to put a pillow under your upper knee. Allow good space between your legs. Avoid hollowing your back when you are lying down too. This is likely to happen if you have a soft mattress and like to lie on your front. If necessary, put a small pillow under your hips so that your back does not cave in.

Whenever you get up from lying on your back, roll over onto one side first, swinging your shoulders round, and push with your upper arm, drawing up your knees at the same time till you are in a kneeling position; tighten your buttocks and then rise from that position (see page 109). This movement will avoid unnecessary strain on your abdominal muscles. It may sound complicated but it can come to be a beautifully smooth, co-ordinated movement, making you feel like Cleopatra rising from her barge.

Aches and pains Although bad posture is often responsible for aches and pains during pregnancy, you may have other aches and pains that are just the result of being pregnant. If this is the case all you can do to relieve them is concentrate on relaxation and experiment with different positions in which you feel more comfortable.

Low backache In late pregnancy, if the baby is facing toward your front and engages as a posterior (see page 218) with the back of its head pressing against your sacrum, you may develop backache. Rest in positions in which the weight of the baby is tilted off the spine, and take every opportunity to get onto all fours. Scrubbing a kitchen floor can provide extraordinary relief from backache. The angry cat (see page 112) is an exercise that combines this position with pelvic rocking to relieve your spine of the baby's weight.

Upper backache This occurs when you try to compensate for the weight of your pregnancy dragging you forward, by flinging your shoulders back and tightening the muscles in the upper back. Roll your shoulders backwards whenever you have the opportunity and do the shoulder roll exercise (see page 113).

Tingling and numbness You may sometimes feel a tingling and numbness in your hand. This is known as the carpal tunnel syndrome. It results from pressure on the nerves and tendons caused by swelling of the hand and wrist. You will be most aware of it in the morning after your wrists have accumulated fluid during the night. To relieve the sensations of discomfort, try the shoulder roll or hold your hand above your head for a few minutes and flex and extend the fingers.

Pain under the ribs You may experience pain below the ribs at either side when the top of the uterus (the fundus) is high after 30 weeks (see page 67). This pain tends to come on whichever side the baby is lying.

You will discover that you are only comfortable when sitting straight on a rather high chair and will not want to slump down onto your uterus. In spite of folklore about the dangers of an expectant mother lifting her arms above her head, it cannot hurt the baby to stretch upward so that your whole rib cage is lifted off the uterus. You can also do stretching exercises with a wall supporting you (see page 113).

Pain in the groin In late pregnancy it is common to have pain around the pubic area, where the pelvic joints have softened in readiness for labor. Avoid standing for long periods, and even when sitting change position often. Symptoms can be relieved by doing the wheelbarrow exercise (see page 113).

Cramp in the leg A few pregnant women get cramps because they are trying to go on a salt free diet. Eating something salty before you go to bed may make the cramp disappear. However, some cramps are probably caused by a calcium deficiency and, if you are plagued by recurring cramps, you may be prescribed calcium tablets. Avoid curling your toes under. Make up the bed loosely so that your toes are not pressed down by the bedlinen overnight.

Lifting your feet above the level of your heart will also help circulation and may relieve cramps. However, in advanced pregnancy this may give you indigestion, so you are left with a choice between two discomforts. While you are lying with your feet up, roll them around in circles from the ankles to help stretch the calf muscles, or practice drawing the letters of the alphabet, with your toe, keeping your legs still. If you do get cramp, ask your partner to grip your heel and push your foot up while pressing down on your knee with the other hand. It is a useful precaution to do this regularly about ten times before you settle down for the night.

Common problems during pregnancy

Although your baby can grow inside you without your having to think consciously or do anything about it, this growth affects your whole body and every system in it. You may worry about these disconcerting changes in your system if you do not understand why they have occurred.

Varicose veins The valves which help direct the blood through the veins back to the heart may soften in pregnancy and become unable to propel the increased amount of blood through the legs.

Avoid all positions which allow pooling of blood in the legs: sitting with your legs crossed or with your thighs pressing against the edge of your chair, for example. Foot exercises will help keep the blood moving. If you are advised to wear elastic stockings, choose semi- or full-support styles and put them on *before* you get up in the morning. Bend a knee, put one leg on and wriggle it up; then do the same with the other.

Swimming when you are pregnant is a good way of maintaining a state of physical wellbeing. . . .

Vaginal varicose veins Sometimes a woman develops varicose veins in her vagina. The discomfort may be relieved by wrapping some ice chips in a clean handkerchief, knotting it and packing it against the sore and tender areas. Obviously you cannot walk around like this, but it is a good excuse to lie down for a while, offering a position in which the whole weight of your uterus is not pressing down on the swollen veins. Sometimes vitamin B6 (pyridoxine) can help (see page 88), and you should take prenatal vitamins which contain B6.

Hemorrhoids (also known as piles) are varicose veins of the rectum and can be caused by constipation. If you have piles, avoid any straining on the toilet. This condition should be treated as quickly as possible because the hemorrhoids can become prolapsed (protrude through the anus) causing extreme pain. Your doctor may give you a prescription for a pain-relieving cream. Alternatively a cotton pad soaked in witch-hazel can also bring relief.

Constipation You are more likely to be constipated during pregnancy because some of the extra hormones produced while you are pregnant cause the intestine to relax and become less efficient. First of all insure that you are eating the right kinds of food (see page 84). Eat plenty of fruit, vegetables, roughage and whole grains and drink as much water as you can. When you are on the toilet, allow your pelvic floor to be fully released and bulging down. Take your time over moving your bowels, and take a brisk walk every day if possible.

Bladder control and infections In the first three months or so of your pregnancy the developing baby and enlarging uterus are pressing against your bladder, while the extra progesterone flowing through your bloodstream softens the tissues. So it is quite normal for a pregnant woman to have to urinate very often. This may be even more noticeable at the very end of pregnancy when the baby has descended into your pelvis ready to be born.

Cystitis Pressure and engorgement of blood vessels in the pelvic area mean that a pregnant woman is more exposed to the risk of urinary infection. If you notice a stinging, burning feeling when you pass urine, this usually indicates that you have developed cystitis. If left untreated, cystitis rapidly becomes very uncomfortable.

If you suspect that you have cystitis, go to your doctor, who will probably prescribe a course of antibiotics to be taken for 10 to 14 days. It is sensible to seek help when you first notice the symptoms as delay can mean that the infection takes hold more firmly. As a general treatment, drink plenty of liquid. Drink a glass of water every time you have used the toilet. Drinking cranberry, orange, lemon or grapefruit juice may help or an alkaline-based drink such as a mixture of sodium bicarbonate and sodium citrate. One natural remedy is marshmallow herb tea.

Wear cotton briefs and avoid any clothing that is tight on the crotch. If you wear pantihose, get some that have a cotton panel or air holes between the legs. Spend time on the toilet to empty your bladder as completely as possible. When the baby is pressing against your bladder in late pregnancy, you will be able to shift position so that the baby moves a little, allowing you to void some more.

Pyelitis If you have a temperature and low back pain, and if it hurts when you apply pressure over your kidneys, on one or both sides, you may have pyelitis (a kidney infection). Sometimes the infection causes nausea and vomiting too. Seek treatment immediately, since this is not only painful for you, but can affect the functioning of the placenta. Antibiotics are effective, but all the measures suggested for coping with cystitis are also helpful and you will probably appreciate a hot water bottle against the painful area. Women with pyelitis are often admitted to the hospital so that a proper diagnosis can be made. The right drugs can usually clear up the problem altogether within two weeks or less.

Yeast infections

It is normal to have an increased vaginal discharge in pregnancy, but if your vulva becomes itchy and your vagina is red, sore and burning, you probably have thrush ("candida" or "monilia"). Vaginal suppositories are usually prescribed. Cut out sugar and white flour and try a diet based on whole grains, fruit, vegetables and protein. Natural, plain (not flavored!) yoghurt may be inserted with a vaginal applicator to restore the natural balance of organisms and reduce itching, but this remedy is not always effective on its own.

Vomiting

For some women the nausea and vomiting that is very common in the first three months of pregnancy (see page 31) goes on much longer, and this prolonged sickness is known by the medical term of hyperemesis. A woman with hyperemesis is really ill because she cannot take any food by mouth. Surprisingly, the cure may simply be admission to the hospital; often no further treatment is necessary. This is why some psychiatrists and obstetricians have suggested that cyclical vomiting in pregnancy is a symptom of disturbed relationships and that, if the woman has a chance to get away from the relentless day-to-day contact with a partner, mother, mother-in-law, or anyone who is part of the stress to which she is reacting, the vomiting will ease off.

If you find that you are vomiting at all hours of the day, cannot be sure of keeping any meal down and are feeling really wretched, it is worth trying to get away, preferably among people you know only slightly or not at all, and who will not fuss over you. If this gives you the opportunity to do something you have never done before (not hang gliding!) or see something you have never had a chance of seeing before, so much the better. There is a phrase that is sometimes used about a person who is "run down":

"she needs taking out of herself". A woman who is vomiting almost without interruption may need to be taken "out" of herself and her usual relationships until she can cope emotionally, and then, when her pregnancy has settled down, she can come back "into" herself with new strength.

Breast tenderness

The normal breast tenderness of the early weeks of pregnancy can be acutely painful for some women, and they walk around with stiff arms to protect themselves in case anyone brushes against them. A good supporting bra (see page 124) is important even if you do not normally wear one, since if the breasts are increasing in size, as they usually are at this stage, their own weight can be uncomfortable. If your breasts become extra-sensitive like this, you will not enjoy your partner's most gentle touch until about the middle of pregnancy.

Inverted nipples

Some women have one or both nipples shaped like dimples. These are called "inverted" nipples. If you have a nipple like this but can press it out, or if it projects when you are sexually excited, the baby will be able to get hold of the nipple well and draw it out further. Otherwise you may find it more difficult to get the baby on the breast and sucking well. However, if you do manage to start the baby off, he or she will suck the nipple into a good projecting shape. It is a fallacy to think that you have to have prominent nipples in order to nurse successfully.

WEARING A NIPPLE SHIELD
Using a dome-shaped plastic nipple shield under your bra in the last 2 months of pregnancy may help your nipple into an easier shape for the baby. The pressure of the shield on the breast coaxes the nipple through the hole in the middle.

Usual nipple shape   Shape of inverted nipple   Plastic nipple shield

Nasal congestion

Sinusitis Mucous membrane inside the nostrils and sinuses often swells up during pregnancy because of the action of hormones flowing in the bloodstream which are also, fortunately, softening up your vagina and cervix. Some women seem to have a permanent cold in late pregnancy for this reason. It does not interfere with your breathing during labor, so there is no need to worry about this, though you may be more comfortable breathing through your mouth than through your nose. This means that you will need to take frequent sips of water or have a small plant spray filled with ice water to spray into your mouth between contractions and lip salve to smooth on your lips. The symptoms will go after delivery.

Nosebleeds are common in pregnancy. These, too, are associated with higher hormone levels and congestion. A tiny blob of vaseline in the nostril will usually stop a nosebleed, and you should avoid blowing your nose hard.

Vaginal bleeding in early pregnancy

Bleeding from the vagina at any stage of a pregnancy is always worrisome. In early pregnancy it may be that the level of your pregnancy hormones is not sufficiently high to avoid break-through spotting. There is no way you can stop this without possibly affecting the developing baby, but it is sensible to take it as a message from your body that you need rest. Go to bed and stay there till the bleeding stops. Cut out unnecessary exertion and, if the bleeding started at a time when your period would normally have been due, take life especially gently then and see if you can manage a few days in bed. Practice deep relaxation every day. There is further information about how to deal with a threatened miscarriage on page 291.

Vaginal bleeding in late pregnancy

If you notice bleeding in late pregnancy it may be a sign that labor is about to start. It is usually blood from around the cervix and, except in those cases where there is a polyp in the cervix that has started to bleed, shows that thinning out and some dilatation is taking place. If your baby is due within a month and the bleeding looks like the beginning of a period, a blood-stained mucous discharge (a "show", see page 202), accept it as a normal sign that your body is in working order for labor and that you may start within a week or two, or even earlier.

Bright red bleeding, which flows as if you were at the height of a period, is another matter. It is called antepartum hemorrhage and, although quite rare, is serious. If you start to hemorrhage, you should call your doctor or go to the hospital immediately.

Placenta previa Sometimes blood flows from the placental site when it is too low lying and partly in front of the baby's head. Intermittent bleeding from 27 weeks onwards is a typical symptom of this condition, known as placenta previa. Placenta previa occurs in about one in every 200 births and it almost certainly means that delivery will be by Cesarean section. During a vaginal birth, as the lower segment of the uterus thinned out, the placenta would be torn away from its roots, depriving the baby of nourishment and oxygen. If you do not have bleeding until you are 37 weeks pregnant or thereabouts, you will be admitted to the hospital and, if bleeding continues, will be advised to stay there until the baby is mature enough to be born.

Abruptio placenta Bleeding can also mean that a tiny part of the placenta, situated in the upper part of the uterus as it should be, has peeled away. This is called accidental hemorrhage (accidental in that the hemorrhage has occurred by chance) or abruptio placenta. The severity of accidental hemorrhage depends entirely on how large a portion of the placenta has separated from the lining of the uterus, but it is always a potentially serious problem, and the doctor should be informed at once. You will be advised to go to hospital for bed rest and, if the bleeding stops and all is well with the baby, will be discharged after four to five days. It is probably wise to avoid intercourse and orgasm until after the baby is born.

Blood pressure Every time you go for a prenatal visit your blood pressure is checked (see page 46). This is because, although slight fluctuations are normal during pregnancy, any significant rise may be an indication of preeclampsia (see below). If the diastolic figure in your blood pressure reading rises by as much as 15, you may be considered to have hypertension. Hypertension can be a signal of preeclampsia, which reduces the efficiency of the placenta. Bed rest will be prescribed, since the placenta will begin to work more efficiently if you stay in bed.

Preeclampsia The full name of this condition is preeclampsia, but it is often called toxemia. It affects between five and ten per cent of all pregnant women, but rarely occurs in the early part of pregnancy. Occasionally it only starts after delivery.

Symptoms Your blood pressure rises, the level of uric acid in your blood goes up, and you retain a lot of fluid. A rise in blood pressure alone does not mean that you have preeclampsia, and neither does an increase in fluid retention. The two symptoms in combination, however, indicate the need for some form of treatment. If mild preeclampsia goes untreated, eventually protein appears in the urine. Babies of mothers with a high proportion of protein in their urine may be born prematurely; once a woman is excreting a lot of protein her pregnancy is unlikely to continue for longer than two more weeks*.

The danger of preeclampsia is not so much to you as to the unborn baby. If allowed to progress, preeclampsia can cause the placenta to fail; this means that labor occurs prematurely, before the baby is necessarily mature enough to survive. In its severest form preeclampsia becomes eclampsia, and then it can seriously affect you as well as the baby, causing convulsions and possibly a state of coma. The following symptoms can be signs of eclampsia: headache, flashing lights, nausea, vomiting and pain in the abdomen. Don't make the mistake of thinking that you have the flu if this happens to you in late pregnancy. Get in touch with your doctor immediately and ask if he or she would take your blood pressure and test your urine.

Causes No one is absolutely certain what causes the disorder, but poor nutrition seems to play an important part. You can do a great deal to avoid preeclampsia by eating well and having a high protein, nutritious diet throughout pregnancy (see page 84). If you have had preeclampsia in a previous pregnancy, start out on a program of good nutrition *before* you conceive again if possible.

You are more likely to develop preeclampsia if any of the following apply: you have diabetes or kidney disease; you have high blood pressure anyway (140/90 or higher); you are having twins or more; members of your family have high blood pressure or have had preeclampsia; you are still in your teens or are over 40; you are under 5 ft 3 in (1.6 m); you have had preeclampsia with a previous pregnancy (in which case there is a one in ten chance of it recurring); you suffer from migraine. If it is your first pregnancy you are also at increased risk.

Treatment Many doctors think that staying in bed at the first signs may avoid further developments. Certainly bed rest coupled with relaxation of body and mind will reduce your blood pressure and improve the blood flow to the baby. Don't lie flat on your back in bed, but on your side or well propped up.

If you have high blood pressure with protein in your urine, or high blood pressure alone above 170/110, your doctor will probably admit you to hospital the same day. You will be kept in bed and your blood pressure and urine will be checked every four hours. Sedatives are sometimes prescribed. After a couple of days you will be allowed up for short periods: if your diastolic blood pressure falls below 90 and stays there, and if there is no longer any protein in your urine, you will probably be allowed home after three or four days.

Many women feel trapped in hospital when they have pre-eclampsia, because they may not feel at all ill. In these circumstances, knowing what is happening to you and why means that you can help to care for yourself rather than just put up with having things done *to* you. Ask questions: find out about your condition and its progress, and understand the reasons for the treatment you are receiving. Counseling is available on the National Toxemia Hotline (914-271-6474).

Eclampsia If your preeclampsia has developed into eclampsia an intravenous drip will be set up through which a drug is introduced into your bloodstream to prevent convulsions; injections will lower your blood pressure.

Sugar in the urine Your urine is tested at every prenatal visit (see page 46). If more sugar than usual is detected in your urine, you may have a tendency to be diabetic which has remained hidden until pregnancy. The diagnosis of diabetes is more likely to be correct if you have a parent who is diabetic.

When you are pregnant, the amount of blood in your system rises and so does the amount of blood sugar to be dealt with by your kidneys. You may be able to reduce the sugar level by modifying your diet and cutting out all sugar, cakes, puddings, sweets and chocolate. If this does not work you may be admitted to the hospital for bed rest any time after 32 weeks, because the accumulation of glucose in a diabetic woman who is pregnant is absorbed by the fetus, which then grows very fast. It is likely that the obstetrician will recommend induction of labor before the baby grows too big to pass easily through your pelvic outlet. Although large, the fetus will not be mature and may need special care after birth (see page 286). Some babies of diabetic mothers are delivered by Cesarean section because the mother's cervix is not soft and ready to open so early in her pregnancy.

If you become diabetic during pregnancy, the diabetes will be controlled by insulin and will probably disappear after delivery.

Anemia   When you are anemic (see page 87), you tend to feel very tired, easily become exhausted when you do anything vigorous and may also have dizzy spells and be short of breath. If you have vomited a great deal during early pregnancy, are having a baby within two years of a previous birth, have had a number of babies in quick succession and are on an inadequate diet, or are pregnant with more than one baby, you are most at risk of being anemic. Women who suffer from anemia in pregnancy are less able to cope with any heavy bleeding at the time of the birth and are more likely to have an infection. The baby suffers because less oxygen is carried by the mother's blood to the placenta and premature labor often results. Adjust your diet so that you get more iron-rich foods, protein, vitamin B, especially B12, vitamin C and a folic acid supplement which your doctor will prescribe (see page 88). All are necessary to ensure that your blood can carry enough oxygen to all the tissues. Your doctor may also prescribe iron tablets. If they make you constipated, ask for another kind. If you have a low hemoglobin level (see page 46) after 30 weeks, injections of iron may be prescribed.

Headache   There is no reason why you should have more headaches when you are pregnant than when you are not pregnant. In fact, some women who usually suffer from migraine find that it disappears throughout pregnancy. You can have tension headaches while you are carrying a baby just as at any other time. If your pregnancy is fraught with anxiety, or you are taking on more than you can handle, you will probably be prone to headaches. Decode the messages from your body, modify your life style and, if you are worried about labor, find out how you can help yourself.

A sharp, blinding headache that affects your eyesight in late pregnancy should be reported to your doctor as it could be associated with preeclampsia.

Digestive disturbances   Indigestion and heartburn are problems of the last three or four months of pregnancy. There seems to be so little room in your abdomen and it feels as if all your organs are being crushed.

It is better to have many small snacks than several larger meals a day, and it is sensible to avoid fried or rich, spicy foods. Some people find that they cannot digest bread or products containing yeast and that, by cutting out these foods, they can eliminate heartburn. Many women discover that they cannot drink during a meal and that meals have to be taken dry. You need to find out what kind of diet suits you personally. There is no perfect diet that is right for everyone.

Since heartburn results from acid normally present in your stomach flowing back into the esophagus, try to find positions for sitting and sleeping in which the upper part of your uterus is not pressing against your stomach. You will probably prefer upright chairs and at night will feel better if you sleep well propped up. Make sure jeans, trousers and skirts are loose at the waist if you want to avoid indigestion.

Shortness of breath When the baby is high, after about 34 weeks and before it drops into your pelvis, you will probably find that you are short of breath whenever you exert yourself or even just climb the stairs. Your uterus is putting pressure on your lungs, and your diaphragm may be shifted out of place by as much as one inch. Again, sitting straight and sleeping propped up can help and you will probably discover that you have to take life rather more slowly in order not to get breathless. There is a rhythm to everything in nature and this is a phase of pregnancy when your body is telling you to slow down.

Daily care and comfort

When you are pregnant you find that you carry around your own very efficient central heating system. You do not need to dress as warmly as usual and in hot weather you will probably feel more comfortable in cotton dresses, skirts and so on and should avoid synthetic materials.

Many pregnant women suffer from varicose veins in the legs, rectum or vagina (see page 115). Boots should not grip so tightly that circulation is impeded. If you wear a panty-girdle, make sure that it does not interfere with the circulation in the groin. Jeans should not be skintight for the same reasons.

Shoes Shoes should allow the feet to keep their normal shape and should not be so high that your weight is thrown forward onto the ball of your foot. In late pregnancy you may find that your feet are wider than usual and so need a wider fitting shoe or an extra half size. Although oxfords give good support to the arches, you may not be able to tie them easily in late pregnancy. For the same reasons slip on sandals are better than shoes that have elaborate buckles.

Bras Since breast changes and enlargement occur from the first days of pregnancy, you will need a bra which gives good support and, if you are heavy breasted, one with straps wide enough not to dig into your shoulders.

Heavy breasts, allowed to hang without support, may develop stretch marks (see opposite), which will leave you with silvery streaks after the pregnancy. A woman with large breasts may prefer to wear a lightweight bra at night too during pregnancy.

WHAT SORT OF BRA?
Bras you wear in pregnancy should have a band around their lower margin and wide straps over the shoulders, adjusted to provide firm support for your breasts. The cotton bra (right) can be adjusted at the back for girth, but opens at the front: it is suitable for nursing as well as pregnancy.

Skin pigmentation   For many women pregnancy is better than a beauty treatment: skin improves, eyes shine and hair is in better condition. But some women develop patches of darkened (pigmented) skin on the face, and this can be distressing. The technical term is "chloasma", but it is also called "the mask of pregnancy". It is a result of the high level of pregnancy hormones and is associated with inadequate folic acid. It is made worse by exposure to sunlight. The kind of cosmetic cream sold as "undereye" cream for minimizing birth marks often disguises it effectively. The mask usually disappears once the baby is born.

You will notice that other parts of the body that are already pigmented become darker, as for example the circles around your nipples and the skin of your labia. You may also develop a dark line down the middle of your tummy from your navel, and this is where the rectus muscle is being stretched (see page 107). It is particularly obvious in dark haired women. This too will disappear once the baby is born.

Stretch marks   Stretch marks (striae) may appear over your tummy, buttocks and breasts. They are dark streaks and are a sign that the skin has been stretched from underneath. They never disappear completely but, after the birth, they change from being brown or deep violet to a silvery shade, rather like the marks on some fine, gauze like fabric that has not been properly pressed. Many women use a rich cream or oil to "feed" the skin, and there are even some on the market especially for stretch marks. However, these are expensive and any cream that is readily absorbed, or even vegetable oil, will do. If your skin is very stretched, and especially if you are having twins, it is marked like this because of pressure on the layers underneath which cannot be reached by anything applied from outside. Still, it can feel good and be relaxing for you to stroke your tummy and, even though you may still have stretch marks, there is nothing to be lost and some pleasure to be gained from regular gentle massage with a rich, slippery cream applied by you or your partner.

Teeth   Although the baby needs calcium to grow strong teeth, your own teeth are no more likely to fall out in pregnancy than at any other time. However, as your gums soften and become spongier along with other tissues in the body as the result of the action of pregnancy hormones in your bloodstream, you may be liable to a gum infection. Good nutrition (see page 84) is the first line of defense against this. Mouth hygiene is also important, with regular tooth brushing, especially after breakfast and before you go to bed at night. Arrange a dental check up when you know you are pregnant and again for midpregnancy. Since it may be difficult to fit in appointments immediately after the baby is born, arrange another shortly before the baby is due. The dentist's waiting room is an excellent place to practice your relaxation for labor, and slow, full abdominal breathing in the dentist's chair works wonders.

Sport

66 I've always been very active physically and was determined I wasn't going to give up because I was pregnant. So I've cycled everywhere and gone on with my yoga and swum every day. 99

Any sport you do well is probably fine during pregnancy: if you are really good at something, you do not waste muscular energy and your movements are smoothly coordinated. As pregnancy advances, you will notice your balance changing as the center of gravity is concentrated in your tummy. This will almost certainly limit your activities, although I heard of a tightrope walker who practiced daily on the high wire until she went into labor—an exceptional woman! Swimming is splendid exercise during pregnancy and dancing too, provided you are not in a stuffy room. Cycling is also beneficial although, if you can avoid heavy traffic, it is kinder on both you and your baby.

Travel

Travel in pregnancy is usually quite safe, but the exhaustion which may result from it is not. It is important to divide up long journeys into short, manageable sections if you can; rest in between. Do not sit immobilized in a car, train or plane for longer than two hours at most without getting up and walking around for five minutes. Sitting for long periods reduces the circulation of blood in the pelvic area. Also remember to empty your bladder regularly as you are more likely to get a bladder infection during pregnancy (see page 117).

Travel in loose, comfortable clothing, and in shoes that allow for a little expansion. Soft slipper-socks are usually the most comfortable. Take any opportunity of dropping off to sleep. Pack an eye shade made of soft material to block out lights.

Flying On an airplane drink water or fruit juice; limit yourself to one alcoholic drink, as air travel is dehydrating, and alcohol will dehydrate you further. If you are over 25 weeks pregnant, most airlines will require a letter from your doctor saying that it is all right for you to travel. Your doctor will probably agree to write such a letter as long as the risk of your going into labor on board a plane is slight. It would be reasonable of your doctor to refuse his consent if, for instance, your blood pressure was high, or if you had suffered a threatened miscarriage in early pregnancy. In such cases a change in altitude could bring on premature labor. Similarly it is unwise to fly in a small unpressurized plane, as the supply of oxygen to the fetus can sometimes be drastically diminished.

You might also bear in mind, if you are thinking of flying a long distance, the strain caused to you by jet lag.

Driving is perfectly safe if you do not find it exhausting and obviously if you are not subject to dizzy spells. Bear in mind that if you drive in city traffic you are almost certainly breathing in other cars' exhaust fumes. This does not do your baby any good, so try to avoid the rush hour if you can. If you have a heavy gear lever, the sheer hard work of changing gear can cause discomfort in the later months. An automatic car makes lighter work of driving in pregnancy. Wear a seat belt, but make sure that it is not too tight or it will cause indigestion and interfere with your breathing.

... and finally deep, relaxing breathing, all the while concentrating on the new life within you.

If you are finding it hard to sleep in late pregnancy the traditional methods of dealing with insomnia are probably the most reliable.

First, a warm luxurious bath ...

... then a soothing, milk drink ...

Rest and sleep

During the first and last three months of pregnancy you will probably feel much more tired than usual, and it is advisable to rest as much as possible, rather than trying to fight off the tiredness. Towards the end of your pregnancy there may be several reasons why you cannot sleep as much as you would like.

Nearly every pregnant woman goes through a period when she either cannot drop off to sleep or wakes in the night because the baby is kicking her, she needs to empty her bladder, or she has been woken by a violent and disturbing dream and cannot get back to sleep. Sometimes the insomnia occurs because she is lying worrying and in the darkness her fears gain the upper hand.

If you have recently given up work, you may feel that your pregnancy has become a time of passive waiting and is stretching out longer and longer, so that you cannot see an end to it. You probably cannot sleep because you need action, and sometimes vigorous exercise during the day can be a remedy for this problem. You could also try the traditional remedies for sleeplessness, such as a hot milk drink after a luxurious warm bath at bedtime.

The stillness of the middle of the night actually provides a marvelous opportunity for practicing your relaxation and breathing. Use the time to center down into your body and become more aware of the developing life inside you. Allow your breathing to flow right down to where the baby nestles deep inside you. Cup your hands over the lower curve of your abdomen and breathe so that the wave of the inhaled breath presses your hands up and, as you give a long breath out, you sink on the receding wave.

Relax and enjoy lying there with your baby. Once you have begun to lose yourself in these feelings, you will probably find that your deep breathing has relaxed you back into sleep.

There are bound to be doubts and
anxieties, but for many women
there is also a new-found
serenity and a sense of
inner fulfillment. . . .

Emotional challenges in pregnancy

Many expectant mothers look and feel radiant. A healthy woman who is looking forward to a much wanted baby, who has a loving and secure relationship with the father of her child, and some knowledge about childbirth and what she can do to help herself, often revels in her pregnancy. Many women say "I feel better than I ever have before" or "I'm really enjoying being pregnant" and are surprised at the vitality and sense of inner fulfillment which they experience.

Everyone's thrilled to bits, except it's me that's got to have it!

Yet probably all of us are assailed by darker thoughts at times when we are overtired or under some special stress. Some of the more negative feelings that women experience in early pregnancy have been discussed on page 32. But as your pregnancy advances, more specific anxieties may preoccupy you at times. Anxiety may grip you in the middle of the night when the baby has kicked you awake or when you have had to get up to empty your bladder and cannot get to sleep again. Every fear is magnified in the darkness as you lie trying to sleep and unable to relax.

Worries about the birth

Labor can be an intensely pleasurable, all absorbing and deeply satisfying activity which it is really possible to enjoy. But just as some people do not like climbing a mountain, even though the view at the summit is magnified and the climb exciting, and just as some feel that sex is overrated and not worth the effort, whereas others think it is one of the best experiences life offers, different women have very different attitudes toward childbirth. This is not just a matter of what happens physiologically or how you are treated in hospital, but also depends on what kind of person you are. Anxiety can cast a shadow over childbirth and produces the speeded up heart rate, high blood pressure, muscle tension and other physical results of stress which actually make birth more difficult. It is important to think through it and to understand why you are anxious.

Anxiety about labor is probably best dealt with first of all by finding out more about it, not just its mechanics, but the physical and emotional sensations of each phase, and the relaxation, breathing and focused concentration which can help you to work with your body instead of against it. The simple process of sharing fears also often results in women feeling much more lighthearted, so that they begin to enjoy their pregnancies. A good childbirth class where discussion is encouraged and women can talk freely about their apprehensions as well as about their hopes is often effective in developing self confidence and helping you to look forward to labor as a peak experience which brings delight and fulfillment, not just an ordeal to be endured.

20 weeks   24 weeks   28 weeks

YOUR CHANGING SHAPE
Some women delight in the physical changes brought about by pregnancy. Others feel threatened by the inevitability of the process. Taking pleasure in your expanding form is good preparation for working with and expressing yourself through your body in labor.

Pain A woman having her first baby often thinks "I have never had anything really painful. How will I stand up to the pain of labor?" and since she has no idea what that pain is like or what contractions feel like, the thought can bring terror. Learning about labor, about how contractions work and how they may feel at different stages of labor, is the most effective way of coming face to face with this anxiety and doing something about it. There is a whole chapter in this book about pain and pain relief (pages 236–244), but the important thing to understand is that for most women the pain of labor is quite different from the pain of injury. Some women describe it as "positive pain" or "pain with a purpose".

Loss of control For many women anxieties about labor are linked with a dread of losing control. For your whole life you have been taught to control physical processes and your own behavior, and suddenly something is about to happen which clearly cannot be controlled and which is about to take over your body. You are told that you may cry out or groan, for example, that you may lose inhibitions and swear and say things you never

32 weeks   36 weeks   40 weeks

meant to, and are horrified to hear that during labor you may involuntarily empty your bowels or your bladder.

You learn that the waters may break suddenly. In any group of women discussing the events of labor, first time mothers nearly always ask those who have already had babies when the waters broke, whether it was sudden, and if so where it was; they express some anxiety that they may break in the supermarket or on a bus. What these women are saying is that they are fearful of letting their bodies function freely because of the embarrassment and social stigma attached. It is as if degrading physical processes, above all dirty ones which involve getting rid of waste products from the body, are taking place in public.

Think through why you find the thought of the waters breaking in public so upsetting. You are having a baby and it is perfectly obvious that you are going to give birth soon. If the waters do break in public, is it really so very terrible? You will attract interest and sympathy, but not disgust. You may see it as a kind of sexual act in front of other people. You are quite right, and understanding this can help you in labor. Birth, just like lovemaking, is a sexual process. If you can go *with* your labor instead of fighting it, the experience can be fulfilling in a strangely pleasurable way. Prepare the way to this through body awareness and relaxation. Touch relaxation (see page 166) is a special kind of release which teaches you to flow toward sensations of pressure and heat. It will help a lot in labor.

Loss of dignity and failure An anxiety closely connected with loss of control is the fear of making a fool of yourself. Some women think doctors and nurses will laugh at them if they find themselves making uncontrollable noises, for instance. You may feel that you are on public display in labor and approach it as a test of endurance. You may also be anxious about "letting down" a partner who puts great faith in your ability to cope, or even of "failing" your childbirth teacher. Some men who participate in classes and the other preparations for the birth become so enthusiastic and obsessional that they are in effect "trainers", rather like athletic coaches. The woman then feels that she is expected to put on a performance and must excel in it. Childbirth classes which are geared exclusively to techniques used in labor rather than focusing on wider aspects of the total experience can reinforce this feeling.

Just as the elaborate techniques performed to "insure" satisfaction in lovemaking can sometimes disturb the spontaneous rhythm of sex and interfere with the intense feeling and play of emotion between the couple, so breathing exercises and "distraction" techniques can sometimes intrude on the experience of labor. Exercises need to become "second nature" and be made a part of yourself. It is like learning to play the piano: there is a vast difference between laborious scales and playing a sonata. The exercises are important because they prepare you for playing music. But the eventual aim is to let the music flow through you, rather than to superimpose tricks and techniques onto it. Such a physical and emotional surrender is simple in labor because of its intensity. Birth involves mind and body working together in a completely absorbing, exciting and passionate way. There is no success or failure in labor. You cannot make a fool of yourself, let anyone down or flunk an examination in birth.

Fear of managing alone Some women approach labor as a medical incident like having an appendectomy, an unwelcome interruption of normal life rather than an experience which can be satisfying in itself. They feel totally dependent on the technology provided by the hospital and worry about whether they will get there on time, or whether the right people will be present to deliver the baby. Such women's dependence is reinforced by contemporary obstetrics and by every program on television which illustrates the latest marvel of science applied to childbearing. The impression is readily given that women must depend on lifesaving machines, and that without them it is not safe to have a baby. The fact is that although these machines can be extremely useful in diagnosing difficulties when a baby is at risk or when special problems are met in pregnancy or labor, the majority of women can give birth perfectly well without them.

It is not advances in medicine but improved conditions, better food and general health which have made childbirth much safer for mothers and babies today than it was 100 years ago. The rate of stillbirths and deaths in the first week of life is directly related to a country's gross national product and to the position of the mother in the social class structure.

It is a disturbing thought that it is twice as safe for a woman in the professional classes to bear a child than it is for an unsupported mother at the bottom of the social scale. The challenge is to find out which mothers and babies are at risk, to offer them everything possible which can make birth safer, but to let those who are at no special risk give birth naturally if they can.

Loss of autonomy Another frequent anxiety is that of being denied the right to function as an adult and fear of being under the control of doctors, nurses and even machines. Many pregnant women resent the feeling that they cannot make their own decisions. Increasing numbers feel that they do not want to hand their bodies over to professional caregivers in pregnancy and childbirth, and are seeking maternity care in which they can share the decision-making with their advisers.

If you are not sure whether your doctor is being quite open with you, or whether the hospital will really let you do the things in labor which you have asked to do, the uncertainty can produce a sick fear in the pit of the stomach. Too often pregnant women are treated like children or as patients in categories of "high risk", "low risk", "primigravida", "multigravida" and so on, who have to be processed through the hospital system, passive receivers of care rather than active birthgivers.

Fear of hospitals For many women hospitals are threatening places. People usually go to the hospital when they are ill. This may be the first time that you have been a patient in a hospital and the sights, sounds and even smells of hospitals may alarm you. Society has given little thought so far to designing and decorating maternity units so that they look more like home, or at least a good hotel. Hospitals are still places with long green painted corridors and white tiles and instrument carts. Delivery rooms in otherwise splendid modern hospitals can be windowless boxes, and prenatal clinics, your first introduction to the hospital, are often forbidding places without pictures and with backache inducing chairs set in rows. Even more important than the physical surroundings are the attitudes of members of hospital staff and the way in which they interact with patients. If you meet cool indifference, rigid authoritarianism or obvious hostility, you may dread going to the hospital, and this anxiety can color your whole approach to labor.

There is a certain kind of emotional climate in which anxieties flourish and unfortunately it is one which our society provides

66 I can still remember when I had my tonsils out when I was 7. I can't stand hospitals. 99

66 All the coming and going and the noise makes me feel really nervous. I can practically feel my blood pressure rising. 99

133

Finding time to concentrate on yourself when an older child is constantly present creates its own particular challenge . . .

for many pregnant women. If there is no one readily available of whom you can ask questions and be answered in terms you can understand, the seeds of anxiety are often sown. They are nourished by the insecurity of seeing different members of staff in the prenatal setting and hospital.

Women often feel apologetic about anxiety, about not being "sensible", as if they were revealing some shameful lack of emotional stamina. They are sometimes regarded as having something psychologically wrong with them if they show evidence of anxiety. But many of the fears you have are not the result of inadequacy but a response to stresses caused by an environment which is alien and unfriendly and by care which is impersonal. In such a situation anxiety is *realistic*.

Although you may not be able to eradicate anxiety about the birth itself, it is sensible to tackle it directly. Ask to have a tour of the labor and delivery rooms, including the machinery which may be used; attend childbirth classes at the hospital so that you can get to know at least some of the staff, and talk with your doctor about the style of childbirth which you would like if possible; ask him or her to note down any particular request on your record card. Read the section in this book on talking to doctors (pages 49–52) before you go.

Loss of attractiveness Some pregnant women are deeply concerned that their sexual attractiveness may be completely destroyed by childbearing. They are frightened of losing their figures; they may also be anxious that the vagina will be slack and changed in shape, and that as a result they will not be able to make love with their partners in a mutually satisfying way.

The fear of a tear or a cut (see page 250) often discussed in childbirth education classes is not so much about pain from stitches, although it is often dealt with by the childbirth teacher in terms of coping with discomfort after the birth. It is really anxiety about genital mutilation.

Episiotomy In many hospitals nowadays, episiotomy is routinely used for all women having their first babies and for a large percentage of those having second and subsequent babies. Knowing this can be very disturbing if you want to avoid having any interventionist obstetric techniques used on you unless they are necessary. Although many obstetricians would disagree, a number of women believe that episiotomy is one of these unnecessary kinds of intervention.

Pelvic floor exercises (see page 103) can help to create the sensitive awareness, coordination and control which helps you in the second stage of labor, preparing you to open your body for the baby to be born and so reducing the stress on the pelvic muscles and the perineal tissues. If you wish to avoid an episiotomy if possible, discuss the subject with your doctor in advance. Say that you would like help at the delivery so that you can breathe the baby out rather than push it out, and ask for this to be noted on your card. It is wrong to think that a woman who is anxious about episiotomy is in any way "neurotic", though doctors sometimes assume this.

Sometimes episiotomy must be performed for the baby's safety or to avoid a large tear. It can help you to understand the healing process afterwards if you know what has happened, and exactly where. Exploring the vagina with your fingers during pregnancy (see page 102) and after the birth, and looking at it in a mirror, can help you to feel that it still belongs to you; you can then rehabilitate the area through pelvic floor movements.

Worries about the baby

❝ I'm not sleeping very well. Things keep running through my mind . . . what if it's got no arms or legs? **❞**

Almost every woman wonders at some stage of her pregnancy whether her baby is normal. Fear of producing a handicapped child is often connected with anxiety about not being able to live up to standards set by somebody else, usually either or both of the woman's own parents. You may feel it almost impossible that you could produce from the dark interior of your body anything which is perfect. This is probably the most persistent, gnawing fear of all, and the only way of coming to terms with it is to develop self confidence, a process which takes time. This is where childbirth education classes which encourage trust in your body and your ability to give birth, rather than dependence on others to get the baby born for you, can help.

One woman who had disappointed her parents academically became pregnant outside marriage, in a desperate effort to show them that at least there was *something* she could do. She now lay awake wondering if her baby was deformed. Talking about this fear in a prenatal discussion group led her to reveal that she was having awful dreams. It then emerged that five out of the twelve women in the group were having very vivid dreams, and that even some of those who had not admitted to any worry about whether the baby would be "all right" were having dreams in which the baby was disposed of because it was not "good enough", or was taken away and looked after by other people because *they*, the mothers, were not good enough. Dreams can often reveal emotional tangles which cause great distress in pregnancy until they are brought out into the open.

Most women who fear bearing an abnormal baby have little reason to expect that the baby will not be perfect. The minority of women who are aware of the possibility of inherited diseases or handicaps in their or their partners' families, or who are pregnant after the age of 40, will realize that they can seek genetic counseling and can have AFP screening (see page 185) and, if necessary, amniocentesis performed (see page 186).

Worries about the future

Loneliness Many women having their first babies move away from their own homes during pregnancy, often to a larger flat or house, so that they find themselves in an area where they know nobody at all. They stop work in late pregnancy and no longer even have the daily contacts with others at work. At home and alone for the first time, they are initially delighted, but often quickly become bored and depressed.

If you are pregnant for the first time and maybe living in a different area, make the effort to meet other people with young families. You will build a new set of social relationships which will stand you in good stead after your own baby is born . . .

If you are in this position, plan to take up some activity which brings social contacts; learn something new, join a club of some kind; attend childbirth education classes; track down interesting places in the locality to which you have moved, and invite people to your home. If you do not know anyone with young children and would like to discover more about what babies are like, seek out your nearest playgroup or nursery school and go when parents are meeting their children, or go to your community center and say that you want to get to know somebody who has a baby. Your doctor or midwife may be able to tell you about other pregnant women or mothers with new babies who live near you. It is worth investigating the possibilities while you are still pregnant. When you are busy with a baby it may be more difficult to make new friends, especially during the winter months, so take the opportunity of making them now.

Change When a woman expresses anxiety about "things never being the same again", it helps to think through what exactly this means for her. If things are irrevocably altered, what might happen? One couple who had a deeply satisfying relationship saw the pregnancy and the upset connected with the birth as an "interruption". "We don't want to change our lives for a child," the woman said, "to be swamped by it. How long will it take before we get back to normal again? Sometimes I'm frightened we'll *never* get back to normal." When I asked what she found frightening about this, after some thought she explained that she did not want to become the same kind of woman as her mother and did not see herself as bound to babies and a home. Most of all she was afraid that her partner would not love her any more and that she would be desexed by maternity.

Social expectations Another woman said that her pregnancy made her feel that at last she was fulfilling a socially acceptable role and that her own mother was proud of her for the first time in her life. In a way, she resented this. Other women acted as if they knew how she felt and what she thought and wanted. The doctors at the hospital expected her to be a "good patient" and be processed through the busy prenatal clinic like all the others with their swelling bumps. She suddenly felt miles away from her former colleagues and the others with whom she had worked, separated from them by the inescapable fact of her pregnancy. But by the end she felt guilty that she had resented the baby at the beginning of her pregnancy. At night as it moved inside her she lay thinking whether she would ever be a good mother. She said, "I sometimes feel so sorry for the little thing in there that I end up crying."

In a prenatal discussion group both of these women had the chance to talk about their disturbing feelings. It emerged that several of the others were also lying awake at night thinking and worrying about much the same things. What had seemed personal handicaps proved to be an experience shared by a number of women in the group.

If you realize that you are not all alone with your fears, and are not being "odd" or neurotic, the anxieties usually become much less disturbing. Thinking about inevitable change may worry you in different ways: you may be afraid that the relationship with your partner will deteriorate; that you have no maternal instincts and will be no good as a mother; that the loss of a job and the money and sense of freedom associated with getting out of the house and earning your own living may bring a real deprivation. You may wonder if you will be able to tolerate being at home all day with a "screaming brat", and whether you will miss all the interesting people at work.

Although such anxiety is realistic in the sense that these changes are dramatic and demanding for many women, most expectant mothers are more aware of anxieties about labor and the baby than they are of how they will cope after the birth. Many take the unknown "afterwards" more or less for granted. It is as if they can only see as far as the birth, which dominates the horizon. The postpartum experience may then come as a shock for which they are not prepared. So some anxiety about life after the baby arrives is a healthy sign, and indicates that the emotional work is taking place which prepares a couple not only for the birth but for parenthood.

Many anxieties during pregnancy, both for the woman and the man, offer clues to the challenges confronting the couple. It is a waste of emotional energy to try to "forget" them or put them to the back of your mind. They are there to be worked with. It is often the man and woman who are determined to take it all in their stride and carry on as usual, and who do not acknowledge apprehension on the threshold of the unknown, who are likely to face the most shattering crises, both in the experience of birth and also when they have a baby in the house.

The discomfort anxiety produces can force you to think through the meaning for you of the coming of a child into your lives. Without stress and challenge of this kind emotional preparation for birth and parenthood may be overlooked. Fears and anxieties are an important element of the emotional changes necessary if you are to face up to the reality of birth and then to the astonishing reality of the new baby.

Becoming a father

66 I reckon that babies have been born for thousands of years and I don't know what all the fuss is about. 99

66 I'm deeply moved by this baby growing inside her. I feel we're very close in a new way. 99

Becoming a father is a major step in a man's life. It can also be a challenging one. Yet it is an experience usually treated as insignificant in comparison with that of becoming a mother. As a result the emotional upheavals and stresses of the future father are little understood and men are not prepared for the impact of pregnancy. If people do notice that a man is finding the going difficult, they tend to laugh rather than sympathize. In fact the nervousness and anxiety of the father to be, and his sheer non-comprehension of what is about to happen to him, are favorite subjects of jokes and anecdotes, ranging from the picture post-card variety—showing a man wide eyed and desperate in the hospital corridor as his wife produces triplets—to those amused tales about male ignorance and incompetence shared between women over coffee.

In childbirth classes and hospital lectures for parents to be a man is often discussed only in terms of how he can help his partner, and his own profound emotional needs are neglected. One result of this is to make him feel isolated and resentful, finding it difficult to reach out and give his partner the support she needs. She is the fairy princess going to the ball and he feels a bit like the back legs of a pantomime horse.

An expectant father may feel jealous of all the attention given to the future mother, absurdly envious of her reproductive powers and sometimes even jealous of the coming baby. Then he feels guilty about succumbing to these emotions and decides to concentrate on his work—because that at least is one thing he can do properly. And the more he immerses himself in his own preoccupations, the more isolated and left out of the pregnancy he feels.

Some men become really depressed during pregnancy or experience violent mood swings similar to those that a pregnant woman may go through. A few even walk out of the relationship because the stress is too great for them to handle. So it is important to remember that usually there are *two* people having a baby and that the man also goes through a transitional period of stress when very deep emotions may be stirred and his behavior may be difficult to understand.

Reacting to fatherhood

The sheer responsibility of having a baby can be frightening. The woman is probably going to give up work outside the home for a time, or even for good, and the man is expected to support the family. The financial burden alone may be too great for some men to shoulder without anxiety. But for many men money problems constitute a rationalization, a reasonable and socially acceptable explanation for anxiety, without getting to the root of what they really find disturbing. In fact, some men find that the prospect of becoming a father brings with it a crisis of identity. Although it is a common occurrence and one which leads to creative change, it is nevertheless still a crisis.

The changing relationship One element in this crisis involves grieving over a relationship that is bound to change with the need for both partners to adapt to being parents. The easy ways, the lack of routine, the spontaneity of the early stage of the relationship, all have to give way to an existence centered around a baby's needs. Some men see their wives as their mothers. When the woman becomes pregnant it is as if the man is losing a mother and is being replaced in her love by a new baby. As she becomes more involved in the pregnancy and the needs of the coming baby he feels increasingly rejected. For a man who feels insecure, or who never came to terms with hostility experienced towards a younger child in the family, this inevitable shift of focus can be very threatening.

The changing woman Some men acquire a wife as a showpiece, proof of their success in hunting down and possessing a desirable sexual object, or evidence of their social success, a demonstration and symbol of a life style which embodies achievement. Delighted as such a man may be to be fathering a child, he may find it difficult to cope with his partner's new concentration on the pregnancy rather than on him. He feels that the physical changes in his partner's body are upsetting as conventional attractiveness is replaced by a very different body—no longer the outline of a neat figure but a melon shaped abdomen and heavy, swelling breasts covered with a network of tiny blue veins. A man who has valued his wife as a status or sex symbol may feel that he is being cheated.

The developing baby It is sometimes difficult initially for a man, who does not have the baby growing inside his body, to feel its reality. He often begins to become more aware of the child at about the time when he feels it bump and kick at night. Some men find this sensation not only astonishing and exciting but rather eerie, and they take a while to adjust to the idea of another being living and growing inside the body of the woman they know so well.

6 6 She's a very determined lady, her mother. When she comes to our house she tries to run it. 9 9

The future grandparents When a couple have a first baby they may have to work through a painful transitional period in which they forge a new adult relationship with their own parents, which allows for the responsibility and commitment they have to the child they are bearing. This in itself may produce stresses with the future grandparents, and a man may get caught up in a difficult relationship with his own mother just as a woman may with hers. When a man's mother is fearful that she is losing her son she becomes demanding. He may feel the pull of her possessive love drawing attention away from the needs of his wife and baby. Sometimes a woman sees this whereas the man is completely unaware of it. It is important to understand that the older women, the ex-mothers, are being replaced, and they may feel hurt and unwanted. If there is a problem of this kind, the couple should talk about it together and be honest about their feelings. Bottling up resentment can sour a relationship.

The father's new role

Having a baby used to be solely the concern of the woman, with her mother standing in the background giving advice. Nowadays it is much more something for woman and man to share, both the preparation for birth and the actual labor and delivery.

There are still some men who say they do not want to get involved in "women's things" and who feel that their manliness is being threatened. They have the uneasy suspicion that learning about childbirth is going to emasculate them and that they will no longer be potent, virile males. Some imagine that it is only "good form" to hand the woman over to the care of experts and retire from the scene. They believe that the professional must know so much more than they do that they are bound to be in the way and have no function in the delivery room.

Even ten years ago some midwives and obstetricians looked askance at men who became involved in the process of childbirth, as if they were slightly odd. Go back forty years or so and men kept well away from anything to do with birth; pregnancy was a "certain condition" which a man pretended he knew nothing about. My mother told me that my father felt embarrassed to go out with her in advanced pregnancy, so that walks they took had to be after dark, with her enveloped in a capacious wraparound coat. And as for a father wheeling a stroller, or changing a diaper—it was unheard of; even a man who might have liked to try his hand at such things rarely got the chance. This was partly because there used to be what one perceptive psychoanalyst called a male "taboo on tenderness". Men were frightened that to become involved with women's activities would humiliate them in the eyes of other men. And childbirth was the epitome of all feminine mysteries. Both women and men were deprived by these rigid rules from discovering their full inner potential.

The modern man is determined to share as much as he can in pregnancy and birth. He enjoys his wife's changing shape and the reality of the baby kicking against his hand. But he still feels a novice at fatherhood. He wonders just how much he can do, since the baby is growing in her body, not his. In a way, the partnership between the mother and her unborn child is complete. And pregnancy often seems to be so carefully managed by the obstetric team that a man can feel an intruder.

But a woman depends on her partner's support and needs the special relationship with him, which is quite different from any others that she has. She may not realize just how much her partner is sharing in the pregnancy emotionally and the heights and depths of his own feelings about it. There is no longer any need for a man to square his shoulders and pretend he is not stirred by what is happening. Take the opportunity to talk together about your feelings.

*The man who fully involves himself in his
partner's pregnancy and his child's birth
is most likely to be uniquely rewarded by
the experience . . .*

Feelings about being present at the birth

Most expectant fathers today approach childbirth with curiosity and interest and in a very different spirit from that thought suitable by their fathers and grandfathers. Though they may wonder whether they are going to make fools of themselves while playing an unfamiliar part, and may be nervous of unpleasant procedures involved in labor, they want to understand what is going on and to help and support their partners. They realize that hospital staff are usually extremely busy and working with more than one patient at a time. It is therefore often impossible for other people to give the constant companionship and loving care which a woman craves as she is swept through the powerful physical and emotional experiences of labor; and the very unfamiliarity of the surroundings can make the most courageous woman apprehensive. She needs her partner or someone else who loves her. She needs someone who is there not simply as an onlooker but as a companion, who has studied what happens in childbirth, who knows what the prenatal preparation has been like, and who is able to help her in labor. (For more about the father's part in the birth, see pages 226–235.)

The man who fully involves himself in the birth shares in an experience which is exciting, challenging, intensely moving and deeply satisfying. It is not only a question of helping his wife have their baby but of an often surprising encounter with his own emotions and a discovery that he is swept into a peak experience which is bigger than anything he anticipated. There may be an astonishing, an almost incredible, joy and wonder at having been close to the beating center of life. In a very direct way, love is made flesh.

Being supportive about prenatal care

The prenatal clinic

Pregnancy can be a time of great emotional upheaval as a woman adapts psychologically to the extraordinary things happening inside her body. She has to go through all sorts of manipulations and physical examinations that are not always conducted in a warm, sympathetic way. It is clear that many women are made anxious by the kind of prenatal care they receive.

Some men find this difficult to understand. They say that they find the sophisticated technology which is used today reassuring and fascinating. But if the man imagines something happening inside his own testicles or penis, he may find it easier to comprehend. How would he feel if his testicles started to swell up and change shape dramatically, forcing him to visit hospital regularly to be prodded, poked and examined by strangers who seemed only concerned with the lower end of his body? He might find it impossible to get information about what was happening to him, knowing only that he faced an ordeal at the end of nine months when whatever was occurring must be terminated and the thing inside him somehow got out. How would he like lying flat on a high table, sometimes with his legs up high and wide apart in metal stirrups, while various white coated women peered at him with little lights and probed his body with special machines? Out of the corner of his eye he could see them writing up case notes full of technical terms and abbreviations apparently suggesting a disease.

A man only has to go to the doctor's office once to get an idea of how intimidating it can be. In the rushed atmosphere of a busy doctor's office women often feel that they have become part of a factory process for producing babies. Questions about treatment or requests for advice go out of their heads, or else seem to interrupt the smooth running of the doctor's office and mean that other women waiting their turn have still longer to wait. All too often a woman returns from the doctor depressed and anxious. If her partner can get away from work to attend occasionally and to meet the doctor, he can give her moral support and comfort, building the foundation for a good working relationship with the people who will be caring for her during labor.

Even if this is not possible, he can still help his partner by providing comfort and security if this is what she needs, and by talking to her about the things that ought to be discussed with the doctor. It is helpful to write questions down and keep a notebook for this purpose, as well as for any instructions given during pregnancy. (The second half of the book can be used as a log book for the birth, so that it is possible to keep track of what is happening and how labor is progressing.)

Childbirth education classes

When a woman starts attending classes in preparation for the birth there is usually an opportunity for her partner to share in some or all of the meetings. He can then learn a good deal about the physiological process and emotional changes of labor, can understand his own part in it, and often has the chance to see films of birth where women are using techniques similar to those that are learned in classes.

Everyday help

In the last three months of pregnancy a man can help his partner by seeing that she has more rest and lies down for a nap every afternoon. Sometimes extra laborsaving equipment, additional help in the house, or the use of services like a laundry, can ensure that she does not get worn out. She should not be carrying heavy shopping so he may take over supermarket duty, or come as well to load the boxes into the car. If there are jobs in the house which entail moving furniture, these are his now. And if the woman cannot get down to bathe the toddler or strip the bed and make it again he can take over these chores too while she does some of the easier tasks. On the other hand the woman does not need to be treated like an invalid, and you can enjoy going out together, especially at the end of pregnancy when time may drag and she feels she has been pregnant forever.

A man can also protect his partner from all the well meaning advice, often very contradictory and confusing, that comes from some older women both before and after the birth. He can support her in doing things the way you have both decided.

With a new baby on the way, a father helps by becoming more involved in the older child's daily routine. . . .

Your changing relationship as a couple

Pregnant women are not only obstetrical patients or even just future mothers. They are also usually in a loving relationship with a man. Pregnancy can be a time of great opportunity for both partners in the relationship to discover things about themselves and each other. However two people feel about each other, the emotional changes and challenges of pregnancy are bound to affect them. If the partners do not communicate easily it can be a time when small irritants turn into major crises.

The couple under stress

There are some couples who find the transition period of pregnancy an especially stressful time. It can put stress on the couple who have an informal, even casual, relationship and who have not attached particular importance to getting married, but who perhaps marry when a baby is on the way. It can put equal stress on a couple who both enjoyed their careers and never saw themselves as parents, but who nonetheless decide to continue with the pregnancy when the woman conceives by mistake. It can bristle with challenges, too, when a woman does not really believe in her bones that she will ever conceive, has been on the pill for many years, stops taking it because the couple think it might be a good idea to have a baby, and then immediately becomes pregnant before she has had time to switch her mind to the possibility of motherhood. For in these different situations rapid adjustment is necessary, and either or both parents may feel trapped, almost at the same time that they are feeling surprised and delighted.

As soon as they tell other people about the pregnancy they may feel that a social machine has swung into action. Some couples say that they felt strong social disapproval from relatives, especially their parents, when they put off having a baby; then when the woman eventually did become pregnant they were overwhelmed by the relief and pleasure these people expressed, as if at last they were doing the socially acceptable thing. In some ways the reactions feel like a public intrusion on their intimate and personal relationship with each other. Some couples find this not just irritating, but threatening.

Sharing the problems

When a pregnancy starts, a man and a woman often begin inhabiting different worlds. He may find that she becomes psychologically unpredictable and vulnerable. In her turn she may see him as unsympathetic, unloving and crude. He may feel he can no longer talk to her about "rational" matters, and that she has lost interest in everything except the coming baby. He may even feel pushed out into the cold, as if he were living with a different woman. Because they are often isolated from other couples facing similar difficulties, they may be under the impression that such problems are unique to them. Talking to other couples expecting babies can help them to see the social pressures on prospective parents, the cultural style of childbirth in modern Western societies which, while making birth safer for mother and baby, can often create emotional stress. Attending classes together can provide a bridge between the different socially assigned gender roles of a man and woman, and can help draw them closer.

Talking in a group At one prenatal discussion group couples discussed together the effect of pregnancy on their relationship. One woman, who was feeling that she had lost her individuality in the universal category of expectant motherhood, remarked that she was frightened of what this was doing to the relationship between her and her husband. Would they, she worried, become just "Mom and Dad" and cease being lovers? Her concern about this was even making her resent the baby at times.

In discussion the members of the group found that other couples too were experiencing these pressures and the same kinds of anxiety. Some of them felt very strongly that they wanted to be different kinds of parents from their own parents, to bring up their children in a radically different way and to have a happier marriage than they thought their parents had. It was agreed that it was important for a couple to share these thoughts with each other and to discuss not just the practical arrangements for preparing for the baby, but their ideas about the kind of parents they hoped to be, and what they thought about their partners as prospective parents too.

Becoming a mother involves emotional "growing pains" which can be no less disturbing than those of adolescence. A similar psychological process often occurs in a man too, but he usually feels he has even less justification to talk about it because *he* is not pregnant. Yet to be able to nurture their young both the man and the woman have to change and become different kinds of people.

Another couple, who had been through this process with an earlier pregnancy, said that talking about it had helped them understand each other better and that they came to like their changed roles. At first the parts of "Mommy" and "Daddy" started out as play-acting, but then they found they were good at it. The new roles made them see new aspects of each other and qualities they had never imagined the other possessed.

One of the things to emerge from that discussion was that becoming parents is not just a matter of physical changes but also of learning. It takes time, and pregnancy is the ideal time to start this process of growing up. Excitement about each other develops into caring. Tenderness felt by the man towards the woman may also be felt by the expectant mother about her man, as well as being directed toward the baby growing inside her.

Developing confidence

Many couples have a funny name for the unborn child, and talk about it as if it were a friend whom they know well but have never met. When doctors prod and poke and the hospital takes the woman over at the prenatal clinic or when she goes into labor, the couple can feel as if a very personal and intimate relationship between the three of them has been invaded. "Our" baby has become "the" baby, or even "the hospital's" baby. A woman needs to feel that the baby really belongs to her. This may be important in pregnancy, and is vital after the birth, if she is to have a chance to fall in love with her baby.

Other couples have problems in family relationships (especially with their in laws), which they imagine to be peculiarly their own and which they do not realize are shared by many others. Each partner may be resenting the other for his or her insensitivity and ineptitude at handling these situations, or for being overdependent on parents. In a childbirth education class there is a chance to talk through these problems, to discuss the future grandparents' feelings and any other situations which are causing stress. The very fact of finding that problems are shared and that they are not alone with such difficulties may help a couple. And often talking will suggest solutions to conflicts which have seemed inevitable and never-ending.

Growing through the experience

Many couples have their babies before they are really emotionally ready for them. As a result, many babies come into the world in spite of, rather than because of, what their parents feel about each other. When a woman decides to continue with an unplanned pregnancy, the accidental product of an impermanent relationship, she needs special emotional support. Even if a man has nothing else to offer a woman he can give her this. It is bound to be painful for them both if they decide to part with the baby, but the experience can be important for both of them and can help them to grow in understanding. In fact, when a couple are unhappy together, there is an even more compelling reason to use the time of pregnancy for joint preparation for the birth of their child, if only because the task can in itself bring a new perceptiveness and sensitivity to the other's needs.

So, in all circumstances, preparation for birth is not merely the acquisition by the woman of a set of instructions and exercises, but a process in which two people start out together on a shared enterprise. It provides opportunities for increased understanding of each other's needs and enrichment of their whole relationship. For both parents pregnancy can be a time of growing up. Any maturation process involves some growing pains. If a man and woman can understand what the pregnancy means to the other partner they are well on the way to growing up *together*. The psychological changes of pregnancy exist for all couples expecting a baby and it helps to realize that others share these experiences and find them just as challenging. Sharing brings relief from anxiety and a new understanding of the emotions involved in having a baby.

Sex in pregnancy

In the prenatal clinic doctors and nurses see you mainly as a patient and out of the context of the loving relationships which have most meaning for you; yet it is on the relationship you have with your partner that society depends if the family is to survive. It is also important for your sense of wellbeing that you are physically loved in pregnancy, whether or not this involves complete intercourse. Stroking, back and shoulder massage, loving touch and sexual pleasuring are all part of this physical expression of the relationship.

Attitudes to sex

66 Sex? What's that? 99

66 I love her luscious, pregnant curves! 99

Many couples make love right through pregnancy. At the beginning nausea and vomiting can mean that the last thing you want to do is to make love, but usually by the middle months lovemaking is enjoyable and satisfying, sometimes for the first time. Pregnancy is a good time for you to learn more about how your body works. A woman who begins to learn about her uterus, vagina and pelvic floor muscles may become sensitively responsive to this part of her body when she was not before. Some women have their first experience of orgasm during pregnancy. Many do not realize the function of the pelvic floor muscles (see page 103) in active lovemaking and some have never looked at or explored the way in which the vagina, labia and clitoris are constructed.

But this is not just a matter of intellectual information and diagrams of the female genitals. Some women dislike and have a general and profound distrust of their bodies. For the first time in pregnancy they can learn to know and be comfortable with themselves. If you have never before allowed feelings to sweep through you, you may find that preparation for the intensely emotional experience of labor, with its storms and currents and the powerful drama of delivery, unlocks a capacity for "letting go" which can apply to lovemaking also.

But some couples (especially in the later months) feel that they do not have the doctor's approval about lovemaking. You may have guilty feelings and be anxious that you are somehow harming your unborn baby. This is one of the subjects that expectant parents often talk about in childbirth education classes. Couples say that they often find sex a very difficult subject to discuss with their doctor.

Positions for lovemaking

The conventional "missionary" position (with the man lying on top of the woman) is rarely comfortable, unless the man gets on all fours and puts no weight on the woman. It is worth experimenting with some other positions in which she is uppermost or in which entry is from the side or from behind (see page 150). The bag of waters cushions the baby and a seal is provided by the mucous plug, which is rather like a stopper in a bottle. Even when your abdomen is bumped hard the only effect on the baby is that it bobs like a cork in a glass of water.

Lovemaking in pregnancy

Whatever position you choose . . .

. . . your partner on top, but with his weight off your abdomen . . .

. . . you on top . . .

. . . relaxed and languorous side by side . . .

. . . almost on all fours . . .

. . . or even if you decide at the end that you don't feel like full intercourse, the important thing is that you feel able to give each other physical pleasure without fear of harming your unborn child . . .

Can orgasm start labor?

Although the female orgasm involves contractions of the uterus, it will not trigger off labor unless everything is ready to start anyway. But it is quite natural after intercourse to feel uterine contractions, which usually die down after a few minutes. The uterus is an active organ and contracts regularly in rhythmic fashion throughout a woman's life. It is especially active in pregnancy and the contractions (known as Braxton Hicks contractions) which you feel in the last months are rehearsals for the labor. If you have had a premature labor before, notice spotting of blood or if the mucous plug has already gone (the show—see page 202), it is wise not to have intercourse. Once the cervical mucus has been disturbed by contractions (and this *can* happen in the last four to five weeks), ascending infection is a possibility.

Using sex to induce labor

If you are "due", especially if induction of labor has been suggested by your doctor, lovemaking is one of the ways in which you may be able to start things off naturally. Some women are thought to be especially sensitive to prostaglandins in the semen. (Prostaglandins cause the uterus to contract, and semen has a higher proportion of them than any other body substance.) It is best to choose a position—such as the woman lying on her back with her legs raised on the man's hips—in which semen is deposited right up against the cervix. But since such a position may be very uncomfortable at this late stage of pregnancy, it should be done gently.

Breast stimulation in late pregnancy also sometimes produces a strongly contracting uterus. This worries some people, but unless you have reason to think that the baby may come too early it is equally harmless, and may actually be a good thing, because the Braxton Hicks contractions which result (see page 203) help to prepare the way for labor, softening and drawing up the cervix, and—just before the baby is due—dilating it a little even before labor begins.

Nipple stimulation during labor

It has been discovered that stimulation of the nipples can reactivate a labor that has come to a halt. Some doctors have tried using it in place of the oxytocin drip (see page 253) to augment a slow labor. Unfortunately they have discovered that it does not always work. It may be that its success depends on how the stimulation is provided: perhaps someone you love may be more effective than simply using a breast pump. The midwife and doctor may agree to go out for a while and leave you to it. Though there may be a few raised eyebrows, it makes sense to try the natural way of stimulating the uterus first.

The emotions you have as lovers are not in conflict with the feelings of compassion and tenderness everyone agrees it is right to have about a baby. The sexual excitement felt by two people bound in love and caring for *each other* as well as for their baby is a good basis for becoming parents able to give love to their baby and growing child.

Pregnant again

Pregnancy the second or third time around is a new experience. It will not be exactly like the first time. It holds different challenges. Coping with them involves flexibility and resourcefulness on the part of both parents. In some ways things are much easier because you know what to expect and have probably developed self confidence in your role as a childbearer. You may sail through the pregnancy with style and thoroughly enjoy it. But there may be difficulties which come as a surprise because you thought that everything would be simple this time.

Reactions to another pregnancy

Other people's reactions The first problem you may encounter is the reaction of other people to a new pregnancy. Whereas your first was greeted with delight, friends and relatives are usually far less interested in the next pregnancy and may even raise their eyebrows and criticize you if you already have three children or if you are pregnant again after a very short interval. They can make you feel that what you are doing is not very publicspirited and even socially harmful. Some women say they were asked "Do you want it?" or "Don't you think you've had enough?", others that sympathy was offered by well-meaning friends, "How ever will you manage?" Being prepared for this reaction will help you cope with it.

Your partner's reaction You may find that your partner is not so excited about the next pregnancy. He may be busy and pre-occupied and even seem totally uninvolved. Many men feel an extra burden of responsibility and financial anxiety when a second or subsequent baby is on the way. One baby was fun but now he feels "trapped" into having to provide for a growing family for years to come. Some women are desperately disappointed at their partners' reactions to later pregnancies and feel that they are missing out on all the joy of the first baby and the companionship that drew them close together the first time round. Talk about your feelings together so that you can come to appreciate what the experience means to each of you.

Finding time to relax

When you already have a lively two- or three-year-old or a group of energetic youngsters to look after, pregnancy can be very tiring. The first time around you were able to look after yourself and luxuriate in afternoon rests, with time for thinking, planning and dreaming. Caught up in the hustle and bustle of family life, ferrying children to and from school, coping with the enormous meals they can consume and facing the everyday battle with egg on the stairs, tricycles in the hall, crumbs on the carpet and dishes in the sink, you may have to relegate pregnancy to the back of your mind. You simply do not have time for it. This may result in your neglecting yourself, your nutrition,

Friends and relatives may be less interested in your second pregnancy than they were in your first, but your first child may be fascinated. . . .

your relaxation, and also missing out on times when you can just "center down" (see page 165) and focus your thoughts and feelings on the coming baby and your changing body.

When you realize this, in the short intervals between your commitments as wife, mother, nurse, psychotherapist, teacher, hostess, house cleaner, chief cook and bottle washer, the chances are that you will feel guilty. You begin to feel apologetic to the little baby growing inside you, and perhaps also fearful that you cannot give him or her the time or even the love that you have devoted to the others. This feeling may be intensified after the birth, when to some extent the new baby has to be fitted into family life rather than your own activities being modified to the baby's needs. If you are sitting a two-year-old on the potty, or calming down three children in the bath having a very splashy game which threatens to submerge the toddler, it is difficult at the same moment to fix the new baby comfortably on the breast and to enjoy the let down of milk.

Talk about these feelings of inadequacy with other women who are facing the same problems. If you do feel guilty, the only solution is to try to organize your life so that every day you have at least some time to think about and plan for the coming baby, or, once the new baby has been born, to give him or her your whole concentration. It is certainly difficult to find even a short space of time for such attention; but you may be able to find someone who is willing to take your other children for a walk some afternoons or your partner might bathe them and put them to bed every evening, giving you a time when you know that you will be able to concentrate on yourself and your new baby.

Taking care of yourself A new pregnancy may produce aches and discomforts which you have not experienced before. Lifting bigger children and the inevitable clearing and cleaning may contribute to backache associated with bad posture. This is accentuated by fatigue and doing things in a rush, while not really caring *how* they are done so long as they *are* done. If your child still wakes in the night, doesn't like the idea of an afternoon nap, *ever*, or wakes very early in the morning and, because he or she is still too young to read quietly, comes jumping into your bed and remains during the hours after dawn, a restless bundle, you may be running short of sleep and long for a solid uninterrupted 10 or 12 hours. Perhaps it is possible to arrange this when your partner is at home at the weekend, but it does need planning in advance and meticulous organization.

The chances are that you look and feel more pregnant with this baby too, partly as a result of poor posture and tiredness, but also as a consequence of the stretching your uterus has had during previous pregnancies. This may mean that you don't feel at all happy about your body and appearance; such a lack of pleasure in yourself is then expressed automatically in the way you stand, walk and sit. It is a vicious circle.

Preparing your first child

Borrow a friend's baby for a few hours so that your child can discover what babies are really like . . .

. . . make a book showing pictures of your first child when he was a baby so that he can see how babies change and grow . . .

. . . let your child feel the baby moving inside you . . .

. . . let father take responsibility for some of your child's daily routine before the new baby arrives . . .

. . . and play at mothering a favorite doll so that the child gets some idea of the way the new baby will be cared for.

Ask your childbirth educator to help you firm up your abdominal muscles. Use buttock and leg muscles to help support your spine and tummy, and do a few rhythmic exercises each day (see pages 104–105). Your older child may enjoy doing them with you. Then make an opportunity to cherish yourself a bit. Buy some massage oil and ask your partner to give you a massage session. Think about what would cheer you up.

Preparing the older child

Some parents worry a great deal about how to prepare the older child for the new baby. This problem can seem almost insurmountable if the older one is clinging and still very dependent. Some childbirth educators* have recently come up with the idea of making a book for the child, illustrated with photographs of himself and starting with a simple description of how a baby grows inside its mother, illustrated with line drawings and a photograph of the mother when she was pregnant. You could show preparations for the birth, and then your child as a newborn baby, being suckled or bathed. These pictures could be followed by a series of photographs of the older child showing him eating, drinking, playing, helping in the house and garden. Perhaps the last page of the book can be left blank for a photograph of the new baby. All this helps the older child to prepare for the new baby and to realize that he was once just as small and incapable as it will be.

If possible borrow a baby for a few hours or have a mother and her small baby in the house for half a day or so. This will help your child to understand the reality of a baby and also how a mother holds and cares for it. Many older children expect a new baby to be either a passive bundle that can be handled like a doll or a playmate who can join in their games immediately.

If you are moving the older child from a crib to a bed, do so several months before the birth, so that it does not seem a consequence of the baby's arrival. And, if you are going to have extra help after the birth, encourage the helper to become friends with the older child well before the advent of the new baby.

When another baby is on the way, the relationship between the father and the older child is of great importance. It is a time when the two can draw closer together and enjoy each other's company for longer periods, something that will help you a great deal after the birth when you are busy with the new baby.

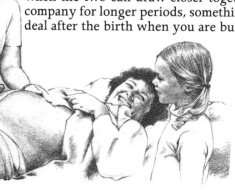

Toward the end of pregnancy take your older children with you to the doctor. Ask if they can listen with a stethoscope to the fetal heart, or help measure your tummy.

PREGNANCY: ANTICIPATING THE BIRTH

In tune with your body for labor
Windows into the uterus
The last few weeks

In tune with your body for labor

Part of preparation for birth is doing exercises, but it is even more important to think about labor in a constructive way. Give yourself time to imagine what is going to happen in your body and what you may feel, and so build up a picture that has meaning for you. This picture will be quite different from illustrations in obstetric textbooks: it is vital that it relates to *feelings* and is not just built up of intellectual information. Only then can the subjective sensations you experience in labor fit into a pattern that makes sense to you and that can help you adjust to each challenge as it comes.

So during pregnancy take time to imagine the birth of your baby. Think of different kinds of labor (see page 218) and how you might cope with them. Avoid restricting your fantasies to only one kind of labor when it may turn out that the labor you have is very different.

Childbirth education
If you are having a baby without having had instruction in childbirth, your body will probably respond naturally. However, education for birth helps you to know more about your body and to feel happy with it during pregnancy. You learn how to prepare yourself so that when you are in labor you can work *with* your body instead of fighting it, so that you can understand the activity of the uterus and the sensations you experience and so that, through relaxation, breathing and focused concentration, you can gradually come to achieve harmony with the birth process.

Choosing a prenatal class

6 6 The discussions in class helped me to face all the possibilities in labor with a minimum of fear. 9 9

Once you have arranged for prenatal care (see page 45), it is time to think about arranging prenatal classes, so that you and your partner can learn about the physiological changes of pregnancy and labor and the possible emotional impact of the stresses likely to be involved. It pays to shop around for classes and discover the different ones available in your area. You would not dream of walking into any hairdressers and asking them to cut and style your hair without first finding out what sort of work they did. Learning your task in childbirth is even more important, and so you should approach childbirth education classes with the same discrimination. For teaching to improve, more critical, informed consumers are needed. Any prenatal teacher worth her salt learns from her students, and continues to modify her teaching on the basis of the feedback she receives from them and the ideas they share with her.

Finding out about classes

66 I didn't realize how scared I was till I went to classes and then it hit me. I'd been kidding myself. But after a few classes I started to feel a new confidence. 99

66 Now I've had the baby I do miss the classes! It was such fun meeting every week. 99

When you inquire about classes, do not assume that they are successful only if those who have attended them have had easy labors and births. If you have to have a forceps delivery or a Cesarean section it does not mean that you have "failed" in applying your teaching in labor. Having a baby is not like passing an exam or winning a race. You are not expected to come out "top" with a two-hour labor, or no pain relieving drugs or whatever. It is much more a question of learning how to adapt your responses—mainly those of breathing and relaxation—to the particular challenges of your own labor. So it can be useful to talk also to women who have had labors that were not straightforward, and to find out from them if attending classes helped them at all.

Even though women all the world over have babies in much the same way, birth can be a vastly different experience for different women; just as, even though sexual intercourse involves certain mechanical and physiological processes which are the same everywhere, what people feel about it, exactly what they do and the meaning the total experience has for them, varies with the individual and the occasion. Childbirth is not primarily a medical process, but a psychosexual experience. It is not surprising that adaptive response to the stimuli it presents should be a matter of subtle and delicate working together of mind and body.

When asking about classes, ask a woman whether she found the techniques that she learned in class helpful when she was actually in labor, and whether she felt confident and as if she understood exactly what was going on. If she says "Nothing helped", implies that the classes did not relate in any way to the reality of labor, or that she was absolutely terrified from beginning to end, it sounds as if the classes did not help her, even though she may have enjoyed getting to know the other expectant mothers.

Your local hospital may have classes, though frequently hospital and clinic classes concentrate on baby care rather than on education for birth. Find out how many of the classes deal with labor: you will need at least five or six sessions on what to do then. Your doctor or midwife may know of classes. If you write to the International Childbirth Education Association or the American Society for Psychoprophylaxis in Obstetrics (addresses on page 337), they will let you know where classes are held by their teachers. The ICEA has a training and study program for its teachers, and in this way aims to continue improving the standards of childbirth education.

What makes a good prenatal class?

Good classes are progressive in the sense that you learn a little more each time; you should not feel at the third or fourth lesson that you have sat through it all before. There should be opportunities for you to ask questions, discuss freely and practice the exercises rather than simply listen to a formal lecture. Breathing and relaxation exercises which can be of practical use in labor

Learning to relax for labor can benefit both of you and be enjoyable too. . . .

should be included. Their relevance to labor should be specific-ally described, and why and how they are used. Relaxation is not as simple as it might sound. It is not just a question of flopping in front of the TV screen or of lying down with a bar of chocolate and a good book, but of learning complete awareness and control of muscle groups all over the body so that they can be contracted or relaxed at will, including muscles you may not even know you possess. Relaxation also means learning how to relax *under stress*, not just lying in a deck chair on a sunny day or in a class-room while a cool voice tells you that a contraction is beginning, continuing and then fading away. You need to learn different levels and rhythms of breathing for the different phases of labor (see page 172). So when you are asking about classes inquire of any woman who has been to them whether she learned breathing in detail.

An effective teacher helps her students realize something of what labor feels like, and the reality and power of its challenge. She also explains things fully, without fear that she is burden-ing her students' minds, and does so honestly and clearly. In some classes there is far too much talking down to pregnant women. You have a right to understand what is happening to your own body and what people are proposing to do to you. A good teacher does not answer a query with "Oh you don't have to bother about that", or imply that everyone will do what is best for you and your baby, and that all you need to do is trust your birth attendants. Discussion should be a real exchange of ideas, not simply a few questions to which answers are given without recognition of the apprehension and the sometimes night-marish fears that can lie behind them.

You can see from this that a good deal depends on the person-ality of the teacher. It is not so much "the method" that is good or inadequate as the quality of the teaching itself, and perhaps most of all the relationship that the teacher has with her students. I have seen teaching in different countries—including Western Europe, the USA and beyond the Iron Curtain—which seemed woefully inadequate or mechanized, or which involved learning a number of rather irrelevant physical exercises, and yet, because of the personality and attitude of the teacher, the women participated actively and joyfully in their labors.

The Dick-Read method

There are different approaches to childbirth education and the names associated with them can be confusing for expectant mothers. The Dick-Read method is named after Dr Grantly Dick-Read;* it is the oldest method and is usually associated with "relaxation classes". The philosophy behind this approach is that ignorance produces fear, which leads to tension, which in turn quickly produces pain. So teachers concentrate on over-coming fear by teaching deep relaxation and the breathing that accompanies it, along with accurate information about the childbearing process, exercises to keep you supple and poised, and discussion of breastfeeding and how to prepare for it.

Psycho-prophylaxis

Psychoprophylaxis is a highly systematized training centered on techniques of breathing rather than relaxation. This method originated in the USSR, was developed in Paris and then adapted in the United States by Elizabeth Bing*. In the past few years free discussion has become an integral part of classes. Psychoprophylaxis classes start by deconditioning the women from their fear and doubts about childbirth, and then recondition them to respond to labor contractions as helpful stimuli and not as pains. Exercises are taught both for limbering up and for use in labor. Full information is given about the anatomy and physiology of pregnancy and labor. This system is that usually taught by ASPO teachers and is one of a range of approaches (including the Bradley method) taught by ICEA teachers.

In the USA, women know psychoprophylaxis by the name of its French originator, Lamaze, whereas in France itself it is often called *"accouchement sans douleur"* (labor without pain), or *"asd"*. This name is thoroughly misleading and might make any woman having pain in labor feel that she is not using the method properly, or that something is going terribly wrong. For most women who have been to classes the pain of labor is not the most important thing about the experience and is a side effect with which many, helped by techniques of adjustment and emotional support and guidance at the time, can cope well without pharmacological aids. Others want some additional pain relief (see page 240), and should have it.

The Kitzinger psychosexual approach

My own *psychosexual* approach grew out of both the Dick-Read and psychoprophylaxis systems of training. It is on this approach that the preparation for birth in this book is based.

Whereas psychoprophylaxis is based on conditioned reflexes, the greatest contribution to the psychosexual method has come from psychoanalytic theory and social anthropology. Labor as a personal experience involves often barely glimpsed feelings about ourselves which have developed through the formative years of childhood: attitudes to and fantasies about our bodies, feelings about the relative size and positions of organs and orifices, and concepts of cleanliness and pollution, beauty and ugliness. All of these are partly social in origin, products of our upbringing and family relationships.

A pregnant woman also needs to discover in what way labor is a social situation, not just a physiological or even a private emotional experience. Because labor involves human relationships at a sometimes tense and demanding time, it helps to know how to talk with the different people assisting at the birth and how to understand what may be in the doctors' and midwives' minds. All childbirth teachers agree that students require plenty of information about how their bodies work and what goes on in hospitals. Most classes include a visit to the hospital and a tour of the delivery room. But it is not just a question of knowing what will happen to you, but of learning how to negotiate to get the kind of birth you want.

Plenty of rest and relaxation will bring you to the end of pregnancy full of health and vitality . . .

The aims of classes

So you will see that there is wide variation in exactly what is taught and how, although there is general agreement that six sessions of one and a half to two hours each are the minimum required. The aim is not to retreat from contractions but to adjust to them and respond actively with control and concentration. Up to date teachers agree that all students should learn correct breathing and relaxation for labor, and that the breathing exercises should include different types of breathing for the different phases of labor (see page 172). Fathers' classes should also be offered, so that prospective fathers can learn how to help their wives in pregnancy and labor and understand something about the feelings involved in becoming a father. Most teachers offer couples classes where the whole of preparation for birth is shared. If you are offered less than this in the classes you attend, you will probably feel the need to supplement them with other classes, reading, or extra private classes if it can possibly be arranged.

When to start classes

Whatever method you finally opt for, do not leave booking for classes or reading up on the subject till the last moment. Start finding out what is available and begin your course of reading four or five months before your baby is due, even though classes may not be offered till the last nine weeks or so. Where teachers run classes which start in the last two or three months of pregnancy there is often an opportunity to have "early bird" classes at three or four months. This is an excellent idea, although some teachers of psychoprophylaxis believe that students get bored if they start too soon. Even if you do not start to practice

By going to prenatal classes with your partner you can prepare for labor together, as well as sharing your feelings about the pregnancy with other couples in the same situation . . .

any breathing techniques till the last weeks, it can only be beneficial to learn good posture in early pregnancy, something about how the baby develops inside you and how to cope with any minor discomforts. It is also an advantage at any time (for men too) to know how deep relaxation can help you get to sleep.

Whatever approach you select, provided you are happy with your teacher and develop confidence in yourself through the instruction, the teaching will be right for you, and you will find that you have a variety of suitable tools with which to adapt to contractions in labor. Labor need not be an ordeal to be feared, but a positive, rewarding experience, and a really *happy birthday*.

Relaxation and massage

Relaxation is the art of letting go and allowing peace to flow through you. The skill is in being able to release your muscles at will and not only when you are in a special mood to relax. It is not just an exercise, but as necessary a partner to—and interlude in—strenuous activity as the breath out to the breath in.

The importance of relaxation

66 I hadn't realized that I clenched my jaw when I tensed up around my eyes or how often I curled my toes when I concentrated. I am much more aware now of how I react when under stress. 99

Relaxation is vital for labor. If you cannot relax you are likely to become exhausted as a result of tightening up muscles all over your body in reaction to the challenging stress of contractions. By tensing muscles unnecessarily you are wasting energy, and if you are exhausted any pain experienced will be felt more keenly and your ability to control it is bound to be diminished.

Generalized tension and anxiety can sometimes affect the way the uterus contracts, producing incoordinate uterine action, which means that the contractions are painful but are not very effective in pulling open the cervix. Because it alters your whole body chemistry, marked tension lasting a long time can also reduce the oxygen supply to the baby. Just as the smooth co-ordination of the digestive system, the beating of your heart and your breathing are all affected by acute tension, so stress and anxiety can slow down the unfolding process of childbirth and make it more difficult.

When you know how to relax you can adjust to your labor with special ways of breathing, positions and other techniques. Relaxation helps keep your mind clear so that you are able to understand what is happening and can respond to it purposefully and creatively.

Centering down

To explore the skills of relaxation, you need to be able to "center down", in an old Quaker term, and be still and enjoy peace of body and mind.

Lie on your back, well propped up with plenty of pillows, or sit in a comfortable chair with cushions supporting all of your back, including the back of your neck. You may also like a cushion under each arm or under your thighs. If you prefer, lie on your side, back rounded, head and shoulders forward, legs and arms bent. Before starting any exercises spend time thinking

Settle into a truly comfortable position for a while each day; make sure that there are no distractions to prevent you from concentrating on your baby's presence inside you . . .

of the journey the baby makes to be born. Read page 210 and then focus your thoughts on that part of your body. Feel muscles and flesh heavy and released.

Touch relaxation

Touch relaxation is a method in which your partner (or a friend) gives you a message with his hands that says, "Relax here". You respond to the pressure and warmth you feel through his hands with immediate release. Start by lying in a comfortable position, well propped up with your legs and arms spread a little and bent, and give a long breath out with a soft mouth, and relax completely. Now you contract different sets of muscles, noticing how they feel when they are tight. Your partner then rests his hands over the part that feels tight. If he is holding his hands against bare skin it is a good idea to sprinkle a little talcum powder over the area before you start, as your skin may feel itchy otherwise. As soon as you feel his touch you relax, with a sensation of flowing *out* towards him. Your partner moves his hands away before you tense up again. Some examples of touch relaxation are illustrated on pages 170–171.

Release of tension By practicing touch relaxation, you and your partner are working very closely together. He learns to notice when there is a buildup of tension in you long before anyone who does not know you well can realize what is happening. Then all he has to do is reach out his hand with a message to relax, before the tension spirals. This is very useful in labor, as you can imagine. If he notices that your shoulders are becoming tense, he can put a firm hand on your shoulder. If he sees that your legs are tense, he can stroke them firmly. If he notices that your arms are tense, he can stroke down your arms. It should be a loving, rather than a bullying, touch. Some men feel that they have to give their wives directions and must "coach" them all the time in labor. This is neither necessary nor desirable. There are times when definite instructions are helpful, particularly at the very end of the first stage, but even then body language and nonverbal communication, confident holding and eye contact can help a great deal.

Your body's response to the doctor or nurse Exploring touch relaxation together also means that you are training yourself to relax towards the touch of the doctor or nurse who examines you, instead of pulling away from it like a snail drawing

66 We are enjoying it a lot. We do it each night when we go to bed and to tell you the truth we like the massage and everything so much that we don't always get round to finishing the exercises! 99

in its horns. So practicing touch relaxation is a useful skill to apply when you are having uncomfortable prenatal examinations.

Pressure from the uterus In labor the stimuli from the uterus itself are remarkably like a very strong, powerful kind of touch inside you, which brings with it pressure and a feeling of heat. At the same time the opening cervix is being pulled wider (see page 208) and this also produces pressure similar to pressure from touch. The baby moving down the birth canal brings enormous pressure too, as if a grapefruit were being pressed down first against the anus and then through the vagina. This pressure also produces a stimulus to which you can respond either by tightening up or releasing your muscles.

Learning to flow along with a contraction You can prepare yourself to relax during labor by imagining the sensations you might feel during contractions. Imagine that you are in labor and that the uterus is producing pressure with a contraction. Feel the pressure of the baby's head. Release and flow towards it. Some women feel each contraction as warmth building up to heat and then dying down again. One mother said that each one was like an oven door opening, swinging open, until at its peak, she received the full blast of heat and then the oven door closed again. If you have learned always to respond by relaxing to the pressure and warmth of your partner's hand, you will react to these messages from inside your body, not by pulling back, but by releasing and flowing toward them. In this way the contractions of your uterus will provide another kind of touch relaxation to guide you through labor.

Puppet-strings relaxation Of course you do not always have someone to help you with relaxation. You can practice relaxation by yourself, using a method that I call the puppet-on-a-string method.

Lie in whatever position you usually sleep. Make yourself really comfortable, well supported by pillows, and give a long, sighing breath out and relax. Imagine that strings are attached to all your joints. Think of one fixed to your elbow, being tightened gradually so that your elbow is pulled up with the string. Depending on the position in which you are lying, your elbow may be moved a lot or a little. Then let it go. Notice the different feelings. Now the angle of the string is different, so feel the pull in a different direction. It lifts your elbow higher and higher. Now the string is released. Do not allow any parts other than those operated by the string to move. The hand hangs limp at the wrist. The shoulder is not lifted. Only the elbow is activated.

Now do the same thing with an imaginary string attached to the other elbow. Let it be pulled in various directions. Continue as if a string were fixed to one big toe, then the other one, the back of one ankle then the other, the left knee, the right knee, the left wrist, the right wrist, the index finger, the middle joint of a finger, one shoulder, the other shoulder, your left hip, your right hip.

Then imagine two strings, attached to your right elbow and right wrist, for example, tightening one after the other till both are drawn taut; first the wrist string is released then the elbow string. Experiment with the strings working in a different order. Keep your mind focused on the tightening string rather than on the muscle you are contracting. Only when the invisible string is taut should you turn your mind to analyzing which muscles are tightened.

Imagine one string fixed to the top of your head, another to the base of your skull. First one is pulled, then the other. One goes slack, then the other. You will find that you can make the strings pull in different directions and at varying angles. This saves it from becoming a repetitive exercise that you do just from habit, without focusing on what your body is doing. It is important that any body movements you do bring awareness, an increased sense of working *with* your body. Mechanical gymnastic exercises have no place in learning to relax.

Go on from this to recreate in your imagination actions that you usually perform without thinking, simple things like writing a shopping list or unlocking a door, and discover exactly how you use your body.

Stanislavsky relaxation

There are acting techniques for increasing body awareness and learning which muscles contract and work together. The precise combination of muscles working together varies with each individual and the nature of the task, the angle at which you tackle it, the weight, dimensions and even the texture of the tools used. You will find that tasks you perform, even ordinary, everyday tasks, often cause you to change your breathing, and sometimes you hold your breath altogether. You may discover too that you tense up muscles that you do not need to use because you tackle a job in the wrong way or overwork at it, or because you are emotionally keyed up about what you are doing. All this is a valuable process of self discovery and you can gradually learn more and more about yourself.

The method of relaxation based on Stanislavsky acting techniques explores different sets of muscles in the body that naturally function together and the way they work in response to different imagined activities and tasks and even thoughts and feelings. You think of certain situations—things you might be doing with your body—and mentally involve yourself in these situations as if you were actually performing them. Notice which muscles have become tense. Once the observation is made, switch off the picture in your mind and deliberately release those muscles.

Start by sitting or lying against a firm support and let the pillows take your whole weight. Listen to the sound of your own breathing. Breathe so that you can just hear yourself—in through your nose, and out through your mouth. Allow the breathing to flow through your mouth, letting the breath out be long and slow. The sound is like a little sigh as you breathe out. You may notice that there is a slight pause after you breathe in as if you have reached the crest of a wave. Enjoy that slight pause. Then give a long breath out. And with each breath out, relax a little more; use your breathing to help your relaxation. It should feel good.

Suggested exercises for Stanislavsky relaxation

The jaw Imagine that you have some very sticky taffy in your mouth, and chew it well. It is sticking to your teeth. Work this great hunk of taffy out of your teeth. Notice what is happening. Then rest and drop your jaw. Let it relax, quite soft and loose. Notice the different feeling of complete release of the jaw muscles.

The eyes We do not usually notice when our eye muscles become tense. Imagine that there is a fireman climbing a ladder to rescue a little dog stranded at the top of a house. Focus on the fireman as he climbs all the way up. Observe the feeling in the muscles behind and around your eyes. Follow him with your eyes—up and up—until he is at the top. He has the little dog under his arm now and is bringing it down and down. Now he is at the bottom. Relax your eyes, and if you want to, let them close. Notice how different they feel when they are relaxed.

The feet Imagine that you are at the seaside standing on a very pebbly beach with no shoes on. Making very slight movements, imagine that you are walking on the beach with the sharp pebbles underfoot, and really feel them under your bare feet. Pick your way carefully over them. Oh! That was a sharp one! Observe the tension in your feet. Now go on to the soft sand. Really feel the difference. Then imagine that you lie down and let your feet relax completely.

The hands Can you recollect the feeling of making a snowball? Imagine that you are picking up snow and are patting the hard, cold mass into a firm snowball. You are hurrying so that you can throw it at someone. As you quickly make your snowball, notice the tension in your hands. Then drop them and let them relax beside your body on the bed or floor again and notice how warm, soft and loose they feel.

Taste Imagine that you are sipping some water. Place the glass to your lips. It is sharp, pure lemon juice! Really taste it. Notice what is happening in your mouth and the tension that is spontaneously produced. Now it is gone. Relax and let the muscles of the mouth soften.

Now you have a large, ripe peach. Take a good bite of it. It is very juicy and the juice is dribbling down. You need to suck it and draw in the juice. Smell it, too. Chew it, swallow it. Now it has gone. Notice the very different feeling in your mouth. Relax completely and think through what happened to the muscle inside your mouth and nose and the other facial muscles as you imagined you ate the peach.

Smell Muscles around the nostrils, in the cheeks and the mouth work together as we smell and taste things. Imagine that you have in your hand a bottle of liquid. Take out the stopper and

Touch relaxation

Tension in labor is bad for you and your baby. Learn how to relax to your partner's touch, so that this will be a spontaneous reaction in labor. Your partner applies firm pressure to the part that is tense. You release to the warmth of his touch, flowing toward him; he draws tension out of you.

The arms
Tighten up the arm nearest your partner. He puts pressure on your shoulder with both hands, then strokes very slowly down to your wrist with one hand on the inside, one on the outside of your arm, molding his hands to its shape. Relax as he does so.

The head
A tension headache can be relieved by your partner placing two fingers on either side of your head, against the temples, pressing firmly then releasing the pressure very gradually. You feel the tension flowing from the center to the sides of your head and away.

The eyes
If you are tense around the eyes, raise your eyebrows until your scalp feels tight. Your partner makes a cap with his hands and rests them firmly on your head, drawing your tension into his hands.

The legs
If your legs feel cold and shaky toward the end of the first stage of labor, your partner can help by stroking them from your thighs to your knees. He points his fingers downward and molds his hands to the shape of your legs (see inset) with a firm stroke down and a light stroke up in a continuous movement.

Abdominal massage
To relieve abdominal tension during labor your partner lightly massages the lower curve of your tummy with his fingers. With one hand following the other, he massages as if stroking the baby's head (see inset).

The shoulders
Many women curl up into a fetal position during labor. Your partner can help you relax by pressing the palms of his hands against the back of your shoulders.

Shoulder tension
Tension in the shoulders can result in hyperventilation. Learn to release this tension toward your partner as he sits facing you, pressing the heels of his hands against your shoulders.

The buttocks
Some women tense up their buttocks in labor when the baby presses against the rectum as it rounds the curve of the birth canal. Contracting these muscles can delay the descent of the baby's head, so practice relaxing them while your partner massages your buttocks firmly, as if kneading dough.

take a good sniff—it is ammonia! Notice how you have become stiff down the back of your neck. Then relax. Breathe fresh, pure, clean air. Let yourself breathe easily.

Here is another bottle. Do the same with this one. It is perfume this time: lily of the valley. You will find yourself drawing in the scent of lily of the valley in long, slow breaths, holding the fragrance as if suffused behind the surface of your face. Now the fragrance has gone and you are just breathing air. Relax.

Breathing for labor

Relaxation and breathing are so closely associated that it is important to learn them as part of a unity. You cannot really breathe correctly for labor unless your body is relaxed. As labor progresses you will spontaneously breathe more rapidly. If you breathe more quickly and at the same time heavily, you are bound to hyperventilate and flush carbon dioxide out of your bloodstream. This can make you feel very uncomfortable and, if severe enough, you will even pass out.

For this reason, in many cultures breathing in labor is deliberately regulated to help a woman work with the forces bringing her baby to birth. Among the Zulu, for example, breathing exercises are taught in pregnancy. A woman is supposed to go to the door of her hut each morning as the sun rises and take careful, controlled, full breaths through each nostril alternately.* She uses the same breathing in labor. In other cultures breathing is regulated by background sounds, including prayers, music, the beating of hands or repeated phrases of encouragement, or by the swaying movement of attendants holding the mother.

Breathing for relaxation — Regulated breathing rhythms can also help release tension and create a state of pleasurable relaxation. In labor this is particularly important because, since contractions come like the waves of the sea, there is a strong natural rhythm built in to the physiological activity. A woman can either resist this, trying to "switch off", escape from or dominate it, or she can go with it and adjust her breathing to the compelling sweep of uterine power. She can only go with the rhythm if she can accept what is happening in her body and assent to it.

So the breathing taught for labor is nothing to do with "distraction techniques" and is certainly no magic method of eradicating sensation or guaranteeing that you do not feel pain. It is another way of getting in tune with your body and especially with your laboring uterus.

Rest your hands over the lower curve of your abdomen. In late pregnancy you have a lovely melon shape there. Breathe as slowly as you comfortably can. As the breath enters your nostrils, allow them to dilate, notice the slight pause between the breath in and the breath out, and then breathe out through a soft, relaxed mouth as if you had on a new, glossy and rather expensive lipstick. Enjoy that breath out. Notice what is happening to your abdomen. Feel it rising under your hands as you breathe in, a gentle swelling a little like a wave building up, and then as you breathe out the abdomen sinks back again and the wave recedes. Feel the slight pressure under your hands as you breathe in and swell up, and the pressure withdrawing as you breathe out and the abdomen goes back to its former position.

The greeting breath

When you are in labor, meet each contraction with your breathing, giving first of all a complete greeting breath. This is a deliberate, slow breath *out*. Imagine an early first-stage contraction lasting 45 to 60 seconds. Breathe slowly through the contraction, with the lower part of your back spreading out and pressing slightly against the bed or floor as you breathe in, and the pressure being lifted a little as you breathe out.

The resting breath

As a contraction fades away, you give a long, slow, complete breath out through your mouth—a resting breath. This is important partly because it gives you complete relaxation at the end of a contraction and you are able to rest before the next one, and partly because it signals to everyone in the room that you are at the end of a contraction. If the nurse or obstetrician wants to talk to you, or ask you to turn over, now is the time, between contractions and never during them.

Full chest breathing

You need a partner to help you practice this. Lie on your side with your back rounded, head and shoulders curved forward, legs well apart and the upper leg drawn up and bent at the knee. Now lift your head as if stretching your spine all the way up the back so that you feel taller. Stretch your neck at the back, stretch all the way up your spine and then simply let it drop back into place; let your head settle comfortably on your shoulders. See that there is a good space between your legs. Then give a long breath out and relax completely. Allow your eyes to close if they feel heavy.

Think of your back. Your spine is not stiff like a lamp post. It is constructed with small vertebrae in a curving shape like a string of sausages. We often act as if our spinal column were very stiff. Yet think of the way a cat moves and how movement ripples up and down the back.

Now your partner rests his hands one on each shoulder and massages with the flat of both hands from the top of your back right down to the bottom. His hands should be relaxed. Tell him if you would like the massage to be heavier or lighter, slower or quicker. Is it in exactly the right place? It should feel good. Relax towards his hands.

Then your partner rests the palms of his hands firmly above your waist on either side of the spine on the ribcage. They should be in a position that is comfortable for you. Notice their warmth and strength. Breathe in through the nose and out through the mouth again so that the main level of breathing awareness is just where you feel the pressure and warmth of his hands, and listen to your breathing. Breathe down to where you feel his hands, expanding your ribcage, so that it is swelling out under his hands as you breathe in, and then it falls away from the pressure of his hands as you breathe out. Listen to it for a moment. Can your partner feel the pressure under his hands, building up as you breathe in and falling away as you breathe out? This is full chest breathing. It can be very useful, once labor starts, to meet the earliest contractions of the first stage of labor. You may be able to breathe like this all the way through your early contractions, concentrating on breathing into this area against which your partner is pressing his hands. When you are actually in labor you will not need the hands there because you will have rehearsed it so that you can do it automatically and the contracting uterus itself will provide sufficient stimulus.

Upper chest breathing

As contractions strengthen, you will want to lift your breathing above them, as if over the crest of a wave. Contractions come like waves and you find that you can cope with them more easily if you breathe more lightly and at the same time more quickly. At this phase of labor they may be coming every four or five minutes and lasting about a minute.

To practice breathing with these contractions, your partner should rest the palms of his hands on your upper back just below your shoulder blades. You breathe so that your main level of breathing activity and awareness is where you feel the pressure of his hands. You will find that you want to breathe more rapidly, perhaps through parted lips. You should be able to hear a crisp little sigh or "huff" with each breath out. Now if you rest your hand over your upper chest you will feel it rising and falling at the same time, rather like a seagull floating on a wave. In labor the wave of a contraction will be underneath and you will be breathing over the top of it. Remember to relax your shoulders all of the time; they are not doing any of the work.

Butterfly breathing

As you go over the most tumultuous waves of contractions at the end of the first stage of labor, just before the cervix is fully dilated and the uterus and vagina become one birth canal, you will need to move up to the quickest, shallowest breathing of all—mouth-centered or butterfly breathing. This is the lightest, most rapid breathing you will need to use in labor. With all breathing you are bound to be using your diaphragm and lungs, but butterfly breathing is easier if you think of it as being centered in your mouth behind your cheeks and not in the throat. If you center your breathing in the throat, you will probably tense up your neck. Think of the space in your mouth, the space behind your warm, plumped up cheeks. Either sit up in a chair or lie well propped up on the bed for this exercise. If you are lying flat, you can easily find yourself gasping and panting heavily when you are doing this type of breathing. So you need three or four pillows behind you; if necessary double the pillow over so that you have a good support.

Preparing for labor need not be a solemn drill: you can make it a natural part of your daily life and involve your other child too. . . .

Resting the plump pads of the tips of your fingers against your cheeks will help you to concentrate on this area. Part your lips in a slight smile like the Mona Lisa. Relax your mouth and you will probably find that you are salivating a little. Breathe regularly and lightly in and out through your parted lips. Start gently, then gradually double the rate of your breathing till it is like the ticking of a wristwatch.

Butterfly breathing may be quite difficult at first. You may feel that you are taking in or letting out too much air. Most people do at first, and find this the most difficult kind of breathing in pregnancy. They think that they will never be able to manage it, but in labor it comes quite naturally and then they do not know how they could have coped without it. You may find that it helps to think in terms of a definite rhythm in which one beat is slightly accentuated: *one*, two, three, four; *one*, two, three, four; or *one*, two, three, four, five, six. If you do this, be careful not to expel a great deal of air on the accented breath or you will gasp in the following breath and start to hyperventilate. If you find it difficult to keep the rhythm or find your throat getting tight, give a quick blow out through pursed lips and carry on with the light breathing immediately after. Try it once again and do not allow your shoulders or the back of your neck to tense up. Drop your shoulders and relax.

BREATHING LEVELS
Experiment with the different sorts of breathing you may need in the first stage of labor . . .

In labor you will want to use this sort of breathing only when you are coping with the biggest contractions, which occur at the end of the first stage and are doing the most work. When you

. . . full chest breathing for the earliest contractions . . .

. . . upper chest breathing, to lift you over the top of the stronger contractions . . .

. . . and butterfly breathing to take you through the end of the first stage.

reach this point, you may feel like a little ship in a storm at sea in the middle of huge waves and confusing crosscurrents. For most women this is the most difficult time of labor. Grantly Dick-Read used to call it "the pain period of labor". This does not mean that you may not feel pain at other times, but it is the time when you will need all your concentration and control.

Sheep's breathing If we watch any mammal giving birth, a cat, for example, or a sheep, we notice that she does not take great breaths in and then "block" the birth canal by holding her breath. A sheep gives birth with rather light, quick breathing. Her breath is involuntarily held as she bears down and then she continues the light, accelerated breathing again immediately.

During the second stage of labor, when the baby is actually traveling down the birth canal (see page 210), most women feel the urge to push during contractions. As a contraction builds up you move from full to lighter, quicker breathing, your cheeks plumped up. Then the surge of desire to bear down comes and you hold your breath. As soon as you can breathe again you do, lightly, and then bear down again—and so on until the desire fades, your breathing slows down and then the contraction ends. You can practice this with only the slightest, most gentle push.

Experimenting with different positions for labor

Once you are fairly confident about your ability to relax and breathe rhythmically, explore some different positions which you may want to use in labor. There is no reason why you should have to be tucked up in bed all the time. There are definite disadvantages with the supine position (lying flat on your back) for your baby, since the bloodflow in the large veins in the lower part of your body may be obstructed by the heavy weight of your uterus and this can reduce the bloodflow through the placenta to and from the baby (see page 205).

During the early first stage of labor you may feel happier walking about or standing up, supported at your back or side by a wall or your partner. If you have low backache, you can lean forward onto a heavy piece of furniture. Once labor is advanced, it will be easier if you already know which positions you are likely to feel most comfortable in. You can try sitting well up, firmly supported right up your spine; kneeling, leaning back over your heels or forward onto a pillow placed on a chair or bed or over the top of the bed head; a knee-chest position with your knees placed either side of your body, rather like a frog; on all fours or squatting, with your back firmly supported. Some of these positions are illustrated on page 180.

Your aim in all these positions is to give the baby as much room as possible in your pelvis by holding your knees well apart and to allow the uterus to tilt forward onto your abdominal wall and away from your spine. In this position it assumes an egg shape, whereas when you are lying flat on your back it tends to be distorted from this natural shape. When you are upright you are also allowing gravity to help the baby down. In all these positions contract only those muscles you need to use to support yourself, and whenever possible use pillows to give you firm support.

You can relieve low backache in labor, especially common when the baby is in an occipito-posterior position (see page 218), by getting into a position in which your abdomen can hang forward, tilting the baby away from your sacrum. It will also be convenient for back massage and counter pressure, and because the longitudinal axis of the uterus is then in line with the birth canal it may help the baby to rotate into the correct anterior position. If the baby is posterior, you will probably have bearing-down sensations before you are fully dilated, and are more likely to be able to control the urge if you take pressure off your rectum.

Pressure on the umbilical cord interrupts the baby's circulation through it. Resulting decelerations of the fetal heart which last after the end of the contractions may be noted if you are having continuous electronic monitoring (see page 257). This will lead your doctor to consider a forceps delivery for fetal distress. If you adopt a position in which your tummy is hanging forward, however, such as on all fours, both the baby and its cord will be tipped away from your spine and the pressure on the cord may be relieved.

Incidentally, it is a good idea to adopt an all-fours position for delivery if the baby has large shoulders that get stuck (shoulder dystocia). It gives the assistant more room for maneuver, as the baby's head can be extended and drawn out and up toward your anus, so delivering the shoulder nearer your front, and the rest will then follow easily.

Sometimes contractions are inefficient from the start of labor and do not seem to pick up or, having been effective, become weak. In either case it is worth trying a position in which the uterus can most easily form a sphere. It may help to stand facing a wall, legs well apart and leaning forward with your hands resting against the wall so that your tummy can drop forward.

Practicing for contractions and pushing

The experience of labor is difficult to imagine before you have had a baby. Will contractions be unbearably painful or hardly noticeable? Some women think of the contractions as bigger and bigger hills they have to climb, each hill having its own peak, until they reach the mountain range at the end of the first stage.

The action of the uterus When the uterus contracts, it is tightening up, just like any working muscle in the body. Make a very tight fist with one hand and raise your arm so that the big muscle on the inside of your upper arm, the biceps, tightens; then feel it with your other hand. You will notice that the biceps has gone hard and is sticking out. If a man does the same thing, his biceps may stick out a good deal more than yours does, because his is probably a bigger muscle. The biceps goes hard as it contracts and it also protrudes. This is because the muscle fibers are shortened and thickened. The same thing happens, on a much larger scale, when the uterus contracts. Like your bulging biceps, the uterus bulges forward in your abdomen when you have a really strong and effective contraction. The strong contractions are the best of all for helping your baby to be born.

Place your hand just above your pubic hair line at the very bottom of the abdomen. The cervix lies under this area and it is here that you are likely to feel the strong, rhythmic pull as it opens, a pull that will feel tightest at the height of each contraction (see page 203).

You cannot actively do anything to help the baby down the birth canal until the cervix is wide open. A relaxed body and a mind at peace are the most important contribution you can make to the birth process at this stage. It is possible to train yourself to respond with neuromuscular release whenever you want to. Your breathing techniques can help your relaxation and your relaxation can help keep your breathing smooth and rhythmic.

Simulating contractions Contractions are felt mainly as powerful pressure which comes whether or not you want it to, so when you are practicing for them work with a partner and allow him or her to simulate the contractions, deciding when they start, how strong they become and how long they last. Meet each contraction with a welcoming breath *out* and use the rhythmic breathing you have learned right through each one, with a long resting breath out at the end.

PRACTICING FOR CONTRACTIONS
By simulating contractions you learn to respond to painful stimuli with the use of breathing. It is best to practice this technique with your partner who acts as your "uterus" by pinching a little flesh on your inside thigh between his fingers. You adjust your breathing levels according to the degree of pressure you feel. . .

. . . and after a while it may be a good idea to change places. "Contractions"—like the real ones—can vary: some short, some long, some easy, some harder; some may even have double peaks. . . . For your partner it may be the first real inkling of what labor can be like.

Practicing positions for labor

There is no reason to spend the whole of labor in bed. In fact lying flat on your back diminishes the oxygen supply to your baby and prevents gravity from allowing your uterus to contract as efficiently as it might. While you are pregnant, try out different positions and work out some which you think will be comfortable.

If you find sitting comfortable, you may like to lean up against your partner or a friend so that you can breathe through contractions together.

Leaning back over your heels with your knees apart is a good way of giving the baby as much room in the pelvis as possible.

In this position your tummy can drop forward so that your uterus is as nearly spherical as possible. If contractions are weak this will help them to become more efficient.

Try leaning forward onto the back of a chair, so that the weight of the baby is lifted off your spine.

Getting down on all fours is one of the best positions for relieving low backache and for reducing pressure on the umbilical cord.

Your partner sits beside you so that you have eye contact with each other. He pretends to be your uterus by taking hold of a piece of your flesh, the inner thigh, say, and squeezing it. He will find that taking hold of a small piece of flesh rather than a big area is more effective. He should be particularly careful if you have a varicose vein, lifting the flesh up off the leg instead of pressing down into the leg, and avoiding the area around the varicose vein. First he squeezes gently, and then tightens his grip to a strong pinch that lasts for about 15 seconds, after which he gradually releases his hold. The contraction should last about 45 seconds in all. This will help him to be aware of what you are feeling and how you react to stress of this kind, so that he can give you emotional support and encouragement.

In between these mock contractions, you can discuss with him how each one felt, and perhaps how he can improve his performance and you can improve yours. In labor this rest space between contractions should be used to prepare you for the next one: do not waste time discussing the contraction that has just ended.

It is a good idea to change places so that you become your partner's "uterus" and he can experience this firm gripping sensation and learn how to respond to it. This is important if he is going to be with you during labor and wants to be able to help you by breathing with you when and if contractions become difficult.

Practicing for stronger contractions

Switch roles again and imagine that labor is progressing, with longer and stronger contractions, each reaching its peak about halfway through. Remember, however, that contractions vary and that it is no good wishing for a "textbook labor" if your own labor proves to be different. Some contractions have their peaks about a third of the way through; some may even have two peaks. The important thing is that if you go with your uterus, you tune in with it rather like an orchestra responding to a conductor. The conductor in this case is the uterus. You have to be able, as it were, to "listen" to your uterus in order to react to it, and be in harmony with it. For these stronger contractions your partner grips your thigh for a minute or a little longer.

When necessary during these longer contractions you respond by lifting your breathing above the contraction—breathing more shallowly and more quickly (see page 174). Relax your shoulders and toes; then, as the contraction becomes slightly less intense, allow your breathing to become slower and fuller.

Pushing

Pushing or bearing down is often described as an extraordinarily athletic activity, as if you could learn to do it the way you learn to do a gymnastic exercise. It should be nothing of the kind.

However you are sitting now, rest your hands beneath the lower curve of your abdomen. Take a deep breath and hold it. Drop your chin forward on your chest and at the same time allow the bulge underneath your hands to press downward and forward, so that *from inside* your abdomen you are pressing your hands out and moving them forward. You probably feel your perineum moving forward too. Allow the movement to carry right down through until you feel the tissues of the vagina spreading out, and then rest. Did you get that feeling of something moving forward? When the baby is ready to be born, this movement helps its head to bulge farther down the birth canal. Though it is useful to learn how to do this beforehand, especially if you practice it without straining and useless effort, most women feel a spontaneous urge to do it anyway during labor (see page 209).

Before going on to practice this pushing movement, make sure that your bladder is empty. Sit on a bed, or on the floor, with four or five firm pillows behind your back, knees flopped apart and your heels drawn up near your buttocks. (Bearing down is really best rehearsed on the toilet as you release the pelvic floor muscles also for defecation and in this way they are not strained. If you happen to be constipated, as many pregnant women are in late pregnancy (see page 117), this movement will help relieve the constipation and is an excellent exercise for encouraging spontaneous, easy bowel movements.)

You will probably feel more comfortable sitting well up, and this will be an advantage during labor, as you will be able to see over the bulge to watch your baby being born if you want to. It is also much easier to let gravity help you. If you are lying flat, or almost flat, you are pushing the baby uphill because the uterus is almost at right angles to the vagina (see pages 210–211). In an almost upright position you can lean on your uterus and press the baby down.

After you have done this pushing movement a few times, begin to work with your partner. He should sit near your head with a pillow over his forearm and support your head and shoulders with it. This gives you a very wide base of support. He puts his hand over your lower abdomen so that he can feel what is happening inside. Drop your head forward onto your chest, so that you do not strain with your throat muscles and produce a grunting sound. Take a breath. Lean forward and press from inside steadily out, slowly, gently; a little bit more; let it go; let the breath out and rest. While you are practicing, your partner's hand pressed firmly against your lower abdomen gives you something to press against and guide you. It is easier to bear down when your baby is actually in the birth canal waiting to be born because you have something to press against. Allow your pelvic floor muscles to bulge forward like a heavy sack of apples. When you have felt and noted the sensation this produces, lift your pelvic floor up again so that it is well toned and not sagging (see page 103). Think of it smiling. Once you know how to do this you do not need to practice it every day, only occasionally, and whenever you do, make sure that you have released your pelvic floor muscles, so that you do not subject them to unnecessary strain.

Windows into the uterus

Apart from the routine urine and blood pressure tests you will have every time you go to the doctor (see page 46), there are certain other investigations that may be done during pregnancy. Whether they are done at all, or how often they are done, will depend not only on there being some specific reason for them, but on the part of the country you are in and therefore on your doctor or the clinic you attend. Teaching hospitals have far more sophisticated equipment and are also engaged in research, so—for example—if you are in a large city you may be offered ultrasound two or three times during your pregnancy, whereas if you live in a small country town you may never have it at all.

Ultrasound

Ultrasound (also referred to as a scan, or an ultrasound scan) works on the principle of bouncing very high frequency sound waves (far higher than the human ear can detect) off solid objects. It is a method which has been used for many years to locate shoals of deep sea fish, and submarines in wartime. Echo sounders in yachts work in a similar way.

Uses of ultrasound In pregnancy ultrasound is used to obtain a picture of the baby in the uterus. It is possible to see the tiny fetus kicking from the end of the second month of pregnancy, and after 28 weeks breathing movements can be observed. There are a number of reasons why scans are done.

66 I found the ultrasound at 16 and 30 weeks exciting because the images on the screen were explained to me. 99

66 I feel I could have been given more information about the ultrasound beforehand. My husband waited for me outside and if I had known what a moving experience it would be I would have brought him in with me. 99

To confirm pregnancy A scan can be used to confirm pregnancy very early, before clinical tests are effective: it is capable of detecting changes in the uterus that cannot yet be revealed in physical examination. You can find out if you are having twins, for instance, when you are only eight weeks pregnant.

To establish the estimated date of delivery Scans are often routinely used in large hospitals, where you may expect to have them done at least two or three times during pregnancy. Your first scan will probably be done at about 12 weeks in order to establish the estimated delivery date. At this stage the age of the baby can be established to within a week (later in pregnancy it is more difficult to be precise because babies of the same age may grow at very different rates). You may then be scanned again in the middle and at the end of pregnancy, or even more frequently, at intervals of a few weeks. This is called serial assessment and does not mean that anything is wrong. Only when the scan is used in this way can the clues that it gives about the rate of fetal growth be taken seriously. In smaller hospitals you may never have a scan at all, unless there is a specific reason for it.

HAVING A SCAN
Because it involves such sophisticated equipment, ultrasound may seem intimidating; if the picture on the screen is blurred and meaningless it may be disappointing; but if it is explained to you so that you can actually recognize your baby, it may be the most exciting moment of your pregnancy so far . . .

To assess maturity in late pregnancy Late in pregnancy a scan is often used to indicate whether or not a baby is ready to be born. It cannot show whether the lungs are mature enough for breathing, but by measuring the diameter and circumference of the baby's head it can establish the approximate age of the baby and its stage of development.

To detect how the baby is lying If it is important to know how your baby is lying in the uterus and a doctor cannot know for certain from manual examination, ultrasound can tell with accuracy. This knowledge may make all the difference to you if you want to have your baby at home, for instance. If the baby is shown to be in a good position, you can proceed with confidence in your plans for a home birth. If the baby is seen to be lying awkwardly, you will accept that it might be more sensible to come into hospital for the birth. Either way, you and your doctor can be guided by the information provided by the scan.

To assess the condition and position of the placenta When there is bleeding in late pregnancy ultrasound can be used to locate the position of the placenta. The danger is that the placenta might be blocking the baby's way out of the uterus (a condition known as placenta previa, described on page 120). In fact a scan done in the first few months of pregnancy often gives the impression that the placenta is lying low on the wall of the uterus, but as the pregnancy progresses and the uterus enlarges the placenta usually proves to be in the right place after all. Occasionally bleeding in late pregnancy means that the roots of the placenta are becoming dislodged with pre-labor contractions, indicating that the baby's lifeline would be cut if labor were allowed to proceed. A scan can show this clearly, and a Cesarean section can be performed to save the baby. Used in this way, or as a preliminary to amniocentesis (see page 186), ultrasound has some advantages.

How ultrasound works

You undress, put on a hospital gown and lie on your back beneath the scanner. Your abdomen is oiled and then a transducer is slowly passed over it in different directions. The transducer is a machine which picks up echoes from the different planes of your own organs and the developing baby's tissues, and which then translates the information into the form of a map on a screen like a television. A scan done in the first few months of pregnancy gains in clarity if your bladder is full and therefore clearly visible, so you will probably be asked to drink a lot of water first and not urinate for an hour or so before the scan. Do not expect to see an immediately recognizable picture of your baby, even in late pregnancy; if a doctor is present, ask to have the picture interpreted, because it may look more like a map of the moon than a baby, and you may find it difficult to make out the different parts of the baby.

AN ULTRASOUND PICTURE
Here is a photograph of a scan of a 14 week old fetus. Unlike many scan photographs, the image of this baby is easily distinguished. Often scans are meaningless to the untrained eye, partly because the baby is hidden behind other organs in the body.

Uterine cavity   Arm

Spine   Head

Leg

The safety of ultrasound

Although ultrasound has not been proven safe, it is probably much safer than X rays (see page 98), which provided the only method of finding out about the baby in the uterus before the scan was developed. High frequency sounds continued for a long time can cause damage to hearing in an adult. Questions have therefore been raised about possible effects on the baby's hearing, since although the sound waves are only bounced off the baby for a short time the baby may be vulnerable at certain stages of its development. Babies are not born deaf after having ultrasound, but no one yet knows if any of them will suffer delayed effects in later life.

AFP screening

Alpha feto protein (AFP) is a substance produced in the early phases of pregnancy by the embryo's yolk sac and later on by the fetal liver. It is known that when the levels of AFP are abnormally high a large number of babies are found to be suffering from neural tube defects such as spina bifida (when part of the spinal cord is outside the baby's body) and anencephaly (the absence of a brain). The baby without a brain cannot live, but babies with spina bifida do sometimes live, although they are usually paralyzed below the waist and often develop hydrocephalus (water on the brain) as well.

Levels of AFP in a pregnant woman's blood double about every five weeks in the fourth, fifth and sixth months of pregnancy, but earlier than this they are usually low. The best time to screen your blood for AFP is therefore in early pregnancy, before the 18th week. Results come through in two to three days and that is usually the end of the matter.

If your dates are wrong and pregnancy is more advanced than you think, you may find that the AFP level seems suspiciously high. The proportion will also be high if you are expecting twins. In both these cases ultrasound will be used to tell you the real age of the baby and whether you are expecting more than one.

If the rate appears to be high for no obvious reason another blood test may be done to double-check; if the level of AFP is then found to be two or three times higher than the median level of a sample group, you will be offered amniocentesis (see below). But this means two or three out of every hundred women having amniocentesis, with the risk attached to it (one or two babies out of every hundred are miscarried). Some people say that the risk of amniocentesis is greater than the risk of bearing an affected baby if your AFP level is high. Because of these differences of opinion within the medical profession, AFP screening is rarely done as routine in the United States of America; the point at which you are offered amniocentesis will also vary depending on the center where your blood is tested.

As with all medical intervention, solving the problem is a matter of a delicate balance between risks and there is no easy answer. If AFP testing shows that your level is high, discuss the matter with your doctor, taking your partner or a family member with you so that you can talk it over together afterwards and make a shared decision about amniocentesis involving both of you and your doctor.

Amniocentesis

Amniocentesis is a procedure which has been developed to detect abnormalities of the central nervous system (spina bifida and anencephaly) and some other forms of mental handicap such as Down's syndrome (mongolism). The sex of the baby can also be determined, so you can discover if any sex linked disorders might have been inherited.

How amniocentesis works Under a local anesthetic a hollow needle is inserted through your abdominal wall into the uterus, where about half an ounce (14 g) of the water in which the fetus is lying is sucked out. This fluid has been swallowed by the fetus and passed out of its body again either through its mouth or its bladder; it is full of cells from the skin and other organs which can provide clues to the baby's condition. The fluid is then spun in a centrifuge, which separates the cells from the rest of the liquid.

In the 1950s, when amniocentesis was first invented, mistakes were sometimes made and the needle penetrated placental tissues, causing occasional miscarriage. But now that ultrasound techniques have been developed, the position of the placenta can be accurately located beforehand and the risks of damage to the placenta have been very much reduced. There still remains a one or two per cent chance, however, that amniocentesis may cause the fetus to abort.

Because of this small but definite risk, there is no point in having amniocentesis unless there is a well above average chance of your baby being born abnormal. You must also have thought carefully about the implications of discovering that something is wrong with your baby and have decided that you would opt for an abortion. In some parts of the country, amniocentesis is offered to all women over 35, since some of the disorders it is designed to detect rise sharply with age.

If an abnormality is revealed, counseling should be made immediately available to both parents. Since amniocentesis cannot be done until some time between the 14th and 16th weeks of pregnancy, at a time when many women have already felt the first fluttering of fetal movement, the decision is often a distressing one to have to make and the abortion is riskier than one performed earlier in pregnancy. The woman who is going through this experience needs generous emotional support from her partner and family.

Fetoscopy

It is now possible to photograph a baby in the uterus by means of an instrument called a fetoscope. This is a fine tube which holds a light and lenses so that for the first time photographs can be taken from inside the uterus. So far fetoscopy is only being done in a very few places in the US, usually experimentally prior to termination, but as it becomes more common it may be a new form of technology used more and more in pregnancy. It can be carried out between the 15th and 16th weeks of pregnancy to determine whether a baby has any kind of brain malformation, and can also reveal some disorders in the blood, allowing treatment in the form of blood transfusions to be given to the unborn baby. Fetoscopy also reveals the sex of the baby, as well as such visible defects as cleft palate and harelip.

How fetoscopy works

A local anesthetic is injected in the abdominal wall just above the pubic bone, and an incision is made through which a tube holding a needle is pushed into the bag of waters. The needle is then taken out, but the tube left in and the fetoscope inserted through the tube. The obstetrician monitors the whole procedure by ultrasound (see page 183) in order not to damage the baby with the apparatus. But the immediate and long term risks for mother and baby and the possible side effects on both are not yet known.

The last few weeks

Your baby is almost ready to be born. The firm body is nestled in the cup of your pelvis, and the little arms and legs are plumper as the last layers of fat form to help the baby's temperature-control system after birth. Sometimes the baby gains as much as 8 oz (226 g) in a week at this stage of pregnancy.

66 I'm really enjoying this time and am looking forward to the birth. 99

Physical sensations

You may feel fewer big body movements but an insistent kicking underneath your ribs on one side or the other. If your abdominal wall is thin you may even be able to hold your baby's foot. There may be other strange movements, perhaps a sudden urgent knocking which continues intermittently for half an hour or more. This can be so pronounced that you may worry in case your baby is having something like an epileptic fit. But it is definitely not that. It could be one of two things: the baby may have got hiccups, perhaps because it was gulping amniotic fluid; or it may have lost its thumb which it was contentedly sucking, and is "rooting" to find it again, with quick, darting movements of the head from side to side, just as later after birth it will search for the nipple. The baby's head feels like a melon or coconut pressing through your bulging perineal tissues, making you sit down with care.

There may also be odd sensations in your vagina. Sometimes there is a sharp buzz like a mild electric shock or a tickle. The baby may be lifting and lowering its head against your pelvic floor muscles in another movement which it will do naturally after birth too, when put down on its front in an alert state. There are times when your baby is sleeping or drowsy and other very active times, often in the evenings.

Mixed emotions

Conflicting emotions are characteristic of these last weeks. You may be tired of being pregnant but on the other hand the state you are in now is a condition you know and understand, whereas in front of you there is an unknown challenge. So sometimes you want the baby out and long to get on with the labor. But at other times you feel safer as you are, and anxious about the future. Some women say that as the birthday draws nearer they feel irritated with the pregnancy and even with the baby. This produces an emotional state which makes them welcome the start of labor. Other women relish these last weeks.

66 It feels as if the pregnancy is just going to carry on for ever and ever, and it is never going to come out. 99

Prenatal depression

It is very common for a woman to feel low and become depressed some time in the last six weeks of pregnancy. If you have been practicing carefully and preparing yourself for a natural birth you may experience a kind of stage fright and be convinced that you are going to forget everything when you are actually in labor. You may also be feeling physically tired with the weight of your burden, heavy and sluggish.

The last weeks of pregnancy are a time of conflicting feelings—uncertainty, impatience and excitement. . . .

Prenatal depression, though usually short-lived and spasmodic, is a fact of life for some women. It is made more severe by anemia (see page 123), so ask your doctor what your hemoglobin level is at present and if necessary have extra iron. It is also partly a result of a need for more rest. You may feel very different if you lie down to rest in a darkened room in the middle of the day, have some early nights and adjust your activity to slower, gentler rhythms if possible.

If you find yourself becoming depressed at this stage of pregnancy have a talk with your childbirth educator who, probably a mother herself, will understand what you are feeling.

Diet in the last three weeks

As you come to within three weeks of the estimated delivery date you will probably find that you need small, frequent meals rather than several large ones each day. There seems to be no room for anything else. This is a time when you can build up reserves of stamina and energy for labor by adopting a diet similar to that used by marathon runners.

One California doctor works with long distance runners, in particular with cardiac patients who adopt running as part of their cure. He describes the typical nutrition of marathon runners as "a fresh, raw, high fiber diet rich in linoleic acid and silicon."* Apparently they experience cravings for certain foods and also share a kind of folklore about what makes for vitality and endurance. Their diet is rich in high fiber foods (roughage), and the active ingredient in all such foods is called silicon. It is also high in polyunsaturated fats, the most important of which is called linoleic acid, found in seeds, nuts and whole grains. Linoleic acid, incidentally, is easily destroyed by exposure to oxygen, heat and light. Marathon runners are mostly vegetarians, avoid greasy fried foods, believe that plenty of onions and garlic is good for them and take large quantities of vitamin C.

As part of your build up to labor in the last two or three weeks you might like to plan a high-energy diet on the same principles as these Californian runners. Start the day with some muesli mixture (which should be kept in a cool place in a covered container), including bran. You can eat this mixed with some raw fruit and yoghurt—two other foods which the runners enjoy—and add some freshly chopped or ground nuts, seeds and grains.

Buy a new book on the preparation of salads at this late stage of pregnancy to stimulate your imagination. A handful of pea-nuts on a fresh vegetable salad will provide you with extra linoleic acid without giving you a high-fat diet. A little finely chopped raw onion and garlic with seasoning added to cottage cheese adds something solid and particularly tasty to any salad. Have an occasional baked potato in its jacket, and wholegrain bread. Otherwise plan to eat mainly unprocessed foods with plenty of raw vegetables, citrus and other fruits of every kind, nuts and lots of yoghurt. You will then be at peak form for the hard work of labor.

What do you need to pack?

Now is the time to be thinking about the things you want to have available during labor and afterwards. Gather them together in a lightweight, easily carried container.

COMFORT AIDS FOR LABOR

Thermos bottle for ice cubes, which are sometimes available in hospital.
Two small sponges to be dipped in iced water and used for sponging your face, wetting your lips and sucking between contractions.
Chapstick or vaseline for dry lips.
Plant spray for moistening face with cold water, or Evian spray.
Baby's hot water bottle or a picnic thermal pack to be heated up in water for use as a hot compress in the small of your back, between your legs, etc.
Talc, cornstarch, or massage lotion to avoid skin friction when massaged.
Rolling pin to iron away backache (see page 220).
Hairbrush and ribbons or bands if your hair is long.
Books, cards, chess, Scrabble, crosswords, etc.
Honey to keep your strength up in early labor.
Eau de cologne or toilet water.
Paper bag to breathe into in case you hyperventilate.
Beautiful object on which you can focus when necessary.
Nourishing snacks for your labor companion.
Camera.
Exercise book to serve as labor log book.
Writing materials.
Phone numbers of relatives and friends.
Money for pay phones if in hospital.

COMFORT AIDS FOR AFTER THE BIRTH

Calendula and hypericum cream from a homeopathic pharmacy, for a sore perineum.
Bottle of witchhazel lotion with which you can soak the sanitary pad next to the stitches.
Sanitary belt.
Soft toilet paper.
Cotton nightgowns that open in the front.
Robe.
Hydrous lanolin for sore nipples.
Nursing bras.
Deodorant (you will perspire heavily in the few days after delivery).
Toilet bag and makeup.
Writing paper and envelopes.
Wax earplugs if in hospital ward.

Thinking ahead to labor

66 I can't help thinking, what if the baby drops out? I might have it *anywhere!* I'm in a state of constant expectation, thinking, is this it, and then deciding no it isn't. 99

You will probably be thinking a great deal about labor at this time, wondering what it will be like. One of the things you can find out is the position your baby is in; remember to ask when you are being examined by the doctor. The ideal position for a straightforward labor (and by far the most common) is head down and anterior. But some babies present in different positions, as posterior or breech for example. Delivery may be less straightforward with the baby in these positions (see pages 218–223).

The baby who is presenting as a posterior

If your baby is lying head down with its back against your spine, limbs towards your front, it may be because you have a roomy pelvis so that it can still move around a lot. Women who think they are due but who really have another two weeks or so to go can have a baby who is still moving freely like this—sometimes posterior, sometimes anterior, sometimes lateral (ear forward). In this case pre-labor and early-labor contractions usually turn the baby into the anterior position without any other help.

If your baby seems to have settled in a posterior position, you may find that you can coax it to change during one of its waking periods by very firm hand pressure. The posterior baby is usually lying with its head on your right side. You want to shift it round and over towards the left. Treat the baby as if it were a sleeping cat which you were trying to scoop off the middle of a sofa and move over to the left side. Curve the side of your hand round the most solid section of its bulk and firmly, little by little, edge it over. Keep the fingers of your other hand over your navel. If you are successful the saucer shaped dip there (the space between the arms and legs of a posterior baby) will become —at least temporarily—a hard convex curve (the back of a baby in an anterior position). You will be able to detect the change as your navel will probably stick out. Talk to your baby as you move it. This is not simply a clinical exercise, but a bit of maternal persuasion.

Once the baby is stretching the uterus to its utmost it is a tight fit and you will probably not be able to move it. You will have to wait and see whether the first-stage labor contractions will do the work for you.

The baby who is presenting as a breech

Most babies tip head down—in the vertex or cephalic position —between the seventh and the eighth month. If your baby is still presenting buttocks first (breech) at around 36 weeks the doctor occasionally decides to try and turn the baby—a maneuver known as external version. This procedure requires skill and should always be done by a doctor—do not attempt it yourself.

How external version is done You empty your bladder and then lie down on your back with your knees drawn up. The doctor will listen to the baby's heartbeats before and after turning the baby. You may be asked to lie on a sloping examining table with your legs up and head down for about quarter of an hour before the maneuver, so that the baby is encouraged to move clear of the pelvis. Spend this time relaxing deeply: use abdominal massage to help you release your tummy muscles and use your breathing to help you as well.

When you feel the doctor's hands on your tummy release and flow towards the touch. Give a long, slow breath *out* and let your lower tummy bulge out in a great wave as you do so.

If the version is successful and the baby turns, walk about for an hour or two, so that there is most chance of fixing the baby in a vertex position. Some babies turn straight back into the breech position. If this happens to you, you will have to accept that your baby prefers it; discuss with your doctor the sort of delivery you will have (see page 220).

EXTERNAL VERSION
Your doctor may attempt this skilled maneuver if your baby has settled in a breech position. Sometimes the version is successful and a normal delivery can follow, but frequently the baby turns straight back into a breech position after the procedure is over. External version must always be done by a doctor; if done by an unskilled person there is a risk of the placenta separating from the uterine wall.

Being "overdue"

Concern about the best things to eat, the position of the baby, and whether labor will be straightforward can be preoccupying in the last few weeks. If you actually go *past* the estimated date of delivery you may really begin to worry; you are now consigned to the category of the woman who is "overdue".

The estimated delivery date

The date that you are given at the beginning of pregnancy for your baby's birth (EDD or EDC) is only a statistical mean. Studies show that only five per cent of babies arrive on that day. If you look at the 95 babies out of 100 who do not put in an appearance on the "correct" date you find that three out of ten babies come before the EDD and seven out of ten come *after* it. This is partly because women's menstrual cycles are of different lengths, and ovulation—and hence conception—may occur at different times within it. But by the time you reach the end of your pregnancy you may not be able to prevent yourself from fixing on the expected delivery date as your goal. If it comes and goes and nothing happens, you may become very depressed. Each day that passes seems like a week, and each week more like a month. Unless you plan for activity and recreation during this time your morale will drop to rock bottom before you start labor.

❛❛ The doctor says he wants to induce me on my due date because my blood pressure is up. I do want to have a natural birth but the time is coming nearer and nearer. It's hanging over me like a date set for execution. **❜❜**

If you find that you are getting despondent, remind yourself that, though very few babies are born on the day predicted for their birth, nine out of ten do put in an appearance within ten days of the expected date. There is nothing abnormal about a baby who is nine days "late". Many women, however, are made to feel "under sentence of induction" if they go as much as a week past their expected date. Some physicians routinely induce labor when the woman reaches the tenth day following the estimated date, and this is done without further investigation. If your pregnancy is normal and you are in good health, being ten days "late" is a very poor reason for induction of labor.

Whether induction (which is described on page 252) is really necessary or not depends entirely on the baby's wellbeing at the end of pregnancy. The baby's wellbeing, in turn, depends on the condition of the placenta.

The aging placenta

At the end of pregnancy the placenta looks like a piece of raw liver about the size of a dinner plate and the thickness of your little finger. Like every other human organ, it has a youth and an old age. An elderly placenta works less well. If labor does not start at the right time (which may be anywhere between two weeks before and two weeks after the estimated date of delivery —and very occasionally later still) the placenta may fail to support the baby's life system inside the uterus well enough. The baby is then deprived of nourishment. This is why obstetricians are concerned if a pregnancy is prolonged much past the date worked out for the birth. Even so, a baby who is thought to be overdue may prove at birth not to be postmature at all.

There are various ways in which the condition of the placenta can be assessed. Some are tests which doctors do to you; probably the most reliable method is one which you can do for yourself (see page 195).

Urinary estriol tests
One way of finding out whether your placenta is functioning well is for the hospital to measure the output in your urine of estriol (a form of the hormone estrogen, important for the baby's growth). Throughout pregnancy your body's level of estriol production rises; just before labor starts, it drops. If you have high blood pressure or preeclampsia (see page 121) the estriol level in your urine also drops, as it will if you have bleeding in late pregnancy, kidney disease or diabetes. A lower level suggests that the placenta may not be doing a good job of nourishing the baby and excreting its waste products. If your doctor is considering whether to induce you, he may therefore perform this urine test.

But the proportion of estriol in urine can vary by as much as 30 per cent with different readings; there are day to day variations, even when everything is normal. You therefore cannot rely on one or two tests alone, and it is important that there should be a series of readings over a period of 24 hours. If you are taken into hospital with preeclampsia, regular urinary estriol tests may be performed. If they indicate that the placenta is not functioning well your obstetrician will suggest induction of labor. But the estriol level is only a clue to the condition of the placenta, and it should not be acted on alone. When levels of estriol output are compared with the information provided by ultrasound to assess the baby's growth, there is often a discrepancy, so obstetricians often use the two types of test together, along with clinical information, to try and find out what is happening.

If there is no urgent need for induction (and your doctor will certainly make it clear if there is), you may first want to monitor fetal activity as an additional check on how the baby is faring (see opposite). There is some evidence that observations you can make yourself are more likely to give an accurate picture of the baby's condition than medical tests*.

Antepartum cardiotocography
This test uses an electronic fetal monitor (see page 257) to see if the baby's heartbeat shows the usual variations. If the heart rate is satisfactory, there is no need to induce labor or to do the more complicated oxytocin challenge test (below).

Oxytocin challenge tests
This test is sometimes called a "stress test" to distinguish it from fetal movement recording (see below), which is a "non-stress test". It is used when a baby is thought to be overdue to see if it would be better off born.

How the test is done The uterus is made to contract with oxytocin dripped straight into your vein; the reactions of the fetal heart are then observed. The heart rate will probably react to each contraction by slowing down. As long as it returns to normal as soon as the contraction ends, the baby is not considered to be under any particular stress and induction is therefore unnecessary.

On the other hand, if contractions affect the baby's heart rate so much that it slows down and remains slow for a time between contractions as well, then this is considered to be evidence of fetal distress. In these circumstances labor may be induced immediately: larger amounts of oxytocin will be introduced into your veins to stimulate contractions, and the delivery will be very carefully monitored throughout; alternatively the doctors may decide to perform a Cesarean section.

Fetal movement recording

66 Just when I think there's never going to be a movement there's a terrific leap and then the baby's wriggling all over the shop. Keeping track of movements has made me much more aware of the baby's waking and sleeping times. 99

One of the most accurate ways of knowing if a baby is doing well while still inside the uterus in late pregnancy is something you can do for yourself. This is to note the baby's movements. In the last weeks of pregnancy, until it engages, the baby usually wriggles, dips and turns, bangs and kicks, and moves like a porpoise from side to side in great sweeps of activity which you can actually see through your clothing. Once it has engaged it often moves less because it is a rather tight fit. Even so, a vigorous baby moves even after it has gone down into the pelvis, though the movements then tend to be just the knocks from knees and feet. You feel as if you have a rolling coconut in your groin or just behind your pubis (the head turning), and later the strange buzzing sensation of the engaged head bouncing against the pelvic floor muscles (see page 188).

You may not normally be aware of most of these movements while you are busy but as soon as you sit down to rest, or lie down hoping to sleep, you cannot help noticing them. They are a good sign that your baby is healthy. Studies of fetal activity show that every baby has its own individual pattern of waking and sleeping inside the uterus, and by late pregnancy you will have probably noticed what your baby's pattern is. But sometimes you may be awake and expecting a kick; if nothing happens it can be disconcerting. In fact, the baby is probably fast asleep; if you have had a couple of drinks or taken sleeping tablets, your baby will probably be affected by them too.

Mothers do vary a great deal in the extent that they observe fetal movements. Sometimes this awareness is related to the amount of amniotic fluid, since the water cushions movements. If you are preoccupied and concentrating hard on something else you may also be less aware of fetal activity. If you are still working outside the home, or busy inside it, there may be too much going on to notice fetal movements. But each woman's experience of the movements is fairly consistent if her baby is thriving in the uterus, bearing in mind that the nature of movements changes after the baby has engaged, as described above.

If for any reason it is thought that your baby may be "at risk" (usually because you have not put on weight for two or more

Often it is when you go to bed that you both notice your child's vigorous movements . . . regular movements are a sign that all is well . . .

It is natural to feel despondent if the hospital is concerned because you are "overdue", but the majority of babies arrive after the predicted date. . . .

weeks, your tummy has not got bigger during this time, or because you are "overdue" in relation to your EDD), you can use your own knowledge about your baby's movements to keep a check on its wellbeing inside you. It is a satisfying feeling to know that monitoring your baby's activity is more likely to be an accurate gauge of how the baby is than a series of complicated tests done by other people. Researchers compared what they called a "daily fetal movement" chart, drawn up by women, with a placental function test designed to measure the total excretion of estriol in the urine over a period of 24 hours (see page 194).* When the amounts of estriol in the urine were low but the mother said that she was aware of a normal number of fetal movements, every single baby was born alive. Unfortunately when the estriol levels were normal but the mother noticed that her baby was hardly making any movements in the uterus at all, three out of ten babies died.

Suppose that you have gone past your dates, and the obstetrician is beginning to suggest taking you into hospital for observation and to talk about possible induction; you can then start to keep a systematic fetal movement chart. If your baby is not being adequately nourished in the uterus and your placenta is failing in its function, fetal movements will diminish over a period of three or four days and some time after that they will stop altogether. If you leave it this late, birth will probably be by Cesarean section in order to ensure a speedy delivery and to care for the baby. But if you monitor the gradual decrease in movements, and tell the doctor as soon as you observe this happening, you will probably be induced, but be able to deliver the baby normally.

When to take action

If you have observed no movement at all over a period of 12 hours and your baby does not wake up at night, go to the hospital or to your own doctor and ask if you can have the fetal heart checked. If you are in hospital, fetal activity can be checked immediately with ultrasound. A sonic aid is placed on your tummy near the baby's heart. You tell the doctor or nurse as soon as you feel movement.

It has been discovered that there is an effective minimum number of movements which can tell you that the baby is all right; ten movements, of any kind, in a 12 hour period indicate that all is well. If you notice fewer than ten movements in that time your baby may *still* be fine, since two and a half per cent of daily counts made by women who have healthy babies fall below that count, but the indications are that the baby would be better off born in the majority of cases.

The "Count to Ten" chart

The "Count to Ten" chart* is a way in which the mother records fetal activity in half hour blocks of time on squared paper. It is very boring to have to observe your baby's movements all day and much easier simply to note down the first ten movements in a 12 hour period and stop when you have

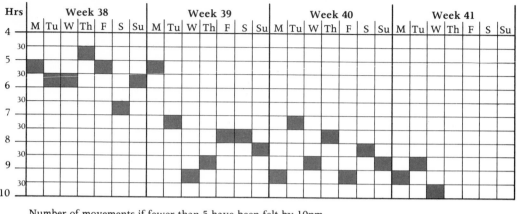

Number of movements if fewer than 5 have been felt by 10pm

FETAL MOVEMENT RECORDING
This way of assessing your baby's wellbeing is especially useful if you are apparently "overdue". Starting at the same point each day, mark the square against the time when you feel your baby's 5th movement. If you do not feel any movements by the end of a 6 hour period, contact the doctor without delay. And if you feel fewer than 5 movements, it is also advisable to call the doctor.

recorded them. The way in which the chart is often used in hospital is to tell the mother to start recording fetal movements at 9 am and go on until ten are recorded. She is told to black in the square corresponding to the time at which she has felt the tenth movement.

If you are going to do this as a record for yourself use squared paper and indicate the days of the week along the top. Down the left-hand side put the hours of the day, beginning with the time at which you have decided to start recording. It is probably better to start late in the afternoon (but it should be at the same time each day), and record during the evening. This seems the sensible half of the day because you are more likely to have a stretch of time when you are sitting down, reading, listening to music, chatting or watching television, and from experience this is known to be a time when fetal movements are often felt. If you start at 4 pm and go to bed at 10 pm or later you then have a clear six hour period for noting movements. On your chart you fill in the block in which the fifth movement occurs. A baby who is not very active will take a longer time to get to the fifth movement. If you do not feel any movements by the time you lie down to sleep at night call the doctor first thing in the morning, say that your baby is hardly moving at all and ask if he will check the fetal heart and activity. (You will probably find that as soon as you settle down to sleep the baby starts moving. If this happens, record the time; but if it is not yet the fifth movement do not shade in the square.)

The point about this method of assessing the baby's welfare is that it is something active you can do for yourself. From both your and the baby's point of view it is completely noninvasive, as well as being incredibly simple.

THE EXPERIENCE OF BIRTH

What happens in labor
Different kinds of labor
Giving support in labor
Dealing with pain
Toward the medical control of birth
Gentle birth

What happens in labor

There are three stages of labor. During the first the cervix is being drawn up into the main body of the uterus and dilating; in the second the baby is pressed down through the birth canal and this stage culminates in delivery; during the third the placenta and membranes are sloughed off the lining of the uterus and expelled.

Having said this, it is important to add that for many women labor is an overwhelming and dramatic experience and you certainly are not sitting around thinking in terms of neat stages. There is no fanfare of trumpets to tell you when the first stage is really under way or when the second stage has started. Some women have a clear physiological message, such as the breaking of the waters or sudden strong, regular contractions, leaving them in no doubt that labor has started and that this is unmistakably *it*, and when they reach the end of the first stage they know with equal certainty that they are now in the second stage and *have* to push. For a great many women, however, the different stages of labor shade over into each other. The experience is rarely as tidy and compartmentalized as books on labor seem to suggest, and the third stage may even pass completely unnoticed as you hold your newborn baby in your arms and marvel at it.

Build up to labor
Labor starts with the gradual softening and ripening of the cervix at the base of the uterus. This can take days and days or can happen overnight, especially if you have had a baby before. Once the cervix is soft and stretchy the uterine contractions—which are occurring anyway in late pregnancy—tend to draw it up bit by bit, so that it gradually changes from being a long canal hanging down in your vagina to being a dip in the bottom of the uterus, the tissues having been pulled up into the lower segment of the uterus.

You are not considered to be in labor when all this is happening. Your labor has not started in medical terms until you are having regular contractions which are effectively dilating (widening) the cervix; it is work that has to be done before it is possible for the cervix to open up. Usually this means you are at least 3 cm dilated (see page 208) before you are considered to be in labor. In fact many women already have a partially dilated cervix by the time they realize that they are having contractions. It is obviously more pleasant for you if your body is working for you while you are carrying on with your work and shopping and eating and sleeping and seeing your friends. You cannot possibly be tensing up and fighting your body when you are busy doing all these things and leaving your uterus to work undisturbed and unnoticed. So carry on normal living for as long as is comfortable.

*hen at last your baby's head slips from
ur body you welcome a new person. . . .*

First signs of labor

Three things can happen to indicate that labor has started or is about to start.

A show appears This is the bloodstained mucous discharge that you have when the cervix is beginning to stretch. Until the start of labor this mucus has acted as a gelatinous plug in the cervix, sealing off the uterus. Its appearance is a good sign that there is some definite activity around the cervix. But it can come out two or three weeks before you actually go into labor and contractions are established, or it may appear when your labor is so far advanced that you do not notice it. So, although you can take it as an encouraging sign, do not drop whatever you are doing and rush off to hospital. Go on with your everyday activities or, if it is night, have a hot milk drink and go back to sleep.

The bag of waters breaks When the membranes surrounding the baby have been pressed down like a wedge in front of its presenting part (usually the head) and pressure has built up, the bag pops. It may do this suddenly with a rush of water or, and this is more likely, with a slow trickle. In fact, you may not be quite sure whether the bag of waters has burst or you are wetting your pants. If you are not sure, forget it (if you can) and carry on as usual, unless you are still several weeks away from your EDD, in which case you should call the doctor at once. If it is more than three weeks before your baby is due it is important for you to be in a place where special care is ready for the baby at delivery.

You will probably have been told to call the hospital or your doctor or midwife if the waters break and you lose a lot of water at once. This is because, if labor is slow, taking 24 hours or more from the rupture of the membranes, there is a chance of your baby becoming infected. Also, if the baby's head does not fit properly into the cervix, there is a chance that the waters might sweep the cord down through the cervix, which in turn might mean the blockage of the oxygen supply to the baby. If, therefore, you do not know how your baby is presenting before you go into labor, you should be prepared to go to hospital immediately after the waters break, in case the baby is breech or its head is high. Today obstetricians usually decide to stimulate the uterus into activity once the waters have broken. So if you are sure of the presentation it seems sensible to give nature a chance and to allow yourself three or four hours of gentle everyday activity before leaving for hospital. In most cases contractions will start during this time.

There is no need to worry about having a "dry" labor, with the baby traveling down an unlubricated birth canal, as there is no such thing. Your amniotic fluid is completely replaced every three hours. Actually a "wet" labor is more likely and can be uncomfortable, since a continual leaking throughout labor is cold and unpleasant. If you find that you are leaking, wear a sanitary pad and change it frequently.

Contractions start They usually feel like a tight elastic belt slung under your bump and around into the lower part of the small of your back, being drawn tighter, gripping for 15 to 20 seconds, and then being released. This sensation occurs again after 10 minutes, or even sooner. These might be the Braxton Hicks "rehearsal" contractions, which some women experience as quite painful at times in the last three weeks or so of pregnancy. These then tend to be called "false" labor. All this means that you thought you were in labor, with good reason, but were not.

If you want to be fairly sure about being in labor, time your contractions over a period of 30 minutes or an hour; make a note of the interval between the start of one and the start of the next, and also note down the length of each contraction. The contractions need to come closer and closer together and to last longer (40 seconds or more) before you can be confident that labor is being established.

MUSCLE BUNDLES
The uterus is composed of spiral muscle bundles which in early pregnancy start to unfold into an open latticework formation at the top of the uterus. If you think of the uterus as a clock, the muscle bundles are spaced out most between 9 and 3 —that is, over the fundus of the uterus. By the end of pregnancy these bundles of muscle have unfolded much more and are stretched lengthways.

During contractions the muscle fibers at the top of the uterus tighten, pressing in and down on the center and producing an upward pull on the cervix. When the baby's head is pressed down by a contraction, the muscles and fibrous tissues of the cervix are drawn apart. In a straightforward labor most of the physical sensations caused by contractions come from this area in and around the cervix, apart from a hardening and swelling felt at the top of the uterus.

Once the contractions are going well, they have a regular rhythm, a wavelike shape, and last longer and longer, while the interval between them is reduced. A woman who did a lot of cooking said she felt her contractions like heat from an oven. First the oven door opened a little and then more till she was in the full blast of heat. Then it closed again.

The first stage of labor Although we do not know for certain what starts labor off, one theory is that when the tissue in the baby's adrenal gland is mature it produces cortisone. This triggers off a remarkable process. It changes the balance between the amount of estrogen and progesterone produced by the placenta, the estrogen level dropping and the progesterone level going up, and this in turn initiates the production of prostaglandins. The prostaglandins act on the uterus to make the contractions you have been having throughout late pregnancy bigger and closer together. So the contractions of early labor may feel just like Braxton Hicks contractions, but stronger and more regular.

These more efficient contractions press the baby's presenting part down to the base of the lower segment of the uterus and against the cervix. This then becomes progressively more stretched and thinned out as the muscle fibers are pulled up into the upper segment. The effacement and stretching of the cervix next trigger off the production of oxytocin from the posterior pituitary gland, and this stimulates the uterus into a steady rhythm of contractions. Labor is under way!

Moving around in labor

Going to bed early in the first stage of labor and becoming more or less immobile can slow down labor or interfere with it starting effectively because, if you are lying in bed, the presenting part may not then be pressed down against your cervix. When you are upright, especially if you are moving around, you have gravity to help you; everything is being pressed down.

It was not till the end of the 18th century in Europe that women began to lie down to give birth. Before that time they had walked around during much of labor and used labor stools or sat up in bed or on a chair. Birth stools were designed like horseshoes with the open part at the front, were low on the ground so that the woman squatted, and sometimes provided support for her lower back as well as handgrips. As a result she was in a physiologically excellent position.

Mauriceau, then the obstetrician to the French court, introduced the lying down position and it soon caught on because people sought to imitate the manners of the court. When forceps were introduced (see page 260), obstetricians found that they were easier to use on a woman who was lying flat. Still later, the lithotomy position, in which the patient lies on her back with her legs fixed to raised stirrups and which was first devised for surgery on bladder stones, was introduced into obstetrics. This highly artificial posture is often terribly uncomfortable for the woman, pressing her uterus against the big blood vessels in the lower part of her body. This interferes with her circulation, causing hypotension (low blood pressure), and also with the production of urine; it can cause fetal distress.

Research on the effect of different positions in the first stage of labor* has shown that most women prefer to be up and about, not lying in bed, and that contractions are stronger and labor shorter with the woman in an upright position. The uterus is working nearly twice as efficiently to dilate the cervix.

When to go to the hospital

Unless you feel strongly that you need to be in the hospital during this time, or your doctor has advised that there is a special reason why you should come in as soon as there are any signs of labor starting, it is best to stay at home and carry on as usual.

USING GRAVITY TO HELP YOUR LABOR
If you move around and carry on with your everyday activities in early labor, your perception of pain may be reduced. At the same time gravity is helping your uterus to contract efficiently .

In this position the uterus is contracting against the force of gravity.

By the time you find you have to stop and breathe through contractions, choose a position such as kneeling or sitting well propped up where gravity is still helping you.

This is partly because of the psychological effect of going to the hospital, being admitted and prepared and getting in to bed. If you have only just begun labor, all this can stop it entirely. There are many women who have gone to hospital with regular contractions that are still more than five minutes apart and who have then gone out of labor and have either had to wait around with their morale dropping steadily or have had an intravenous oxytocin drip inserted in an arm vein to stimulate the uterus into action.

Knowing that your contractions will be coming one every two minutes and will last about one minute or longer just before the baby is born may give you some perspective on your labor when it is just starting. Having contractions every five minutes can be tiring and some women experience this for 12 hours or more (usually when the baby is in a slightly awkward position, facing the mother's front instead of her back, see page 218), but the baby cannot possibly be born when contractions are coming this far apart, so if you are happier at home, stay there. Keep a careful record of what is happening, time the contractions now and then, and be ready to go to hospital as soon as the membranes rupture or contractions come more often than every five minutes.

Of course you must bear in mind the distance from your home to the hospital and the difficulty of getting there. If you are going in your own car, it is as well to have done a trial run beforehand during rush hour to see how long it can take and to be sure that you know the way, even in deep snow, hail or fog, and also any short cuts that may be convenient. Your partner should drive steadily, but not fast, and certainly not braking suddenly at corners or at lights. Decide early what you will need to make the journey comfortable and whether you would prefer to be on the front or back seat. If you are calling an ambulance, find out well in advance how to do this and, if you are relying on getting to hospital by cab, have a list of several numbers pinned up by the telephone in case one is not immediately available.

Admission procedures When you arrive at the hospital, a nurse will take you to a little room where you will be "prepped" (prepared) for labor. She will ask you questions about how labor started, if the waters have broken, and if so when, how often contractions are coming, and so on. She will do some of the things you are already familiar with, such as requesting a urine sample, checking your blood pressure, feeling the position of the baby through your abdominal wall and listening to the fetal heart. She or a staff doctor will feel through your vagina and into your cervix to tell if you have started dilating. If you are already partly dilated, the waters may be broken (see page 247). This is done routinely in many hospitals at 3–4 cm dilatation. If you want your membranes to remain intact until they rupture spontaneously, it is important to say so before your internal examination has taken place.

In many hospitals the hair surrounding the vagina is shaved off, and some hospitals remove a greater part of the pubic hair. If you would prefer not to be shaved, it is not essential to have it done; if you have to have an episiotomy (see page 250), the area around where the cut is to be made may be shaved just before this is performed. It is also the practise to give an enema to empty the lower bowel. This is a good idea if you have been constipated. It can also help trigger off contractions if they are weak or very irregular. But, again, it is not essential and if you have had loose movements, which many do have as labor starts, tell the nurse about them as she may then consider that the enema can be omitted.

Then you will don a hospital gown which is a cotton version of the kind worn at the hairdresser's. It is usually fastened at the back, but if you hope to have your baby at the breast immediately following delivery it may be easier to wear it opening at the front.

Your partner may be asked to wait while you are prepped, but more and more couples are asking to stay together. It can seem a very long time to be separated and if your partner has been helping you cope with contractions up till now, it is good to go on having the same kind of support. It also gives the doctor or nurse a chance to talk with the father, which means that he or she is meeting you not as an isolated patient but in your relationship with your man.

A doctor will come into the room too to assess your progress. If you have any questions, take this opportunity of asking them. If you are planning on a natural birth if possible, want to walk around in labor as long as is comfortable, or have any other wishes about your birth, remind the doctor or nurse of these and ask if they have been or at least now can be noted on your medical chart.

Countdown for birth at home

If you are having your baby at home, plan ahead and make sure that any major chores do not pile up. When you think you are in labor, start to prepare for the birth. Put a plastic sheet—a shower curtain works well—on the bed and if the bed is not already at right angles to the wall move it to this position. Put out the things that the midwife has asked you to have ready on a small table, arranged on a freshly washed towel, or pillow case and cover them with another piece of cloth. Arrange the lighting so that the midwife can direct some light onto your perineum for delivery and so that the other lights can be dimmed or turned out if you so wish. Put the baby's clothes out and a change of nightgown for yourself. Boil some water: this will be used mostly for tea, but is also useful for washing your perineum after delivery.

Then turn your mind to what you are going to eat and drink for the next three days and also what you may want to offer visitors. You will have been wise to have stocked up your cupboard and freezer well in advance. If you put anything in the oven at this stage, take a timer with you when you go to the bedroom and write a reminder to yourself, pinning it in a prominent place, or your labor may be accompanied by the smell of burning food.

Call the midwife, if possible before she goes out on her rounds, to let her know that you may be needing her later, and pin all important phone numbers by the phone. She will probably call to check how you are doing and will leave phone numbers of where she will be throughout the day.

Transition

66 Every time a big contraction came part of me said "No no" and I answered mentally "Yes, yes". 99

66 I liked to feel a warm hand on my arm through the contractions. 99

Toward the end of the first stage, when you are between 7 and 8 cm dilated, you are in transition.

For most women the very end of the first stage is stormy and challenging. Contractions follow each other relentlessly with hardly a pause between, and they tend to become arhythmic, with sharp peaks and sometimes with more than one to each contraction. The build up of energy with each may be so sudden and tumultuous that there is no time for slow breathing and you must adapt straight away and breathe much more lightly and quickly if you are to soar over the top of it with your breathing. The very length of the contractions may demand every bit of concentration and determination you are able to summon, and you will need strong emotional support and unfailing encouragement. Your partner's attention must not waver for a minute and he should repeatedly communicate to you his confidence in you and his love.

At the same time other physiological signs may occur which can be unsettling, until you remember that they are indications of progress and that if you are aware of three or more of them, you are very likely to be 8 cm dilated and hence in transition. Feeling hot then cold, then hot again, your cheeks flushed and your eyes shining bright, suggests that you are in transition. So does a fit of hiccups or belching, or you may even feel nauseous and actually vomit. Perhaps your legs feel icy cold and begin to shake uncontrollably. One of the surest signs is feeling that you have a large grapefruit pressing against your anus or that you want to empty your bowels. You might have a catch in your throat that stops your easy rhythmic breathing or you involuntarily hold your breath or start to grunt. You may suddenly feel that it is all too much hard work and that you cannot go on and would like to go home and forget about having a baby. Or you may become irritable with everyone around you and hypercritical of the help your partner is giving.

Not all women experience these signs, but a sufficient proportion do to make it a good idea for your partner to memorize them, so that at the right moment he can say: "I think you are in transition". You may have forgotten you are having a baby by this time and are simply concentrating on the work of handling each contraction. You are also very likely to feel that you are not making any progress at all and have lost all sense of time. Since in transition you may get an urge to push before you are fully dilated, you may be told to continue breathing and not to hold your breath until you absolutely must.

Pushing powerfully and for a long time against an incompletely dilated cervix can make it puffy and swollen so that the opening actually closes rather than opening wider. This is why you may be asked not to push until you cannot avoid pushing. This is wise advice, because then you can be quite certain that your body is really ready to push and you will also enjoy the

2 cm   6 cm   10 cm

DILATATION OF THE CERVIX
The cervix has to be 10 cm dilated (widened) before the uterus can press the baby out. The time taken to reach full dilatation (shown right, lifesize) varies enormously: some women are 3 cm dilated before they realize they are in labor, others take many hours to reach 5 cm.

2 cm   4 cm   6 cm   8 cm   10 cm

surrender to the great sweeps of energy that come with the contractions in a way you cannot if you are just pushing because someone has told you to do so.

Transition may be very brief—just a few contractions—or it may last an hour or more. It is likely to last longer if the baby is in an occipitoposterior position (see page 218). The cervix has to dilate to 10 cm before the baby can be pressed down through the opening. At full dilatation (10 cm or the width of the palm of a large man's hand including the thumb joint) the cervix is open enough for the baby's head, its largest part, to ease through. There are spaces between the baby's skullbones, the fontanels, which can close up as the baby slides down the birth canal, so shaping its head to make the journey much less arduous, even for a 9 lb (4 kg) baby. This is why, especially in first labors, the baby's head is molded, sometimes into a rather peculiar shape which disappears in the first week or so after the birth (see page 283). As soon as the cervix has dilated to 10 cm, the second stage starts.

The second stage of labor

66 I felt wonderful sensations of involuntary pushing. The midwife examined me and I heard the blessed words, "There's no cervix left." 99

The second stage of labor is the most exciting. During the first stage the cervix has thinned out and opened. At the end of the first stage the cervix is open to 10 cm, making the uterus and vagina one birth canal. Then follows a wonderful time when you can begin to push. The second stage of labor is often described as if it were sheer, grinding, hard work, but you will *want* to do it. You will probably have an overpowering urge to bear down and press the baby through the birth canal. This is passionate, intense, thrilling and often completely irresistible, and for some women it is the nearest thing to overwhelming sexual excitement. Pushing is not something you decide to do with a rational part of your mind, but a force that sweeps through your body and culminates in the delivery of your baby.

There are a few women who do not feel much of an urge to bear down. Sometimes women who have had other babies do not experience a strong pushing urge. The whole process may be gentler; the mother seems not to need to do much bearing down because that baby is going to be born very easily anyway.

There are three to five urges to bear down with each second-stage contraction, though sometimes we talk about these contractions as if they were all push. Frantic pushing results in your becoming desperate, straining to press the baby just that little bit farther. This is not necessary, because surges of desire to bear down come with each contraction, and it is important to go with each as it comes; allow yourself to hold your breath, bear down and open up with the surge, which usually lasts five or six seconds, no longer. Only you can know when these surges are there. Some people think it is a good idea for a woman to hold her breath for as long as she possibly can in the second stage and only then is she really working hard. However, research suggests that prolonged breath holding is not only exhausting for the mother, but can also be dangerous for the

The journey through the pelvis

About 80 per cent of women have good, well-rounded pelvises for childbirth. Problems may be encountered if your pelvis is narrow: an android pelvis, for instance, is shaped like a triangle at the brim, which is hard for the baby to negotiate. Even when the pelvic shape is not ideal, the uterus works to press the baby into a neat package which, given time, can often make the journey without difficulty. Basically the baby consists of two balls which move against each other. The ball with the largest diameter is the baby's head. The other ball is the baby's trunk with the limbs well tucked in. The action of a uterus that is contracting well results in the baby being molded into the right shape for the journey down the birth canal.

1 *The vagina is almost at right angles to the uterus. So the baby has to negotiate an angle similar to that of the foot putting on a high boot. But there are several bones that may stick out and hold up the baby's progress. The sacrum is the big bone in the spine which forms, together with the pubic bone at the front and the hip girdle at the sides, the pelvic brim. Once the baby's head has traveled below the pelvic brim, it is in the pelvic cavity.*

Normal female pelvis

Android pelvis

baby because it reduces the oxygen content of the blood. So trust your spontaneous feelings and do what comes naturally.

Your baby's head appears

When the top of your baby's head can be seen for the first time, it looks like a wrinkled walnut in the vagina, not like a baby at all. Your partner will probably see this before you can, and he will be able to tell you the color of the baby's hair. With the first baby the second stage may take one to two hours. With the second or subsequent baby it may take only ten minutes. So with the first baby you must be prepared to wait quite a long time before you actually see something waiting there to be born.

Then there comes a time when the widest part of the baby's head is just at the birth opening and does not go back in between contractions. You feel stretched to your utmost. At this moment of "crowning" it is important not to go on pushing, even though you feel very much like it, otherwise you might tear the surrounding perineal tissue. The doctor or midwife may perform an episiotomy if they think you might tear (see page 250). If you want to avoid having one, just before the head crowns start to *breathe* the baby out instead of pushing it out (see page 177), and in this way it may slip forward without being forced. The midwife or obstetrician checks to see that the cord is free of the neck and may insert a mucus catheter in the baby's mouth and suck any mucus out.

The baby's head slips under your pubic bone and extends, the chin being automatically lifted off its chest. As the head

2 *Once the baby has negotiated the pelvic brim, it moves on to the pelvic outlet, bordered by the coccyx (the tiny bone at the base of the spine) at the back, the bottom of the pubic bone at the front, and the ischial spines, which are the two projecting crests on the side walls of the pelvis. The coccyx slips out of the way as the baby's head comes through.*

3 *Usually the downward pressure from above that is provided by good contractions will ease the baby's head down so that as it comes through the steepest curve at the beginning of the vagina the muscles at the back of the neck extend. In effect this means that the baby is facing downward just before and as it is delivered.*

emerges, damp and sticky with mucus, it is often a violet or purple color, since the child has not yet taken that first great gasp of air that will oxygenate the blood.

The baby may be covered in vernix, a cold cream like substance which coats the baby's skin in the uterus and makes it look as if it has been spread with cottage cheese. The head has been molded by its journey down the birth canal, so it may be an odd, pointed or bumpy asymmetrical shape, and the forehead may recede and the baby be almost chinless. The nose is often flattened like a prizefighter's and there are little red marks between the eyes and on the eyelids.

66 I felt the baby's head pop out and she was born. And she was a girl! All the time I had been desperate for a son but I didn't mind. I held her and she just lay there and liked it. 99

At delivery, the baby's head is facing downwards but the shoulders are still turned sideways inside you. Once the head is free, it turns to come in line with the shoulders. You may need another push for the shoulders. The doctor or midwife usually presses the baby's head down so that the shoulder nearer your front slides out first, then the head is lifted up so that the lower shoulder slides out next. Then the whole body slithers out and your baby is born! There is often a great gush of water, and the baby may be already breathing and crying, its limbs lashing and its face puckered up with what looks like rage. The lower end of the body seems very small in comparison with the head end, apart from the genitals which often look extraordinarily large. All this is normal. If the baby is not yet breathing, attendants suck out the respiratory tract again, and hold the child's head down, or they may give oxygen with a small mask. If you are well propped up, you will be able to reach your baby, provided he or she is lying over your thigh or has been delivered up on to your tummy, and you may want to reach down right away and take your daughter or son in your arms.

The third stage of labor

Though you may not feel the contractions, your uterus continues to contract after the birth of the baby. This makes the placenta separate from its lining, since the placenta cannot contract. As the uterus squeezes down into a firm, hard ball the placental mass is automatically peeled off. This process has been compared to stretching a piece of rubber on which a postage stamp has been stuck; when the rubber moves, the stamp becomes detached. The sinuses in which the placental blood vessels were rooted are closed by the tight squeezing of the uterus, and these contractions prevent excessive bleeding.

When the placenta has detached itself, the midwife or doctor may pull on the cord (see page 251). Take a breath, hold it and bear down at the same time to help this process. Or you may be asked to push again and do it by yourself.

There is a squelchy, slippery feeling as the placenta slides out. The person who delivered you examines the placenta carefully to see that every part is there. Pieces of placenta left inside could cause unnecessary bleeding, pain and infection in the postpartum period. Though the placenta looks like a large piece of raw liver, it was the tree of life for your baby. You may be interested to examine it yourself and see the difference between the rough side, which was against the wall of the uterus, and the smooth side, which lay towards the baby like a soft, velvety cushion, and to note the network of blood vessels that provided your baby with its life support system.

The nurse will help you on with a couple of sanitary pads, as there will be some bleeding now and for several days, resembling the height of a heavy period. The length of time during which there is a bloodstained vaginal discharge (lochia) varies greatly among women. Some bleed for just a few days, others for as long as five or six weeks.

In many hospitals the staff tidy up at this point. They wipe and weigh the baby, examine you to see if you need stitches, give you a wash, change your gown, shorten the baby's cord and reclamp it. But practise is fast changing and many now give the parents the opportunity for a quiet time with their baby immediately following the birth, only doing the basic essentials and leaving the couple for about half an hour to get to know their baby. Being together should always come first. Tidying up can be done later. It is far less important. If you need stitching, it is usually possible to have the baby with you throughout this procedure. Suturing (the technical term for stitching) is done under local anesthetic and may take a long time, sometimes as long as an hour, since careful embroidery has to be done and the underlying layers of muscle must be correctly aligned. So keep your baby in your arms or near enough to touch.

The second stage of labor

The cervix is fully dilated to 10 cm and the midwife feels the position of the baby's head as it moves down the birth canal. The mother is now free to go with the great sweeps of energy that accompany the overpowering urge to bear down and is caught up in an act that requires intense concentration. She is supported by her partner who gives himself fully to helping her cope with each contraction.

Once the cervix has dilated, the baby's head moves down through the pelvis.

The appearance of the head
The baby's head has slipped under the mother's pubic bone and emerges. Because it has rotated in the birth canal, it is now facing downward. The midwife feels to make sure that the cord is not around the baby's neck.

The head rotates and begins to emerge from the birth canal.

Rotation of the head

The baby's head starts to rotate again, so that it is once more in line with the shoulders. Now that she has pushed the head out, the mother is relaxed and happy, and sits up to catch the first glimpse of her child.

After the head is born, it rotates again to come in line with the shoulders.

Birth of the body
*The baby's body follows, helped out by the midwife. He is already
breathing. The hair is damp and the skin still crinkled up like a
rose petal before it has opened. The parents look on in wonder.*

*The shoulders slide out, one
after the other, followed by
the rest of the body.*

Becoming a family
The long awaited moment. Joy and a celebration as the mother holds her child in her arms for the first time. Still attached to the placenta by the umbilical cord, he lies safe and warm against her tummy after his journey to life.

When the baby has been born, the uterus continues to contract strongly to expel the placenta.

217

Different kinds of labor

However much people may advise you not to have any preconceptions about your labor, just to be ready for whatever comes, it is difficult not to have some, because it is almost impossible to prepare yourself to cope with a situation that you have not imagined in advance. So it is useful to think ahead to the major variations on the theme of childbirth which you might confront. However, it is still vital to keep in the forefront of your mind the normal, rhythmic and harmonious pattern of a straightforward labor. Otherwise all the medical technicalities may seem bewildering, and you may interpret each uncomfortable physical sign as an indication that something has gone wrong.

This chapter looks at some different types of labor, all of which can throw you unless you understand what is happening.

Labor with a posterior baby

When the hard back of the baby's head presses against your sacrum or slightly to one side of it, the baby is said to be in an occipitoposterior position. Most women have some backache in labor, but women with posterior babies may have it all the time, so much so that the labor can be described as a "backache labor". Few women with posterior babies do not have backache, which can be the most tiring and stressful thing about a labor—especially if, as is often the case when the baby is posterior, it continues *between* as well as during contractions.

Another characteristic of labor with a posterior baby is that it starts very slowly, often over a period of several days, and contractions are usually experienced as one big one followed by a feeble one. Plan for morale boosting activity during a long first stage. Don't go into the hospital too soon. A walk in the park or the country is probably better. Eat and keep up your strength in early labor and have plenty of fluids, remembering to empty your bladder regularly. Your partner also needs stamina in a backache labor, to keep you going by giving you his total attention during difficult contractions.

The baby will probably rotate at the very end of the first stage or the onset of the second and things will be smooth sailing from then on. About five per cent of posteriors do not rotate and then the hard work has to be continued with the second stage and you may need obstetric help (see page 260) to deliver the baby. But the chances are that the baby will swivel around and then slide down your birth canal with ease.

Ways of dealing with a backache labor

You may find some of the following things helpful in the first stage of a backache labor.

Changes of position Keep upright and moving around for as long as possible. In this way you tip the baby down to press through the pelvis and birth canal instead of right into the small

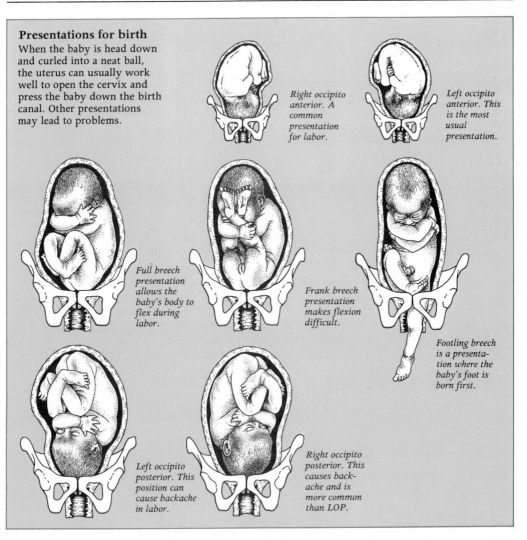

Presentations for birth

When the baby is head down and curled into a neat ball, the uterus can usually work well to open the cervix and press the baby down the birth canal. Other presentations may lead to problems.

Right occipito anterior. A common presentation for labor.

Left occipito anterior. This is the most usual presentation.

Full breech presentation allows the baby's body to flex during labor.

Frank breech presentation makes flexion difficult.

Footling breech is a presentation where the baby's foot is born first.

Left occipito posterior. This position can cause backache in labor.

Right occipito posterior. This causes backache and is more common than LOP.

of your back. Crouching, leaning forward, kneeling, squatting, getting onto all fours, and side lying with your back well rounded, your head and shoulders curved forward and a good space between your legs, may all be positions in which pain is eased and rotation of the baby's head is encouraged.

Heat A hot water bottle wrapped in a towel, or a hot compress (in the form of a face towel or small towel wrung out in really hot water) may bring relief, applied to where you feel most pain.

Pressure Ask your partner to provide firm pressure, either right over the place where your pelvis joins your spine or to the left or right of this if the pain is more to the side. He should use the heel of the palm of one hand, with the other resting over it, and press his body weight down through his arm. Or you may prefer the feel of knuckles. It is sometimes comfortable to sit on your own knuckles, one hand under each buttock, so that firm pressure is applied there as your own weight is put on them.

Stimulus on pressure points may help you to handle the pain more effectively. One place where deep pressure of a thumb or finger may feel good is on your bottom, level with the top of the slit between your buttocks and a little more than the width of your palm out towards the leg on each side. Experiment to find the spot: it feels tender, but pressure on it is satisfying. If you are in a position in which you are tilted forward, your partner can apply pressure to the spot on both of your buttocks at once. If you are on your side he will only be able to reach one, but even this may help. These areas are called "pain prevention points" in one system of psychoprophylaxis.

Acupressure This Chinese system involves exerting pressure on parts of the body far away from where you are feeling pain, but where a really strong stimulus can offer almost miraculous relief. One place is just below the center of the ball of the foot: try sitting up well with good back support, while your partner holds both your feet and uses light counterpressure over each foot. It is surprising how strong the pressure from finger and thumb can be on the right spot. This can be effective for strong contractions, wherever they are felt.

If you are in the kind of environment where you can really do as you please, your partner can sit on the bed with his pelvis against your lower spine and lean back against you. This provides welcome rest for someone who after several hours of working to relieve backache may develop back pain himself!

Massage Massage may feel better than pressure, or can feel good alternated with pressure. The massage that suits most women best is firm, slow and steady, moving the flesh and muscle on the bone. You can use talcum powder, cornstarch or massage oil to avoid skin irritation, and your helper should have some cream to rub into his hands if he has to give a massage for a long time.

Another highly effective way of giving a massage is to use a rolling pin. You can knot a face towel or even a hot compress towel around it to get more grip.

Labor with a breech baby

Labor with a breech sometimes starts with the waters leaking. This is because the baby's bottom does not fit the opening cervix as well as the oval of the crown of the head, and so part of the bag of waters becomes wedged between its bottom and your cervix. It is important that you call the hospital if this happens to you and the baby is not yet engaged. The risk is that the cord might slide down as well and be caught between the baby and the cervix, so that the oxygen supply to the baby is cut off.

If the waters do not break early in labor, stand up and keep walking around through the first stage, until they break spontaneously. There is a strong case to be made for not doing an amniotomy (see page 247), since if a breech baby is left in its bag of waters there can be no pressure on the cord.

Relieving a backache labor

Pressure above and to either side of your buttocks can greatly relieve a tender and aching back . . .

. . . or you might prefer a hot water bottle wrapped in a towel held against the area that feels most painful.

Your partner can apply firm pressure to your sacrum by leaning over you and allowing his full weight to pass down through his arm . . .

. . . and, by pressing the back of his pelvis against your lower back, he can make you more comfortable while having a rest himself.

After the waters have broken, the best positions are on your hands and knees or on your side. You may have backache (see above) and if so your partner should exert firm pressure with his knuckles over the small of your back.

The second stage of a breech labor

You may be moved to an operating room before the second stage starts, in case you should need an emergency Cesarean section. Often your partner is shown to the waiting room at this time. If you want to stay together make this clear.

Many doctors prefer to deliver breech babies with the woman in the lithotomy position (see page 204), since they feel that they have most control over the birth this way. But you will probably be more comfortable sitting up, with your partner positioning himself so that his shoulder and arm are behind you to give you a firm base, or even—if you are in a setting where you feel able to do what suits you—sitting on the bed behind you.

It is usually best to let the second stage proceed with no voluntary exertion on your part until the body is born and the head is about to slip out, so that the baby's body is born on contraction waves only. (It may be easiest to do this if you are on all fours.) Concentrate on total release: breathe, rather than push, the baby out.

If the baby has both feet up by its head, the doctor may slip a gloved hand in to draw down a leg and turn the baby into a footling (see page 219). Relax and breathe as this is done. Once the foot is down the baby can then take the curve of the birth canal more smoothly, as its legs are no longer alongside its spine.

Birth of a breech baby
Breech babies can be born vaginally as long as the pelvic outlet is wide enough for the baby's head.

1 *The buttocks are usually delivered first, followed by the legs.*

2 *The baby turns so that the shoulders can emerge as easily as possible.*

3 *The baby's own weight draws the head down and its legs are then lifted to deliver the head.*

If you are not having an epidural (see below), an injection of local anesthetic is given in your perineum before the baby's head is delivered. It takes one or two minutes to be effective. Then usually an episiotomy is done (see page 250).

Most obstetricians do a large episiotomy with a breech so that the head can be delivered unimpeded, and some do two cuts, one on each side of the perineum (a bilateral episiotomy). But if you give birth with breathing instead of pushing, your tissues may fan out well and an episiotomy may not be essential. Since there is unlikely to be an opportunity for discussion at the time, when things will be happening fast, talk about this earlier on in your labor (between contractions, of course). Otherwise the doctor will probably do an episiotomy.

Once the episiotomy is done, the doctor can deliver the head, using hands or forceps to cradle it. You will be asked to push for the head and will probably find that only one bearing down effort is necessary.

Sometimes women can help to deliver their own breech babies by leaning forward and lifting the baby's legs up, while the doctor or midwife controls the delivery of the head and supports a shoulder. I first saw this done by mistake when a very helpful midwife told a first time mother to put her hands down and touch her baby while its head was still inside her. The mother was so excited that she held the baby's legs, lifted them, and as she did so the head slipped out without an episiotomy.

Epidural anesthesia (see page 242) is often used for breech deliveries and indeed has largely replaced general anesthesia. It means that you only feel a pulling sensation, and that even if delivery is complicated you are awake and aware and can hold your baby as soon as it is breathing well. An increased number of obstetricians routinely do Cesarean sections (see page 262) for all first baby breeches. Discuss this with your obstetrician. Even if a Cesarean section is the safest option for your baby, there is no need to be unconscious if you do not want to be.

Short sharp labor

66 She came so quickly there was no time to get to the delivery room. All was calm and peaceful. A mother in the next bed slept right through. 99

It is wrong to assume, as do some obstetric textbooks, that a short labor is bad for the baby. In many apparently short labors the cervix is dilating gently (see page 200) over a period of days before you realize you are in labor. And some short labors can be delightful. But however easy it might be physically, a violent precipitate labor is emotionally demanding and may leave you feeling drained and shocked.

If, from start to finish, your labor lasts less than an hour or two, you may need a great deal of active help from your partner: in effect it is like starting straight in at the very end of the first stage. Your partner needs to concentrate with you; he needs to maintain eye contact and breathe with you. Remember that breathing has to be light to avoid hyperventilation. Your partner may hyperventilate if everything is happening very quickly and he becomes anxious or excited. So remind each other to keep the breathing butterfly-light.

When you feel the baby pressing like a grapefruit against your anus it may be easiest to avoid pushing if you turn on your side, with your knees drawn up. But whatever position you choose, push only when you have to and then for as short a time as you can. Open your mouth, drop your jaw and relax your lips. Then continue breathing in and out through a relaxed mouth and concentrate on releasing all the tissues around your vagina as they fan out and open wide.

If the baby is coming very fast in the second stage you will probably need to blow as well as breathe quickly to stop yourself from pushing. If you feel as if you really must push, blow as if you were extinguishing a candle flame to reduce the intensity of the push (see page 177). You will not stop the push altogether, because the expulsive power of the uterus is there whatever you do, but you can limit it to a certain extent.

Some women feel after a labor of this kind that they want the baby inside them again; they wish that they could go back to the beginning, because everything happened so fast that they cannot make sense of it. Some even feel "cheated". If this is so with you, talk through each event of labor with your partner, fitting the pieces of the puzzle together, and relive the birth in your thoughts until you can see its shape.

Long drawn out labor

A lengthy labor can be psychologically taxing as well as physically exhausting. You need constant confident emotional support from someone who loves you and does not leave you. Yet unfortunately a prolonged labor tends to make the man anxious about what is happening, unsure of his role and often feeling that he ought to leave it all to the professionals.

A long drawn out labor can seem prolonged for two reasons: you may be unable to differentiate clearly between the lead in to labor proper—sometimes called the "latent" phase—and active labor; and active labor itself may then be prolonged because contractions are faint and infrequent, or because they are not achieving dilatation of the cervix. In these cases, psychological support, accurate information and an opportunity to rest are vitally important. Even if contractions seem ineffective and dilatation is slow until you reach 4 cm, everything may seem to coordinate suddenly so that from then on labor goes like a bomb. Over 90 per cent of women having a lengthy latent phase go on to have a normal labor and delivery if given the chance.* So don't immediately assume that if labor takes several days to start it is going to be like that right through. Have relaxing hot baths, sleep or rest in different beds if possible so that you have a change of scene and automatically take up different positions. There may be a couch, an easy chair or even a rug to lie on as a change from your usual bed. Do not go into the hospital until you think you would feel happier there. Even if you have a long first stage the second may be completely normal.

The progress of your labor is assessed in terms of the rate of dilatation of the cervix (see page 208). Provided the baby is all

A position which may seem unusual can bring unexpected relief in the course of a long first stage.

right and its heart tones are regular, *slow dilatation at the onset of labor does not harm the baby*, however tiring you find it. Slow dilatation in the early phase is not the same as complete lack of progress over several hours once active labor has started (that is after about 3 cm); then the baby may be exposed to special risk and the heart rate may slow down. Do remember that it is difficult for people to be accurate about dilatation: you may be examined by someone who says you are 5 cm dilated, but an hour later someone else says you are only 4 cm or perhaps 5 cm dilated, when by then the first person examining you would have felt you to be 5½ cm dilated.

Ways of dealing with a long labor

66 Throughout labor I was conscious that I could only go with the contractions. It was like a marathon. 99

In the hospital it is often difficult to walk about and alternate periods of rest with sessions of activity. But if you can do this, it is the best natural way of helping a uterus which is contracting ineffectually to start working far more efficiently.

Be sure that you are taking enough fluids, as you can forget to drink and become dehydrated. You may be given an intravenous "cocktail" of glucose solution to keep up your strength and insure that you do not become dried out. If this is the case, get into an upright position beforehand so that you are not then stuck lying down with an IV in your arm. If you have to stay in bed, take up positions in which the long axis of the uterus is in line with the birth canal. You can do this by kneeling or squatting, and it is one of the most effective noninvasive actions you can take. You can do this *before* taking drugs for pain relief (see page 240), having a spinal or epidural (see page 242), or accepting hormone acceleration of labor (see page 256).

Sometimes fear or anxiety seems to prevent a uterus from functioning well. If physical difficulties have been ruled out, work together with your partner on facing up to any worries that may be on your mind. Together create an atmosphere which is psychologically positive, concentrating on the reality of the baby who is coming to birth and on the visual image of the cervix opening up. In parts of New Guinea when labor is long drawn out the woman is urged to confess any hidden anger she may feel because it is thought that labor will proceed easily once she has got rid of the negative feelings she is bottling up.

Dysfunctional labor

One of the things that may be holding up labor is incoordinate uterine action. Unfortunately it is possible to have massive contractions and yet for the upper segment of the uterus not to be able to draw up and pull open the lower section. It is as if one part of the uterus is working against another part. The result is dysfunctional labor with powerful contractions and failure to progress. With this kind of labor effective pain relief (as from an epidural) and augmentation of labor with an oxytocin intravenous drip set up may well be the answer. If this happens to you there should be time for a rest to overcome fatigue and then —once dilatation progresses—the epidural can be allowed to wear off so that you can push the baby out yourself.

Giving support in labor

It is now accepted in most hospitals that many fathers want to be present during labor and that couples expect to be together. But if the father wants to do more than just watch, it is important for him to learn in advance exactly how he can help most effectively. Childbirth education classes can be very useful in helping him understand what is happening and teaching him what he can do to help his partner (see page 158).

The father at the birth

The man who knows what he can do to help is in a much better position than the one who is merely invited into the labor room, but who has no idea of what is going on. He has every opportunity to be an informed and knowledgeable participant. It is not just a question of holding his partner's hand, although this can be a way of giving emotional support, but of being able to judge where and when she needs guidance and encouragement with relaxation.

He has also learned how to breathe "over" the contractions so that he can breathe with his partner at times when she needs extra support. He knows how to rub her back and do gentle, light massage over her lower abdomen when the uterus is opening up, and perhaps provide other kinds of stroking and firm pressure for her shoulders, arms and legs.

The father's role in the hospital

It can be one thing to learn how to give support in the friendly atmosphere of a small prenatal class where couples are working together, often with much discussion interspersed with laughter, and quite another to put that learning to use in a large, perhaps rather impersonal, hospital. Confronted in labor with masked figures in white or green whom he has never met before, whose names he does not know, in a strange clinical environment, he can feel out of place in spite of consent by the hospital to his presence at the birth.

This is why it is a good idea for him, as well as for his partner, to have seen around the hospital and especially the labor room before the labor. Women sometimes say that it was when they were approached with some unfamiliar piece of equipment in labor that they began to tense up, and that if they had known what it looked like and how it worked they would have found it much easier to stay relaxed. And men who have been giving good support to their partners before apparatus of this kind is used sometimes give up, as they feel that the machinery is controlling the labor.

This is understandable, because when an IV stand or monitoring equipment is brought to the bed it is physically more difficult for him to get close enough to his partner, and because a monitoring belt which fits around her abdomen may make it impossible for him to massage that area. In most hospitals, too, once the

66 We didn't plan on him being there for the birth. But the doctor took it for granted that he would come into the room, so he did. And he was pleased as punch! He was grinning from ear to ear afterward and he told everyone that he had been at the birth. His family thought it was disgusting. 99

labor is monitored and speeded up, a nurse stays with the patient all the time, so the intimacy that the couple may have had together in earlier labor is lost, and this can lead to them feeling that the experts and machinery have taken over.

If the baby's father cannot be with his partner, it is important that she has a companion, one who knows what she is doing and why, and who can help her. This might be another woman. Whoever it is, she (or he) should, if possible, have attended some or all of the childbirth education classes too. Although this chapter is addressed mainly to fathers, it is also meant to give guidance to any attendants at the birth.

The kind of support you can give

66 It is not a question of just being there for her sake, but for your own. You don't know what you're missing if you're not at the birth. It was the most tremendous experience of my life! 99

The first and most important thing for a companion helping a woman during the long first stage of labor is to be relaxed. This is difficult in an exciting situation, but any tension or anxiety is immediately communicated to the mother. If labor is different from what you expected, awareness of what is happening can worry you more than the woman, who is enveloped in the force sweeping through her body and who may actually shut out all irrelevant stimuli. You, however, may be made anxious by the doctor's tone of voice, the nurse's remark to a colleague, or by the (quite normal) appearance of bloodstained mucus during a contraction. Ask for information, because if you are in doubt about anything, it is better to find out *early* rather than late. In many hospitals you will not be given full information unless you ask. Speak slowly and quietly. Move slowly and deliberately. Touch your partner without haste, resting a relaxed hand on her body and, when you lift your hand away, do so slowly. If you are massaging her, stroke very slowly.

Distractions in the labor room

When helping her to achieve focused concentration on what is happening in her body during contractions, never break that concentration by chatting to anyone else, watching a machine or allowing yourself to be distracted by what is going on around you. As well as causing the woman in labor to tense up, modern equipment often fascinates her companion; who may become so involved with watching the monitor, for example, that the pregnant woman takes second place and feels that emotional support has been withdrawn. You should not forget that, however sophisticated the machinery, it is in fact the woman who is having the baby. Once labor is well under way, your attention should be on her, and encouragement by word, touch or look should be given with every single contraction.

On the hospital's side too an induced or speeded up and monitored labor becomes an interesting clinical exercise. Nurses, doctors and students may come in to watch. Teaching may go on at the bedside. Discussions about the equipment sometimes take place while the woman is busy with a contraction and would appreciate silence so that she can concentrate better.

227

Although you cannot insist that everyone is quiet during contractions, you can indicate politely by your own silence and attention to the woman in labor that you are not available for conversation during contractions, and by doing this can help her to enter a "circle of solitude" with just you, and the baby coming to birth.

Occasionally machines break down and engineers arrive. This can be very distracting for the woman in labor, and may even be alarming. Fortunately she is not dependent on the monitor or other pieces of equipment to have her baby. Give her your full and undivided attention. Be on the same level, at the head of the bed, not towering over her. Use eye contact to give her nonverbal emotional support. If she is coping well, she may like to close her eyes and handle contractions without looking at anybody, but if the going gets difficult, it is a good idea to suggest that she open her eyes and that you go through it together. This is likely to be of special help at the end of the first stage of labor, when her cervix is anything from 6 cm to fully dilated.

Hold her firmly but gently and give her encouragement with each contraction. . .

Positive support during contractions

Everything you say should be positive. Avoid saying "You're not relaxed here" or "Your shoulders are tightening". Instead say something such as "Your feet are beautifully relaxed. Do the same with your hands" or give her positive instructions such as "Pull your shoulders down and now let them go". When she is doing well, tell her so: "Good. Good. Beautiful. You're doing really well." This helps most as contractions reach their peak. It can be useful to hold her shoulder firmly during big contractions, and if she has practiced relaxation techniques that help her flow out towards your touch (see page 166), these will help her keep her shoulders loose and so avoid hyperventilating. Between contractions talk together about where she likes to be stroked or held, as different women like different things.

She may find it helps her to work with her contractions if you describe to her what is happening as the uterus goes into action: "You are opening up wider and wider. Your cervix is being pulled up and open and the baby's head is pressing right down." Ruth Wilf, an experienced midwife at the Booth Maternity Center in Philadelphia, suggests that if the woman seems out of touch with her body the support person should quietly discuss with her between contractions what she is thinking about as they occur. This gives you something to work on during the next contraction. Create an image for the next one—the baby pressing down, the cervix opening up—and use your hands to suggest gradual opening. Then ask after the next one, "How was that compared to the last contraction?" The woman may be able to suggest other things you can do.

Understanding the labor's progress

As well as needing to be told what progress she is making, she also needs information about what is being done by her birth attendants. Being in labor can be very disorienting. Chloe Fisher, a community midwife and midwifery tutor in England, who has the art of helping women get in touch with their bodies in labor, says that fear of the unknown is the main reason why women panic in labor and that a request for painrelieving drugs is usually one for reassurance and for understanding about what is happening. A woman may be distressed because she does not realize the progress her labor is making and has not caught up with it. She loses all sense of time and each contraction may be so enveloping that she cannot see the pattern of her labor. So be clear about progress, however slight, and if you can, prepare her also for what is about to happen. For instance, if the waters have not broken by the time contractions are coming every two minutes, you can be fairly sure they will break soon. If she is about to have an amniotomy (see page 247), prepare her for the renewed strength of contractions after it and discuss with her how she might change her breathing to cope with them. In the second stage remind her that the hot, throbbing, tingling feeling is a sign that the baby is just about to be born and will soon be in her arms.

Know when to be quiet. This depends very much on your empathy with her. Talk when it helps, but keep quiet when you can give other forms of support. Facial expression, gesture, touch and massage are important. One of the best ways of helping is to rest a hand on her shoulder with the other hand at her wrist and to keep them there as she goes through the contraction. If she has backache, she will welcome firm pressure or massage over the sacrum, or slightly to one side of it (see page 219).

How to help with breathing

Breathe with her through difficult contractions. Do not wait until she is tense to start the breathing. Begin with a relaxed breath out together. Keep closely in rhythm with her own breathing at the beginning of the contraction so that there is a partnership. Do not impose a radically different level or rate of breathing on her or it will become a fight between her breathing and yours and will introduce tension. If she starts to drag through the contraction with heavy gasping breaths, this is the time to differentiate your breathing from hers.

When appropriate, move your hand in a light butterfly wing movement to stress the lightness of breathing necessary when the uterus is at its tightest. As soon as she catches on and lifts her breathing let her know that what she is doing is right.

Help her enjoy complete relaxation between contractions. This is especially important in stressful labors, as otherwise the woman carries her tension from one contraction to the next and it is cumulative. When she is relaxed, you can talk together about how to meet the next contraction. Avoid complicated anatomical and physiological terms. When you speak about the uterus or cervix, remember it is "your" uterus and "your" cervix, just as it is also "your" or "our" baby. Words used during contractions should be simple, rhythmic and repetitive.

Coping with pain

Labor companions are often unsure whether or not they should mention the word "pain". For some it is taboo. It is imperative to acknowledge pain when it exists and not pretend that it is not there. To do so is to deny a woman the validity of her own experience and to say in effect: "You aren't feeling what you think you are feeling, and if you are there must be something wrong with you or with your labor." If she tells you it hurts, agree and say, "I understand" or "Yes, I realize that". It might be the moment to add, "Your uterus is working very hard" or "The baby is pressing right down" and also to help her see the pattern of her labor. If she is more than 6 or 7 cm dilated, you will know that she is at the most difficult part of labor. Show her with your hand how far she is dilated. Help her change position, freshen her up with a face wash, brush her hair, use massage. Give her your total, undivided attention. Emotional support of this kind can take the place of drugs for pain relief.

Sometimes it can help her just to know that you are there. . .

The most undermining thing you can do to a woman in labor is to encourage her to feel sorry for herself. The woman who is told, "Oh, my dear, I can't bear to see you in such pain," or words to that effect, is being deprived of emotional support. Even the expression on a helper's face can give that message, sometimes more clearly than words. We would not think much of someone who leaned over the side of a boat and called to the person in the water, "It looks terrible down there. The waves are so huge and, poor thing, you look as if you are drowning. Do you want an injection?" Yet this is the equivalent of the sympathy and the offer of "something to take away the pain" that some attendants offer to a woman in labor. The woman who has prepared herself for labor often wants help to cope with the mountainous waves rather than the offer of a drunken stupor or sensation free childbirth. If she wants drugs for pain relief, this should be her own decision. If she does ask for Demerol or an epidural, she should do so freely, not because she has been persuaded or coerced.

Staying together

If you feel queasy or that you must have a break, just tell your partner you will be back in a moment and stroll out. Although you may be asked to go out when the doctor comes in or when examinations are done, this is not really necessary. It seems that fathers are sometimes asked to go out because doctors and nurses are embarrassed to do things to the woman in front of her partner. But women often feel they especially need support when they are being examined or when drugs for pain relief are offered, and for you to go out then can be the worst time. This is one point in labor when the woman, who is at the focus of all the care provided, can herself speak up and state her preferences. She could say, "I'd very much like my husband to stay, please. Don't send him away. I really need him," or "I don't think I'll be relaxed if he goes out." If the doctor or nurse is doubtful, she could add, "He's learned about what happens and under-stands it pretty well. He's being a wonderful support!" You have no legal right to insist on being present so, if the doctor is adamant, you must go out, but you can ask if you may come back in at the earliest possible moment and linger outside, making your message clear. Problems of this kind may not arise, and in labor reports couples often say how helpful and friendly every-one was, but it is wise to have a contingency plan in case every-thing is not straightforward. It should not be forgotten whose labor it is: in normal labor the hospital staff and any machines should be there to assist, not take over.

Start and stop labor

Some labors seem to come to a full stop for a time and a woman may be stuck at 4 cm dilatation or more for several hours. This is a sign for a change of activity and if possible a change of scene. Lying flat on one's back is not a good position for labor, from either the woman's or the baby's point of view. You can see that she does not slip down in the bed. Remember that when she is

231

lying on her left side or is upright the blood flows more freely through the placenta to the baby than it does when she is lying flat on her back.

It is not a good idea for the woman to lie still for long periods and you can suggest that she may like to roll over onto the other side occasionally or to sit well up. If she is sitting up, supported by four or five pillows, there is not the same problem of decreased blood flow to the baby. It is also fine if she wants to squat, kneel, sit upright, stand, or adopt any of the many positions which women often spontaneously choose in labor (see page 204). But these are obviously limited if drips and machinery are in use.

If no machinery is being used when labor comes to a stop, encourage her to get up and move around. If she is already walking about, suggest a shower, perhaps a back massage, and then rest in bed with hot water bottles wherever she aches. Jamaican folk midwives give the woman a good wash down and then wrap her in hot towels and offer a drink of hot thyme or mixed spice tea when labor fails to progress. Perhaps we could learn something from this.

A full bladder can hold up labor and cause unnecessary pain. Remind the woman to empty her bladder every hour and a half, or more frequently if she seems to need that. If progress is slow, help her to feel that her natural pace is the right pace. Each labor is different and having a baby is not a competition to see who can do it fastest or who can most nearly conform to a norm. Especially when labor is long drawn out, affirm your confidence in her own body rhythms.

Between 8 and 10 cm dilatation the woman may feel lost and tossed in the sweep and turmoil of contractions following on each other almost without a break. Keep eye contact and breathe with her through each contraction. Letting her know that you trust her own natural rhythms is nowhere more important than at this point, when many women are made to feel that it is a race to the finishing line. Her legs may feel very cold and begin to shake, and you can help her by firmly massaging the inside of her thighs.

Support for the second stage

When the woman begins to push the baby out, it is a help if she can be propped well up with her back supported firmly by your arm and three or four pillows. The ideal position is one in which her back is rounded with shoulders forward and chin resting on her chest. You can help by cradling her in your arms so that she is comfortable and by reminding her to keep her head forward, without making any attempt to push it forward. From time to time give her a wrung out cloth or ice cubes to suck if her mouth is dry.

In the second stage, do not mention the word "push". Say "open up" instead, as straining only wastes energy and results in uncoordinated expulsive efforts. If you suggest she does not push at all unless she feels she has to, she will push in the right way at the right time. If the pushing urge is strong and difficult

Yours to share — the birth not only of a new human being but of a new family . . .

to control, help her to lie on her side, as this may lessen the impulse. Encourage her to put her hands down and feel even before any part of the baby's head is oozing through the vagina, then use a mirror for her to see the top of the head as it crowns. If you see that the crown is moving forward, but she is still holding her breath, say quietly "*Breathe*". She should immediately breathe out and go on breathing in and out with a dropped jaw.

Sharing in the birth

Many women are anxious that they might be too small. Reassure her that there is room, and her own feelings of openness and flexibility will help to make room. The power of suggestion is so great that each word and phrase used can affect positively or negatively her ability to work with her body.

When you are with a woman in childbirth, you share with her a journey into the unknown. The helper is like the lookout on a yacht sailing at night, watching for the coastline and helping to steer her through. She needs your constant presence and to be left alone is the most frightening thing of all. Giving support in labor requires vigilance, skill, patience, an understanding of that particular woman—her rhythms, her responses to stress—an awareness of what she is thinking and how she is feeling at each moment, and your complete commitment to this task. Sometimes it demands endurance and courage. It can be hard, exhausting work. But yours, too, is the excitement, the deep satisfaction and the joy of the journey's end when a child is born.

Surprise delivery

If you are with a woman in labor who is giving birth before a doctor arrives or before you can get to the hospital, the most important thing is for you to stay calm and give her quiet, confident support. Drop your shoulders and relax! Tell her she is doing well. Hold her in your arms and help her feel secure.

Making her comfortable

If the room is cold, heat it. The baby will need a warm environment after birth. If you can, place a pile of newspapers or a plastic sheet or tablecloth under the mother. She may like to sit on a firm cushion, bolster, or a bean bag. Cover whatever she is sitting on with a sheet if there is one available. Find some big towels, a blanket or something else warm to wrap the baby in. Offer her sips of water if her mouth is dry.

Put pillows or some sort of support behind her back, shoulders and head to allow her to sit up comfortably unless she prefers some other position: her own feelings about this are likely to be right. If traces of feces appear at her anus, wipe with cotton or toilet paper down and away from the vagina.

Put the kettle and a few saucepans of water on to boil, then pour the boiled water into heatproof bowls and leave it to cool. This cooled water can be poured between the mother's legs after delivery to clean her up. Wash your hands and scrub your nails thoroughly.

If she is already pushing, remind her to "open up" and not to hold her breath or push at all unless she feels she needs to. As the head crowns, tell her to pant, so that from then on she breathes the baby out instead of pushing it out. She can push gently between contractions if delivery is slow.

If there is a loop of cord around the baby's neck as its head slides out, hook a finger around it and lift it over the head. *Do not pull the baby or the cord*, as this may detach the placenta from the wall of the uterus before it has stopped being the baby's life support. If a membrane is over the baby's face, lift it off. When the head is born, allow it to hang by its own weight and this will tend to draw forward the shoulder nearer the mother's front. Either you or she can catch the baby. Cradle it in your hands and lift it up onto the mother's upper thigh or tummy, head slightly down so that any mucus can drain.

After the delivery Cover mother and baby with a coat or blanket, or better still a quilt, which is light and warm. Put a bowl between the mother's legs ready to receive the placenta as soon as she feels more contractions. There is no need to cut the cord immediately. Enjoy the peace after delivery as you together admire the baby and wait for the placenta. Make her comfortable. She may be shivery and appreciate a hot water bottle. She might like a hot drink and may even be ravenously hungry. When the baby is ready to suck put it to the breast and see that the nipple is well back in the mouth. Telephone for a midwife or doctor.

If this surprise delivery happens in a car, away from any help or home comforts, there is no need to do anything about the placenta or cord. However, if you have a plastic bag or some newspaper, you can wrap the placenta in it and keep it slightly above the level of the baby, if you can do this easily.

If you are at home and are not able to get a midwife, boil up shoe laces or soft string for tying the cord, and scissors for cutting it. If the placenta does not come after about 20 minutes, get the mother to kneel and press on her own lower tummy. It will almost certainly slip out then. (Above all do not pull on the cord.) Put a bowl under the woman's buttocks and pour some of the warm boiled water over the area between her legs. Then help her on with two sanitary pads and find her some clean clothes. She can keep her uterus contracting and so reduce bleeding from the placental site by massaging it firmly with one hand.

Tie the cord about 4 in (10 cm) from the baby and again about 6 in (15 cm) and cut with sterilized scissors or a new razor blade between the ties. Check that there is no bleeding from the baby's cord stump. If there is, do another tie nearer to the baby.

The greatest heat loss from a newborn baby is from its head, so cover the back of the head with any warm piece of clothing. Keep mother and baby cuddled together. Babies stay warm when they are held close. When labor comes by surprise and proceeds fast it is very unlikely that anything will go wrong. This is just nature at its most efficient.

Dealing with pain

"I've got a very low pain threshold. I can't stand going to the dentist, so I can't *think* what labor is going to be like! They'd better knock me out."

"The idea of the pain really worries me. I've never really experienced severe pain, and I can't imagine what it's like to be in pain for hours and hours and hours."

"What is labor pain like? I mean is it like breaking your arm or a bad headache or menstrual cramps or indigestion—or what? If I knew a bit more what it was going to be like I think I could face it better."

These three statements express what many women who are pregnant for the first time feel, but perhaps do not acknowledge or put into words: fear that pain is going to be overpowering, a sense that they have never experienced pain that tested their inner resources, and ignorance of the kind of pain that is likely to be felt in childbirth.

Putting pain in its context

People often think that pain is just a matter of a "high" or "low" threshold. There are very few women who think that they have a high threshold and can bear pain as well as other women. In fact, the idea of simple thresholds like walls, with some of us possessing high walls and others low ones, is a myth.

It is now known that in human beings the pain sensation threshold is exactly the same.* In one study, members of Italian, Jewish, Irish and Old American ethnic groups were all given electric shocks ranging from mild to fairly strong, and every single person said pain occurred at exactly the same point. Yet obviously people do not *react* to pain in the same way and there are times when a pain which you once bore easily becomes too much to take and you cannot stand it any more. Toothache that you can cope with when you are busy and preoccupied can be absolutely shattering when you go to bed, lie down and try to sleep. So you cannot judge the degree of pain by how an individual reacts.

People may see a pain producing stimulus as a test of their power to *endure* pain, and so may not be ready to admit to being hurt. In the Sudan, for instance, a young man who cannot bear pain loses social esteem and is unlikely to find a girl to marry him. As in many cultures, the ability to bear pain stoically is part of a code of values.

In every society there are cultural stress points, situations which are seen as threatening and thus predispose people to feel pain. When we know what makes people anxious in a particular society, we can begin to understand these stress points. In many societies some painful stimuli are linked with pleasure. Take lovemaking for example: slightly painful stimulation may be deliberately sought because it is sexually exciting.

The context within which pain occurs is important. As an experiment*, electric shocks were given to test people first when they were feeling relaxed and cheerful, and then when they had been made anxious. The electric shocks were felt as much less painful when the subjects were feeling cheerful. In another study*, as many as 35 per cent of a doctor's patients experienced marked pain relief when given a placebo, an inactive substance which they believed was a painkiller. It has also been found that the degree of pain tolerated bears a direct relation to the rate of increase in pain, rather than to the level of pain reached.* A person experiencing a pain stimulus that gets worse rapidly feels it more than someone experiencing just as strong a stimulus, but one which takes a longer period to reach the same point.

This may have particular relevance to very rapid labor, especially an induced labor (see page 252), when the pace is more than a woman can cope with. We sometimes talk about labor as if a long labor were difficult and a short one easy. This is far from being the case. Speed alone can give no indication at all of how a woman experiences her labor.

Pain perception always involves not only a recording of the stimulus by the brain, but judgment as to its importance, its precise significance, and its place in the scheme of things—the meaning of the total situation in which the stimulus occurs. Labor pain, like all other pain, is a function of the whole person, and we can go even farther than that and say that the experience of pain in labor is profoundly influenced by the values of the society in which the woman grew up.

So labor pain is partly a product of personal and social values about the meaning of childbirth. The way we eat, sleep, empty our bowels, make love, have babies and die makes them more than simple biological acts. They all express ideas, for the most part shared, about good and evil, beauty and ugliness, the pure and the polluting, what is healthy and what diseased, and what normal and what abnormal.

Pain relief in other cultures

There are two myths about the ways in which women in the Third World give birth. One maintains that labor is always horrific and dangerous, but that women do not cry out because of strong taboos against showing that they are in pain. The other suggests that the women all have completely painless births, and just squat down in the fields and have their babies before getting back to work again. The truth is probably in between. In many Third World countries healthy women have straightforward labors. Other malnourished women suffer a great deal.

Most cultures have methods of relieving pain in childbirth, so there is obvious recognition that it exists. But the ways in which pain is relieved and labor made more comfortable are radically different in the technological Western countries. We can give complete relief of pain and remove all sensation from the waist down with regional anesthesia. This is what a spinal does (see page 242). We have other forms of pain relief which partially remove pain or which eradicate the memory of it. We rely on pharmacological substances to do this for us. Herbal medicines are used in the Third World and some of them have narcotic or mood changing properties, just like modern drugs, though it is much more difficult to prepare the right dose when you are using plants. There are also other kinds of help which are much favored in these countries and which used to be employed in the West but tend to be ignored in hospitals today. They include religious and magic rites, different kinds of counter stimulation, massage, hot and cold compresses, changes in position, and emotional support from others sharing the experience with the woman in labor. These supporters hold her, stroke her, rock her back and forth, and live through the birth *with* her rather than do things *to* her as a patient.

Much of what is done by birth attendants in other cultures is meant to provide simple, practical help based on the handed-down experiences of generations of women. It is also intended to have a psychosomatic effect, helping the baby to be born by influencing the mind of the woman in labor. This practical and psychosomatic help in labor may be forgotten or not understood in our modern hospitals. Yet there are advantages in being able to cope without drugs if possible, because all powerful drugs have side effects and they all go through the mother's bloodstream to her baby.

Imagining your labor in advance

In preparing for birth it is a good idea to work out how you might like to be helped to be more comfortable and also how you can use your mind to help your body through relaxation, focused concentration and ideas and mental images that produce a pattern and harmony between what is going on inside your uterus and the way you think about it. This may be difficult to conceptualize before you have a baby.

Trying to master your body or running away from the sensations you are experiencing can actually produce pain, because you are bound to become tense and then chemical messages are sent instantaneously into your bloodstream which affect your whole metabolism. This causes changes in blood pressure and heart rate, breathing, sweating and skin, digestion and defecation, and also causes involuntary contraction of the pelvic floor muscles. Psychosomatic factors can even change the action of the uterus itself in ways we do not yet fully understand. A woman who is very anxious may have a long labor because her uterus does not work efficiently or stops contracting altogether.

What labor feels like

In a normal labor any pain experienced is quite different from the pain of breaking a leg or being injured. The physical feelings produced by a strongly contracting uterus are powerful and challenging. They are likely to involve a combination of sensations, a very tight squeeze, a pulling open of tissues and the firm downward pressure of the solid ball of the baby's head through a passage which is being slowly stretched wide.

In films you sometimes see a pregnant woman suddenly double up, her hands clasped over the top of her abdomen. The director is telling viewers that labor has started. But it *never* happens like this in reality. Instead there is likely to be a sensation of being gripped by tightening muscles low down in your abdomen or in the small of your back. All the sensations are at hip level. Nor is the feeling a sudden one. It has a wavelike shape, building up to a crest and then subsiding and disappearing until the next contraction. There is always a rest period between each. As contractions get stronger, longer and closer together the tightening may extend right round your body, so that it feels more like a circle of thick, wide elastic across your pelvis which is being steadily drawn in, held firm, and then slowly released again. Or you may be conscious of expansion during contractions and be most aware of the top of the uterus spreading and rising, tilting forward in your abdomen, while the great muscle squeezes its lower part open and presses the baby down.

"Pain with a purpose" The feelings that this produces may be painful, but it is pain with a purpose and different from the pain of injury. Contractions are not painful in themselves, and in fact the uterus contracts strongly and rhythmically at intervals in the second half of pregnancy usually without causing any pain. It is the peak of the contraction, when the muscle is working hardest and is making most progress, that is most likely to be perceived as painful, and this may last as long as 30 seconds or as little as 15 seconds.

The idea of a pain that is *qualitatively* different from other kinds of pain is difficult to accept for anyone who has not experienced it. Yet sheer physical effort, like that involved in running a race or climbing a mountain, produces just that kind of "functional" pain, the ache of muscles that are working very hard. If the athlete thought only of pain instead of about winning the race, she would give up. If the mountaineer thought that her aching muscles were the sign of some dreadful physical injury instead of the natural result of working them so hard, she would forget all about her goal and lose the feeling of triumph when she reached the summit.

Pain in labor is the byproduct of the body's creative activity. Contractions are *not* pains. They are tightenings which may be painful, especially when they are being most effective. There is an art in approaching each new contraction, thinking "Splendid! Here's another one!" and later, as you approach the end of the first stage, when they are at their biggest, "Oh, this is a really good one!"

When you are in the thick of labor, your whole self is involved. It is almost impossible to think about other things or to hold a part of yourself back in any way. The intensity of labor can be frightening, especially for the unprepared woman who does not know what to expect, or for one who wants to keep it all at the level of a learned skill, doing her exercises in much the same way as she might carry out a three point turn in a driving test. This is why preparation merely for handling contractions is never enough. You also need to prepare yourself mentally and emotionally for the overwhelming nature of the sensations and feelings of labor.

Drugs for pain relief in labor

There is a variety of pain relieving drugs available, and different drugs suit different women. It is important to understand what can be used and how each type works so that you can make your own informed decision as to whether you want the help of a drug, and if so which kind.

All drugs for pain relief in labor, whether given by injection or inhaled, pass through the mother's bloodstream to the baby. They all affect the baby—some more than others. None of them actually does the baby any good. When you are considering whether or not to accept drugs in labor, bear in mind also that some forms of anesthesia and analgesia can interfere with your first meeting with the baby and subsequent bonding.

Tranquilizers and analgesics

Tranquilizers are used to relax you if you are anxious and tense and also to lower your blood pressure. Given intramuscularly, tranquilizers take effect in 15 minutes; taken by mouth they are effective in 30 minutes. If taken during labor, tranquilizers tend to make the baby limp and floppy at birth, and probably also slow to suck. They interfere with the newborn's temperature control, too.

They are sometimes used in combination with analgesics, Demerol for example (see below), to increase their effectiveness, though some obstetricians are critical of this practise.

Valium The effects of diazepam (Valium) last half an hour to four hours and pass rapidly to the baby. The manufacturers of Valium report that it reduces the woman's recall of labor and delivery and that in 70 per cent of cases complete amnesia occurs. Twelve per cent of women cannot even remember whether they have had a boy or a girl.*

Valium, when given to the mother in labor, is known to change the pattern of the baby's heart rate.

Demerol The most widely used drug used for analgesia (taking the edge off pain) in labor is a narcotic, Demerol. It is usually given by intramuscular injection in doses of 50 to 150 mg. It takes effect in 15 minutes and lasts for two to four hours. Some women like it and say it helped them cope with difficult contractions by making them feel relaxed and slightly drunk. Others hate the effects of Demerol and call it "stupefying" and say they were woozy and out of control.

A fairly common side effect of Demerol is nausea. One or two women out of every ten vomit when they are given Demerol. It is sometimes combined with an antihistamine to prevent sickness, but this tends to make you even sleepier.

❝ I felt very woozy and out of control. I didn't really know what I was doing after I had it. I couldn't concentrate on my breathing or remember what I had learned in classes. And I was just overwhelmed by the pain, but helpless to do anything about it. Never again. **❞**

Large amounts of Demerol are present in the baby if this is injected within five hours before delivery, and especially in the three hour period before delivery. When it is given intravenously the concentration of Demerol in the baby's cord blood is only slightly below that in the mother's bloodstream. Demerol can cause breathing difficulties in the newborn, who may then need to be given oxygen at delivery.

Other side effects of Demerol and similar narcotic analgesics include emotional depression, lowered rates of respiration and heartbeat, nausea and vomiting.

Gas anesthetics Inhalant anesthetics such as nitrous oxide (laughing gas) and halothane are often offered for the actual delivery. This leads women to believe that the birth of the baby entails excruciating pain. It is a shame to have gone all the way through labor only to be "put out" for the most rewarding part, the culmination of nine months' waiting. Not only does the mother miss her baby's first cry but she may remain too sleepy and disoriented to be with her baby and breastfeed right after the birth. Other possible side effects include respiratory depression, hemorrhage, irregular heart rate, nausea and vomiting. Babies born under a heavy dose of anesthesia may have difficulty breathing and adjusting to life outside the uterus.

"Twilight sleep" A combination of a tranquilizer, an analgesic and an amnesiac is known as "twilight sleep". Many women have described it as "twilight nightmare" because of its side effects. The usual amnesiac scopolamine (also known as "scope" or "the bomb") can cause total disorientation which may not end when the labor ends, thus its nightmarish quality. It is supposed to make women forget their labor but, in fact, most women report hazy memories of having felt like an animal howling in pain.

It is sensible to remember that no drug has been proven safe for the fetus: labor is soon over but the damage that overmedication can cause lasts a long time afterward.

Local anesthetics Local anesthetics can also cross the placenta but they are least likely to affect the baby when they are injected into the area around the vagina and the perineum. This is done before an episiotomy (see page 250) and before a forceps delivery (see page 260) if other anesthesia has not been given.

When local anesthetics are used to bathe nerves that cover a large area of the body, they are usually referred to as *regional* anesthetics.

Paracervical block is a series of injections of local anesthetic around the cervix. It affects the baby immediately and in three out of ten babies the heartbeat becomes slower (a condition known as bradycardia)*. Some babies have died as a result. Paracervical block is becoming less common for this reason.

Spinal anesthesia is given by injection into the cerebrospinal fluid in the lower back. Its effect is to numb the woman from waist to knees. It takes about five minutes to work. If you have a spinal you have to lie flat for around eight hours after delivery to avoid a postspinal headache and should be careful not to lift your head quickly. Spinals are considered dangerous because blood pressure drops and hence the oxygen supply to the baby is reduced, progress slows down and a forceps delivery is usually necessary. However, they give good pain relief.

Pudendal block is an injection numbing the nerves in the perineum given just before or at full dilatation. It is often given before an episiotomy.

Epidural anesthesia is injected into the space between part of the spinal cord and the dura, the outer membrane around the spinal cord. Additional injections can be given through a fine plastic tube which is left in place after the first injection. This is preferable to another injection, as an epidural takes about half an hour to set up. An epidural may be given with you sitting up and curled forward or lying on your left side.

HAVING AN EPIDURAL
It is important to make your back as convex as possible when you are being given an epidural so that the vertebrae are spread out. This makes it easier for the anasthesiologist to insert the needle between the bones. You must, of course, stay completely still while this is being done.

❝ Nearly every mom in this hospital has an epidural; anyway they wire you up to things and do so many things to you that I thought, well, at least I won't feel all that. I mean, they might have forgotten that I *could* feel if everyone else couldn't. ❞

An epidural can provide complete relief from pain and can even be used as an anesthetic for a Cesarean section. It removes sensation from the waist down, or sometimes from your navel down, either completely or partially, while allowing you to remain conscious and to see what is happening if you want to. It is a great advantage in obstetric anesthesia. For a painful labor which is difficult or prolonged it seems the perfect answer. Many women have said how marvelous the epidural was, but it should be your own choice. Some hospitals give epidurals to all first time mothers, unless there is no time to give one.

Epidurals do not always work. It may be difficult to inject into the right place or the anesthetic may take on one side only, so that you get the odd lopsided feeling of contractions occurring in half your body, which can be disconcerting.

The anesthetic used is similar to that used by dentists, and you feel it like liquid ice numbing your tummy, bottom and legs. Even though it only anesthetizes part of you, it must be given by a skilled anasthesiologist and under sterile conditions.

An epidural lowers blood pressure, sometimes drastically, so that other drugs have to be given to raise your blood pressure again. Because of this effect, an epidural is sometimes given to a woman whose blood pressure is high, even though she may not be having a painful labor. In one study 39 per cent of women having epidurals experienced hypotension, though it did not last longer than one hour. The proportion went up to 47 per cent when women were also receiving an oxytocin intravenous drip (see page 253)*. When your blood pressure suddenly drops, you feel sick and faint and may vomit. This sudden lowering of blood pressure and the reduction in the amount of blood coming from your heart affects the baby too, since the oxygen bearing blood supply is pumping more weakly and slowly through the placenta.

Having an epidural may mean that a whole train of other procedures is started which you did not bargain for. Because you have no feeling in your bladder, it will need to be emptied by catheter. Because you may not feel any urge to push, the obstetrician may rotate the fetal head with forceps or manually.*

Since there is an increased chance of having a forceps delivery once an epidural has been given, it is a good idea to let the anesthetic wear off as you reach the very end of the first stage and to refuse more. On the other hand, if you have not felt first stage contractions at all and have to cope with the long strong ones near full dilatation, the experience can be an overpowering one.

The epidural anesthetic passes into the baby within ten minutes and studies are still being carried out on the possible effects of an epidural on the baby.* Some studies suggest that the baby becomes nervous and jittery while others show that it is very drowsy after delivery,* but this may vary according to what drug is used.

Caudal A caudal is like an epidural, except that it is injected into the epidural space around the sacrum and only blocks that area rather than the larger area blocked by an epidural. A greater dose of anesthetic is necessary with a caudal, and a caudal is usually given for short term pain relief to a woman having a very difficult second stage.

Dura
Epidural space Spinal cord
Catheter Vertebrae

Syringe

If you have an epidural a needle containing a catheter is inserted between the vertebrae into the epidural space and then withdrawn; the catheter is left in place in case more is needed.

Hypnosis A method of pain relief that is effective for some women is hypnosis. This has the great advantage over chemical anesthetics in that it cannot reduce the baby's oxygen intake. In fact, about a quarter of women having had hypnosis in childbirth say that they experienced no pain, but results do vary and most women who have hypnosis need chemical pain relief as well.

The common belief that hypnosis involves some kind of magic trickery and that you can be made to do anything the hypnotist wishes is very inaccurate. Hypnosis is simply a state of increased suggestibility and you can prepare yourself with a good practitioner so that you can, if you wish, use autohypnosis, making the suggestions yourself.

People who are able to go into a deep trance are completely immune to pain while in the trance and can have a forceps delivery or be stitched up after an episiotomy without a local anesthetic. It has been calculated that two out of every hundred women can go into such a deep trance that they could even have a Cesarean section without feeling any pain.*

If you agree to have hypnosis in childbirth you are usually trained in progressive relaxation to remove anxiety, and taught to think positively about the joy of childbirth. If you want to do autohypnosis, the hypnotist will suggest that you can put yourself to sleep and wake up when you wish. After the birth the doctor will suggest that you will in future only be hypnotized by a medical person for a therapeutic purpose, so that you need not be afraid of being put into a trance by anyone using hypnosis for their own purposes or for fun.

It may be that all good prenatal classes teach an element of autohypnosis, though prenatal teachers would not usually like to admit this. Yet in many ways thinking ahead to labor constructively, when one is deeply relaxed, is using the power of suggestion. Whether or not you decide to try hypnosis, you can use autosuggestion and anticipatory fantasies about labor and the baby in a creative way to prepare yourself for childbirth, knowing that this is the safest analgesia of all.

The future of drugs in childbirth

Hospitals should provide an environment and the kind of personal care in which every woman is free to accept or reject painrelieving drugs as and when she wishes. Whatever drugs are given to you in labor, your consent should always be obtained beforehand.

Fear, anxiety, loneliness and feeling you are part of a factory for producing babies all increase the experience of pain. Understanding what is happening inside you and what is being done to help you and your baby, knowing what you can do to help yourself, feeling you are among friends and having someone you love with you all make pain much more easily bearable. If you do decide you need painrelieving drugs, they will be most effective if they are given when you are in a calm state of mind.

Modern obstetric anesthesia, used only when necessary, is fairly safe for the baby, but one consultant anesthetist, warns that "numerous questions about the effects of drugs given to the mother on mother-baby interaction and future child development require an answer"* and stresses that long term studies should be carried out to assess exactly what risks are being taken. For the present this still remains a largely unexplored field of research.

Toward the medical control of birth

You have the right to decide what happens to your body before, during and after childbirth. You are not bound, either in law or out of politeness, to agree to procedures and investigations which you are unwilling to accept. If things are done for which your consent has not been obtained it is a form of assault. Your consent is implied when you are forewarned about some kind of obstetric intervention and concur by remaining silent.

You are also entitled to be given full information about anything that is being done to you and your baby, can reasonably expect to be able to ask questions about it and to be given honest answers. If you do not ask questions, professionals may take it for granted that you do not want to know any more and even that to offer further information might make you uncomfortable.

Your right to choose

In all medical procedures it is a question of carefully balancing the relative risks of a policy of intervention on the one hand and a policy of "wait and see" on the other. To be able to make an informed choice you may value the counsel of skilled professionals, but ultimately *you* make the decision. This applies both to *where* you have your baby and *how* you have your baby. If you want natural childbirth, go all out to get it. Plan for it, prepare yourself for it and do everything you can to create the right setting for it to take place. But also be flexible so that if something in your physical condition or that of your baby indicates that modern technology can be used with advantage you do not miss out on its undoubted benefits even if this means that the birth is less "natural"

A woman having a baby has responsibilities as well as rights. One of the most important of these is the responsibility to give the baby the best possible start in life. Some obstetricians believe that whenever a machine or a procedure is available which permits greater medical control of childbirth it ought to be used. An equally valid view is that one should be selective in the use of modern technology, employing it where indicated, but bearing in mind that birth is also, inevitably, a psychological experience which affects the relationship between mother, father and baby perhaps for a long time after.

The best environment for birth

The highest quality childbirth and the best welcome into life must include emotional as well as medical aspects of birth. If you accept medical help, it does not follow that you give up concern about the psychological dimensions of the experience. Technology need not, and should not, be permitted to ruin a woman's personal experience of childbirth.

When machines are used *in place of* warm and friendly human relations they seem to take over. But when they take second place to emotional support and encouragement and you feel free to reach your own decisions about how much aid to accept, they can be a useful adjunct to good nursing care, especially when the risk to a baby is higher than usual.

Many couples can bear witness to ways in which sophisticated modern apparatus made them feel more secure in childbirth and was used to help rather than hinder. But for this to happen the environment provided for birth has to be a very special one and all those coming into contact with the expectant parents need to be able to give of themselves and not only their technical skills. For it is only in such a setting that there can be trust, honesty and self confidence.

The growing use of technology Obstetricians are discovering new ways of controlling a process which 20 years ago was left to nature. Many now say "Why stand by watching and only intervene when something goes wrong?" and believe that instead labor should be regulated from start to finish. To do this effectively they need to be able to monitor exactly what is going on in the uterus and what is happening to the fetus at every second and to intervene at any point to ensure that cervical dilatation, the strength of contractions and the biochemical state of mother and fetus conform to a predetermined norm. This is called *active management of labor**. Such a policy is only made possible because of the development of a sophisticated technology of obstetrics.

Many inventions are appearing on the market which obstetricians, quick to seize an opportunity to reduce the perinatal mortality rate, want to buy for their units. Some women hate this intrusion of machinery into what they feel should be a natural process and question its benefits for the labor and the baby. Others feel security in knowing that labor is controlled by the obstetrician with all his machinery, like knowing exactly when the birthday will be and are relieved to know that labor will not last longer than 12 hours at the most. In some hospitals the love affair with technology is gradually giving way to a new concern about the quality of human relations. Yet many doctors and midwives still have no idea how the setting for birth can be humanized.

Common procedures in labor

When you arrive in hospital, you may be given an amniotomy, linked to a fetal monitor and hooked up to an intravenous drip. During the second stage, an episiotomy may be performed to hasten delivery. Some women experience many kinds of intervention during the course of their labors and unless you specifically tell the obstetrician or midwife that you do not want your labor controlled in this way there is a chance that you will have at least one of them during your labor.

Artificial rupture of the membranes

Artificial rupture of the membranes (ARM for short) or amniotomy has come to be accepted as a normal routine in most hospitals and is often performed as part of the "prepping" done after you are admitted. The membranes surrounding the fetus are punctured with a small tool like a crochet hook through the open cervix. Routine amniotomy is now open to question, however. When the membranes are allowed to rupture spontaneously, they tend to do so towards the end of the first stage of labor.* In 12 per cent of women the membranes remain intact right through to delivery. Some membranes rupture spontaneously when the midwife or doctor touches them during a vaginal examination.

Since there are no nerve endings in the membranes their rupture is not painful. All you feel is a gush of warm liquid. Be prepared for contractions to increase in intensity after this has happened. ARM can speed up labor if the membranes have not ruptured spontaneously by the end of the first stage, since the baby's head is pressing harder against the cervix once the cushion of fluid has gone, and this produces a rush of oxytocin in your system which triggers off stronger contractions.

RUPTURE OF THE MEMBRANES
Spontaneous rupture of the membranes usually indicates that the cervix is starting to open. The baby's head then presses right against the cervix and contractions are intensified. This may also happen after artificial rupture of the membranes.

Membranes intact   Membranes ruptured

Reasons for amniotomy

Besides being a part of induction, rupturing the membranes also allows the obstetrician to assess the state of the amniotic fluid. When a fetus is in distress it passes meconium, the first contents of the bowels, into the water, which is easily seen in the fluid released. Many obstetricians believe that amniotomy is important to assess the condition of the baby. Once it has been done, it is possible to insert an electrode in the baby's scalp so that its heart can be recorded throughout labor (see page 257); amniotomy is often done for this reason.

The risks of routine amniotomy

Pressure on the cord Intact membranes protect the baby's head. The amniotic fluid equalizes pressure on the head and amniotomy takes away the cushion of water in which the fetus lies, so exposing its head to the direct effect of contractions. Rupture of the membranes also gives rise to the possibility of pressure on the cord which may hinder the flow of blood through it. It is not rare for a baby to have the cord round its neck, though this does not matter at all if the membranes are intact. It is these babies with the cord round their necks who are most vulnerable to pressure on the cord. It has also been suggested

247

that once the amniotic fluid has gone, the fetal surface of the placenta is compressed, which may reduce the flow of blood to and from the baby.*

Pelvic infection Amniotomy introduces the possibility of pelvic infection.* Since infection is more likely if labor is allowed to continue for more than 24 hours after amniotomy, operative delivery may be necessary if the baby has not been delivered naturally by that time.

Deceleration of the baby's heartbeat Some studies have demonstrated that after amniotomy there are more early decelerations in the baby's heartbeat. These early decelerations come at the start of a contraction and the heart is back to normal by the end of the contraction. The slowing down is slight, by less than 40 beats a minute. Many obstetricians consider this innocuous and quite normal.* Because babies born after amniotomy have been demonstrated to be in good condition, with high Apgar scores (see page 280), some obstetricians have concluded that the procedure does not subject the fetus to any special stress during labor.

Head molding Some obstetricians are concerned about head molding and disalignment of the cranial bones, which may be increased after amniotomy. There is some disagreement about this but, either way, the molding of the baby's head gradually disappears during the first week or two of life and is not a permanent feature.

So amniotomy raises many questions which have not yet been adequately answered. It is a subject that you may want to discuss with your obstetrician. You have a right to be fully informed. You can, if you wish, request that amniotomy be done not as a routine but only if the baby is showing signs of distress.

The intravenous drip

In many American hospitals an IV, or intravenous drip, is set up for every woman in labor. A fine catheter (hollow tube) is introduced into a vein in your arm or hand and fixed with adhesive tape so that fluids can be infused straight into your bloodstream. The argument for setting up an IV is that once a vein is open emergency action can be taken rapidly and your strength can be kept up without your eating and sometimes even drinking anything. This means that if a Cesarean section is necessary (see page 262) and general anesthetic is used, your stomach is likely to be almost empty already and there is not a great deal of risk that you will regurgitate or inhale the contents of your stomach.

Glucose may be given through an IV to act as a "pick-me-up" in labor. Since it bypasses the stomach you do not have to digest it. Glucose is useful if labor is long and tiring and you are becoming dehydrated, or if lactic acid builds up in the course of a difficult labor, causing acetone to appear in the urine. Often, however, it is unnecessary.

If you have an IV set up, it is especially important to remember to empty your bladder regularly: every hour is not too frequent. You will be accumulating fluid and should urinate frequently to stop urine building up in your bladder.

Once an IV is set up, other substances can be introduced by the same route. This may be done without your consenting to or even being aware of the administration of drugs. If you have an intravenous infusion and the bag or bottle is changed, ask what it is. Your partner will be able to get close enough to read the label. Oxytocin is introduced by this means. The label may read "pitocin". You can read more about this in the section below on induced labor.

You need not consent to an intravenous drip unless you are confident that there are good reasons for it. It is yet another way in which women are sometimes made needlessly uncomfortable in labor. It can be very useful when needed, but used routinely merely makes it difficult for you to move. In most hospitals where intravenous drips are used routinely it is taken for granted that the woman in labor stays in bed.

Episiotomy

An episiotomy is a surgical cut made to enlarge the birth opening. It is done with scissors just before the baby is born. It can be midline (down from the bottom of the vagina toward the anus) or mediolateral (sloping out to the side; away from the anus, or down and then out in the shape of a hockey stick). Occasionally an episiotomy is done each side, for example when a breech baby with a large head is being born. This is known as a bilateral episiotomy.

Since the incision is made through both skin and muscles, careful repair of the wound must be done afterwards. The local anesthetic given before the episiotomy was performed is usually enough for the repair. If not, more can be given. The suturing is done with a curved needle and may take an hour or more. The stitches can be left in as they are the kind that dissolve. Episiotomy is increasingly performed in American hospitals and in some it is done on almost 100 per cent of mothers. You are more likely to have an episiotomy with your first baby than with subsequent babies.

HAVING AN EPISIOTOMY
An episiotomy is usually done as the baby's head crowns and between contractions. The local anesthetic, combined with the numbing effect of the baby's head pressing against the perineum, means that the cut is rarely felt.

Here the two most common incisions are shown.

Midline
Mediolateral

Being linked to a monitor does not mean that you have to do without support . . .

Reasons for episiotomy

Some obstetricians believe that all primigravidas should have an episiotomy to relieve strain on their tissues and to get the baby delivered quickly. If the baby is showing signs of fetal distress an episiotomy can speed delivery and make birth easier for the baby. You may be told that it is a good idea to have an episiotomy because "a straight, clean cut is better than a messy, jagged tear" which is also more difficult for the obstetrician to sew up. Sometimes episiotomy is done to save tissues inside the vagina when there is evidence of "buttonhole" tearing (that is, a series of very tiny lacerations deep inside the perineum).

Problems with episiotomy

Research studies on episiotomy are few and far between and where they have been done suggest that a first degree tear (that is, a surface one) heals better and more comfortably than an episiotomy. If done too early—before the perineum has thinned out—it can cause you unnecessary bleeding and sometimes the cut is much larger than the tear would have been. Sometimes a woman would not have torn in any case. Many women say they feel terribly uncomfortable when making love for several months after having an episiotomy. Quite often the stitches get infected too and antibiotics are necessary.

Managing the third stage

A now widely accepted method of controlling the third stage of labor, the expulsion of the placenta, is to give an intramuscular injection of oxytocin after the delivery of the shoulder nearest your front (the anterior shoulder). The placenta then usually separates from the lining of the uterus with the next contraction and is expelled within five minutes of the birth.

However, if the placenta does *not* separate completely after the injection, it can be trapped by the powerfully contracting uterus. So attendants very often clamp and cut the cord as soon as the baby is born and then press a hand on the top of the uterus, pulling on the cord at the same time.

If the placenta is left to separate naturally, it may take half an hour or more. Clamping of the cord immediately at delivery may make a retained placenta more likely. If the cord is not clamped until after it has stopped pulsating there is much less chance of a retained placenta and postpartum hemorrhage. This may be because when the cord is clamped blood cannot flow out of it, so encouraging the placenta to be peeled away from the uterine wall. Instead the placenta stays firm and full.

If the third stage is allowed to proceed naturally, your first physical contact with your baby produces a rush of emotion that is accompanied by the release of oxytocin. This *natural* oxytocin keeps the uterus firm and causes further contractions. Once the placenta has separated the midwife gently places flat hands over your lower tummy, just above the pubic bone, and you push against the hands, so delivering the placenta and membranes. It is often a help to have a hand to push against like this. The alternative is to squat over a bowl or pail and to deliver it with gravity to help.

CONTROLLED CORD TRACTION
After the birth of your baby, your uterus continues to contract strongly to expel the placenta. You can help to push the placenta out, once it has peeled off the wall of the uterus, by pushing against the doctor's or midwife's hand placed against your lower abdomen, while he or she gently pulls on the cord with the other hand.

There is no reason for a cord to be clamped before the placenta has been delivered except for convenience, in the rare cases when the cord is so short that it is impossible for the mother to hold her baby unless it is cut first, or when it is twisted in a succession of loops around the baby's neck at delivery and so is cut to enable the baby to slide out. In fact, if a woman is Rhesus negative and her baby is Rhesus positive (see page 99) there is a strong case for delayed cord clamping. If the cord is clamped before it has stopped pulsating, the flow of Rhesus positive blood back into the mother's circulation increases.

Induced labor

6 6 It was fantastic! I really enjoyed myself. I would choose to be induced again... 9 9

Induction is the medical way of starting off labor, and keeping it going. When labor begins naturally, the uterus becomes sensitive to hormones present in your bloodstream at the end of pregnancy. When labor is induced the doctor tries to obtain a similar result by flooding your system with hormones, until they reach a level much higher than that which occurs naturally. This can be done by introducing synthetic oxytocin hormones into your bloodstream, through a continuous intravenous drip, or by inserting prostaglandin pessaries into your vagina. Both these methods are usually combined with artificial rupture of the membranes.

Induction procedures

At present a great deal of research into these methods is taking place in hospitals. Remember that you have the right to receive full details of what is going to be done and why, *before* being admitted to the hospital for induction, and you can choose to accept or refuse it once you know the facts.

Artificial rupture of the membranes (see page 247) may be performed as a means of induction if you are near your due date. Most obstetricians believe that, once the membranes are ruptured, the baby ought to be born within 24 hours, especially if there have been many vaginal examinations, because there is some risk of infection if labor is a long drawn out one. So you need to be aware that if your labor is started by ARM, but is slow to get going, it may then have to be accelerated.

Prostaglandin pessaries A new way of inducing labor is to use pessaries of prostaglandin gel which are introduced into the cervix. If the gel is inserted during the evening, labor may have started by the following morning. In fact, it may be unnecessary to have amniotomy and an oxytocin drip as well, and prostaglandin gel has the great advantage of allowing you freedom to move about in labor.

Oxytocin drip If induction involves being connected to an oxytocin IV, ask if the syringe can be introduced into the arm or the hand you use least. If the connecting tube is short, you cannot easily move your arm or change position without dislodging it, but there is no need for it to be short, and you can ask for it to be securely fixed so that you can still change position. Many women have discovered that when they are in labor they get backache simply from lying in one position for too long, quite apart from the backache that is often a result of contractions. A glucose solution is often passed through the IV first. The drip can be turned down or even stopped once 5 cm dilatation of the cervix has been reached. It is usually kept in until after the end of the third stage since it can control bleeding from the uterus by keeping it contracting hard.

Why induction may help Induction is an invaluable obstetric technique when a baby must be born without delay. Many doctors believe that between 15 and 25 per cent of women and their babies benefit from either induction or acceleration of labor. Some believe that these figures are too high, while others again that 60 per cent or more of labors ought to be induced. If you have symptoms of pre-eclampsia (see page 121), including high blood pressure, albumin in the urine, sudden excessive weight gain, and edema (puffiness resulting from fluid retention), this is a good reason for induction, since the baby may not continue to be well nourished inside your uterus if the pregnancy is allowed to go on. If you have had a previous forceps delivery because a baby was a tight fit, inducing the next baby before it is at term may allow you to give birth more easily.

Induction before the EDD Some babies stop growing because the placenta, through which they receive nourishment and oxygen, is not working well at the end of pregnancy, even before there is any question of being "overdue", and even though the mothers may be feeling fit. Such babies may do better outside the uterus.

During an induced labor, it is important that your partner is with you all the time to help you with breathing and relaxation as you adjust to the sudden, sometimes overwhelming, contractions.

Induction after the EDD If you are 42 weeks pregnant and your baby is known to be overdue, there is a chance of the placenta not functioning so well because it is aging. However, *premature babies are most at risk,* so the obstetrician needs to be sure that the baby really is overdue before inducing it. Some doctors make it a rule to induce if you are more than a week overdue, others like all their patients to deliver at about term and bring you into hospital if you are a few days past your date. Tests can be done to find out whether the placenta is working efficiently (see page 194).

The length of induced labors Although you may have a rapid labor with induction, this cannot be guaranteed. Some obstetricians prefer labors not to last longer than ten, eight or even five hours and deliver with forceps or by Cesarean section if labor is longer than they believe it should be. Since there is so much variation, it may be a good idea when discussing the possibility of induction with the doctor to ask what his or her practise is. Depending on whether or not you want a short, sharp labor, this may affect your decision about whether to agree to induction if it is not urgently necessary for your baby's sake.

Possible problems Induction is a form of intervention which, while extremely useful when really necessary, is not without risk, and in coming to a decision the relative risks of leaving the baby inside your uterus and inducing labor have to be assessed.

Unripe cervix It has been stated that "the major factor governing the success of induction is the state of the cervix."* When the cervix feels soft—like your lips when you hold your mouth slack—then it is ripe and ready for labor. Unfortunately, induction is often done before the cervix is ripe, and in consequence the uterus may not respond vigorously to the hormones. If the membranes have been ruptured, then the only way to get the baby born is by Cesarean section.

Powerful contractions If, however, the uterus is triggered to work harder, labor is more violent than it would be if it started naturally. In an induced labor there are often two "peaks" to each contraction, and each may last one minute or longer. Women who have had babies before, and whose previous labors were not induced, say that contractions start more powerfully and that there is not much lead up to each contraction, but instead a sudden "explosion". There may be only a short interval between them; just time to let out one relaxing breath and then you are into the next one! You may find you need to go straight into the breathing techniques corresponding to the ones you will have learned for about half dilatation (see page 174).

Interrupted blood flow Extremely powerful contractions are likely to interfere with the blood flow through the uterus and so cause fetal distress. In one study it was discovered that fetal distress was significantly more common in women having oxytocin, that the babies were more likely to have low Apgar scores (see page 280), and that far more babies went to the nursery to have special care.*

So it is important to have expert assistance if you are being induced and essential for the baby's heart to be continuously monitored. If you experience a contraction that lasts longer than 90 seconds, let the obstetrician know immediately. Even with a small dose of oxytocin some women have a prolonged contraction in which the uterus clamps down on itself—and on the baby. There is no test by which the sensitivity of your uterus to oxytocin can be known beforehand, so it is best to start with a small dose and gradually build up until good contractions result. The aim should be to simulate normal labor.

Accelerated labor Labor is said to have been accelerated (or augmented) when it has already started and then, for some reason, has been speeded up by the use of an oxytocin drip. If a drip is used *before* the cervix has started to dilate progressively, even though you have felt contractions and have had a "false labor" or many Braxton Hicks contractions, you are being induced, not accelerated.

Labor may be accelerated when there is uterine inertia or incoordination, that is, when the uterus is not working effectively (see page 225). Some of the most difficult labors are long ones, and if you are becoming tired out with back pain for example, acceleration may help you cope.

If it looks as if labor ought to be induced or accelerated, there are breathing skills you can use to deal with the challenge. These are described in detail on page 174. You need not give up, feeling that the doctors have taken over.

Induction with epidural anesthesia

In some hospitals you may be offered a "package deal" of induction combined with spinal or epidural anesthesia. (For more about these see page 242.) Women who accept the package deal offered know that labor will take place on a certain day and that complete pain relief will be available. This new style of childbirth is attractive to many obstetricians and to many women too.

As with any intravenous drip, if you are receiving a large quantity of fluid, you should remember to empty your bladder regularly. If you cannot pass urine (and you usually cannot if you have had an epidural) the nurse will insert a catheter and draw off the urine for you. A full bladder makes contractions painful and slows up labor by acting as a barrier between the baby's head and the base that forms the front of your pelvic arch.

Elective induction

Elective induction, also called induction for convenience, is induction that has no medical benefit.

Some doctors believe that most women should be induced. Some think it is the only way in which *all* labors can be efficiently managed. They say it is important for women to be in labor when staff are on duty, that hospital organization is easier when it is known how many women will be in labor each day, and that it is better if women are not in labor at night.

There will always be those women who go into labor spontaneously at inconvenient times, but the earlier they are induced the less this is likely to happen. So some obstetricians believe that induction any time after 38 or 39 weeks is right for most women. The logical development of this approach to obstetrics is that spontaneous labors will be considered "emergencies" and the "normal" labors will all be induced.

The Federal Drug Administration has, after considering the research, withdrawn approval for the use of oxytocin for the elective induction of labor, asserting that it can be dangerous for both mother and baby, but there has been no notable decline in its use.

Coping with induction

While there are basic questions that women need to ask about induction and acceleration of labor in terms of our whole style of childbirth in the West, these may not seem very relevant if your doctor advises you that your labor should be induced. It may come as a shock. You may even feel that all your careful preparation for birth is pointless now.

Many women have enjoyed induced labors and coped with them well. But unfortunately many whose labors were induced say that they did not have any choice and that they are given inadequate information. Yet the British Department of

Health and Social Security has stated: "A mother should have learned about induction at antenatal classes and if later it appears that induction would be the safer course of action for her, she should have every opportunity of discussing it with professional advisers. Knowing what is likely to be involved, she can make a fully informed decision about it."

A woman has a legal right to be informed of all decisions made about her care and the care of her baby. Many hospitals in the US have adopted a "Patients' Bill of Rights" which specifically deals with this right of "informed consent" and other rights. It is important to remember that you have the legal right to refuse any drug, test, procedure, or treatment. Before giving your consent you should understand the risks and benefits of the proposed procedure and you should be able to give your consent only after you have weighed the relative importance of the risks and benefits.

The important thing is to ask questions. Do not wait and hope that the obstetrician will explain things to you. Discuss it all fully, learn about what happens and share in the decision-making rather than feeling it is all being decided for you. When you have the facts and your obstetrician's advice, take time to weigh it and choose what seems to be the best way, but always leaving your mind open to new evidence which may later point to a different course of action. It is your baby and your body and the experts are there to help you.

Electronic fetal monitoring

The electronic fetal monitor is used to track the fetal heartbeat and to record the pressure of the uterus during contractions. Either a transducer is placed over your abdomen near the baby's heart (external monitoring) or an electrode is inserted through the opening cervix and clipped to the baby's scalp (internal monitoring). A printout, which is usually in the form of a continuous graph on a long spool of tape rather like ticker tape,

ELECTRONIC FETAL MONITOR
The monitor is usually near the bed and you can see when the next contraction is starting even before you feel it, and can get ready to meet it with your breathing. On the right of the monitor is a print out which shows the fetal heart-beat on the left and contractions on the right.

shows the baby's heart rate in relation to the work done by the uterus. The monitor is a compact box which can amplify the baby's heartbeat so that it becomes clearly audible. It incorporates a flashing light which also registers the baby's heart, but this can be turned off. If anything goes wrong it sounds an alarm, though this often indicates something wrong with the machine rather than with the baby.

The external monitor An external monitor has two straps which are attached to your abdomen. One strap holds the tochodynamometer (a pressure gauge to record contractions), the other holds a transducer which registers the baby's heartbeats.

The internal monitor The internal monitor, which is more accurate, is inserted through your vagina and cervix and fixed to the skin of the baby's head. It is connected to a catheter leading to the machine and another catheter is inserted into the uterus to record the pressure of contractions or you may wear a single strap around your abdomen to hold the tochodynamometer. An internal monitor cannot be used until the membranes have ruptured spontaneously or have been ruptured artificially, and until the cervix is dilated at least 1 or 2 cm.

Advantages of monitoring The monitor is particularly useful in high risk pregnancies and when labor is induced or augmented with an oxytocin drip, since the length, power and frequency of the contractions produced by the drip must be carefully watched and their effect on the baby observed lest they prove too stressful for it. Until recently induction was often done "blind", and enormous, turbulent contractions were produced which sometimes cut off the fetal blood supply. This is much less likely nowadays since, by monitoring all these artificially aided births, it has been discovered that small amounts of oxytocin are effective.

Another undoubted advantage of monitoring is that the monitor indicates when the next contraction is beginning, so that, however drowsy you are feeling during labor, you can breathe out and relax, and get ready to breathe over it.

Problems of monitoring Many women say that the abdominal strapping for the external monitor is very uncomfortable. Some even say that the pressure of the transducer on their tummies was the most painful thing about labor. Sometimes the internal electrode slips off the baby's head or, if an external monitor is being used, the baby moves and its heartbeat is lost. Some new external monitors have transducers which track the position of the baby's heart so that they do not lose it in this way.

As with an intravenous drip, having an external monitor means that you must remain more or less in one position lest the transducer slips off. As we have seen this immobility means discomfort for you (page 250) and possibly problems for the baby. So monitoring may actually sometimes produce the failing fetal heart rate which it then records. If you are being monitored, turn on your side before the monitor is put on, although even this position can become uncomfortable after a while.

Some women in labor are wired up to the monitor only to find that nothing is being recorded at all because the machine is not operating. It is very irritating to be immobilized and connected to a machine when it cannot possibly be doing anything to help. Yet staff sometimes appear shocked at a woman's request for the transducer to be detached so that she can move about and get on with her labor unhindered. If this happens to you, you are entirely justified in being insistent. But when the monitor is working well many women find it reassuring to know that every heartbeat of the baby is being recorded.

Telemetry Monitoring by telemetry (radio waves) is an advance on the older method and allows you to be up and about in labor unattached to wires but continuously monitored at the same time. The equipment is less cumbersome and the machinery can be placed at some distance from you. Most women prefer it, labors seem to go faster and babies do better. Because you are able to be upright, you may feel less pain, and the uterus can work more efficiently, producing stronger contractions.

But even monitoring by telemetry still needs to be invasive to be really accurate, as an electrode has to be clipped to the baby's scalp. Any invasive technique (one which entails entering your body) introduces added risk of infection. This is a risk worth taking when there is a reason to suspect the baby is encountering difficulties, but *not*, many people would think, when everything seems to be straightforward.

Though we cannot be certain, it is possible that a scalp electrode causes the baby some pain. (It is uncomfortable to prick your finger with one.) It remains on the baby's head till after delivery. In 85 per cent of newborn babies a rash appears at the site of the electrode and in 20 per cent a small abscess develops.* Sometimes the child is left with a permanent bald patch.

Interpreting the data Although it is estimated that the fetal monitor enables an obstetrician to save one life for every 1000 babies monitored, the interpretation of data is of first importance. The machine by itself can do nothing to make childbirth safer. It is only too easy to interpret normal variations in the fetal heart as pathological, sometimes because of the design of the machine, or to miss out on clinical signs that something is wrong because the monitor indicates that everything is normal. Obstetricians and midwives experienced in auscultating the fetal heart and assessing clinical conditions have a skill which is being neglected today as more and more confidence is put in electronic machines.

In four out of every 12 babies there are some irregularities of heartbeat during labor, and usually this is of no significance. The baby's heart rate is usually between 120 and 160 beats per minute. A quicker rate than this is termed tachycardia, and a slower rate bradycardia. Incomplete understanding of the normal range of variation in the fetal heart rate during and between contractions leads to more forceps deliveries and Cesarean sections being performed, and the introduction of the monitor in a hospital is associated with sharply increased rates of operative delivery, though these often drop after a while.

Testing the baby's blood Some obstetricians believe that the baby's blood should be tested to confirm the findings when the monitor's reading suggests fetal distress, since, if the baby is in difficulty , this always shows up in the blood chemistry. This extra check could cut down the number of unnecessary Cesarean deliveries. A new type of electrode is being developed which both records the baby's heart rate and tests its blood.

Helping the baby out

In most hospitals about one woman in every four or five is delivered by forceps, though the rate is higher in some hospitals.

Forceps delivery Forceps look like metal salad servers and dovetail into each other so that they cannot press too far in on the baby's head. If the woman has not already had an epidural an injection to numb the birth outlet is given first. The curved blades are inserted one at a time and cradled around the baby's head, one at each temple. Forceps are of different shapes for different situations: most bring the baby down the birth canal though some are simply used to lift the baby out. If the baby's head is occipito transverse or occipito posterior (see page 218), the obstetrician may first turn the head manually or may use curved Kielland forceps for the delivery to rotate the head from the transverse or posterior to the anterior.

Vacuum extraction Sometimes a vacuum extractor is used instead of forceps. This works like a miniature vacuum cleaner to suck the baby out. A vacuum cup is attached to the baby's head. It may take between 10 and 20 minutes to be applied. During this time if you want to push, push. Once the cup is on, it helps if you can bear down, pressing the baby down from above as well as it being pulled by the suction applied from below.

Reasons for forceps or vacuum delivery Forceps or vacuum extraction is used when delivery needs to be hastened because your blood pressure has risen dramatically, for example, or because there are signs of fetal distress, or when the baby is in an unusual position, making its journey through the pelvic outlet more difficult. The obstetrician has to use clinical judgment to decide whether this particular baby will pop out like a cork from a bottle given a firm, long pull or whether it is so firmly wedged that it might harm both the baby and you to deliver vaginally. Sometimes after forceps have failed a Cesarean section is performed (see page 262).

HELP WITH DELIVERY
These forceps (right) are the kind used simply for lifting the baby's head out of the birth canal. Vacuum extraction (far right) can sometimes avoid a difficult forceps delivery, and the suction cup may be attached to the baby before it has started to descend the birth canal.

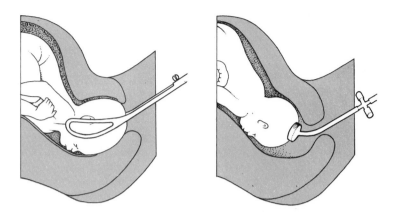

Forceps may also be used if you have had an epidural (see page 242), as you may still feel too numb to work with contractions.

A forceps delivery is frequently advised if you are having a prolonged second stage. Different obstetricians have different ideas of what a prolonged second stage is. Some would say that it is any second stage of longer than half an hour in which there are no signs of progress. Many set a definite time limit on the second stage and instruct nurses to call them when it looks as if this stage is extending. Some believe that this is rather doctrinaire and that the important thing is to observe whether or not the baby is coming down the birth canal progressively, while checking its condition carefully and regularly.

Some women seem to be able to cope with long second stages without tiring whereas others quickly become exhausted. If you have already had a long labor and then a slow second stage it is difficult to retain enthusiasm and, unless given a great deal of encouragement, you might hope that someone would just come and take the baby out of your body one way or another.

Sometimes a woman may be given too much encouragement to push or is persuaded to hold her breath too long, when she does not feel any spontaneous urge to bear down. This is because the nurse knows that the delivery will be by forceps unless the baby is born within the time decreed by the obstetrician, so hopes that getting the mother to push more strenuously will help the baby to be born before the deadline comes.

Avoiding a forceps delivery

If you have been struggling to push the baby out and it is suggested that forceps may be necessary either because the second stage is taking too long, you are becoming too tired, or the fetal heart rate is slow, explore the effect of *not pushing*. You may find that you do not need to push at all for several contractions—a welcome rest for both you and the baby—and then there is an unmistakable and irresistible pushing sensation which is much more effective than pushing just because you are following instructions. It is a good idea to stand, squat or kneel so that gravity can help the baby out.

261

66 The doctor gave me an internal exam and said, "It's not dilating any more–I'll have to do a C-section on you." And I remember saying, "Oh no, I don't want to have a C-section!" I was so emotionally involved in this whole process that it was like robbery. 99

Cesarean section

If the obstetrician tells you that you need to give birth by Cesarean section, this means that you will be anesthetized and your baby will then be delivered abdominally rather than vaginally.

The most common reason for Cesarean section is cephalopelvic disproportion, when the baby's head is too large to pass through the pelvis. Some obstetricians prefer to deliver abdominally all breech babies, or all breech babies of first time mothers, because they believe it is safer for the baby. But size of the baby in relation to the maternal pelvis and the way the baby is lying are factors which should also be taken into account. If fetal distress is picked up by an electronic monitor and the obstetrician becomes anxious about the state of the baby, he or she may decide to do an emergency Cesarean section. Abdominal delivery may also be performed for twins, or when it has been discovered by amniocentesis that a baby is damaged, for very low birthweight babies and on women suffering from diseases such as diabetes, renal disease and chronic hypertension.

The rise in Cesarean births

Cesarean rates vary, but make up between 10 and 15 per cent of all births. Cesarean section is more commonly done in the USA and Canada, where in some hospitals 25 per cent or more of all babies are delivered abdominally.

Where in the past the obstetrician would have corrected a baby's bad position by external version through the mother's abdominal wall (see page 192), the tendency now is to deliver by section rather than attempting to turn the baby first. As a result many doctors nowadays no longer know *how* to perform external version.

More and more women are now being included in the category of "high risk". The age at which a woman is considered obstetrically high risk went down from 40 to 35, then to 30, and now in some hospitals anyone over 27 is included in this category. If you are over 27 and it seems likely that there may be problems with your labor, you may find that you are advised to deliver by Cesarean section.

Throughout North America it is also the practise to do *repeat* Cesarean sections even when the conditions which resulted in the first section are not present in a subsequent pregnancy: "Once a Cesarean, always a Cesarean." American doctors argue that the uterine scar might break open during a subsequent labor, but British obstetricians differ. They normally use a "trial" of labor, allowing the labor to proceed naturally but being ready to do a Cesarean if necessary. One British professor of obstetrics says that problems of scar separation are "much less than the one per cent that is often quoted" and that even if the scar is pulled open by strong contractions "careful monitoring of the fetus and mother usually means that any harm to either is rare".*

The classic Cesarean incision is vertical. Though still used in emergencies, the horizontal incision ("bikini cut") is now more common, mainly for cosmetic reasons.

Planned Cesarean section The decision to perform a Cesarean section is often made days or weeks in advance. A section will usually be planned if it is known that the baby is in a difficult position to be delivered vaginally, or if there is evidence of cephalopelvic disproportion. The baby must be delivered abdominally if the placenta is lying at the bottom of the uterus in front of the baby's presenting part (placenta previa). Surgery is either arranged for the 39th week or in some cases you are allowed to go into labor naturally, knowing that a Cesarean section will be performed.

Emergency Cesarean section Some of the reasons for a planned Cesarean section (such as cephalopelvic disproportion) may also apply to an emergency section, when they have not been obvious until labor. An emergency section may also be decided on during a long labor in which no progress is being made, if you have severe preeclampsia (see page 121), if the placenta has failed to service the baby or if it is detaching itself from the lining of the uterus causing antepartum hemorrhage (see page 120).

Anesthesia for Cesarean section Cesarean section has traditionally been performed with the patient under general anesthetic, but epidural anesthesia (see page 242) is becoming more common for this operation. Though general anesthesia has to be used when a very quick decision is made to do a section, those women who have had epidural anesthesia usually like being awake and aware of what is going on and being ready to welcome the baby as soon as it is lifted out.

General anesthesia If general anesthesia is used, you are given as small a dose as possible for the baby's sake, and you may be unconscious for only a few minutes. All the preparation for the operation is done while you are awake and you are often given pure oxygen to breathe in during this time. It should be possible to arrange for the baby who is in good condition to be held by the father while you are unconscious.

Epidural anesthesia You are given the epidural after being taken to the operating room—the dosage is larger for this surgery than it would be if an epidural were being given just for pain relief. An anesthetist checks carefully to see that the anesthesia is sufficient for the operation and is ready with general anesthesia should the epidural not take effectively. There is no postoperative nausea and vomiting as there often is with general anesthesia. An epidural is also safer for you because you cannot inhale your stomach contents and safer for the baby, who does not receive a knock out dose of anesthesia.

Horizontal or vertical incision Incisions for Cesarean section are either horizontal or vertical. The classical incision is vertical but is rarely done now unless there is no time to spare. The main advantages of the horizontal incision are that it is done low down near the line of the pubic hair, in the area which would be covered by a bikini, and that a horizontal scar is less likely to break down than a vertical scar.

What happens during a Cesarean section

66 I felt no pain. I could feel the skin incision like a finger being run over my abdomen. When the uterus was cut open it felt rather as if somebody was rummaging in a chest of drawers. 99

66 They told us it was a girl so I thought she'd been born and asked if she was all right. "Have a look" they said and pushed the screen down to show us her spindly little legs sticking out from my body. A few seconds later out came her head and I felt wonderful. I don't think I've ever enjoyed anything so much in my life. 99

Before you have a Cesarean section a nurse will shave off your pubic hair and slip a catheter into your bladder so that it is kept empty. In the operating room sterile drapes are put around your tummy and if you are going to be awake a screen is erected at about waist level so that you do not see the surgery. Your tummy is washed in antiseptic solution. If there is anything you want to know, ask.

You will be given an epidural or general anesthetic. When your whole tummy is numb or you have become unconscious, a small cut is made through the lower abdominal wall below your navel to reveal the lower uterine segment. Packs of surgical gauze are pressed in to keep other organs out of the way. A horizontal slit is made through the muscle and the bag of waters bulges through it. The obstetrician pops the bag and sucks out the amniotic fluid—if you have had an epidural, you may hear the glug-glug-swoosh sound—and uses one blade of the forceps or a hand under the baby's presenting part to ease it out of the small opening, at the same time pressing with one hand on the upper part of the uterus so that the baby is pressed down through the incision.

If you have had an epidural, it may be possible for you to watch the birth at this stage. Ask the doctor to put the screen down for a few moments. You will see your baby emerging and, from your horizontal position, will not see anything gruesome. In fact you will only have eyes for your baby and will not think about the surgery that has been done. The baby is lifted out, suctioned with a mucus catheter, and once it is breathing well can be handed to you or your partner. The whole birth process from the beginning of surgery need take only about four minutes.

As the baby is being delivered you may be given an injection of oxytocin to make the placenta peel away from the wall of the uterus. It will then be lifted out through the abdominal opening that has been made. The obstetrician then stitches the cut in the uterus, layer by layer. Suction instruments are used to draw out blood and amniotic fluid, and then the obstetrician repairs the abdominal wall.

Having your partner with you

66 It was Joanna, our prenatal teacher, who convinced us not just to accept the word of a doctor who said "No, husbands cannot be present at a Cesarean birth." 99

Not all couples want to be together during surgery. You may worry that perhaps it will be too much for your partner to cope with or he may expect to find it so distressing that he will be unable to give you any support. Those who do want to be together do so because they feel that the birth of a baby, by whatever route, is something they want to share, that it should be family centered, and that, if the mother is not able to cuddle the newborn baby, the father should be there to do so.

If you do want to be together and your Cesarean is planned try getting to know your obstetrician well in advance. Once you have built up a relationship, ask if your partner can be with you at the birth. If the answer is no, ask politely for the doctor's reasons. If it is not normal practice at that hospital, you may convince the doctor that you are both concerned enough to want to be the first couple to experience a Cesarean birth together there. There is always a first time. If your partner is present, he is up by your head supporting you emotionally and does not need to watch the operation, since the screen restricts his view.

After the delivery

After the operation say you want to see your baby if he or she is not already beside you. An intravenous drip is left in for some hours so that you can be given plenty of fluids straight into your bloodstream if necessary. If you had general anesthesia, you may feel sick and weak for the first day or so. As soon as you feel you can move around in bed a little, do so. Even wiggling your toes and rotating your ankles is good and prevents pooling of blood in your legs.

Whatever anesthesia you have had, the chances are that the nurses will help you get up later the same day. Though it hurts, moving around is important to avoid thrombosis. To move off the bed, work your way to the side of it, pressing your buttocks together and taking some of the weight of your body on your hands. As you get up you may have a lot of bleeding from the vagina. This also happens after a vaginal delivery and it is simply the blood that has pooled in your pelvic region while you were lying still. Stroll around the room to encourage good circulation and use the slow, complete breathing you learned in classes.

Drugs for pain relief are available and if you feel you need them ask for them. Though you probably want to be awake to enjoy your baby you cannot really do this if you are in severe discomfort. The more your partner can be with you, even while you doze, the more you can relax, feeling that the baby is being looked after by someone who loves her.

Dressings will probably be removed three or four days later. Because the obstetrician has had to cut through muscle, your tummy will look very big and soggy. Once the dressings are off you will be able to have a bath. The stitches inside your body dissolve naturally, but the external stitches will be removed towards the end of the first week. Do not worry about them bursting open—with every layer stitched separately there is little chance of any such damage occurring.

After general anesthesia fluid collects in the lungs and has to be coughed up. A nurse will teach you how to do this so that it causes least discomfort. The breathing you learned in pregnancy can help you too.

It is natural to feel a flood of conflicting emotions after Cesarean birth. Some women say they are grateful to have the baby but at the same time feel "cheated".

A Cesarean birth is a surgical operation and you need time to recover from it as from any abdominal surgery. For the first six weeks after the birth you should avoid any heavy lifting. If it is possible to arrange for extra help at home, especially if you already have a toddler who expects to be lifted, it is an enormous benefit to have someone else to do the more strenuous work.

Still damp from birth, the gently delivered baby is alert to learn about the world . .

Gentle birth

At birth eyes open for the first time on a new world. Your baby's life outside your body begins. Yet your baby already has nine months' experience of life inside the uterus. The ancient Chinese dated life from conception rather than from delivery and perhaps this corresponds more nearly to reality. The baby started off as the chance collision of a ripe egg and a sperm. Forces which have their origin far back in creation long before this tiny speck of being had even the possibility of separate existence poured energy into the cells, nourishing and multiplying them to make an embryo budding on a stalk and drawing sustenance from your uterus. Gradually as the days passed a fully formed being developed, albeit in miniature, and there was already at the third month a fetus whose main task was one of growth and maturation. As week followed week its senses became sharper so that it was increasingly aware of its surroundings, responding to your movements, and to bright light, loud sounds and music. This long drawn out period of preparation culminates in the dramatic journey into the brilliance and bustle of our own world outside the uterus.

What is it like to be born?

Birth is an intense experience not only for you: for the baby, too, it is the climax of a time of growing and waiting. The new human being is caught up in a rush of powerful uterine activity, which squeezes it out from the confines of the tight muscle firmly enveloping its body and the cradle of bone in which it has been rocked, into a separate existence.

Traveling from the depths of the uterus, under the arch of bone and out through the soft, opening folds of the vagina, the baby passes through a barrage of different kinds of sensory stimulation. It is the original magical mystery tour and must be more astonishing and full of surprises than any tunnel of love traveled through in search of excitement in a fairground.

The baby's experience of labor — Pressure builds up over the crown of the baby's head where it is directed through the dilating cervix, which is pulled up over its head like a turtle neck sweater. Pressure is also directed over the baby's buttocks as the uterus contracts down on them and propels the baby forward. So the baby is fixed between the uterus gripping its bottom and the cervix being progressively drawn over its head. This pressure causes the baby to roll up into a neat ball, head tucked in and knees bent up, arms folded over its chest. The upper part of the head, not yet hard bone all over, is firmly molded so that the brow is pressed backward.

As the baby is forced downward the crown of the head also confronts resistance from the pelvic floor muscles, which are springy and firm and which are also gradually eased over its head. The passage is narrow but yielding and the baby's whole body is massaged vigorously with each contraction as it slowly descends.

Beneath the stretched abdominal skin and the thinned translucent wall of the uterus itself the baby in the last weeks of pregnancy has been aware of glowing light whenever bright sun or artificial light shone on your body. It must be rather like firelight or the light cast by a red shaded lamp. When the journey to birth begins, the baby is pressed deeper into the cavity of the pelvis, under arches of bone and a canopy of thick supportive ligaments and muscles. Perhaps it is a sensation rather like traveling through a long, dark avenue of overhanging trees.

The baby is not just a hunk of flesh or a lifesized doll. It is a human being fully equipped to feel pain and pleasure, a *person* coming to birth. The baby cannot remember or anticipate in the same way that we can, but it nevertheless feels keenly and is a fully sentient being. The uterus holds and presses tightly in on the child not yet born, with steadily escalating power. By the end of the first stage of labor it is embracing the baby tightly for one or two minutes at a time. Each hug begins gently and grows tighter and tighter till at the height of the contractions the baby is being gripped fast for 20 to 30 seconds. Then the wave of pressure recedes again and the baby floats once more in its inner sea: it is in labor along with you.

Newborn reflexes used in labor

In some obstetric textbooks the fetus is described simply as "a passenger", and purely in mechanical terms, as two ovoids, the head and the trunk, the long axes of which are at right angles to each other and which can take the curve of the pelvic axis independently. While this is accurate as a description of the mechanics of fetal descent, it leaves out any mention of what the baby might be doing during this process and how the reflexes with which it is born and which are unmistakable after delivery are probably also functioning during labor.

The baby changes its position in response to the power unleashed in your body, and does this not only because of mechanical forces which act on it but probably also because it is making active movements. It is working *with* you toward birth, your partner in the struggle, not just a passenger, and can do this because of inbuilt reflexes (see page 281). A newborn baby turns his head in the direction of a touch, moves his head up and down against a firm surface, curls his toes down when pressure is applied to the ball of the foot, lifts his foot up and puts it down at a higher level when pressure is applied over the top of the foot, and makes forward stepping movements when tilted forward with his feet against a firm surface. Two of these actions probably operate to help the baby onward in its journey. One is the reflex to move its head up and down against firm resistance, which means that it actually wriggles its way forward through the cervix and the fanned out tissues of the vagina with much the same action that we make when putting on a new sweater with a rather tight neck. The other is the stepping movement when resistance is offered to the feet, so that in effect the baby pushes away from the solid wall of the uterus as it tightens around it.

The impact of the outside world

In the second stage the head has to take nearly a right angled bend. The pressure builds up until it swivels the neck around so that the baby is facing downward ready to slide out. You can imagine that this provides a very sharp stimulus to the baby, a message which says unmistakably "Things are changing. Wake up! It's all systems go!" At last the crown of the head oozes through the vagina and remains there. Perhaps you reach down with eager hands to stroke the damp, warm top of your baby's head. This is the first greeting.

The head slips out and suddenly the baby encounters space and air. The shoulders and chest slide forward, followed by the whole body. There is a gasp and air rushes into the lungs, inflating them for the first time. The damp inner surfaces of the lungs, previously clinging together like wet plastic bags, open up with the first cry with which the baby meets life.

Air, space, the baby's own limbs moving in an unfamiliar medium, weight, strange sounds, glaring lights, cold hands picking the baby up, turning it over—all at once a myriad of new sensations assails the newborn. Not only must lungs fill with air and start to function rhythmically for a lifetime, but the circulation must find new pathways.

Labor as a stimulus

In his book *Birth Without Violence**, Dr Frederick Leboyer calls the mother "a monster" because of the pain he believes she cannot help but inflict on the baby as it passes through the throes of birth. But the process of being born can also be seen to involve stimulation and awakening for which the baby is ready and which prepares it for life. Looked at from this point of view, muscles hold and embrace the baby, triggering powerful sensations, then soften again in a rhythmic pattern. The space between contractions is like the trough between two waves. Inevitably the next wave comes and again the muscles tighten firmly around the child.

Though labor is undoubtedly traumatic for some babies, others look extraordinarily peaceful and contented after delivery. It may feel to you as if you are swimming in a stormy sea when you reach the end of the first stage of labor. You may be anxious that these massive squeezings of the great muscle of the uterus are causing your baby suffering. Yet in spite of the relentless onslaught of contractions as full dilatation approaches, the baby who is pressed through the cervix and down the birth canal in this way responds more vigorously to life than most babies do who are merely lifted out through an abdominal incision. You might think that Cesarean section would be easier for the baby, but the 9 in (23 cm) journey squeezes out fluid and mucus from its nose and mouth so that the baby born vaginally has less mucus in its respiratory tract than one delivered by Cesarean section and is better prepared for the great new activity of breathing.

Welcoming your baby Have you thought about how you want to welcome your baby into the world? Frederick Leboyer believes that just as our attention has now been drawn to the mother's experience of birth, so we must focus on the baby's needs and learn how to reduce its suffering. For him this is not just a matter of safe or speedy delivery, a question of making sure that the baby has enough oxygen or is not traumatized by delivery, but one of greeting the baby with consideration and gentleness.

Most babies cry at the shock of birth and this first cry insures that a rush of air enters the lungs. But if they *go on* crying Leboyer asserts that there is something wrong. The crying of abandonment and distress is quite different from the healthy crying of the newborn, yet people often take persistent crying for granted and even smile indulgently and say, "He's got a fine pair of lungs!" or "She'll grow up to be a singer". The newborn baby continues to scream because of insensitivity to her needs and the lack of a sufficiently caring environment. If the setting for birth is changed and, above all, if the attitudes of those assisting are different, so that the baby is treated with respect, Leboyer says, the child will become quiet, will open her eyes, will reach out with her hands and start to discover herself. But if this is to happen the birth room must be calm and hushed, the lights dimmed and those handling the baby must do so slowly, carefully and lovingly. This is *gentle birth*.

Creating a caring environment

Gentle birth need not start only as the baby is born. In the way that labor is conducted and in the whole atmosphere of the labor room an environment of peace and serenity can be created. Though Dr Leboyer is concerned with what is done to the baby *after delivery*, a mother and baby are so close and in such a subtle and yet intense relationship that everything done to you during labor must affect the way in which you are able to respond to your newborn baby. If you are treated as if your body is merely the container from which a baby is removed, or as an irresponsible child who has to be given orders, you will find it very difficult to be in harmony with the forces which are bringing the baby to birth, with your own body in its work of creation and also with the baby. The caring environment for the newborn starts with a caring environment for you, a respect for your rhythms, patience to wait and watch and loving support.

Dimming the lights It is irritating for you to labor under bright lights, just as it is for the baby to confront brilliant fluorescent light at delivery. For a gentle birth all unnecessary lighting is switched off so that the room is softly illuminated, with a clear light only on the

Slowly, carefully, lovingly . . . sensitive handling is what your newborn needs most after the turbulent journey from womb to world. . . .

perineum. Instead of lying flat on your back or with your legs suspended in lithotomy stirrups you need to be in a position you find comfortable and in which you can be an active birthgiver. Many women like to be sitting up, crouching or kneeling so that they can catch the first glimpse of the baby's head and can put their fingers down to touch it even before it has started to emerge through the vagina. We have already seen (on page 205) that an upright position has many advantages for the mother in terms of mechanical function. If you are well raised you are also in a splendid position for greeting your baby.

When the head crowns, some women put their hands down to caress the top of the baby's head. It feels warm and firm and as it eases forward you touch more and more warm, damp, silk hair. This first contact between mother and child is beyond excitement; it is a moment of awe and for some women something close to spiritual ecstasy.

Then the head slides out and turns to align with the shoulders still inside and you can see your baby's profile; with a rush the shoulders and whole body are born. As the baby slips out and starts to breathe the lights can be dimmed further so that the baby can take its time to open its eyes in the half light. Many years ago Maria Montessori, the educator, stressed that babies are assaulted by bright light. She said that they should be able to begin the gradual exploration of the world with their senses in a soft glow and shadows, similar to the uterine environment they have just left. Yet in the past we have subjected newborns to harsh hospital lights and have acted as if they were unable to see or hear.

Reducing the noise level In nonviolent birth there is no unnecessary conversation and those attendants who speak do so in hushed voices. Leboyer believes that the mother should be quiet too and that excited voices can startle the baby. He thinks that there is too much emphasis nowadays on the father's presence in childbirth and that fathers sometimes get too emotional. Couples who value sharing birth together would not agree with him. I feel myself and know many women who also feel that it would not have been possible to go through labor and birth without the child's father there.

In fact couples often do cry out with astonishment and wonder when they see their baby leap into life and this is a spontaneous outpouring of emotion, an integral part of childbirth with joy, which *in itself* is a life enhancing experience for both parents. We don't work out carefully exactly what we are going to do when we are caught up in other sorts of peak experience, we don't weigh up the different factors and come up with a calculation: to do so would be to diminish the experience. Life is exultant and we are borne along with it. Birth is that kind of climactic process. It is an act of love, the continuation and culmination of the passion which started the development of that baby.

Physical contact

66 It was a forceps delivery. But the doctor took the forceps off after the head was born and said "Come on, deliver the rest of your baby yourself!" I reached down and lifted him up. And they dimmed the lights and he lay making sucking noises on my tummy. 99

It is because birth is a peak experience that arms reach out to take and hold the baby and draw it close. It is not just that this small, wrinkled, vulnerable baby is yours and that therefore you decide to take it in your arms (though unfortunately this is just how it is for some women in a loveless, uncaring environment); if the right atmosphere exists you are totally enveloped in a rush of intense feeling. This does not mean that the baby is neglected in an orgy of self indulgent emotion, as Dr Leboyer believes. The baby is drawn into the warm circle of love between the parents and becomes part of it. This is what it is for not only a baby to be born but also a *family*.

In nonviolent birth the baby is handled gently and slowly without haste. There are no rough, quick movements. He or she is delivered up onto your tummy or over your thigh. If you ask beforehand it is often possible to do this yourself and the midwife or doctor will remind you to reach out and draw the baby onto your body and against your skin.

The baby can be delivered straight onto your tummy for its first moments of life; there it is in direct contact with your warm skin and can also still hear the familiar, reassuring sound of your heart.

Frederick Leboyer believes that the baby should be lovingly and gently massaged until he or she stops crying and becomes calm. Only then does he think the baby is ready to go to the mother's arms. In his own obstetric practice he used to do this massaging. But many women think that this is yet one more way in which professionals, however caring, attempt to take over childbirth and to intrude on the mother's natural role. Wherever gentle birth is done today it is usually the mother who holds and caresses her baby. You do not have to learn how to massage your newborn. The way you explore and stroke it is spontaneous and right. But this is only possible if the baby is naked and in skin contact with you. Babies are often bundled up in wrappings in case they lose heat. It is true that new babies quickly become chilled unless they are in a warm atmosphere and are held close. Research now taking place shows that the baby, even the low birthweight baby, keeps warmer in flesh to flesh contact with his mother and nestling against her breast than the baby who is wrapped up and put in a crib. So ask a helper to slip your gown down over your shoulders or to take it right off before delivery.

A blanket can easily be thrown over you and your baby or a heater can be placed over both. Mothers often feel chilled and shaky after delivery and appreciate the warmth themselves.

If your baby is handed to you bundled up in a cloth, unwrap the covers and cuddle it close. Do not be afraid to talk to your baby. He or she will respond to the sound of your voice and will be especially sensitive to the higher pitched tone of a woman's voice.* The baby is also getting to know your unique scent and by the time she is a few days old will already prefer a cloth which has been against your body to one which has been close to another new mother's body.*

Delaying the clamping of the cord

Frederick Leboyer believes it is important to wait to clamp the cord until it has stopped pulsating. Midwives always used to wait, but nowadays the whole of birth is so often rushed that the cord is sometimes clamped and cut immediately while blood is still flowing. Even though this blood is not particularly well oxygenated—because the placenta begins to peel off the wall of the uterus as soon as delivery takes place—it is blood which really belongs to the baby. Unless there are reasons for clamping (such as a Rhesus negative mother who has already produced antibodies against her Rhesus positive baby—see page 99) it seems a good idea to wait a few minutes for the cord to become flaccid, when the baby has no further use for it. There is no reason why the cord has to be cut at all until after the placenta is delivered and it is separated only for convenience.

You can rest your fingers on the cord to feel the blood throbbing through it and wait for the moment when it stops completely. Cutting the cord between two clamps is a very simple procedure and something which a father may enjoy doing. If you would like to do this, ask in advance to see if it is at all possible.

Some obstetricians are concerned that blood could drain back into the placenta and the baby even become short of blood if it is placed above the placenta with the cord still unclamped. This is not a good reason for early clamping or for refusing to place the baby against your body. The baby can be rested over your thigh, where it will be below the placenta and you can easily see and touch it if you are well propped up. If the baby is held with its head tilted lower than its bottom mucus drains out naturally, though a mucus extractor will also be used.

Waiting for the rooting reflex

Your baby may emerge from your body already wanting to suck. But many babies are not quite ready and need time to feel secure before they reach out to find the nipple. The rooting reflex (see page 281) is a sure sign that the baby is ready to be put to the breast. It is better to wait until the baby shows interest than to stuff your breast into his or her mouth.

Leboyer believes that mothers often try to feed before the baby is ready and that then even breastfeeding can be another assault on the newborn. Many women today are anxious to feed immediately after delivery and perhaps their anxiety to do this in an alien environment, and one which they may even feel is hostile, makes them rush things. Be patient if you can. Let the baby rest against your bare breast and in his own time he will start to explore with mouth, hands and eyes. This time is precious for you and your baby. It cannot be speeded up without interfering with spontaneous, natural rhythms. After a while the baby will probably begin to lick your nipple and then will seek it and, with a little help as you lift your breast into its searching mouth, will latch on.

The Leboyer bath

An important part of the Leboyer style of birth is the warm bath in which the baby is supported shortly after delivery and in Leboyer's own film this is given even before the mother holds her baby. Leboyer believes that the baby needs time to feel safe again in the medium which it has just left in the uterus—water, and that suspended in a bath the baby becomes peaceful and sometimes positively beatific, discovers itself and starts to open its eyes and explore the world around. It is true that some babies seem to enjoy the bath very much, but only if it is done slowly and calmly and if the water is deep enough for the baby to float. The ideal way of giving a bath is to use a deep container with a thermal lining (such as a picnic ice chest) and to have an air heater over the bath.

You may find that the hospital where you are having your baby does not allow a bath because of the risk of hypothermia (chilling). Unfortunately cold air ventilation ducts have been incorporated into the design of many modern maternity units and the baby in water or exposed to this air is likely to get chilled. Many hospital pediatricians are concerned that the baby can lose a great deal of body heat while wet or in a bath, through evaporation, and say that if it is done at all it should be done speedily, which defeats its purpose. You obviously cannot add hot water to a bath when the baby is in it and you know yourself how shivery you feel when you get out of a hot bath into a relatively cold atmosphere. It is much harder for the baby, who cannot shiver yet and whose largest area of heat loss is her big head, to keep warm.

The baby can maintain heat by using its body fat to create warmth, just like a hedgehog or any cold adapted hibernating animal, though a low birthweight baby does not have enough body fat to do this. Muscular activity and crying also help the baby keep warm, and a baby in a cool room will hyperventilate, though one with respiratory depression cannot do this. Another way in which heat loss is reduced is that blood vessels near the surface of the skin tighten up, so increasing tissue insulation, rather like double-glazing over the surface. But babies who have received some drugs from their mothers' bloodstreams, including

Demerol and Valium, are not only sedated but unable to prevent heat loss efficiently. So if you want the Leboyer bath to be given, bear in mind that you should not have had Demerol or Valium in the last five hours, that your baby should be full term, weigh more than $5\frac{1}{2}$ lb (2500 g) and should not have had breathing difficulties at delivery.

Parents are sometimes very doubtful about the advantages of the bath, preferring to be in skin contact with their baby and to let him or her suck at the breast indefinitely instead. If a baby is happy lying against his mother and ready to go to the breast after a little while it seems purely ritualistic to insist on putting him in a bath because of preconceived ideas about what babies *ought* to like and how they *ought* to behave.

One doctor* uses the bath, but with a difference. The baby goes first to the mother's arms and sucks if he is rooting; only then is he immersed in a bath, and instead of the doctor bathing the baby the father takes over this responsibility, but close enough to the mother so that she can see and touch too. It can be moving to watch a father doing this first service for his newborn child and to see them both looking for the first time into each other's eyes. A midwife described what happened in one case when a father bathed his baby in this way: "The baby, who had been resting quietly with its mother, gradually opening its eyes, now seemed to wake to its surroundings and gaze serenely around. It is this serenity which is so remarkable and such a joy to watch. The baby's body was totally immersed in the water, which kept it warm, and gave it total relaxation.

"After five to ten minutes a midwife took over and gently lifted the baby on to the warmed towel below the overhead heater. Not one cry while all this was going on, and all handling was done with an awareness that the baby had never been handled before and that its skin was acutely sensitive. There were no sudden jerks, movements, or pulling while the baby was being dressed. I now realize that the crying which so often accompanies these tasks is the result of sheer fright."*

In some births both parents give the Leboyer bath together and in a few home births the mother bathes with her baby in a well heated bathroom.

After the delivery

Gentle birth does not finish with the minutes after delivery. It is part of a continuum, a flow of interaction between you and your baby beginning in pregnancy and going on into the weeks following childbirth. It is not just a question of how the delivery is conducted or even whether you are able to hold your baby right away. It is a matter of creating an environment in which throughout the 24 hours you have free access to your baby, feel it yours and can act spontaneously. You need to know that everyone round you understands what you are feeling, and to be confident of emotional support as you learn to be parents and start to discover more about this unique being who has come into the world.

YOU AND YOUR NEWBORN

The first hours of life
The baby who needs special care
Losing a baby
The first ten days
The challenge of new parenthood

The first hours of life

The hours immediately following birth are for many women some of the most intense they experience in their lives. A peak experience like that of giving birth does not suddenly end after you have had half an hour holding the baby or terminate conveniently when the lights are turned out. After such a dramatic and exciting time it is not surprising that some women are unable to sleep for a while, and that many remain in a party spirit for hours or even days after.

Unfortunately many hospitals treat the time after birth as a time when, once clean and tidy, you should be quietly resting; if you are too excited to sleep you may be offered sleeping pills or tranquilizers. Most hospitals do not make provision for the continuity of passionate feeling which insures that motherhood becomes part of you as a person and is not just something which you are trying to learn. These overpowering emotions impel you through the interim period between the time when you feel you do not know anything about your baby and are meeting him or her as a stranger, and the moment when you realize you know *everything* about your baby and have become centered in this tiny new existence as much as you are in yourself.

Your first meeting with your newborn

You look down at this new little person, feel the weight of the body as he or she begins to relax after the struggle to birth. The head is the biggest part, the hair silken and perhaps still wet and curled in damp fronds or streaked back as if after a swim. Ears are tiny and carved like convoluted shells and the fingernails too are like the little pink shells you picked up from the sand when you were a child. If the baby is still crying the mouth looks huge, a most efficient organ capable of reaching out and grasping on to the breast for its essential nourishment. And the cry itself, a high pitched, almost animal wail, (though when the baby is sleepier it is more of a lamblike bleat) is well adapted to summon immediate attention, to drive you to find out what is wrong and how you can answer the baby's needs, and to be intensely anxious until you have stilled the crying. It is a biological mechanism of vital importance for survival.

As you hold the baby, the hands start to scan the air, encountering space, meeting the face, perhaps brushing against your body or hand. The fingers move and undulate like sea anemones. Though they seem aimless, they are starting on the important task of finding out about this new world.

If lights have been dimmed the baby will open wide eyes and look straight at you some time during this process of unfolding. It has been discovered that newborn babies find the human face the most attractive thing to look at, far more so than woolly bunnies or painted ducks, and the moving, speaking human face is best of all.

Testing the newborn

The diameter of the baby's head is measured . . .

. . . his weight recorded . . .

. . . length measured from head to foot . . .

. . . jaw and hips tested for dislocation . . .

. . . and his mouth for cleft palate. These are just some of the standard procedures which are done routinely to all new babies.

The experience of bonding

The Leboyer approach to childbirth focuses on the importance of the environment into which the baby is born and the attitude of all those handling the baby. This is important not only for the baby's sake but for yours too and for the relationship between you. There has been a great deal of research in different countries which demonstrates that it is far more difficult for a mother to feel her baby belongs to her and she to it—to *bond*— if she does not have a time immediately following birth to begin to get to know her baby.* An important element in this is naked skin contact. The baby should not be wrapped up and turned into a solid little package which you are allowed to hold but not to explore. Instead it should be delivered onto your naked body and you should be able to put the baby to the breast as soon as it is ready to suck.

Marshall Klaus and John Kennell*, working at a hospital in Cleveland, recommend that mothers should be able to hold their babies naked on the delivery bed and have undisturbed time to get to know them, and should then be encouraged to look after them themselves, with help available if they need it. They should have their babies with them and be completely responsible for them for at least five hours a day and be given ample emotional support from hospital staff.

Still in many hospitals the hours after birth are considered to be time in which you and your baby are medically processed, during which you must pass tests of fitness before being pronounced not "at risk" and discharged into society.

What tests are carried out?

As soon as the baby is born the midwife or doctor assesses the baby's condition and rates it according to something known as the Apgar scale. This is done by simple observation of the baby's breathing, skin color, muscle tone and general vitality. The highest number of marks is ten and most babies get seven or over. Once you have had a cuddle a further check is made on the baby. Many women say they like this checkup being done close beside them so that they can see what is happening and can discuss anything that they find worrying with the pediatrician. If the baby stays by your side and never leaves you this will happen as a matter of course.

The Apgar scale	What is tested	Points given		
Immediately after birth your baby is tested on five basic points; it is tested again when it is about five minutes old. Even babies who get low marks the first time usually score nine or ten when they are tested again.		**0**	**1**	**2**
	Heart rate	Absent	Below 100 beats per minute	100 beats per minute or more
	Breathing	Absent	Slow or irregular	Regular
	Skin color	Blue	Body pink, extremities blue	Pink all over
	Muscle tone	Limp	Some movements	Active movements
	Reflex response	Absent	Grimace only	Cry

Newborn reflexes
Babies are born with reflexes to help them adjust to life outside the uterus. The most important are the reflexes to breathe, suck and swallow, but some others are illustrated below.

The baby is born with a strong grasp reflex and will usually grip your finger tightly.

If the baby is handled abruptly or roughly the Moro or startle reflex will be seen. The baby throws up its arms and trembles.

The baby opens its mouth, often screws up one eye and turns its head. This is known as "rooting" for the nipple.

When you stand a newborn baby up it will make "stepping" movements.

The baby's weight and length are recorded. The depth of breathing is noted, whether or not his or her extremities are still blue, whether he or she responds vigorously to stimuli and seems strong and healthy. Certain specific things are looked for, too. These include the head size, a check that the genitals are normal and—in a boy—whether both testes are descended. If the baby has not already passed meconium, the anus is checked to insure that it is formed normally. And the baby's heart is listened to (auscultated). The upper part of the mouth is examined to insure that the palate is complete, and the legs are gently bent up and circled outwards to make sure that there is no dislocation of the hips. Gentle feeling of the baby's tummy will discover whether the liver and spleen are the right size and feeling around the top of the baby's head reveals the state of the skull bones. In many states it is the law that silver nitrate must be introduced into the baby's eyes.

Relating to your baby

Such tests are reassuring. But unfortunately sometimes the adjustment of mother and baby to each other is treated as of secondary importance to this process of medical screening. As a result many new mothers lack confidence in handling and relating to their babies. In our society it is almost as if women are *expected* to be unsure of themselves, awkward and readily depressed. In fact much of what is usually called "postnatal depression" probably results from a mother's inability to relate to her baby and feel comfortable as a mother because other people have taken over responsibility and it feels to her as if the baby belongs not to her, but the hospital.

It can be even more difficult for a man to feel that his baby belongs to him than it is for a woman. In one Stockholm maternity hospital men were shown how to handle, change, bathe and weigh their babies and were helped to understand the emotional and physical stresses of pregnancy and birth on their partners. This was done on two separate occasions while the women were on the postpartum ward. It was discovered that these fathers became more involved in baby care later on and that their partners thought they were more understanding than a control group of fathers who had not been given the chance to become involved with their babies in this way. Research shows that *both* parents need an unhurried and peaceful time with their baby in the hour following delivery.

How your baby may look

Your new baby may have a low, sloping forehead, a receding chin, hair in sideburns (low on the brow, in the nape of the neck and sometimes down the back as well), an odd, bumpy-shaped head which has been molded like a ripe grapefruit in its passage down the birth canal, a squashed boxer's nose and blotchy skin. Yet to most new parents their baby looks beautiful! You respond in a protective, caring way to the wonder of this new human being who has come out of the inner depths of your body, having been pressed and kneaded and squeezed out of the uterus and down the vagina to the outside world and into your waiting arms. The experience of meeting your newborn is unique and precious.

Even if you are unaware of feeling anything remarkable at the time, you will probably look back at those moments as being special, as you piece together the fragments of the birth experience and place it in its setting of life lived. This kind of reflection and thinking back is especially important after a difficult labor and probably comes spontaneously to most women if they allow themselves time and do not try to forget about what happened to them.

How the baby has had to adjust

Enormous changes occur as the baby adjusts to the challenges of an extrauterine existence. One of the most dramatic things that happens, though unseen, is the change from fetal to newborn circulation with the blood flowing along different pathways. When the baby is inside you, all blood flows in and out through the umbilical cord and bypasses the lungs which do not need to function (see page 65). And since the placenta is doing much of the work that will later have to be performed by the baby's liver and kidneys little blood needs to be carried to these organs in the intrauterine state.

At birth the first great gasp of air causes pressure changes in the whole circulatory system so that blood enters the lungs, liver and kidneys. The increased pressure in these organs brings about the collapse of the umbilical blood vessels and of the bypasses around lungs, liver and kidneys. Once these pressure changes have taken place the system goes on working for a lifetime and the blood vessels which are no longer used waste away.

Why your baby may look strange

Some babies are born without any covering of vernix; others are still quite thickly coated with it.

There are many things you may notice about your baby which can worry you. It helps to understand the wide range of the normal and to realize that the baby may look very different once it has uncrumpled after a few days.

Lanugo The dark hair which may be over large parts of the newborn's body, especially if it is premature, is called lanugo and drops out over the next week or so. The hair on the baby's head is often a different shade from that which will grow in a couple of weeks' time as the original hair gradually disappears. One of my babies was born with almost black hair and in a few months was a flaxen blond.

Vernix The creamy substance which may be on the baby's skin, sometimes covering it thickly, is vernix. It is produced by skin cells as they drop off into the amniotic fluid and forms a protective coating for the baby's skin. Vernix is gradually absorbed, so it is not necessary to wipe it off, except on the head, where it tends to stick to the hair and is best gently washed off, and in the folds and creases under the arms, in the neck and the groin.

Caput Some babies are born with a peculiar bump like a large blister on their heads, often to one side or the other of the center. This is where the head was pressing down through the inadequately dilated cervix before the second stage of labor; the swelling produced as a result is superficial, does not affect the baby's brain in any way, and will gradually go. The bump is known as a caput.

Sugar loaf molding Usually the brow is sloped back and rather low in a newborn baby, but some babies have high, domed heads like figures in an Egyptian hieroglyph. This is the result of molding of the head of a baby who was posterior, and is called sugar loaf molding.

A baby who was presenting by the face is usually very swollen, bruised and puffy but, again, this gradually goes away.

Mongolian blue spots look like bruises and fade with time.

Mongolian spots Some babies have patches of slate blue skin on their tummies or backs. These are called "Mongolian spots", have nothing to do with mental handicap or Down's syndrome, and are completely harmless. They occur most often in families of Asian and Mediterranean origin.

Sexual characteristics A newborn baby's genitals can look very large, especially if the baby is premature. Sometimes there is milk in the breasts of both girl and boy babies (called "witches' milk"). It is harmless and disappears without treatment. It is a result of withdrawal of estrogen received from the mother's bloodstream and the action of prolactin released by the baby's pituitary. Some baby girls even have a kind of period—pseudomenstruation—as the result of the withdrawal of maternal estrogen. Again, it is nothing to worry about, and stops within a few days.

Cocooned in the cradle of your arms . . .
. . . the most comforting security
in the first hours of life. . . .

Bonding as a gradual process

Some of the reactions that you have to your newborn baby are instinctive. You respond to the sight of the baby's plumpness, the rounded head, the large forehead, the smell of the skin, the bright gaze of her eyes which look as if they say "So that is who you are!", to the baby's cry, her exploring hands and mouth, and to her vigorous movement and the extraordinary compactness of her neat little body. But even instinctive behavior needs the right setting if it is to be released and unfold into appropriate nurturing. Then you can go on from instinct to learning from the baby how to respond to her signals and try to meet her needs.

Bonding is often talked about as if it were instant glue which sticks a mother and baby together the minute after delivery. Some women who do not spend the time after the birth with their babies worry that they have failed a kind of examination in motherhood at the very beginning and are anxious that this will have lasting effects on their relationship with the child. In fact bonding is a gradually unfolding process which only *starts* then and develops during each hour you and your baby are together. During all this time you are learning about each other and further physical changes in you are triggered off by stimuli provided by the baby. The most obvious of these is the let down reflex (the release of breast milk), which is stimulated by the baby's crying and searching for the nipple, the touch of his mouth against the breast and his sucking.

One aspect of hospital care which Klaus and Kennell stress is the way in which doctors and nurses can support the family, not just the mother, father and baby, but also other children. They believe that older brothers and sisters should be able to have close contact with the baby too and be made welcome in the hospital, whereas in practice many hospitals are very restrictive about sibling visiting and some do not allow it at all*.

The importance of the time after birth

Wherever you are having a baby, and even if you are "high risk" and need obstetric help, provision should be made for a quiet, intimate time together after birth during which you can begin to feel that you belong to each other. It can be done in a big teaching hospital just as it can in a small unit and *it is part of the job of the hospital to create that environment for each mother, each father and each baby.* Discuss it with your doctor. It is only when doctors and nurses know what women want that they will be sufficiently tuned in to consumer wishes to offer the caring, loving environment which is every baby's birthright.

The minutes, hours and days after birth are a time for emotional "work" which may be no less significant in the lives of the newborn baby and of both parents than the sheer physical work of labor. The hospital should provide an environment which helps and supports these unfolding emotional processes. New mothers and fathers do not need to be shown how to develop a relationship with their babies. They do need, however, to feel that they are among friends, to be handed the baby at birth and to be left in peace and privacy together.

285

The baby who needs special care

About six per cent of all babies weigh $5\frac{1}{2}$ lb (2500 g) or less (the internationally agreed definition of a low birthweight baby). Such babies can be divided into two categories—preterm and small for dates—and they will probably require special care.

Half or more of low birthweight babies are born too soon—preterm or premature babies. There seems to be no obvious reason why such babies should be expelled from the uterus so early, and research is still being carried out into the causes of preterm delivery.

Small for dates babies are born at the right time but have not flourished in the uterus in the last months of pregnancy because of a variety of reasons. Sometimes this happens because of malnutrition in the mother, her smoking, high blood pressure or preeclampsia, because the placenta has not been working well (placental insufficiency), or because she was carrying twins or more. These undernourished babies often have difficulty during labor, are short of oxygen and have problems with breathing after delivery. They may suffer from hypoglycemia (low blood sugar, see opposite) and have seizures. A few small for dates babies, however, are small right through pregnancy for genetic, chromosomal or other reasons which limit their growth from the very beginning.

The baby with poor temperature control

Low birthweight babies may have problems during labor too and are also more likely to have poor temperature control, because there is very little fat under the skin. They may be jaundiced, difficult to feed and susceptible to infection. Their skin is usually red because the blood vessels are visible through the thin layer of fat. Such babies are kept warm in a nursery which is warmer than the wards and are cared for in incubators. A thermostat may be strapped to a baby's tummy so that the temperature can be regulated according to his or her needs. Sometimes a baby is placed under a plastic heat shield and wears a hat. Tiny babies who are kept warm grow faster.*

The baby with breathing difficulties

Premature and low birthweight babies may have interrupted breathing (apnea) in the early days. This is why a very tiny baby is nursed on a special mattress which sets off an alarm if breathing stops. All that is usually needed to start the baby's breathing is a little stimulation of the baby by touch.

One in every ten premature babies has insufficient surfactant in its lungs. Surfactant reduces the surface tension in the lungs and stops them deflating entirely with each breath out, and it normally develops before the baby is ready to be born.

A baby usually inflates its lungs with the first breath after delivery and they pop open like parachutes. With the first breath out half the air is retained, so that breathing after this is much easier. The baby who has not enough surfactant has to work hard to breathe and may become exhausted in the struggle to get enough air. It breathes very quickly, its chest collapses with each breath out, and it looks blue and grunts as it breathes. This condition is called respiratory distress or hyaline membrane disease. It is obviously important in these cases to give the baby oxygen and to help its breathing.

Other babies who may suffer from respiratory distress are those born to diabetic mothers (even though they are large babies), those who have not had sufficient oxygen during labor, those delivered by Cesarean section (see page 262), and babies who develop pneumonia as a result of infection.

If the pediatrician decides to give the baby oxygen, a small catheter is inserted through the cord stump into an artery so that blood samples can be taken about every three hours to test the amount of oxygen in the baby's blood.

Oxygen can be given with continuous positive pressure so that the baby's lungs are kept open. A tiny catheter is inserted through the baby's nostrils, or a face mask or headbox is used. Another method is to apply negative pressure around the baby's chest so that he or she does not have to work hard to breathe. The baby is put into a machine that looks like a miniature iron lung with a neck seal, so that all you can see is the head. Sometimes a mechanical ventilator is used, which takes over all the work of breathing for the baby.

The baby with low blood sugar

A baby may have low blood sugar (hypoglycemia) if it has a low birthweight or is premature and also if its mother is diabetic or if the delivery was difficult. The hypoglycemic baby may have breathing difficulties and be jittery or lie limp and apathetic. Treatment involves making sure that the baby is getting ample nourishment, so the pediatrician may decide to set up an intravenous glucose drip. It is because of the risk of hypoglycemia that a very tiny baby may be given additional feedings, even though there are no obvious symptoms of low blood sugar.

Neonatal jaundice

If your baby looks beautifully suntanned as if just back from a cruise in the Bahamas, he or she has jaundice. A newborn baby has a surplus of red blood cells which are broken down after birth. During this process a substance called bilirubin is produced. Sometimes the baby's liver is unable to cope rapidly enough with the bilirubin which is circulating through the baby's system and the baby becomes jaundiced.

Physiological jaundice About half of all babies develop jaundice. It is usually harmless and is then called physiological jaundice. Jaundice is most likely to develop after the second day of life and to disappear after a week. In premature babies

*Even if your baby has to spend
some time after birth in special
care, she still needs your
loving presence. . . .*

jaundice tends to be most marked on about the fifth or sixth day of life and to go on longer—often for ten days or more.

A jaundiced baby needs sunlight and frequent feeding. If you have the chance, put your baby beside a window and, if it is warm enough, uncover the baby so that light can reach its limbs and trunk.

Jaundiced babies tend to get very sleepy and do not readily wake for feeds. Yet they should have plenty of fluids to cope with the bilirubin, so need to be roused for feeds. Every two hours is not too often.

If the bilirubin level is high, the pediatrician may decide to use phototherapy on a baby to bring the level down. This light treatment produces a photochemical breakdown of bilirubin into substances which are then passed out in the baby's urine. The baby is blindfolded so that the light cannot possibly harm its eyesight. This can be especially distressing for a mother who feels out of touch with her baby when she cannot make eye contact with it. When you lift your baby out from the lightbox for its feed, take off the eye covering.

Hemolytic jaundice Pediatricians always watch the jaundiced baby carefully because, although neonatal jaundice is a common and not very serious complaint, the baby may be jaundiced as a result of a blood group incompatibility between the mother and baby. This is called hemolytic jaundice and can damage the baby's nervous system and brain cells. Sometimes, too, the jaundice is associated with infection, with a metabolic condition such as low blood sugar or even with the administration of drugs to the mother in pregnancy.

Feeding the baby in special care

It has been shown that very small babies do best if they are fed soon after delivery,* so a low birthweight baby is given a milk feed within two hours of birth. The best food for a baby is its own mother's breast milk, but this will take a few days to be produced in quantity. The baby can, however, be put to the breast if strong enough to suck, to give it the benefit of the protein and antibodies in the colostrum that is already there.

If the baby cannot suck, it is usually fed through a small, soft catheter, a nasogastric tube, which is passed through a nostril down into the baby's stomach. Feedings should be small and frequent—about every half hour—or a slow continuous drip is often best for a sick baby. If your baby is being fed in this way it is usually possible for you to help with the feeds once you can express your own breast milk. If you have any difficulties, contact one of the breastfeeding organizations, which are listed on page 337.

Relating to the baby in special care

It is distressing for parents to see their baby in intensive care, attached to tubes and wires, isolated in an incubator. They may feel as if the baby is just another interesting specimen. Very low birthweight babies look so fragile and strange that it can be

Your baby may look lost and lonely if she has to be cared for in an incubator. You will feel she belongs to you if you talk to her and touch her reassuringly through the portholes.

difficult to see them as real people: your baby may look to you like an odd little misshapen doll or a little animal and not your child at all. On the other hand you may feel passionately that the baby belongs to you and want to grab it away from all the machines and other contraptions so as to hold it close. The obvious skills of those working with sophisticated technology can make parents feel clumsy and awkward so that they lack confidence to handle their baby. Yet it is important to do this. *All* babies need touching and talking to and, if they are well enough to be taken in your arms, they like being cuddled. If your baby is in an incubator, you can stroke it through the portholes. Tender, loving care may be just as important for the health of your baby as modern medical technology and you and your partner are the people who can give it best.

Many hospitals now have rooms where mothers of babies in special care can stay to be close to them, help look after them and breastfeed them. It is better for both mother and baby and makes it easier to build close links between them if the mother stays in the special care unit rather than merely visiting. When a woman can start to look after her baby herself, she begins to feel that she is a mother whose baby belongs to her not to the hospital. One intensive care unit has rooms where babies are cared for by their mothers, with a glass wall at the side of the baby's cubicle so that nurses can keep a constant eye on the babies. A nurse in this unit said: "One thing the nurses must not do is to take away responsibility for the baby. We always try to make a mother feel it is her baby, even when it is very small and sick."

66 I looked at her lying there with tubes and adhesive tape everywhere and I felt a wave of longing to grab her and pull out all the equipment and take her away with me. **99**

Losing a baby

Many women know what it is like to have an interrupted pregnancy, although the distress caused by even an early miscarriage is often underestimated. Stillbirth, on the other hand, is now rare. But still today, for a small number of women, the birth is also a death.

After all the happy expectations and preparations a woman goes through a labor which culminates in the delivery of a stillborn baby or of a weak and possibly handicapped baby who dies within the first week after birth. Her arms are empty and in spite of the drama and intensity of the experience she is left alone. The more we reduce the perinatal mortality, the more isolated is the woman whose baby dies.

Miscarriage

A miscarriage usually comes as a shock, yet one in every five pregnancies probably ends in miscarriage or "spontaneous abortion" as obstetricians call it. In three out of four cases this occurs before the tenth week and sometimes even before the woman realizes she is pregnant.

Threatened miscarriage
In the first three months of pregnancy, if you notice a heavy feeling around your pelvis and in the pit of your tummy and have any periodlike twinges and aches, stop everything and go to bed if you possibly can.

Sometimes you may have bleeding that is really a suppressed period. This happens when there is insufficient pregnancy hormone to stop your period, even though it will be scanty. Such bleeding is not a miscarriage and the blood comes from the endometrium, not from the placenta or the baby. Sometimes this too occurs at the time when each period would have been due, and right through the early months of pregnancy each would be period is marked by slight bleeding.

Again, if you have any bleeding or pinkish staining of mucus from your vagina the best treatment is rest in bed. The blood that you see is not the baby's blood but yours, and comes from the maternal side of the placenta where it is not adhering to the uterus, or from around the cervix. Lying down increases the blood flow to your uterus and, if the placenta is not firmly rooted, gives it a chance to attach itself more firmly to the lining of the uterus.

Inevitable abortion
An "inevitable abortion" is a miscarriage which occurs because the baby is no longer alive and, whatever you do and however much you rest, the bleeding is bound to continue. If the fetal heart cannot be detected by ultrasound (see page 183), the abortion is inevitable and you might just as well be up and about

and let it run its course. If ultrasound picks up the baby's heartbeat, there is only a ten per cent chance that you will miscarry, even though you may go on bleeding for a while.

Possible causes of early miscarriage

66 Don't believe it when they say it doesn't matter if you lose a baby early in pregnancy. This was my baby and I wanted her, not just any baby, but that special baby. 99

The cause of early miscarriage is often not known. Fortunately defective embryos with abnormalities that would not allow them to survive after birth are usually miscarried, and a large proportion of miscarriages are probably the natural way of getting rid of imperfect babies. Sometimes there has been no development beyond the very early stages of segmentation and what is termed a blighted ovum is passed. It is estimated that one in six miscarriages results from fertilized eggs that do not develop properly.

After it had been noted that more women than usual miscarry in early pregnancy during flu epidemics it was discovered that a high fever can result in miscarriage. There is more about this on page 98. Sometimes the presence of uterine fibroids (common in older mothers) or an oddly formed uterus means that there is not enough space for the pregnancy to develop.

Late miscarriage

Incompetent cervix Miscarriage after the 12th week of pregnancy is about three times less common than early miscarriage. Late miscarriage is often the result of a weak or "incompetent" cervix which starts to dilate long before it should. The bag of waters is wedged between the baby and the cervix and ruptures as the cervix starts to dilate, so the first sign may be the breaking of the waters. This type of miscarriage is particularly likely if a woman has already repeatedly miscarried in midpregnancy. An incompetent cervix may be the result of a previous termination, if it was done after the 12th week, or a previous difficult labor. There is more information about an incompetent cervix on page 101.

Placental insufficiency Miscarriage after the 20th week may mean that the placenta has failed to function in servicing the baby. (After 28 weeks the loss of the baby is termed a stillbirth.) If there is evidence of poor placental function and inadequate growth of the baby in the uterus, bed rest will allow a better flow of blood through the placenta to the baby. One of the ways in which you can affect the efficiency of the placenta is by making sure that you have a good diet during pregnancy. If you have had a miscarriage, it is a good idea to start an especially nutritious diet before you become pregnant again (see page 84). If you have had a series of miscarriages, keep any large blood clots from the latest one (a large jar is suitable) for the doctor to see. It may be worth having these tested in a laboratory.

Miscarriages are more likely to occur as you grow older (over 35), if you have had difficulty in conceiving (if it has taken more than six months) and if you have had two or more previous miscarriages. If you have had only one miscarriage before, there is no obvious reason why the next pregnancy should not be straightforward. After three miscarriages there is a 50/50 chance of miscarrying again, so talk to your doctor *before* you become pregnant and make plans for care and for extra rest from the first days after possible conception.

Guilt about a miscarriage

Every woman who has had a miscarriage wonders if anything she did or failed to do caused it. A miscarriage can happen at any time so that most women will be able to think of some event that might have triggered it off. You had a fight with someone in the office, your mother-in-law came to stay, you slipped in the street, had just had intercourse, or were overtired from a party the night before. But, whatever your guilty suspicions, none of these things has been shown to cause miscarriage. However, it can be difficult to convince yourself that you are in no way responsible. If you feel guilty, you are just like most of the women who have experienced miscarriages.

Grieving for the lost baby

Talk with your partner about your feelings. Even if you have not yet felt fetal movements, the loss of your baby is sometimes emotionally shattering. If you have had miscarriage after miscarriage or are slow to conceive, you may experience every single period as the loss of a baby and grieve as a result. This grieving is necessary for you to be able to look forward to the future with confidence in yourself as a "real woman". Suppressed grief always causes trouble later.

Your partner, however, may not have accepted the reality of the pregnancy by the time you miscarry and so it can be difficult for him to understand why you need to mourn, but it will help you if he can give time to listen. Or you may find you can talk with another woman who has been through a miscarriage herself more easily than with your partner.

After it is all over, the longing to start another pregnancy can interfere with relaxed and spontaneous sex. No man enjoys being treated as if he were a stud bull. And the more anxious you are to conceive the more tense you become and the less likely to get pregnant. If you feel that you are getting anxious and that this is spoiling your sexual relationship, try having a vacation from each other and coming together again at the time when you expect to be ovulating.

Stillbirth

"I'm so sorry. Your baby has died."

Almost every expectant mother has thought at some time that someone might say these words to her. For some women it is a nagging fear which haunts them and threatens to punish them for negative feelings they have about the baby and becoming a mother or for daring to expect too much of the birth and the baby. Sometimes, not as often as in the past, but nevertheless in about 16 out of every 1000 births, it really happens and the baby dies before, during or shortly after birth.

The experience of loss

6 6 We were left alone together and we sat and held her. She was perfectly formed. We wept together. It was a very important time for us. 9 9

6 6 I wish I'd asked to see him. It all happened so fast. Now I long to have seen him and held him. But it's too late. 9 9

In spite of everything that anyone can do you are suddenly confronted with the experience of loss. This is a loss not only of the baby, but of all the hopes and expectations of yourselves as parents and the new images of the self that have been built up through the months of pregnancy.

Nothing can take away the suffering that comes as a result of stillbirth. This is so even when the care given to you is loving and sympathetic, though such emotional support can help you gradually deal with the experience and eventually come to terms with it. Unfortunately some members of hospital staff cannot cope with their own feelings of guilt and distress when a baby dies, and you may be left alone in your room and avoided as much as possible by nurses and doctors who do not want to "upset" you by referring to what has happened. When they do talk to you, they may urge you to put it behind you, say that you will forget what happened when you have another baby, or tell you to think of your husband. The more such advice is given, the longer the experience may take to live through.

The task of grieving is a personal and intimate one. It consists of slowly and painfully—and sometimes you may feel that you will never succeed—integrating the experience into the total pattern of your life and finding a place for it in which it has meaning. Once you have done this you will be able to stand back from it a little and see its significance, and will no longer be overwhelmed by it. This process cannot be hurried and, if an attempt is made to force the pace, grieving will be delayed and you may be overpowered by grief at a later stage of your life.

Stillbirth in Third World societies

A hundred years ago everyone expected a certain proportion of babies to die. You bore ten and reared six if you were lucky. In many Third World countries even today babies are not named or publicly spoken of for the first few weeks because the chances are that they will not survive. It has been suggested that the mothers themselves are able to remain slightly emotionally detached from a new baby whose life may be transitory.*

In these societies death is incorporated into the web of life and there are supportive rituals to deal with it, whereas we are ill prepared in Western society for facing death. We each struggle to find our own way and often feel that we are the only people who ever faced such emotional upheavals. Death is a shocking intrusion into the normality of existence.

Facing up to the loss

If professional helpers know that something is going wrong with your birth, you have a right to expect them to give you information, discuss the difficulties openly and honestly and stand by you as you try to cope emotionally with what is happening, rather than treating you merely as a patient for whom "the less you know, the better". Women who have been through this ordeal say that it helped to realize that they were being told the truth and to be fully involved rather than artificially shielded from the event by the mystique of medical practice.

If your baby dies while still inside the uterus, you know that you are carrying a dead baby. It is as if your uterus, a place of life, has become a grave. The obstetrician may advise that it is safer to wait to go into labor naturally, which often happens within a couple of weeks, but may offer you induction if you wish. Many women feel an urgent need to "get it over with".

When something so distressing happens, there is no easy "solution", no one course of action that can wipe out the anguish. Sometimes a man asks what he can say or do to help his partner and to make the suffering less, or other family members or friends want to help but do not know what to do. People are so different in their responses to loss that the most helpers can do is to make themselves available, to reach out and be ready to receive whatever the bereaved person wants to tell them, without holding back for fear of exposing themselves or intruding or feeling embarrassment at her grief, and to be willing to listen if she feels she wants to talk. The most valuable thing they can offer is a *waiting silence*, without tension or unnecessary words, so that the sufferer's pain can flow into them.

Mourning for the baby

This may sound simple, but in fact it can be very difficult, because grieving is not just a matter of tears and sadness, but also numb shock and guilt and anger, all of which are felt at different phases of the experience. It is not easy to acknowledge destructive guilt, and perhaps even harder to cope with anger which may involve hostility against people, including doctors and nurses, who tried to help.

For you the time immediately following the death of a baby may be one of frozen half-awareness of what has happened and it is often not till three weeks or so afterwards that you begin to live through these other phases of grieving.

It is sometimes difficult for a mother to mourn her stillborn baby because she never really knew this person over whom she is grieving. It can be still more difficult if you have not *seen* the dead baby and realized that your bulging tummy held a living creature that has since died. This is why some psychotherapists and pediatricians think it is a good idea for a mother to touch her stillborn child and even encourage her to do so.

The baby's burial

You and your partner may wish to discuss together arrangements for the baby's burial. Some women do not wish to know where the baby is buried but others want to know. It is up to you to learn as much or little as you wish to know. Some women feel afterwards that perhaps the baby was a figment of their imagination and never existed at all. It was removed from them like a tooth which was causing trouble and extracted. You may think of your baby's body being handled with indifference and lie wondering what "they" did with it.

Allowing you to choose whether or not to see the baby and hold it and to plan a funeral is not simply a therapeutic remedy for grief: it is a way of treating you as an adult.

The effect on your relationships

Being depressed affects all our relationships with other people, including those we love and need most. Though the death of a baby may draw you and your partner closer together, it introduces stresses into the relationship which may be too severe for you to cope with. You may both need help from other people, and if you turn only to each other the burden may be too great to bear. Your partner has to grieve too and yet may feel that it is "unmanly" for him to show weakness and that he must be strong to support you. The result may be that he simulates a matter of fact acceptance of the inevitable and leaves you feeling rejected and isolated because he does not understand.

If the baby lived for a time and went to the special care nursery, your partner probably had a chance to go there and see and touch the baby while you may have stayed in your room, out of touch. So you rely on his descriptions and the details he can give you to be able to build up a complete picture. Yet a man who is himself depressed and grieving may find it difficult to talk about such things without showing his own distress and may resist it, so giving you the impression that he is holding back on vital information.

Losing a baby almost invariably causes a deterioration in the couple's sexual relationship too. It is difficult to feel sexually excited when you are depressed. And even as time goes on, when you are beginning to "function" again, feelings of pleasure can be followed by a rush of grief. When you start to enjoy life again, even when you start to feel sexually aroused, you may both feel at times that you are betraying your dead child.* So grieving after the death of a baby is a process in which both of you need to give understanding to each other.

If you have lost your baby and want to be in touch with others who have also gone through this experience, contact your childbirth educator or one of the organizations listed at the addresses given on page 337.

The next pregnancy

If you are pregnant following an abortion or if you have lost a previous baby as a result of miscarriage or stillbirth, or if your baby died after birth, the previous experience tends to cast its shadow forward. Strangely, this tends to happen even if you really did not want that particular pregnancy to continue and you felt glad at the time to "be yourself" again.

A woman who has lost a baby through accident, who has had miscarriages, for example, or a crib death, may feel angry that the emotions of one who has had an abortion should be discussed in the same context as her own ordeal and even that the woman who got rid of a baby deserves whatever happens to her. Yet the experience of loss may be equally haunting and the sense of guilt the same, or even greater.

We tend to compare and contrast the progress of the present pregnancy with past pregnancies. If a previous pregnancy had an unhappy outcome, it colors our view of the whole experience and it is natural to become acutely conscious of risks and dangers. We do not always realize that this is what we are doing, since a common way of trying to deal with fear and anxiety about repeating a previous distressing experience is to attempt to shut out thoughts of it. We try to protect ourselves from the painful experience of yet another failure.

A woman who feels guilty about aborting a previous baby or who feels somehow responsible for a miscarriage may transfer this guilt to the present pregnancy and be anxious that she is going to have a terrible labor, bear an abnormal baby or lose the baby as a kind of retribution or punishment, either for deliberately getting rid of a baby or for being negligent and selfish or not wanting the baby enough. It is not a rational or even necessarily a conscious thinking through of the risks, but a kind of primitive expectation that automatic punishment comes from the gods.

If you try to forget what happened before or to put it to the back of your mind, you will be unprepared for the flood of emotions that may assail you in situations of stress, when you lie on the examination couch to have a vaginal examination or when you go into the same hospital. And when labor starts you may find that you cannot help thinking back to the sensations and events surrounding the loss of the other baby.

You may tell yourself to be sensible and not to dwell on negative thoughts. Though understandable, this is rarely successful. You are right to acknowledge your feelings and also justified in getting those who care for you to take them seriously. But do not leave this till the end of pregnancy and certainly not until you go into labor. Try and find the kind of preparation for birth and parenthood that includes discussion about feelings and in which there is frank and open acceptance of any previous unhappy experience.

In a pregnancy following the loss of a baby women often experience painful, disturbing dreams about bearing a damaged child or losing the baby and feel that in some awful way this is their own fault. The dreams may be clearly about birth and babies or may be heavily disguised. The baby is often represented in such dreams as a doll or small animal or one's own tooth or limb, and death as the irretrievable loss of anything that is treasured.

You may feel that you are carrying a baby of the same sex as the previous one or even that you are pregnant with the child you lost before. That is one way of trying to cope with the painful experience. In fact, some people even say, "Have another baby and you'll forget about it". But of course you cannot really substitute one baby for another or replace a lost baby by getting pregnant again. It is vital both for your own wellbeing and the wellbeing of the baby you are now bearing that you work through to an acknowledgment that this baby is its own unique self, not a substitute for that other baby.

The first ten days

It is recognized that a woman who bears a child who is handicapped or ill, or who has a baby who dies, needs to pass through a period of grieving. It is less well understood that for *any* woman the time immediately after birth is experienced as a loss which she needs to grieve over, however perfect the baby. As a new mother you are on the threshold of a new beginning which entails the death of some aspects of your self and, with the birth of a first baby, the relinquishing of the self as child and as adolescent.

Emotions after delivery

Unexpected emotions

Many women need time to part with the fantasy baby which they carried inside them before they can come to terms with the real baby who has been born. The real baby is often astonishingly different from the one they imagined they were bearing. The death of a fantasy which has been cherished can be a painful process. It is especially threatening if the baby is premature and needs to have special care, or if it suffers from any form of handicap. But even a healthy, mature baby may be so unlike what you expected that you cannot come to terms with its reality or with the fact that it turns you into a mother with different responsibilities from those you had before, who is unavoidably committed to that baby for every minute of every day.

66 I was very depressed but told no one, as no one asked and I felt too awful about it to bring up the problem. 99

Changes in mood

All the intense feelings you have during the hours and days after giving birth have a biological survival value for the baby. Without them you would be just a caretaker. Sometimes your emotions are mindblowing and if you had not just had a baby would rightly be thought pathological. But during the first week after birth they are perfectly normal and experienced by many more women than ever openly admit to them.

It is not just a matter of depression. In fact you may feel you are on a permanent high. But it is likely that at some time during the first five days after the birth you will experience an abrupt drop in mood and a sudden feeling of depression. Your stitches are uncomfortable, the hospital routine is intolerable, you start to worry about the baby or whether you will be a good mother, or you simply feel flat because the party is over and it is now "the morning after the night before". Then again you may experience violent mood swings and feel you are on an emotional rollercoaster in the days immediately after the birth. You are probably more likely to feel like this if you usually have pronounced mood swings anyway. Our society often has a very romanticized stereotype of the new mother in a frothy pink negligée, a cherubic baby in her arms. The violent mood swings of the postpartum period can come as a shock because they are so different from the way you think you *ought* to feel.

*A mother "teases" her newborn with the nipple . . .
soon her baby will be enjoying one of the great
pleasures of the early months of life . . .*

Needing to behave spontaneously

You do not become a different person once you have had a baby: it is just that all the colors of your personality may become more vivid. This is why you may want to cry and then a short while later laugh helplessly at something which is not really very funny. And this is why indignation you may feel about something or someone in the hospital—and above all longing for your baby if he or she is in a nursery—seems to have a physical impact, knotting your stomach, drying your throat, burning you up.

Some women who have their babies in hospital are emotionally unstable until they get home. For them an institutional setting for the postpartum experience is unsettling and confusing. They seem to have a great need to be *in their own place*. There is nothing abnormal about you if you feel like this. The important thing is to acknowledge the kind of person you are and for your partner to accept it too and make arrangements decisively and as speedily as possible.

If all seems to be well with you and the baby, the best thing is to arrange to leave hospital as soon as possible. Ask to see the pediatrician and let him or her know how you feel. A visiting nurse may visit you at home if you wish.

6 6 The hospital was so busy and there was so little opportunity to sleep that I came out exhausted. 9 9

The complexity of your emotions

Your partner may be experiencing violent emotions himself at this time; he too may be torn between laughter and tears after the delivery. Our society tends to stress that men ought to be strong and offer broad shoulders for the new mother to lean on, but in fact some men are so deeply touched by the experience of birth that they are undergoing much the same emotional turmoil as the new mother. A new father may suffer acutely on leaving the hospital, because he is surrendering you and his baby to the care of strangers. In spite of the rejoicing and excitement there may be a strange undercurrent of grief. The intimate bond linking him to the woman who has borne his child has to be cut by an enforced separation. When he returns to hospital it is to come as a visitor.

6 6 The awful thing was having to go away and leave them both in the hospital 2 hours after the birth. The separation then was very hard to bear and I felt quite sick. 9 9

Being in a hospital ward where the atmosphere is friendly means that you can discuss your baby and any worries that you might have with other new mothers.

Your changed body

After you have had a baby you encounter your body in a dramatically changed state. Whereas before you enjoyed your smooth body heavy with fruit, the curve of your abdomen like an enormous melon still awaiting the harvest of birth, you may feel after delivery astonishingly alone, bereft and empty. If you are in hospital without people you love near you, in the care of people who treat you as just another "mom" or worse still as an involuting uterus, a sutured perineum and a couple of lactating breasts, you need time to come to terms with your changed body and to rediscover yourself as a person.

For many women the euphoria of having given birth and of having produced a real baby, which comes as a delightful surprise at first, gives way to this confrontation with the body. Changes in the breasts associated with breastfeeding can be an ordeal for some women. Many set their sights at the birth, seeing labor and delivery as the challenge, and are ill prepared for the new challenges that follow immediately after. One mother who felt a revulsion at her much changed body exclaimed: "But it was all supposed to be *over*!" Once the baby had arrived she wanted her self back again.

Weight loss Immediately following delivery you probably feel beautifully slim and lightweight. You have lost the combined weight of the baby, the placenta, the amniotic fluid and membranes. It is only when you first put your hand down on your tummy that you become aware of the folds of skin, like a soft and soggy cream puff. When you first catch sight of yourself naked in a full-length mirror you may be horrified at the amount of weight you have put on: the thickened waist, the heavy thighs and (if you are breastfeeding) the ballooning breasts—which you and your partner may enjoy if you were small and flat before, but which can be too much of a good thing if you were top heavy anyway.

Water loss During the week after childbirth most women sweat out the excess fluid they no longer need, and any puffiness you may have noticed in your legs and ankles will disappear; so will the plumped out facial features and the fluid which might have been retained in your fingers, making them fatter than usual.

Restoring muscle tone If you use your abdominal muscles your tummy will flatten after a few weeks, but you cannot achieve this if you go without exercise. Some exercises suitable for the early postpartum period are illustrated on pages 302–303. Brisk walking is good for abdominal muscles: if the weather is suitable, put the baby in a carrier against your body and walk, in the country if possible.

At first your pelvic floor muscles may feel as if they are sagging like a heavy hammock, but their tone will be gradually restored over the next three months and if you use them regularly, without straining them, rehabilitation will be complete.

Postnatal exercises

Many of the exercises recommended during pregnancy are also good for getting your figure back after delivery. It is important to remember, though, that postnatal exercises should be progressive. Do only the gentlest exercises for the first day or two then move on to the more strenuous ones shown here. Never do an exercise that hurts you.

1 *Lie on your back with a firm pillow under your head. Draw up your knees and rest your hands on your thighs.*

Toning the abdomen

To restore the muscle tone of your tummy after childbirth, try gentle leg sliding (see page 105) for the first few days then practice these abdominal exercises five times each. Always raise your head on a breath *out*.

2 *Raise your head and stretch your arms toward your knees. Count five, then gently relax.*

3 *Repeat, but stretching both arms first to the outside of one knee, relax, then to the outside of the other knee.*

Lift one leg and cross it over the other till your foot touches the floor.

Abdominal exercise

A gentle exercise for toning up abdominal muscles is done lying on your back with the small of your back pressed against the floor or bed.

Lying comfortably

If you have had stitches, lying on your front may be the most comfortable position for you. Pillows placed under your hips help your pelvic organs to return to their usual position and allow you to practice pelvic floor exercises and pelvic tilting. A pillow under your head and shoulders will take pressure off your breasts.

Wrong

Never lie on your front propped up on your elbows, as this hollows your back and stretches your tummy muscles.

Put two pillows under your hips not your abdomen, so that your back is not hollowed and the abdominal wall is relaxed.

Repairing the rectus muscle

If your rectus muscle has separated, this exercise, done from about three days after delivery, can help.

Lie on your back, knees bent and hands crossed over your tummy. As you breathe out, raise your head slowly, pulling in your tummy and holding the rectus muscle together. Do this exercise a few times twice a day.

Roll your right shoulder slowly backward around and around in a complete circle ten times. Then do the same with your left shoulder.

Encouraging the milk flow

Many women find that their milk flow slows down when they are resting. The first sign is usually a red patch of inflammation, often in the outer lower quarter of the breast where your arm has been pressing against it. If your breasts are not too tender, the answer is vigorous arm movement.

Grip your wrists with your hands and hold your arms in a square in front of you with your elbows high. Push the skin of your wrists hard towards your elbows, gripping firmly. Do this ten times.

Breasts and breastfeeding

The sooner you put your baby to the breast the sooner its gut will be lined with colostrum, a substance which forms a protective "paint" and a barrier to invading bacteria. Colostrum also provides the baby with antibodies to diseases to which you yourself are resistant. Ready in your breasts at the end of pregnancy, it is the earliest form of milk, rich in protein and an ideal first concentrated food for your baby.

The let down reflex

When your baby sucks, the action stimulates an area in your brain (the hypothalamus), which in turn stimulates the pituitary gland at the base of your brain to release oxytocin into your bloodstream. Oxytocin flows into the blood vessels in your breasts and causes specific cells around the milk glands deep inside your breasts to contract. This has the effect of squeezing the milk out through the tiny holes in your nipples.

You will probably feel the warm, tingling glow of the let down reflex immediately preceding the flow of milk. This occurs as the oxytocin carrying blood rushes into the breasts and you feel them getting warmer. Infrared photographs of lactating breasts show that they really do grow hotter in response to the baby's cry. The term "let down" has nothing to do with being depressed and in some ways is an unfortunate term; it simply means that the milk which was in your breasts is released so as to be made available to your baby.

The first feedings Notice what happens when you put the baby to the breast. She should have the nipple deep in her mouth and as much of the areola as will make a good mouthful. Cuddle the baby close and wait. Drop your shoulders: if they feel really stiff *pull* them down and then let them go. It may take a few minutes for the sensation to come and then suddenly it is there: deep inside both breasts, not just the one the baby is sucking, there is a prickling, buzzing feeling as if champagne is flowing through your veins and at the same time a wave of heat flowing toward your nipples. And then you see the baby's jaws beginning to work, and the strong steady movement of the bone at the top of the baby's jawbone, just by her ear, as she begins to swallow as well as suck. The let down reflex can happen when you just think about feeding the baby or if you hear her cry. If she is not in your arms, you can press the palm of a hand firmly against your breast and the milk flow—which will be a slow but steady dripping from the nipple—will come to a stop.

The difference between sucking and feeding

It is not enough to have milk in your breasts. Obviously the important thing is to release it so that it flows into your baby. For nutritional purposes it is not enough to have a baby sucking at your breasts, though he will enjoy this anyway. He needs to *swallow* and until this happens is not feeding. Hospitals are more relaxed than they used to be about the time babies spend at the breast, but if you are in one where feeding time is still restricted, you should count this time from the moment the baby is actually feeding, not from when he is just sucking.

Even before the let down occurs the baby gets some milk, because it collects in the ducts just behind the nipple. This is called "foremilk" and is rich in protein. It usually keeps the baby happy until the rush of milk comes with the let down. But if you give a baby foremilk only, because he is not sucking for long enough to stimulate the let down reflex, your milk supply will dwindle or never build up.

If you feel embarrassed or selfconscious or experience strong emotions of anxiety, fear or anger, the let down will probably be slower in coming and sometimes does not occur at all. This is why the setting for breastfeeding in the first days after birth is so important and why emotional support from someone who understands how you feel is helpful. Even though you may think you have emptied a breast, a fresh let down can occur when you put the baby back to it again. A breast is not like a pitcher of milk, but has a constant milk supply provided that the right stimulus creates a let down.

Little and often If you are concerned about the amount of milk the baby is taking, the frequency of feeds is more important than the length of feeds. Though some babies, especially in the first four to six weeks of life, enjoy sucking more or less continuously at certain times of the day, the main nutritional content of the milk has been obtained during the first five to seven minutes. This is why many short feeds, the baby dropping off to sleep in between, is for many mothers and babies the perfect style of feeding in these first weeks. You may be able to unplug the baby's mouth gently from your nipple by depressing the breast with a finger or by slipping a finger just inside the baby's mouth to break the vacuum—but don't, whatever you do, just pull.

Babies who like sucking for comfort Some babies always wake up and fuss when you do take them off the nipple. These are usually babies who have such a strong need to suck in the first six weeks or so that they never drop off the nipple for long. Then it makes sense to consider providing the baby with a pacifier for alternative sucking satisfaction, and with some additional help in dropping off to sleep, such as rocking, regular rhythmic sound or the oldfashioned lullaby.

You may feel very "drained" when feeding takes a long time: if you are tired and the baby is constantly demanding to be fed, it is easy to think that you cannot be providing enough milk. Though this is sometimes the case, many babies want to go on feeding nonstop because they like it so much, not because they are starving. So after about ten minutes sucking it is sensible to put the baby down or hand him or her over to a friend or your partner for a cuddle. Relax a bit, top up with some more breast milk at whichever side feels most generously supplied at that moment; then have another break, and so on.

Each baby's feeding pattern is different

Breastfed babies do not suck all the time through a feed. They enjoy bursts of sucking, stop for a while, then start again. This is normal. If you think about meals you enjoy you will realize that you do not chomp away nonstop either. Nor do you want the same quantity of food at each meal. Babies are the same.

Think of each feed as divided into different courses. Some will be seven- or eight-course banquets, but others will be only two courses. You will gradually be able to work out when the baby likes the banquets, and then you may be able to cater for them by arranging your day to fit in with this pattern. Somehow anticipating and preparing for feeding sessions of this kind makes them much easier to cope with and you are less likely to feel exhausted by them.

Is breast milk enough?

You may wonder if and when your baby needs any food other than your breast milk, especially if you secretly feel that your baby is not having enough milk from you.

Water Most hospitals advise giving babies water. Since hospitals are so hot this may be a good idea while you are still in hospital, but it is usually not necessary once you go home. The baby needs milk, not water. If your baby is producing six or more wet diapers in the 24 hours and is having no other fluid, and if the urine is pale amber or colorless, this is an indication that she is having enough milk from you. You will probably find that *you* are thirstier than usual. Drink as much as you like, though there is no point in having more than you want, since it will not produce more milk.

Supplementary bottles If you are concerned that your baby is not having enough milk and you start to give supplementary bottle feeds, the amount of milk you are producing will diminish, since it is demand that stimulates supply.

Using a bottle for supplementary feeding or to replace breast-feeding (supplementary bottle feeding) in the first two months of life can mean that the baby grows accustomed to the type of sucking action which is used at the bottle. The large bottle nipple can provide a sort of superstimulus to which the baby responds more readily than to your nipple. And if the nipple has a large hole in it so that the milk comes quickly she may soon come to prefer bottle to breast.

Solid foods When you introduce solid foods be prepared for your milk supply to be automatically reduced. This is one reason why the early introduction of solid foods is counterproductive. It replaces food the baby needs, human milk, with food which she does not need until she is about six months old. A baby's appetite cannot possibly cope with human milk *plus* all the other foods which are on the market. Manufacturers of so-called "baby foods" are often responsible for breastfeeding difficulties which start at three to four months, a common time for mothers to discover that they are failing to produce enough milk.

Test weighing Weighing the baby before and after a feeding (test weighing) is a method of finding exactly how much breast milk he or she has taken. It is pointless unless done over 24 hours, since the baby takes different quantities at different times; even then it tends to increase your anxiety and make you feel inadequate. A much better guide to a baby's wellbeing is feeling good muscle tone and noticing if she is alert and responsive.

More frequent breastfeeding When you want to increase the quantity of milk you are making, put the baby to the breast more often. If the baby has not gained weight, or has lost weight, it is a good idea to feed him every time he stirs over a 24 hour period. If the baby is very sleepy, wake him after every two and a half hours if you can, except at night. Unwrap him, talk to him and "woo" him with the breast. I call this my *Twenty-Four Hour Peak Production Plan*. It works in the first weeks after birth and is also useful at about six weeks.

Breastfeeding difficulties

Engorged breasts Many new mothers find that they are engorged on the third or fourth day after delivery when the milk really floods in. The longer you go between feedings the more likely you are to be painfully engorged. A cold compress, such as a diaper with some ice inside, resting against your breast, will ease the pain of engorgement, and with the baby's frequent sucking will help you through this difficult transitional phase. The hospital will have a breast pump that you can use if it is important to draw off some milk and if you find it difficult to express by hand, but only draw off enough for comfort.

Sore nipples Nipple soreness, especially when the baby is a vigorous sucker, is common in the first few weeks and does not mean that you will fail at breastfeeding. Studies show that those mothers who go on to enjoy breastfeeding include many women who have had initial trouble with sores and cracks, and that the only difference between these and others who give up is that they persevere. Go topless whenever you can; avoid using soap on your nipples or using breast pads against them, and let them dry off after a feeding, exposed to warm air. There are various creams and sprays on the market for treating sore nipples.

Cracked nipples Sometimes a crack appears at the point where the nipple joins the areola. This is almost invariably because the baby has not fixed well on the surrounding tissue and obtained a really good mouthful. If a baby drags on the nipple stem and does not draw the nipple into the back of the mouth, not only will you have problems with sores and cracks but also the baby will not be able to take enough milk after the first spurts.

A soft, flexible nipple shield made of rubber with a wide brim like a Mexican sombrero can sometimes help to relieve soreness caused by cracks. However, such shields reduce the stimulation essential for milk production, so stop using them as soon as possible. Avoid using plastic-lined breast pads, since if there is any leaking your nipples will be sitting in the damp.

When you want to express milk, you have to replace the baby's stimulation by gentle massage. First stroke the breast down toward the areola. Then place your thumb firmly halfway up the breast (right) and move it down to the areola (far right), pressing in and then up as you go. You should not press or pull on the nipple itself when you express: the pressure on the areola is enough.

Breast tenderness If you develop a red patch on a breast, feeding more often can help. Exercise your arms to increase the circulation to your breasts (see page 303). If an infection develops and you run a temperature at the same time as having a red patch, cold compresses and oral antibiotics prescribed by the doctor will quickly treat it. Continue feeding the baby, as this makes it far less likely that you will develop an abscess.

Excitable babies Some babies feed with great vigor and excitement, spluttering and coughing and really making a meal out of it. In the first weeks they suddenly draw back as they start to choke, pulling on the nipple at the same time. Or they may let go for a second and then grab on again, but because they have jerked their heads back they now have only the nipple stem in their mouths so that they are dragging on the place where the stem joins the areola. These babies need a calm environment in which to feed. Talk to yours soothingly and reassuringly, and reposition her firmly and securely. If your milk comes with a sudden rush after the let down reflex has occurred, turn away the breast until the flood has subsided, or see if a little boiled water or mint tea, which can be given by spoon or in a mini-feeder dummy, encourages her to be more relaxed at the breast. If your milk streams out fast you may need to express a little at each feed before putting the baby to the breast.

Sore abdomen After a Cesarean section breastfeeding may be difficult because you find it almost impossible to settle with the baby in a position where she is not pressing on the wound. Try lying on your side, or pop the baby's legs under one arm so that she is facing you.

Giving breast milk in a bottle When you desperately need sleep and your partner wants to give some feedings, it can be a good idea to express some breast milk after each feeding, and store it in the refrigerator (perfectly safe up to 24 hours). Use a sterile plastic container. If you want to keep your milk longer than 24 hours, freeze it. Express after each feeding of the 24 hours, either immediately or about 30 minutes later. If you find that milk shoots out of one breast when you put the baby to the other you can collect this milk too. If you are not good at expressing by hand buy a small breast pump. There are different varieties on the market.

Bottlefeeding

If you decide to bottlefeed or want to give occasional bottles for convenience, the formula you choose for your baby should be as much like your own milk as possible. No manufacturer has yet been able to invent anything but a product which *approximates* to human milk, because your milk adapts to your baby's individual needs. Substitute milks are a great improvement on unmodified cow's milk, however, and those which are "humanized" have the proportions of fats, sugars and trace elements changed so that they are more like the real thing. Discuss with your doctor, midwife or nurse the different choices available. Most babies thrive on artificial milk. But you do need to be scrupulously hygienic in preparing feedings.

Preparing a bottle

If you are using bottles, it is vital that your kitchen and all utensils are clean and that you sterilize both bottles and nipples carefully, following the instructions that come with the sterilizer or that are on the can of formula. You can make up enough feeds for 24 hours straight into the bottles, put caps on them and store them in the refrigerator. It is then easy to feed your baby whenever he or she shows signs of hunger. If you use disposable bottles, only the nipples need sterilizing.

Never leave warm milk for more than a few minutes as bacteria will multiply. Always throw away any milk that has been heated, clean out the bottle immediately and leave it soaking in antiseptic. Keep nipples in sterilized covered containers. When you go out, do not take warm milk with you. Take it cold, straight from the refrigerator, and reheat it in a pan of hot water or an electric bottle warmer. It is tempting to tuck the bottle under the carriage covers to keep it snug and ready immediately the baby wants it. But if you do this you are running the risk of feeding your baby milk which is harboring bacteria capable of causing gastrointestinal illness.

Though it seems pleasanter for a baby to have warm milk, this is not strictly necessary; if the baby is impatient for a feed and you are in a hurry it is quite all right to give her a cold bottle.

Powdered milk must be thoroughly mixed. Some brands dissolve more easily than others. Even the tiniest lumps can block the hole in the nipple and, if your baby splutters or vomits, can be inhaled and cause trouble with breathing. When you are making up dried milk, measure it very carefully and never put in an extra scoop to make it richer, as this overloads the baby with minerals which his system can absorb only with difficulty.

The baby who is fed on artificial milk may go longer between feeds since the milk takes longer to digest. If you were worried about whether your baby was having enough breast milk it can be very reassuring to know how much he or she has had from the bottle. But avoid trying to make the baby finish the bottle just because it is there. In hot weather give drinks of water too and introduce sips of fruit juice, since the bottlefed baby will need extra vitamin C. But artificial baby milks do contain some extra vitamins, so do not give vitamin supplements unless advised to do so by your doctor, not exceeding the prescribed dose.

Feeding for pleasure
When bottlefeeding, remember to hold the baby close, cheek against your breast, just as if you were breastfeeding. Though it may produce a less comfortable cushion for the baby's head, a man can do this too. The baby may sometimes like to lie nestled against your partner's bare skin, and fathers who give a feed in the middle of the night like this say how much they enjoy it. Never prop a baby up to feed on its own in a crib, however rushed you are. It can be dangerous, and it means that the baby misses out on one of the most important experiences of early life.

Sleep and crying

After being awake and alert, eyes wide open, for an hour or so after birth, the baby often sinks into a deep sleep for about 24 hours, waking only to suck and then dropping off to sleep again while still at the breast. It is a period often followed by another lasting about 24 hours, in which the baby may be sucking almost continuously. This is a normal pattern. It is the frequent sucking which stimulates your milk supply. Some babies suck in short bursts, get drowsy, then suck again. Others will sleep for two to three hours between more prolonged sucking sessions. Some babies start a pattern of evening fussing when they are one or two weeks old which may continue for three months. Though tiring and perhaps worrying for you, this is also normal.

Sleep patterns of newborn babies
When your baby is asleep you will sometimes notice that the eyelids flicker and the eyeballs are moving behind them. This is rapid eye movement (REM) sleep similar to that which adults have—the dreaming time. It has been discovered that REM sleep is essential for mental wellbeing and if people are not to become exhausted.* These little eye movements also stimulate the flow of blood to the brain. Even if the baby seems to be stirring and is making little jerking movements or fussing noises, this is not a time to wake him or her. This kind of sleep is probably just as important for babies as it is for adults.

The meaning of your baby's cry
Another innate biological mechanism is your baby's cry on waking, which alerts you to care for him or her. The baby may also cry whenever you undress her and seem to hate being without clothes. This is nerveracking for the new mother and father, especially if you are about to bathe the baby. But remember that the baby was held firmly inside your uterus, hugged by its tightly enclosing walls. If your baby startles and cries when you change a diaper or when you start taking off her clothes, keep your movements slow and firm. With one hand hold the baby's arms over its chest, as they would have been folded inside the uterus at the end of pregnancy, and speak soothingly.

You will soon discover that the baby has a different kind of cry to express different needs. But in the first weeks the cry nearly always means *hunger* and the right thing to do is to let the baby suck. A wet or dirty diaper does not really matter to the baby.

Practical care

There is a great gap between studying something in a book and doing it in practice. Experiment and see what works for you.

Bathing your baby

It does not matter how you bathe your baby, for example, so long as he or she is head above water, keeps warm and has a chance to enjoy it. Many babies hate being undressed and abhor being bathed in the first weeks of life, and make you feel you must be a tyrant for ever doing either of these things to them. And because they cry you are convinced that you must be utterly incompetent and hopeless as a mother. But try not to feel this way! The single most important thing to remember is to talk to your baby while dressing, undressing and bathing him.

If you do not want a very hot bath yourself, you can take the baby with you into your own bath. This provides the baby with a personal swimming pool. Start by placing him or her facing you on your knee and have a conversation. Then you will discover that you can work out little games together and the baby will find out what fun it is to splash. Have the biggest bath towel you can find for afterwards and make the patting dry fun too.

Changing diapers

Diaper changing can be done any way you like. At first take it gently and give yourself time and privacy so that you can work out your own style of doing it. A firm surface helps. Have everything you need close at hand before you start, including a bucket into which you drop the soiled diaper (which you can then carry to the toilet, tipping any lumps straight in, before putting the diaper to soak in whatever antiseptic solution you are using). Stick the safety pins in your clothing or you will not be able to find them when you start to do the baby up again.

Your older child will not feel left out if you involve her in looking after the new baby. . .

Content, asleep and oblivious
of the world your baby may
well be dreaming . . .

How you decide to fold your diapers will depend on whether you have a boy or a girl, and will also vary according to how big your baby is. It helps to fold a whole pile ready in the shape you like them. You may decide that it is simplest to buy diapers which are already shaped so that they do not need folding at all, but if you enjoy making geometric patterns it is not difficult to work out what suits you in practice: the only thing you need to remember is that the baby should not be in a permanently bow-legged position because of the material between its legs.

You don't need a layette! Though it can be fun to collect together tiny clothes, it is not really necessary, and since the baby will quickly grow out of these first and even second size garments there is little point in spending much money on them.

Diapers You will not be able to manage without diapers. The choice is between disposable and washable diapers. Disposables come with a plastic backing. Their obvious advantage is that they eliminate washing. They come in different sizes, shapes and absorbencies. Washable diapers are cheaper than disposable ones, as well as being highly absorbent. Bear in mind that babies often dirty their diapers before, during and after a feed, and that many like to suck every two or three hours at first. You will have to decide how often you are prepared to change your baby! You may find you need as many as 24 diapers to see you through the 24 hours, and possibly more if you do not have an efficient tumble drier. Diaper service is also available.

Clothing New babies lose heat rapidly, so need to be kept warm and cosy. You can do this in any way you like, but several fine layers are usually warmer than one thick one. When you can, choose things which do not have to be pulled over the baby's head, as most babies hate narrow neck holes. In very cold weather the baby's head ought to be covered outdoors.

Avoid strings and ribbons near the baby's mouth and hands, and large holed lacy knitted jackets and shawls in which the baby will catch little fingers and toes. You are bound to be given bootees and mittens; these are wriggled off, lost, and get dirty and probably germ ridden. Stretchy one piece suits are better for keeping feet covered, and babies should be able to get at their hands and explore with them when they are awake.

A baby carrier is not strictly clothing but is important for your mobility. The most useful item of clothing is something for you, not the baby. It is a big wraparound overcoat, cape or other voluminous top garment. Then you can tuck the baby in a baby carrier against your body underneath your wrap with just her face peeping out, and you know that your own body heat is providing warmth and that the outer garment is holding the warmth in around the baby. The baby carrier you use to begin with should be one of those where the baby is held in front of you and the head is supported.

The challenge of new parenthood

Though most women look forward to the day when they will have their baby at home, taking an important part in family life, the first days at home alone with a new baby can be days of worry and even panic. You may suddenly feel like a stranger in your own home as you try to understand and cope with the needs of this demanding new person. You will soon learn to interpret the different cries of your baby, however, and you may want to take advantage of your local available visiting nurse service.

Visiting Nurse Service

Your doctor may arrange for a visiting nurse to come to your home after you leave the hospital. She will assist you with the aspects of baby care that you are unsure of. If your baby was premature or sickly, she will teach you any special procedures you need to know. The visiting nurse is concerned with the physical and emotional wellbeing of every member of the family, not only with the baby.

Postnatal checkup

Your postnatal checkup will be arranged for between five and seven weeks after the birth, and is an important way of insuring that you have complete physical rehabilitation after childbirth. The obstetrician will give you an internal examination to see if your pelvic floor muscles are well toned and the uterus and bladder correctly positioned, and will check on the state of any scar tissue. If sexual intercourse is difficult and uncomfortable or if you are feeling depressed and unhappy, tell the doctor at this visit. If you are dissatisfied with any aspect of care you have received or seek further explanation of things that have happened to you in labor, take the opportunity to discuss these things with the doctor.

Sex after childbirth

For many women the full flood of passion is slow to return after childbirth. So much has happened in your body that you may need time to find yourself again and get in touch with your feelings. If labor was unpleasant or delivery traumatic you need time, too, to *like* yourself again and to trust your body.

If you have had stitches you may feel at first as if you will never want to make love again. If you are one of the minority of women who do not have stitches you may not be able to wait to make love. So there is a great difference in attitude, depending very much on the state of your perineum. The initial healing of the episiotomy wound (and it is a wound) often takes two weeks or longer and even then you may be very conscious of scar tissue at the side or the lower end of your vagina.

Rediscovering each other's body

Make sure first of all that your partner knows which areas are likely to feel sore and help him discover what feels good and where. Do not attempt to have intercourse at first and certainly do not try to *prove* anything to yourselves. Choose a quiet time when you need not be rushed, perhaps after a feeding when you know the baby is most likely to settle and sleep soundly. Use a lubricant jelly, squeeze a little on your partner's fingers and, taking his hand in yours, guide him, showing him where you like to be touched. Many couples need two or three exploratory sessions like this before they feel sufficiently confident and passionate to have complete intercourse. If you rush it, you may have unexpected discomfort and will then tense up in anticipation of pain next time, and because your pelvic floor muscles have contracted will experience more pain.

When you feel you are ready for intercourse, adopt a position in which your partner's weight is not going to drag on the lower part of your vagina or, if you are breastfeeding, is not on your breasts. For example, if you lie or sit with your legs over the side of a low bed, feet on the floor, your partner is able to penetrate you gently without pressing against or pulling on any tender areas. You will probably feel extraordinarily full. Release your *throat* and this will help the release of muscles around your vagina. Do not aim for simultaneous orgasm. It is usually much more comfortable and pleasurable for you in the weeks immediately after having a baby if your partner comes to orgasm first and then stays still inside you for a while, allowing you to maneuver your pelvic floor muscles more effectively until you have an orgasm too.

Adjusting to your changed body

You will learn a lot about each other and sometimes sex will be funny, sometimes tender, occasionally passionate. Even if you do not feel that you are making a wild success of your sex life in the first few months, lovemaking helps you and your baby by releasing oxytocin into your bloodstream which helps the uterus contract so that it returns to its previous size and shape and encourages the flow of breast milk. When you do have orgasm, milk may actually shoot out from your nipples.

You will probably find that your shape has changed after a first baby. The labia, like the outside petals of a flower, are softer and fleshier, and away from the site of the episiotomy you may find the entrance to the vagina also more yielding. If your uterus is still involuting, you will feel after contractions following lovemaking. This is a good sign. If they are uncomfortable, use a hot water bottle against your lower tummy or back.

Even if you thoroughly enjoyed lovemaking, you may feel sore afterwards, once the sexual intensity has faded. Again, this is normal. A cold witchhazel compress may feel soothing.

Painful intercourse   For some women intercourse after childbirth is acutely painful and no amount of trying to relax does away with the pain. This is called "dyspareunia". It can occur when stitches have been inserted too tightly and the surrounding flesh has become puffy and swollen (edematous) and perhaps is infected. Ask your doctor or midwife to look at the sore area as soon as possible. Sometimes it is just a question of nicking a few stitches, sometimes a matter of taking antibiotics. Occasionally, too, the pain is deep inside. If you have pain up near your cervix, it may be that the transverse cervical ligaments have been torn and it takes time for them to repair themselves. Make sure that your doctor knows that you are having this sort of pain.

Many women worry that they have become "frigid" after childbirth. Often a lack of interest in sex is caused by tiredness. Try and rest with your feet up and if possible sleep at some time during the day when your baby sleeps. Even the most active baby sleeps sometimes, and it is a question of discovering your baby's pattern and taking advantage of it. This is more difficult if you have a toddler too, but many toddlers enjoy a cuddle in bed or on the sofa.

Although you may not feel like making love for some time after childbirth, it is sensible to have explored sensations and had intercourse *before* your postnatal checkup. Most women with new babies are so busy that it is not easy to fit in another appointment to discuss sexual difficulties and they hope that if they do not notice the problems will disappear. Make a note of where and when you feel pain and let the doctor know that you are experiencing dyspareunia and that you want help.

Sex after childbirth takes you on a new journey with your partner. It involves discovery, change, in some ways for many women a fresh awareness of the depth and drama of their sexual feelings, and for both of you a new closeness and tenderness as parents of the baby who has been born of your love.

Contraception after childbirth

There is no easy answer to contraception and what pleases one couple is completely unsuitable for another. Many couples now consider the matter in advance so that they can have intercourse safely whenever they feel ready. You may find that a combination of methods works best for you but, whatever kind you select, study carefully the correct method of use and never deviate from the routine. It is not worth being worried about another pregnancy when you are only just beginning to enjoy the results of the last!

Breastfeeding   If you are breastfeeding, your periods may not come back till you wean the baby or start introducing solids. Ovulation, and hence the possibility of conception, can occur a couple of weeks or so *before* you have this first period. Breastfeeding tends to reduce fertility but is not an effective contraceptive unless

As you gain confidence, caring for your baby becomes a pleasurable opportunity for you to learn more about each other . . .

you are suckling the baby intermittently right through the 24 hours and are giving him or her no other food or fluid at all.

Coitus interruptus

Hoping that your partner will withdraw before ejaculation, and deposit semen outside your vagina, is not a reliable method either, though it is very common throughout the world. In spite of working well for some couples, it demands great control on the man's part and may lead to dissatisfaction for you both. Sperm can flow from the penis *before* ejaculation and if you have intercourse again within a short time live sperm may already be present in your partner's urethra and be introduced into your vagina before ejaculation. Sperm does not have to be deposited right inside your vagina for you to become pregnant, and even a drop or two of semen leaking against the labia may contain a million sperm or more.

The rhythm method

The rhythm method is the only method of birth control officially approved by the Catholic Church. You need to predict the time in your cycle when you are most fertile and avoid having intercourse during that time and for several days beforehand and afterward. Your time of ovulation can be worked out by different methods, which can be combined for greater efficiency — your doctor will advise you on these.

Because few women's menstrual cycles are consistently regular, the rhythm method is not very reliable. It is even less effective before you have reestablished a regular pattern of ovulation after childbirth. This may take six months or even a year if you are breastfeeding.

The condom

The condom (sheath) is the most widely used of the barrier methods and, employed carefully, is effective and safe. The one big disadvantage after childbirth is that your vagina may not be well lubricated and may be tender following episiotomy. Unless you use a lubricant cream the latex rubber sticks and drags, interfering with pleasure and reducing confidence. So have some artificial lubrication ready, but avoid vaseline, as this rots rubber. Do not use old condoms; their shelf life is about two years.

The diaphragm

If you used a diaphragm before you became pregnant you will probably need a larger size after you have had a baby, and it must be fitted by a doctor, who cannot do it accurately until about six weeks after childbirth. Do not leave the diaphragm in place for longer than eight hours if you have had any kind of bladder infection during pregnancy or following the birth, since pressure of the rubber rim on your bladder can sometimes cause irritation and exacerbate an infection. Use one teaspoonful of spermicidal cream on the diaphragm, and never use vaseline. It is probably best not to dust with talcum powder as some manufacturers advise, since some kinds of powder contain carcinogenic substances. The diaphragm is completely safe to use when breast-

The diaphragm is more effective when used with a spermicide.

feeding and the spermicidal cream or jelly cannot harm the unborn baby if you should conceive accidentally. The failure rate ranges from four pregnancies for every 100 years of use to as high as 29, but the efficiency of the diaphragm depends very much on motivation and care of the user.

Sometimes ligaments running across the cervix are slack after childbirth and the diaphragm cannot be wedged snugly up under the pubic bone but slips out of position, especially when you bear down. In this case you may want to consider a cap.

The cervical cap

This is a rigid, thimbleshaped rubber dome which fits by suction right over the cervix itself and has to be placed in position very carefully by you. It can remain in place the whole month, from period to period. It is not easy to find, but some women's groups import them from England.

Spermicides

Foaming spermicides are more effective than creams or gels because they effervesce into every crevice. However, you may find that this characteristic in itself interferes with your pleasure in intercourse. Spermicides in the form of foaming tablets or pessaries are not so reliable, because women often do not place them sufficiently high up in the vagina.

If you note any vaginal irritation with a particular brand, try changing to another. Some spermicides come in prefilled applicators; others have to be measured out into an applicator. One problem is that you are supposed to lie on your back so that the spermicide does not drip out before intercourse, and this may not be your position of choice.

Spermicides are safest used in combination with a diaphragm, cap or condom. The pregnancy rate is anything between five and 30 pregnancies for each 100 years of use, depending on the care with which they are used.

The intrauterine device

It is usually easier for an intrauterine device (IUD) to be inserted into your uterus and retained without excessive cramping once you have had a baby. So it may be that the IUD will suit you. The failure rate is between one and five pregnancies for every 100 years of use, depending on the skill of the doctor who inserts it. Some IUDs need to be replaced every few years and after each insertion you may feel faint and sick. You should not have intercourse for the first few days, and may notice some bleeding after intercourse during the first month or so.

Pelvic infection is common with an IUD and is more likely when there is a string attached to it, since infection ascends from the vagina up through the cervix. Infection can, and should, be treated with antibiotics, all of which pass through into your milk, though the only obvious effect on the baby may be that his or her bowel movements become rather loose. In some ways the thread is reassuring, since occasionally an IUD is expelled or buries itself in the uterine lining and many women like to have some means of knowing whether their IUD is still there.

The copper 7 is the type of IUD most commonly prescribed.

Rarely an IUD actually perforates the uterus, and this is more likely to happen when it is inserted within a short time after delivery when the uterine wall is thin and soft. An IUD with a rounded rather than a spiky edge is less apt to do this, so you may want to discuss this with your doctor.

The contraceptive pills

Though the pill is the most reliable method of contraception so far invented, you need to ask some questions about it if you are breastfeeding.

There are certain conditions, some of which are not evident until pregnancy, that indicate that you should not choose the pill as your postnatal contraceptive. If you have high blood pressure which continues after the birth or if it has been discovered during pregnancy that you have diabetes, you should *probably* not go on the pill. If you are suffering from severe postnatal depression, it may be wiser to avoid the pill.

If you developed varicose veins during pregnancy, you should watch for any pain in your legs which could be a sign of a blood clot. If you have had a blood clot in a vein (thrombophlebitis), you should *not* take the pill.

Progesterone changes the bacterial flora of the vagina and some women develop thrush for the first time when taking the minipill. If you have already had thrush this may not be the contraceptive you should choose.

The pill also needs reassessment as you get older. If you are over 35, the risk of a cardiovascular disorder is increased significantly. If you smoke heavily as well, you should not be taking the pill, as you are running grave risks with your health.

The combined estrogen-progesterone pill, almost 100 per cent effective in preventing pregnancy, is definitely *out*. It affects your metabolism and therefore indirectly the baby. It may alter both the quantity and the quality of milk and there may possibly be long term effects on the child.

The progesterone only pill Many women who breastfeed are prescribed the progesterone only pill, the "minipill". Since it contains no estrogen, it probably does not prevent ovulation but works by thickening the cervical mucus, making it difficult for sperm to travel beyond the cervix, and by preventing the normal cyclic changes in the endometrium (the lining of the uterus) which allow a fertilized egg to implant. It is a less effective contraceptive but has fewer side effects. The failure rate ranges from one to four pregnancies for every 100 years of use. It has to be taken every day without a break and must be taken at about the same time each day to be effective.

Many women say that though their milk supply was diminished for a few days after they started taking the minipill, feeding on demand more or less continuously if necessary for a day or two brought the supply back to normal. On the other hand, we do not really know what effects, if any, these powerful synthetic hormones may have on the baby.

Gaining confidence as parents

Many women in our society have no experience of babies and some have never had a newborn baby in their arms before. They are anxious that they will not know when the baby is hungry, that they will drop or drown it in the bath, that they will never be able to stop it crying or that the baby who is not crying has stopped breathing. New mothers are often too ashamed to talk about such feelings and may even repress recognition of them. If you feel like this, talk with other mothers and you will discover that you are not alone with such anxieties. Talk about the good feelings too, when the baby falls asleep and lies heavily in your arms in perfect contentment, the soft, downy head resting against the skin of your neck, when he opens his eyes wide and gazes at you with excited attention, or when you watch her satisfied sucking at your breast.

Twins can give you twice the pleasure if you take time to enjoy them. . .

You are not just a caretaker of the baby but a partner in a unique and evolving relationship. Both of you start out knowing very little about each other and go on from there to learn more every day, synchronizing with each other rather as dancers do. You both respond to nonverbal cues, to facial expression, eye movement, muscle tension—even breathing—quite spontaneously. And when you act like this *you are invariably doing the right thing*. When you become selfconscious and critical, you miss steps in the dance and confidence drains away.

The developing relationship between a mother and her baby is a process that needs time to unfold and blossom, patterned, just as a hyacinth bulb or a crocus is patterned, by the laws of its own inner energy.

Yet this is only part of the dance. The baby's father too has his own special kind of interaction with his child as well as with you. When a man is fully involved with his baby, enjoying her, responding to her needs and getting to know her as intimately as you do, the pattern becomes even more intricate and exciting.

Sharing in parenthood

Parenthood is a shared task. In the past fathers missed out on the baby's early months and were supposed to be interested in their children only when they started to play games and talk. Babies have astonishingly strong personalities and are different from each other even in the early weeks. It is worth getting to know the person who is your child from the outset. Sharing in parenthood is part of the concept of marriage as a partnership, but it involves skills which have to be worked at. The man who turns his back on this opportunity to share in the relationship with the newborn baby may be denying a whole aspect of himself and the chance to discover how very good he is at fatherhood.

Being a parent is not just an endless series of repetitive tasks or a heavy responsibility, though all parents see it like that at times. It is a journey of discovery—discovery of the baby's personality, of who you are, who your partner is and who you are *becoming* together.

Pregnancy week by week

This is a week by week guide to what may be happening to you and your baby throughout pregnancy. As different women's pregnancies develop at different rates, do not expect to be at exactly the same stage for the week described. Read the information for the two weeks either side, too.

Since pregnancy is dated medically from the first day of your last period, the record begins with what is termed the third week of a 40 week pregnancy, the week of conception.

Space has been left for you to jot down reminders and appointments for each week.

Week 3

You have ovulated and an egg is traveling along one of the two fallopian tubes towards your uterus. During intercourse one of the millions of sperm your partner has ejaculated has fertilized the egg while still in the fallopian tube.

Your baby is a cluster of cells which multiply rapidly as they continue the journey along the fallopian tube.

Week 4

You have probably not noticed anything different, though some women have a strange, metallic taste in their mouths.

The fertilized egg has arrived in your uterus and, after floating in the uterine cavity for about three days, has embedded itself in the uterine lining. It is nourished from blood vessels in the lining of the uterus, and the placenta begins to form around it.

Week 5

You are beginning to think that you may be pregnant. Your period is late, but you can't be sure, because you may feel as though it is about to start at any time. Your breasts are slightly enlarged and tender and you may find you need to urinate more often than usual.

The embryo is about $\frac{1}{10}$ in (2 mm) long and would be visible to the naked eye by now. Its spine is beginning to form and the brain has two lobes.

Week 6

You may be feeling sick first thing in the morning or when you are cooking a meal. Your vagina will have become a bluish or violet color. From the 10th day after your period was due it should be possible to find out by a urine test whether or not you are pregnant. Your uterus is now the size of a plum.

The baby has a head and trunk, and a rudimentary brain has formed. Tiny limb buds are beginning to appear. By the end of this week its circulation is beginning to function. The jaw and mouth are developing and 10 dental buds are growing in each jaw.

Week 7

You may sometimes feel dizzy or faint when you stand for a long time. Your breasts are noticeably larger and small nodules (Montgomery's tubercles) may appear on the areola at about this time, while your nipples may become more prominent. By this date the doctor should be able to confirm your pregnancy by a vaginal examination.

The limb buds have developed rapidly and now look like tiny arms and legs. At the end of these limbs are small indentations which will later become fingers and toes. The spinal cord and brain are now almost complete and the head is assuming a human shape. The baby is now about $\frac{1}{2}$ in (1·3 cm) long.

Week 8

You may find that you have "gone off" certain foods. Many pregnant women can no longer drink alcohol, even if they previously enjoyed it, and a dislike of cigarettes or tobacco smoke is common. Your hair may seem less manageable than usual. You may also have a slight vaginal discharge. This is quite normal as long as it is not irritating or painful.

The baby now has all its main internal organs though they are not yet fully developed. The eyes and ears are growing, and the face is taking on a recognizably human shape. The baby is just under an inch (2·5 cm) long.

323

Week 9

You may notice changes in your skin because of the pregnancy hormones in your system. Any wrinkles you have may be less obvious. Your gums may be softening, again because of these hormones, and you need to be especially careful about dental hygiene now and through the rest of the pregnancy. The thyroid gland in your neck may be more prominent.

The baby's limbs are developing very rapidly, and fingers and toes are beginning to be defined on the hands and feet. The baby is moving about gently to exercise its muscles, although you cannot feel these movements. At this point the baby weighs only about as much as a grape.

Week 10

Your uterus has expanded to the size of an orange, but is still hidden away within your pelvis. You should be wearing a bra with good support by now. If you buy a bra that fits your breasts but is adjustable to allow for later chest expansion, you should not need to get another size during pregnancy.

The placenta, to which the baby is attached, begins to produce progesterone in a process which is completed by the end of the 14th week, when the progesterone produced is sufficient for the placenta to take over the function of the corpus luteum. The baby's ankles and wrists are formed, and fingers and toes are clearly visible. The baby has grown to about $1\frac{3}{4}$ in (4·5 cm) long.

Week 11

If you have been nauseous during the last weeks, the sickness should gradually lessen from now onwards. The amount of blood circulating through your body has started to increase, and will go on increasing until about the 30th week. You should be thinking about arranging prenatal classes, as they often tend to get booked up early.

Your baby's testicles or ovaries have formed, as have all of its major organs. Since these organs will not develop much further, but will merely continue to grow during its time in the uterus, the baby is relatively safe from the risk of developing congenital abnormalities after the end of this week.

Week 12

You will probably have your first doctor's visit this week. You will have a complete medical examination and the doctor will be able to feel the uterus by external examination, as it has risen above your pelvis. Arrangements are made for you to have appointments once a month until you are 32 weeks pregnant. This first visit is the time to ask about anything bothering you.

The baby's head is becoming more rounded and it has eyelids. Its muscles are developing and it is moving about inside the uterus much more. It is now about $2\frac{1}{2}$ in (6·5 cm) long but still weighs only $\frac{1}{2}$ oz (18 g).

Week 13

If you have had morning sickness this will probably have gone completely by the end of this week. From now on your uterus will be enlarging at a regular and noticeable rate.

The baby is now completely formed. From now on its time in the uterus will be spent in growing and maturing until it is able to survive independently of its mother.

Week 14

You will be feeling less tired than you were at the beginning of your pregnancy and feel quite fit. You may notice a dark line (the linea nigra) down the center of your abdomen. This will probably start to fade after your baby is born. Your nipples and the area around them are also starting to darken. Your uterus is the size of a large grapefruit.

The baby now has eyebrows and a small amount of hair has appeared on its head. Its heart can be heard by ultrasonic scan. The baby drinks some of the amniotic fluid and can pass urine. It is now receiving all of its nourishment from the placenta and measures about $3\frac{3}{4}$ in (8–9 cm).

Week 15

Your clothes will be getting too tight for you. It is best not to try and cram yourself into tight jeans. To cope with the increased amount of blood circulating in your body and the baby's need for oxygen, your enlarged heart has increased its output by 20 per cent.

The hair on your baby's head and brows is becoming coarser. If it has a gene for dark hair, the pigment cells of the hair follicles are beginning to produce black pigment at this stage.

Week 16

Your second prenatal clinic is now due. Some doctors do a scan at this visit. You will be able to see the outline of the baby's head and body. You feel butterflies in your stomach that just *might* be the baby moving. Your waistline will be starting to disappear. If you have not already done so, book childbirth education classes now. Sometimes an "early bird" class is available to discuss diet, exercise, posture, emotions and health.

Lanugo (fine down) is starting to form all over the baby, following the whorled pattern of the skin, and the baby has fingernails and toenails. It is $6\frac{3}{4}$ in (16 cm) long and weighs nearly 5 oz (135 g).

Week 17

You may find that you are sweating more than usual (the extra blood circulating in your system) and also that your nose feels congested. This is a common result of pregnancy and will end after delivery. Vaginal secretions may increase now.

The growing baby has pushed the top of the uterus to halfway between your pubic bone and your navel. From now on the baby weighs more than its placenta. It is probably aware of—and may be startled by—sounds outside your body.

Week 18

If this is your first baby, this is the time when you may feel the first prod which is definitely nothing to do with indigestion! At last you know that there really is a baby in there! Trouble in sleeping at night will be helped by increasing the number of pillows supporting you.

Measuring about 8 in (20 cm) long, your baby is now testing out its reflexes. As well as kicking, it is grasping and sucking. Some babies find their thumbs and are confirmed thumbsuckers before they are born.

Week 19

Now is not too early to start practicing deep relaxation and steady, rhythmic breathing. Keep aside some time each day for this. You may notice that you are putting on weight on your buttocks as well as your abdomen.

Buds for permanent teeth are forming behind those that have already developed for the milk teeth.

Week 20

You will notice your baby being more and more active, and may even be able to see some of its movements. The growing uterus is pushing up against your lungs and pushing your tummy outwards. Your navel may suddenly pop out and stay that way until after delivery. Your chest (rather than breasts) has expanded and, if you do not already have an adjustable bra, now is the time to buy one.

Sebum from the sebaceous glands mixes with skin cells and begins to form the vernix. This protective vernix clings to the lanugo all over the skin, especially on the hairier parts and in the creases. The baby is now about 10 in (25 cm) long.

Week 21

You may start having heartburn—a burning sensation in the lower part of the chest—and may also bring up small amounts of acid fluid. Get your doctor to give you some antacid tablets to neutralize the acid.

The baby weighs just under 1 lb (450 g). It is still moving about freely in the amniotic fluid and can be felt kicking sometimes high in your tummy, at other times down near your pubis.

Week 22

Your gums may be swelling because of the pregnancy hormones in your system. Do not forget that dental hygiene is important throughout pregnancy.

The baby is settling into a pattern of activity and sleep. It is probably at its most active while you are resting.

Week 23

The different parts of the baby can be felt (palpated) through your abdominal wall. You may feel a stitchlike pain at times down the side of your tummy; this is the uterine muscle stretching and the pain should go after you have had a rest.

At about this time the Braxton Hicks "rehearsal" contractions may become more pronounced, gripping and massaging the baby at regular intervals.

Week 24

Your next visit to the doctor—by now the doctor will be able to hear the baby's heart through a stethoscope. The top of your uterus (the fundus) now reaches to just above your navel.

The baby is growing rapidly—it is now about 13 in (32 cm) long and weighs over $1\frac{1}{4}$ lb (0·5 kg). Although its vital organs are quite mature by now, its lungs are not yet sufficiently developed for survival outside the uterus.

Week 25

You may get a cramp now and later. Avoid pointing your toes down. The baby may also be pressing against your bladder, causing you to go to the toilet little and often.

The baby's bone centers are beginning to harden.

Week 26

You should make arrangements for maternity leave and discover to what benefits you are entitled.

The baby's skin is beginning to change from being paper-thin and transparent to being opaque.

Week 27

You will be putting on weight fairly regularly now until about the 36th week. It may be a good idea to start thinking about what to get for the baby before you become so big that shopping becomes an unpleasant chore.

The baby's skin is very wrinkled, but is protected and nourished by the covering of vernix.

Week 28

Colostrum may leak from your breast. From now on you will probably be visiting the clinic every two weeks. If you are Rhesus negative, an antibody check is done.

At this stage of development, the baby is considered legally viable, which means that if delivered it must be registered. It is about 14 in (38 cm) long and weighs around 2 lb (0·9 kg).

Week 29

You probably feel as if all your internal organs are being crowded out by the baby. There is pressure on your diaphragm, liver, stomach and intestine.

By now the baby's head is more or less in proportion with the rest of its body.

Week 30

It is important to remember to maintain good posture when you are standing or sitting, even though the weight of the baby seems to be dragging you off balance.

The baby is probably very aware of the Braxton Hicks contractions, even when you do not notice them.

Week 31

You may be getting very breathless when you climb stairs or exert yourself. In fact, the tidal volume of your lungs has increased from about 500 cubic cm of air with each breath in to 800 cubic cm.

However breathless you feel, the baby is getting enough oxygen. It now weighs about 4 lb (1·8 kg).

Week 32

At each clinic visit the baby's position is felt, its rate of growth assessed and its heart checked.

The baby is 16 in (42 cm) long. It is perfectly formed but the fat reserves beneath its skin are only gradually laid down. Born at this time it would still need to be cared for in an incubator.

Week 33

You may be able to distinguish the baby's bottom from a foot or knee. You feel its movements more as prods and kicks—it may be too big now to swoop around in the amniotic fluid.

Your baby has probably adopted the most usual head down ("vertex" or "cephalic") position, in which it will now stay until delivery.

Week 34

You will be attending prenatal classes by now.

The baby's skin is becoming pinker. The baby can differentiate between dark and light, and is bathed in a red glow when sunlight is on your tummy.

Week 35

You may have some backache at about this time. This is because the ligaments and muscles supporting the joints in the small of your back relax.

The fetus measures approximately 18 in (44 cm) in length and weighs around $5\frac{1}{2}$ lb (2·5 kg).

Week 36

Doctor visits will be every week from now on. If this is your first baby, it will probably engage some time this week or soon after, and may have done so already. Your lump will settle lower down and you should find that your breathing becomes easier, though you may also need to urinate more often.

The baby is almost fully mature and any time now the presenting part may drop into your pelvis ready for birth. It is about 18 in (49 cm) long.

Week 37

You may have a chance to tour the maternity floor and labor room of the hospital in which you are planning to give birth.

The baby may be rehearsing slight breathing movements, though there is no air in its lungs. In this way amniotic fluid passes into the baby's trachea, giving it hiccups!

Week 38

You may notice that the baby moves less now and that, instead of whole body movements, there are only jabs from the feet and knees, and the strange buzzing sensation inside your vagina of the head moving against your pelvic floor muscles.

The baby may be putting on as much as 1 oz (28 g) in weight a day at this stage.

Week 39

Your cervix is ripening in preparation for labor. You may feel heavy and weary and be experiencing quite strong Braxton Hicks contractions.

The amniotic fluid is renewed every 3 hours. The baby's bowel is filled with greenish black meconium, excretions from the baby's alimentary glands mixed with bile pigment, lanugo and cells from the bowel wall.

Week 40

The long awaited day is near, and perhaps after the long wait you are now wishing that it had not come so quickly! You will soon hold your child in your arms.

The baby is about 20 in (55 cm) long. The presenting part is in the lower segment of your uterus and pressing through the softened, partially opened, cervix. It is about to leave the security it has always known and then it will need all your love and care.

Appendix 1

Health and hospitalization insurance

An amendment to Federal Law now makes it mandatory for all employers with 15 or more workers to provide equal benefits for male and female employees. This means that if you receive a health insurance benefit, it must cover pregnancy and birth in the same way as any other medical condition. This does not mean that the employer is required to give health insurance but if he does give it, it must not discriminate against the pregnant woman, whether married or not. Contact your insurance carrier for the precise details of your policy.

Most policies cover the hospital costs of a semiprivate room. If you wish to have a private room, you will be asked to pay a supplement. Your doctor will probably supply you with hospital registration forms or arrange to have them sent to you. At this time inquire about fees, deposits, and estimated costs. The obstetrician's fee does not usually include tests such as amniocentesis, nor does it include vitamins. Most health care policies do not cover the full cost of the obstetrician and may not cover any part of the cost of a midwife. In addition you may be asked to pay a standby fee for an anasthesiologist and a fee for a pediatrician. These may or may not be covered. The conditions of coverage for well baby care vary with the policy. Some insurance policies do not cover prenatal classes. It is worth while for women to group together to put pressure on the company to cover these costs. You should be aware that most policies do not pay until after the baby is born. Therefore it is important to make financial arrangements with your birth attendant regarding the time of payment, so that if possible you can pay when it is most convenient for you.

Childcare leave

Some employers allow a woman to have maternity leave without loss of benefits or seniority. It is now a Federal Law that companies that give maternity leave must not discriminate against fathers.

Disability benefits

These are determined by company policy. Federal Law states that if employees are covered by disability insurance, pregnancy and childbirth must be included. For further information about disability benefits, contact your State Department of Labor.

Union benefits

Contact your shop steward regarding union benefits since these vary widely.

Public assistance

If you have been receiving public assistance, visit the doctor or clinic as soon as you suspect you are pregnant. You will need a letter stating your expected date of delivery to qualify for an additional allowance for your expected baby. This will begin at the beginning of your fourth month of pregnancy and is the equivalent to the allowance for an additional person. The expected baby is not entitled to food stamps or rent allowance. Contact your local Bureau of Public Assistance or Department of Social Services.

Medicaid

If you cannot afford prenatal care, contact your local Bureau of Medical Assistance or the Department of Social Service office at your local hospital or clinic. If your medical bills are excessive, you may qualify for Medicaid even though your income is otherwise adequate.

Free clinics

Contact your state or local Board of Health and local Women's Health Center for information about free or low cost clinics.

Women, Infants and Children's Supplementary Food Program (WIC)

This program supplies supplementary foods to women, infants and children at nutritional risk. Each state determines the standards for nutritional risk but two of the common criteria are inadequate weight gain and anemia. Women should apply through the appropriate state agency; in most instances this is the Department of Health or Department of Social Services. A woman is eligible as soon as her pregnancy is confirmed; she remains eligible until six months postpartum if she is bottlefeeding and twelve months postpartum if she is breastfeeding. The income regulations differ from area to area but in 1980 in New York City a family of four may gross almost $16,000 a year and still be eligible. Nutritional risk is determined by a physician, registered nurse, dietician or nutritionist. Currently the supplementary foods include milk, cheese, eggs, juice and cereal for the pregnant and lactating woman, and infant formula, infant cereal and infant juice for the bottlefed baby. It is expected that peanut butter and dried beans will soon be added to this list. The WIC program came into being in recognition of the fact that the pregnant and lactating woman needs an additional source of protein to produce a healthy baby.

Appendix 2

These research references relate to the asterisks in the main text. Where there is more than one asterisk on a page, the references appear in order, with each entry on a new line relating to a different asterisk.

p. 45   J. R. Ashford, "Policies for maternity care in England and Wales", *The Place of Birth*, (ed. Sheila Kitzinger and John Davis), OUP, 1978.

p. 49   Sheila Kitzinger, *The Good Birth Guide*, Fontana, 1979.

p. 50   Sheila Kitzinger, *The choice of birth at home for those thinking of having a home confinement*, NCT, 1976, and Sheila Kitzinger, *Some women's experience of induced labour*, NCT, 1978.

p. 84   Sir Dugald Baird, *Journal of Biosocial Science*, VI, 113, 1974. R. W. Smithells *et al.*, "Maternal nutrition in early pregnancy", *British Journal of Nutrition*, 38, 3, 497–506, 1977 and *Nutrition and Fetal Development*, (ed. M. Winick), John Wiley & Sons, 1974. H. A. Kaminetzky and H. Baker, "Micronutrients in Pregnancy", *Clinical Obstetrics and Gynecology*, 20, 2, 363–380, 1977 and R. M. Pitkin, "Nutritional support in obstetrics and gynecology", *Clinical Obstetrics and Gynecology*, 19, 3, 489–513, 1976.

p. 85   Gary K. Oakes and Ronald A. Chez, "Nutrition in Pregnancy", *Contemporary Obstetrics and Gynecology*, 4, 147–150, 1974. Ellen Buchman Ewald, *Recipes for a Small Planet*, Ballantine, 1977.

p. 86 and p. 89 Jacqueline Gibson Gazella, *Nutrition for the Childbearing Year*, Woodland Publishing Co., Wayzata, Minn., 1979. R. W. Smithells *et al.*, *Lancet*, I, 8164, 339–340, 1980.

M. Robinson, "Salt in Pregnancy", *Lancet*, I, 178–181, 1958. B. S. Worthington, J. Vermeersch and S. R. Williams, *Nutrition in Pregnancy and Lactation*, Mosby, 1977. B. S. Worthington *et al.*, op. cit.

p. 90   *Drugs adversely affecting the human fetus*, Ross Laboratories Columbus, Ohio, 1971. The thalidomide disaster took place in the early 1960s. In some cases when the mother had taken the drug for only a few days the baby was badly affected, as the effect of the drug on the babies depended on the stage of growth the embryo had reached when its mother took the drug. Early suspicions about the drug were reported by a doctor in Australia, who had noted a sudden very high proportion of babies born with deformities following the expectant mothers' use of thalidomide, but it was some time before the drug was withdrawn.

p. 91   Federal Register, 43, 114, US Department of Health, Education and Welfare, 1978.

p. 92   *Perinatal Problems*, (ed. N. R. Butler and E. D. Alberman), E. & S. Livingstone, 1969. M. B. Meyer, "How does maternal smoking affect birth weight and maternal weight gain?", *American Journal of Obstetrics and Gynecology*, 131, 888–893, 1978. J. Kline *et al.*, "Smoking: a risk factor for spontaneous abortion", *New England Journal of Medicine*, 297, 793–795, 1977 and R. L. Naeye, "Relationship of cigarette smoking to congenital anomalies and perinatal death", *American Journal of Pathology*, 90, 289–297, 1978 and M. B. Meyer and J. A. Tonascia, "Maternal smoking, pregnancy complications and perinatal mortality", *American Journal of Obstetrics and Gynecology*, 128, 494–502, 1977.

p. 94   Ross Laboratories op. cit. Cree *et al.*, *British Medical Journal*, 4, 251, 1973. J. V. Kelly, "Drugs used in the management of pregnancy", *Clinical Obstetrics and Gynecology*, 20, 395–410, 1977.

p. 95   Peter Parish, *The Doctors and Patients Handbook of Medicines and Drugs*, Knopf, 1977.

p. 97   Federal Register, 41, 115, 1976. Roger Hoag, "Perinatal psychology", *Birth and the Family Journal*, 113, 1974. Parish, op. cit.

p. 98   Studies of babies born in England and Wales between 1943 and 1965 revealed that the children of mothers who had pelvic X-rays during pregnancy were almost twice as likely to develop leukemia before they were 10 years old than those who had had no X-rays. The greatest risk is in the earliest weeks, when the mother may not even know she is pregnant. The risk of cancer was increased 15 times when X-rays were done in the first three months of pregnancy. See A. Stewart and G. W. Kneale, "Radiation dose effects in relation to obstetric X-rays and childhood cancers", *Lancet*, I, 1495, 1970. David W. Smith, Sterling K. Clarren and Mary Ann Sedgwick Harvey, "Hyperthermia as a possible teratogenic agent", *Journal of Pediatrics*, 92, 6, 878–883, June, 1978, and Peter Miller, David W. Smith and Thomas H. Shepard, "Maternal hyperthermia as a possible cause of anencephaly", *Lancet*, I, 8063, 519–521, 1978.

p. 110   Aidan MacFarlane, *The Psychology of Childbirth*, Harvard UP, 1977.

p.111   E. Noble, *Essential Exercises for the Childbearing Year*, John Murray, 1978.

333

p. 121   Christopher Redman, "Old-fashioned alertness is the key", *General Practitioner*, 1979.

p. 123   Pregnant women often have "physiological" anemia. There is a greater volume of blood circulating in their bodies; hence the red blood cells are dilated. This is normal and does not mean that they are suffering from anemia.

Having iron supplements when you do not need them may do more harm than good; excess iron enlarges the red blood cells (macrocytosis) until they are too big to pass through some of the capillaries in the mother's and the baby's circulatory systems. This deprives the baby of essential nutrients and can lead to its growth being retarded. See T. Lind, *British Journal of Obstetrics and Gynaecology*, 83, 760, 1976.

p. 156   Sherry L. Jimenez, Linda C. Jones and Ruth G. Jungman, "Prenatal classes for repeat parents", *MCN*, 4, 305–308, Sept./Oct., 1979.

p. 161   Grantly Dick-Read, *Childbirth Without Fear*, Harper & Row, 1972.

p. 162   Erna Wright, *The New Childbirth*, Pocket Books, 1969.

p. 172   Sheila Kitzinger, *Women as Mothers*, Random House, 1980.

p. 190   T. J. Bassler, "Dietary practices of marathon runners", in *Health Aspects of Endurance Training, Medicine and Sport*, 12, Karger, 1978.

p. 197   J. F. Pearson and J. B. Weaver, *British Medical Journal*, I, 1305, 1976.
J. F. Pearson, op. cit.

p. 204   Professor Mendez-Bauer discovered that dilatation of the cervix and the efficiency of contractions is much greater when a woman is standing up than when she is lying on her back. The uterus works nearly twice as well.[1]

Professor Caldeyro-Barcia, looking at the difference between contractions when a woman is lying on her left side and on her back, found that contractions were as frequent when a woman was standing as when lying flat on her back but that they were stronger. He concluded that for the uterus to work really effectively the woman should be standing up.[2,3]

Eleven hospitals in seven Latin-American countries joined in a study of the effects of the mother's position in labor. At each hospital half the mothers were told to lie in bed during the first stage and the other half were encouraged to get up or sit or lie in bed as they liked. It was discovered that 95 per cent of the women did not want to lie down. The membranes were not ruptured artificially, and the waters went at the end of the first stage or the beginning of the second in 85 per cent of the women. First time mothers who stayed upright had shorter first stages than those who were lying down. The majority of the women said they were more comfortable when they stayed upright.

To find out whether an upright position could produce traumatic pressure on the baby's head the researchers looked at the incidence of caput and also at the effect on the baby's heart and discovered that, when the membranes had not ruptured, there was no increased rate of caput if the mother was standing, nor was there an increase in deceleration of the fetal heart as recorded by an electronic monitor. They concluded that in normal labor an upright position is fine for the baby, shortens labor and reduces pain.[4]

Further research at the Queen Elizabeth Hospital, Birmingham, came up with the same results.[5] See 1 Peter M. Dunn, "Obstetric delivery today", *Lancet*, I, 7963, 790–793, 1976.
2 R. Caldeyro-Barcia *et al.*, "Effects of position changes on the intensity and frequency of uterine contractions during labor", *American Journal of Obstetric Gynecology*, 80, 284, 1960.
3 Yuen Chou-liu, "Effects of an upright position during labor", *American Journal of Nursing*, December 1974.
4 R. L. Schwarcz *et al.*, "Fetal heart rate patterns in labors with intact and with ruptured membranes", *Journal of Perinatal Medicine*, 1, 153, 1973.
5 A. M. Flynn, J. Kelly, G. Hollins and P. F. Lynch, "Ambulation in labour", *British Medical Journal*, II, 591–593, 1978.

p. 224   Emanuel A. Friedman, *Labor. Clinical Evaluation and Management*, Meredith Publishing Co., 1967.

p. 236   Ronald Melzack, *The Puzzle of Pain*, Penguin, 1973.

p. 237   Melzack, op. cit.
ibid.
ibid.

p. 240   *Obstetrics*, a drug-information publication produced by Roche.

p. 241   Dianne Houslow *et al.*, "Intrapartum drugs and fetal blood pH and gas status", *Journal of Obstetrics and Gynaecology, British Commonwealth*, 80, 1007–1012, 1973

p. 242   Michael Rosen, "Pain and its Relief", *Benefits and Hazards of the New Obstetrics*, (ed. T. Chard and M. Richards), William Heinemann Medical Books, 1977.

p. 243   M. B. Wingate, "Effects of epidural analgesia on fetal and neonatal status", in *American Journal of Obstetrics and Gynecology*, 119, 1101–1106, 1974, and B. S. Schiffrin, "Fetal heart rate patterns following epidural anaesthesia and oxytocin infusion during labour", *Journal of Obstetrics and Gynaecology, British Commonwealth*, 79, 332, 1972.
Andrew Doughty, *Journal of Royal Society of Medicine*, December, 1978.

A. D. Noble et al., "Continuous lumbar epidural using bupivicaine", Journal of Obstetrics and Gynaecology, British Commonwealth, 78, 559, 1971.
Kay Standley et al., "Local-regional anesthesia during childbirth; effect on newborn behaviors", Science, 186, Nov. 15, 1974.

p. 244   Josephine A. Williamson, "Hypnosis in Obstetrics", Nursing Mirror, 27 Nov., 1975.
Michael Rosen, op. cit.

p. 246   Kieran O'Driscoll, John M. Stronge, Maurice Minogue, "Active management of labor", British Medical Journal, 3, 135–137, 1973.

p. 247   R. Caldeyro-Barcia et al., "Adverse perinatal effects of early amniotomy during labor", Modern Perinatal Medicine, (ed. L. Gluck), pp. 431–439, Year Book Medical Publishers, Chicago, 1974.

p. 248   A. Huch et al., "Continuous transcutaneous monitoring of fetal oxygen tension during labour", British Journal of Obstetrics and Gynaecology, 84, Suppl. 1, 1977.
G. C. Gunn et al., "Premature rupture of the fetal membranes", American Journal of Obstetrics and Gynecology, 106, 469–477, 1970.
P. J. Steer et al., "The effect of membrane rupture on fetal heart in induced labour", British Journal of Obstetrics and Gynaecology, 83, 454–459, June 1976.

p. 255   Allan Gordon "The time for forceps or Caesareans", General Practitioner, 1 June, 1979.
A. W. Linston and A. J. Campbell, "Danger of oxytocin-induced labour to fetuses", British Medical Journal, 3, 606–607, 1974.

p. 257   Reducing the Risk, Department of Health and Social Security, 1977.

p. 259   D. M. Okada and A. W. Chow "Neonatal scalp abscess following intrapartum fetal monitoring", American Journal of Obstetrics and Gynecology, 127, 875, 1977.

p. 262   Stuart Campbell, Letter published in Sharing, Maternal Health Committee of Social Planning and Review Council of British Columbia, Summer 1979.

p. 269   Frederick Leboyer, Birth without Violence, Knopf, 1975.

p. 274   Aidan MacFarlane, Getting to know each other, Farley Products, 1979.

p. 276   Michel Odent of Pithiviers, Bien-être, Seuil, 1976; Genèse de l'homme écologique, EPI, 1979.
Johnson's Baby Newsline, Autumn 1978.

p. 280   There has been a great deal of research in different countries which demonstrates that it is far more difficult for a mother to feel that her baby belongs to her—to bond with her baby—if she does not have time immediately after the birth to begin to get to know her baby. Much of the original research was done with monkeys: Robert Hinde discovered that rhesus monkey babies separated from their mothers shortly after birth became very distressed and stayed hunched up in a corner of the cage. He suggested that separation from the mother might be bad for a newborn human baby too.[1] Other research has even gone so far as to indicate that mothers who had greater contact with their babies, and continued this contact through early childhood, produced children whose IQ, when tested at the age of five, was significantly higher than average.[2] Those who advocate bonding between mother and baby at birth also suggest that the importance of skin-to-skin contact between mother and child is important. Criticisms have been voiced that the child could become chilled, but a study of heat loss in warmed cribs as compared with that in the mother's arms showed that there was no significant difference between the temperature of babies lying in heated cribs and others left with their mothers.[3]
See 1 Robert Hinde in Proceedings of the Royal Society, 196, 29, 1977.
2 F. S. W. Brimblecombe, Separation and Special care Baby Units, William Heinemann Medical Books, 1978.
3 C. N. Phillips, "Neonatal heat loss in heated cribs vs mother's arms", Journal of Obstetrical, Gynecological and Neonatal Nursing, 6, 11–15, 1974.
Marshall Klaus and John Kennell, Maternal-Infant Bonding, Mosby, 1977.

p. 285   Klaus and Kennell, op cit.

p. 286   L. Silverman, W. A. Silverman and J. C. Sinclair, Pediatrics, 41, 1033, 1969.

p. 289   P. A. and J. P. Davies, Lancet, 2, 1216, 1970.

p. 294   Cicely Williams and Derrick B. Jelliffe, Mother and Child Health, OUP, 1972.

p. 296   Harriet Sarnoff Schiff, The Bereaved Parent, Crown, 1977; Penguin, 1978.

p. 310   Rudolph Schaffer, Mothering, Harvard UP, 1977.

p. 316   If a woman has never had German measles (rubella), the obstetrician may advise her to have a rubella vaccination after delivery. Since this vaccine could affect any baby conceived within the next three months, it is vitally important for her not to conceive during this time. If the woman is unsure about what kind of contraceptive to use, she may be offered an injection of a long acting contraceptive called Depo-Provera. Women who intend to breastfeed should not have this injection which introduces hormones into the baby's bloodstream.

Useful reading

G. J. Annas, *The Rights of Hospital Patients: The Basic ACLU Guide to a Hospital Patient's Rights*, Avon, 1975.

Boston Women's Health Book Collective, *Our Bodies Ourselves*, Simon & Schuster, 1976.

G. Bourne and D. N. Danforth, *Pregnancy*, Harper & Row, 1975.

T. G. R. Bower, *The Perceptual World of the Child*, Harvard UP, 1977.

Berry Brazelton, *Infants and Mothers*, Delacorte, 1969; Dell, 1972.

Berry Brazelton, *Toddlers and Parents*, Delacorte, 1974; Delta, 1976.

G. S. Brewer (ed.), *The Pregnancy-After-30 Workbook*, Rodale, 1978.

G. S. and T. Brewer, *What Every Pregnant Woman Should Know: The Truth About Diets and Drugs in Pregnancy*, Random House, 1977; Penguin, 1979.

D. Brook, *Naturebirth*, Pantheon, 1976.

A. Cartwright, *The Dignity of Labour*, Methuen, 1979.

G. Corea, *The Hidden Malpractice*, Morrow, 1977; Jove, 1978.

G. Dick-Read, *Childbirth without Fear*, Harper & Row, 1972.

M. Eiger and S. W. Olds, *The Complete Book of Breast Feeding*, Bantam, 1973.

D. and R. Ewy, *Preparation for Breast Feeding*, Doubleday, 1975.

G. Flanagan, *The First Nine Months of Life*, Simon & Schuster, 1962.

S. Fraiberg, *Every Child's Birthright: In Defense of*

Mothering, Basic Books, 1977; Bantam, 1979.

J. G. Gazella, *Nutrition for the Childbearing Year*, Woodland, 1979.

M. Howell, M.D., *Healing at Home: A Guide to Health Care for Children*, Beacon, 1979.

D. B. and E. F. P. Jelliffe, *Human Milk in the Modern World*, OUP, 1978.

S. Kippley, *Breast Feeding and Natural Child Spacing: The Ecology of Natural Mothering*, Harper & Row, 1974; Penguin, 1975.

S. Kitzinger, *Birth at Home*, OUP, 1979.

S. Kitzinger, *Education and Counselling for Childbirth*, Schocken, 1979.

S. Kitzinger, *The Experience of Breast Feeding*, Penguin, 1980.

S. Kitzinger, *The Experience of Childbirth*, Taplinger, 1972; Penguin, 1978.

S. Kitzinger, *Giving Birth*, Taplinger, 1971; Schocken, 1978.

S. Kitzinger, *Women as Mothers*, Random House, 1980.

S. Kitzinger and J. Davis, *The Place of Birth*, OUP, 1978.

La Leche League International, *The Womanly Art of Breast Feeding*, La Leche League, 1963.

F. M. Lappé, *Diet for a Small Planet*, Ballantine Books, 1975.

P. Leach, *Your Baby and Child*, Alfred A. Knopf, 1978.

F. Leboyer, *Birth without Violence*, Alfred A. Knopf, 1975.

F. Leboyer, *Inner Beauty, Inner Light: Yoga for Pregnant Women*, Alfred A. Knopf, 1978.

F. Leboyer, *Loving Hands*, Alfred A. Knopf, 1976.

J. Liedloff, *The Continuum Concept*, Alfred A. Knopf, 1977, Warner, 1979.

A. Loader (ed.), *Pregnancy and Parenthood*, OUP, 1980.

A. Macfarlane, *The Psychology of Childbirth*, Harvard UP, 1977.

A. Montagu, *Touching*, Columbia UP, 1971.

L. Nilsson, *A Child is Born*, Delacorte, 1977.

E. Noble, *Essential Exercises for the Childbearing Year*, Houghton Mifflin, 1976.

E. Noble, *Having Twins*, Houghton Mifflin, 1980.

R. and R. N. Rapoport and Z. Strelitz, *Fathers, Mothers and Society*, Basic Books, 1977.

R. Schaffer, *Mothering*, Harvard UP, 1977.

B. and G. Seaman, M.D., *Women and the Crisis in Sex Hormones*, Rawson, 1977; Bantam, 1978.

D. R. Shanklin and J. Hodin, *Maternal Nutrition and Child Health*, Charles C. Thomas, 1979.

L. B. Shettles, M.D. and R. Rugh, *From Conception to Birth: The Drama of Life's Beginnings*, Harper & Row, 1971.

D. Stern, *The First Relationship: Infant and Mother*, Harvard UP, 1977.

P. S. Williams, *Nourishing Your Unborn Child*, Nash, 1974; Avon, 1975.

Useful addresses

American Academy of Husband-coached Childbirth
Box 5224 Sherman Oaks,
California 91413
(213) 788-6662

American Academy of Pediatrics
1801 Hinman Avenue
Evanston, Illinois 60201
(312) 869-4255

American College of Nurse Midwives
1012 14th Street N.W.
Suite 801
Washington, D.C. 20005
(202) 347-5447

The American Fertility Society
1608 13th Avenue South
Suite 101 Birmingham,
Alabama 35256
(205) 933-7222

American Public Health Association
Maternal-Child Health Section
1015 18th Street N.W.
Washington, D.C. 20036
(202) 789-5600

American Society for Psycho-prophylaxis in Obstetrics (ASPO)
4711 K Street
Washington, D.C. 20005
(202) 783-7050

Association for Childbirth at Home, International
Box 1219
Cerritos, California 90701
(213) 668-1132

Birth, Family & Health Bookstore
P.O. Box 2232
Buena Park, California 90620
(714) 761-1012

Birth Right
101–25 104th Street
Ozone Park, N.Y. 11416
(212) 847-8800

Cesareans/Support, Education and Concern (C/Sec)
66 Christopher Road
Waltham,
Massachusetts 02154
(617) 547-7188

Circumcision Hotline
(415) 889-1053

Consumer Product Safety Commission
5401 Westbard Avenue,
Room 745-A
Bethesda, Maryland 20016
(301) 492-6600

Cooperative Childbirth Network
14 Truesdale Drive
Croton-on-Hudson, N.Y. 10520
(914) 271-6474

Couple to Couple League
(Natural Family Planning)
P.O. Box 11084
Cincinnati, Ohio 45211
(513) 661-7612

Feminist Women's Health Centers Federation
6411 Hollywood Blvd.
Suite 202 Los Angeles,
California 90028
(213) 469-4844

Home Oriented Maternity Experience (HOME)
c/o Esther Herman
511 New York Avenue
Takoma Park
Washington, D.C. 20012
(202) 585-5832

International Childbirth Education Association (ICEA)
5636 W. Burleigh Street
Milwaukee, Wisconsin 53210
(414) 445-7470

La Leche League International
9616 Minneapolis Avenue
Franklin Park, Illinois 60131
(312) 455-7730

Lamaze
See American Society for Psychoprophylaxis in Obstetrics

National Association for Parents and Professionals for Safe Alternatives in Childbirth (NAPSAC)
P.O. Box 267 Marble Hill,
Missouri 63764
(314) 238-2010

National Foundation/March of Dimes
1275 Mamaroneck Avenue
White Plains, N.Y. 10605
(914) 428-7100

The National Midwives Association
P.O. Box 163
Princeton, N.J. 08540
(609) 799-1942

National Organization Mothers of Twins Clubs
5402 Amberwood Lane
Rockville, Maryland 20853
(301) 460-9108

National Sudden Infant Death Syndrome Foundation
310 South Michigan Avenue
Suite 1904
Chicago, Illinois 60604
(312) 663-0650

National Women's Health Network
224 7th Street S.E.
Washington, D.C. 20003
(202) 543-9222

Parents Anonymous
(800) 421-0353

Resources in Human Nurturing, International
(Breastfeeding Information and Publications)
3885 Forest Street
P.O. Box 6861
Denver, Colorado 80206
(303) 388-4608

Sex Information and Education Council of the U.S. Inc.
84 5th Avenue
New York, N.Y. 10011
(212) 929-2300

Society for the Protection of the Unborn through Nutrition (SPUN)
17 N. Wabash Avenue #603
Chicago, Illinois 60602
(312) 332-2334

Toxemia Hotline
(914) 271-6474

United Infertility Organization
P.O. Box 23
Scarsdale, N.Y. 10583
(914) 723-7122

Women, Infants & Children's Supplementary Food Program (WIC)
Contact your State Department of Health for local office.

Glossary

Abdomen The part of the body containing the intestines, stomach, bowels and uterus.

Abortion (Miscarriage) Either spontaneous or induced delivery of the fetus before the 28th week.

Abruptio placenta (Accidental hemorrhage) The peeling away of part of the placenta from the wall of the uterus in late pregnancy, which may result in heavy bleeding.

Accelerated labor The artificial augmentation of contractions, after the cervix has started to dilate, by the injection of oxytocin through an intravenous drip. Often used to speed up a long labor or to get a "tired" or incoordinate uterus working more effectively.

Active management of labor The constant monitoring and technical control or induction of labor.

AFP See *Alphafetoprotein*.

Albumin A protein present in all animal tissues. Albumin in the urine of a pregnant woman can be a sign of preeclampsia.

Alphafetoprotein (AFP) A substance produced by the embryonic yolk sac, and later by the fetal liver, which enters the mother's bloodstream during pregnancy. A very high level can indicate neural tube defects of the fetus—such as spina bifida or Down's syndrome—but can also mean a multiple pregnancy.

Alveoli Milk glands in the breasts which, when they are stimulated by prolactin, produce a flow of milk.

Amenorrhea The absence of menstrual periods.

Amino acids The main organic chemical constituents of proteins found in all foods produced from animals, but only in limited and varying combinations in vegetables.

Amnesia Loss of memory, usually short term, which can be a side effect of certain drugs, especially Valium.

Amniocentesis The surgical extraction of a small amount of amniotic fluid through the pregnant woman's abdomen. Usually done as a test for fetal defects or fetal maturity.

Amnion The layer of membrane immediately enveloping the fetus and the amniotic fluid inside the uterus, it is also referred to as the amniotic sac, or the bag of waters.

Amniotic fluid The fluid surrounding the fetus in the uterus.

Amniotic sac See *Amnion*.

Amniotomy The surgical rupture of the amniotic sac, sometimes done to speed up labor. Referred to as ARM (artificial rupture of the membranes).

Amobarbital See *Barbiturates*.

Analgesics Painkilling agents not inducing unconsciousness.

Anemia A condition in which there is an abnormally low proportion of red corpuscles in the blood, treated by iron (Fe) supplements.

Anencephaly The congenital absence of the brain.

Anesthetic Medication that produces partial or complete insensibility to pain.

Anesthetic, general Anesthetic that affects the whole body, usually with loss of consciousness.

Anesthetic, local Anesthetic that affects a limited part of the body. See also *Caudal; Epidural; Paracervical*.

Antepartum hemorrhage Bleeding from the vagina occurring after the 28th week of pregnancy. A rare but serious condition. See also *Abruptio placenta; Placenta previa*.

Anterior position See *Occipito anterior*.

Antibacterials Chemical agents that limit the growth of, or destroy, bacteria. See also *Sulphonamides*.

Antibiotics Substances capable of destroying or limiting the growth of microorganisms, especially bacteria.

Antibodies Protein produced naturally by the body to combat any foreign bodies, germs or bacteria.

Anticholinergic drugs Used in the treatment of nausea and vomiting partly by limiting the impulses through the nervous system and partly by restricting the secretion of stomach acids.

Anticoagulants Drugs that prevent the blood clotting.

Anticonvulsants Drugs that combat convulsions, especially epilepsy.

Antihistamines Drugs used in the treatment of nausea, vomiting and certain allergies.

Apgar scale A general test of the baby's wellbeing given immediately after birth to ascertain the heart rate and tone, respiration, blood circulation and nerve responses, named after Dr Virginia Apgar.

Apnea Interrupted breathing which may occur in preterm and low birthweight babies.

Areola The pigmented circle of skin surrounding the nipple.

Arhythmic contractions Irregular contractions.

ARM See *Amniotomy*.

Aspirin (Salicylate) A mild analgesic. Taken in pregnancy, it may interfere with the clotting of blood in the fetus.

Bag of waters See *Amnion*.

Barbiturates Powerful and highly addictive tranquilizers.

Bearing down The pushing movement made by the uterus in the second stage of labor.

Bile pigment See *Bilirubin*.

Bilirubin Broken down red blood cells, normally converted to nontoxic substances by the liver. Some newborn babies have levels of bilirubin too high for their livers to cope with. See also *Jaundice, neonatal.*

Birth canal See *Vagina.*

Blastocyst An early stage of the developing egg when it has segmented into a group of cells but is not yet implanted.

Blighted ovum An abnormal development of the egg in which the cells do not develop in the usual way to form a baby. It results in miscarriage.

Bradycardia A slow heart rate. In the fetus and newborn baby, this is a rate of less than 120 beats a minute.

Braxton Hicks contractions (Rehearsal contractions) Contractions of the uterus which occur throughout pregnancy, but which may not be noticed until the ninth month.

Breast pump Apparatus for drawing milk from the breasts.

Breech presentation The position of a baby who is bottom down rather than head down in the uterus.

Brow presentation The position of a baby who is head down in the uterus, but with chin up, so that the brow comes through the cervix first.

Candida See *Thrush.*

Caput A small, temporary swelling on the crown of the baby's head caused by the head being pressed against an incompletely dilated cervix.

Carpal tunnel syndrome Numbness and tingling of the hands arising from pressure on the nerves of the wrist. In pregnancy it is caused by the body's accumulation of fluids.

Catheter A thin plastic tube inserted into the body, through a natural channel to draw off urine from the bladder, or into a vein

to maintain a constant input of fluids, or into the epidural space to introduce anesthetic.

Caudal (Caudal epidural block) An anesthetic injected into the base of the spine. See also *Epidural.*

Cephalhematoma A temporary swelling on the side of the baby's head caused by pressure during labor.

Cephalic presentation The position of a baby who is head down in the uterus. This is the most common presentation.

Cephalopelvic disproportion A state in which the head of the fetus is larger than the cavity of the mother's pelvis. Delivery must be by Cesarean section.

Certified Nurse Midwife A graduate of an approved program who has passed National Boards and is licensed to practice by her state.

Cervical dilatation See *Dilatation.*

Cervical erosion Superficial inflammation of the cervix which sometimes occurs during early pregnancy, and may if infected produce irritation and yellow vaginal discharge.

Cervical incompetence A disorder of the cervix, usually arising after a previous mid-pregnancy termination or damage to the cervix during a previous labor, in which the cervix opens up too soon, resulting in repeated midpregnancy miscarriages. It is sometimes treated by suturing to hold the cervix closed, but this is not always effective.

Cervicograph See *Partogram.*

Cervix The lower entrance to the uterus, or neck of the womb.

Cesarean section Delivery of the baby through a cut in the abdominal and uterine walls.

Chloasma Skin discoloration during pregnancy, often facial.

Chloral hydrate Nonbarbiturate hypnotic tranquilizer. See also *Tranquilizers.*

Chorion The outer membranous tissue enveloping the developing fetus and placenta.

Chorionic gonadotrophin See *Human chorionic gonadotrophin (HCG).*

Chorionic villi The layer of tiny fronds which forms around the fertile ovum, allowing it to become embedded in the uterine wall.

Chromosomes Rodlike structures containing genes occurring in pairs within the nucleus of every cell. Human cells each contain 23 pairs. See also *Gene.*

Circumcision An operation to cut the foreskin from the penis, usually performed soon after delivery if desired.

Cleft palate A congenital abnormality of the roof of the mouth.

Clitoris Sensitive small organ at the upper end of a woman's genitals, just under the pubic bone and between the folded external labia.

Club foot A congenital abnormality where the foot is twisted out of shape.

Codeine An addictive pain-killing agent derived from opium.

Colostrum A kind of milk, rich in proteins, formed and secreted by the breasts in late pregnancy and gradually changing to mature milk some days after delivery.

Conception The fertilization of the egg by the sperm and its implantation in the uterine wall.

Congenital abnormality An abnormality or deformity existing from birth usually arising from a damaged gene, the adverse effect of certain drugs, or the effect of some diseases during pregnancy.

Contractions The regular tightening of the uterine muscles as they work to dilate the cervix in labor and to press the baby down the birth canal.

Corpuscles Constituents of blood, divided into red and white varieties.

Corpus luteum A glandular mass which forms in the ovary after fertilization. It produces progesterone which helps to form the placenta, and is active for the first 14 weeks of pregnancy.

Cortisone A steroid produced by the adrenal gland which appears in the amniotic fluid immediately before labor.

Crowning The moment when the largest part of the baby's head appears in the vagina and does not slip back again.

Cystitis An inflammation of the bladder and urinary tract, producing a stinging sensation when water is passed.

D and C The surgical *dilatation* (opening) of the cervix, and *curettage* (removal of the contents) of the uterus.

Dehydration An excessive loss of body water.

Demerol See *Analgesics*.

Depression, respiratory Breathing difficulties in the newborn baby.

Dextrostix A test to assess the level of sugar in the urine.

Diabetes Failure of the system to metabolize glucose, traced by excess sugar in the blood and urine.

Diastolic pressure The blood pressure between heart beats. See also *Systolic pressure*.

Diazepam (Valium) See *Tranquilizers*.

Dilatation The progressive opening of the cervix, caused by contractions of the uterus during labor.

Distress See *Fetal distress*.

Diuretics or "water pills". Drugs that reduce blood volume. They should not be taken during pregnancy unless a medical condition such as congestive heart disease has caused blood volume to expand beyond the needs of the pregnant woman.

Diuril See *Diuretics*.

Dizygotic See *Twins*.

Doppler A method of using ultrasound vibrations to listen to the fetal heart.

Down's syndrome (Mongolism) A severe congenital abnormality producing subnormal mentality.

Drip See *Intravenous drip*.

Dura The outer membrane protecting the spinal cord.

Dystocia, shoulder A state in which the baby's shoulders get stuck during delivery.

Eclampsia The severe form of preeclampsia, characterized by extremely high blood pressure, headaches, visual distortion and flashes, convulsions and even coma and death. It is now rare since the symptoms of pre-eclampsia are treated immediately.

Ectopic pregnancy A pregnancy which develops outside the uterus, usually in the fallopian tube. The mother has severe pain low down at one side of the abdomen at any time from the 6th to 12th weeks of pregnancy. The pregnancy must be surgically terminated.

EDD The estimated date of delivery.

Edema Fluid retention, which causes the body tissues to be puffed out.

Elective induction Induction done for convenience rather than for medical reasons. See also *Induction*.

Electrode A small electrical conductor used obstetrically for monitoring the fetal heartbeat, usually during labor.

Electronic fetal monitoring The continuous monitoring of the fetal heart by a transducer placed on the mother's abdomen over the area of the fetal heart or an electrode inserted through the cervix and clipped to the baby's scalp.

Embryo The developing organism in pregnancy, from about the 10th day after fertilization until about the 12th week of pregnancy, when it is termed a fetus.

Endocrinological changes Changes in the secretion of the endocrine glands which occur in pregnancy or the puerperium.

Endometrium The inner lining of the uterus.

Enema The introduction of fluids into the rectum to induce the evacuation of the bowels.

Engaged (Eng/E) The baby is engaged when it has settled with its presenting part deep in the pelvic cavity. This often happens in the last month of pregnancy.

Engorgement The over-congestion of the breasts with milk. If long periods are left between feedings, painful engorgement can occur, and can be relieved by putting the baby to the breast or expressing the excess milk.

Epidural (Lumbar epidural block) Regional anesthesia, used during labor and for Cesarean sections, in which an anesthetic is injected through a catheter into the epidural space in the lower spine. See also *Caudal*.

Episiotomy A surgical cut in the perineum to enlarge the vagina.

Estriol A form of estrogen. Its level in the urine or blood may be tested in late pregnancy to find if the placenta is working well.

Estrogen A hormone produced by the ovary.

Ethacrynic acid See *Diuretics*.

External version (External cephalic version, or ECV) The manipulation by gentle pressure of the fetus into the cephalic position. This may be done by an obstetrician some time between the 32nd and 34th week of pregnancy if the baby is breech.

Face presentation The position of a baby whose face is coming through the cervix first.

Fallopian tube (Oviduct) The tube into which a ripe egg is wafted after its expulsion from the ovary, along which it travels on its way to the uterus.

False labor Braxton Hicks (rehearsal) contractions that come so strongly and regularly that they are mistaken for the contractions of the first stage of labor.

Fertilization The meeting of the sperm with the ovum to form a new life.

Fetal distress A shortage in the flow of oxygen to the fetus which can arise from numerous causes.

Fetus The developing child in the uterus, from the end of the embryonic stage, at about the 12th week of pregnancy, until the date of delivery.

FH Fetal heart.

Fluid retention See *Edema*.

FMF Fetal movement felt.

Folic acid A form of vitamin B essential to the constant production of blood cells and hemoglobin, the shortage of which can produce anemia in the fetus. It is sometimes supplemented during pregnancy.

Fontanels The soft spots between the unjoined sections of the skull of the fetus.

Foremilk Milk which accumulates naturally in the ducts behind the nipple and precedes the main let down of milk.

Fraternal twins See *Twins*.

Fundal palpation Feeling through the abdominal wall for the top of the uterus to assess its height.

Fundus The upper part of the uterus.

Gamma globulin A protein-based antibody.

Gene The part of every cell which stores genetic characteristics.

Genetic counseling Information and advice on the probability of recurrent

hereditary abnormalities or diseases.

Gentle birth One term used for a method of delivery proposed by Frederick Leboyer in which the shock of birth upon the baby is minimized and the baby is welcomed by loving hands, skin contact and soft lights and is able to discover itself in a deep, warm bath.

German measles See *Rubella*.

Gestation The length of time between conception and delivery.

Glucose A natural sugar found in certain organic materials and in the blood; the main source of energy. Used in labor to supplement the level of blood sugar, usually introduced by intravenous drip.

Glycogen The natural source of glucose; glycogen stores carbohydrate materials and is formed by the liver and muscles.

Gynecologist A doctor who specializes in all aspects of female medicine.

Hb See *Hemoglobin*.

HCG See *Human chorionic gonadotrophin*.

Hegar's sign The softening of the lower part of the uterus that gradually occurs during the first 6 weeks of pregnancy.

Hemoglobin (Hb) A constituent of the red blood cells which contains iron (Fe) and stores oxygen.

Hemorrhage Excessive bleeding.

Hemorrhoids (Piles) Swelling of the veins around the rectum.

Hormone A chemical messenger in the blood which stimulates various organs to action.

Hormone accelerated labor See *Induction*.

Human chorionic gonadotrophin A hormone released into the bloodstream by the placenta from about 8 days after the last period due. Its

presence in the urine means that a woman is pregnant.

Hyaline membrane disease Respiratory distress affecting some preterm babies resulting from a lack of surfactant which holds the lungs open.

Hydatidiform mole A rare abnormality in which the egg fails to develop after becoming implanted in the uterine wall, so there is no baby, although the placenta and chorionic villi go on developing. The growth must be removed.

Hydrocephalus A congenital abnormality in which the baby's head is swollen with fluid.

Hydrodiuril See *Diuretics*.

Hyperemesis gravidarum Almost continuous vomiting during pregnancy.

Hypertension High blood pressure. In pregnancy this can reduce the fetal blood supply.

Hyperventilation Abnormally heavy breathing which flushes carbon dioxide out of the bloodstream, so that the normal chemical balance of the blood is lost.

Hypnosis A state of mental passivity with a special susceptibility to suggestion. This can be used as an anesthetic.

Hypnotics See *Tranquilizers*.

Hypoglycemia Low blood sugar sometimes apparent in babies who have suffered a difficult delivery, preterm babies, or those of a diabetic mothers.

Hypotension Low blood pressure.

Hypothermia A very low body temperature.

ICEA International Childbirth Education Association.

Identical twins See *Twins*.

Implantation The embedding of the fertilized ovum within the wall of the uterus.

Incoordinate uterine action See *Uterine action, incoordinate*.

Induction The process of artificially starting off labor and keeping it going.

Insulin A hormone produced by the pancreas which regulates the level of carbohydrates and amino acids in the system. It may be used as a means of controlling the effects of diabetes. See also *Diabetes*.

Internal monitoring See *Electronic fetal monitoring*.

Intramuscular injection (IM) An injection into a muscle.

Intravenous drip (IV) The infusion of fluids directly into the bloodstream by means of a fine catheter introduced into a vein.

Intravenous injection (IV) An injection into a vein.

Invasive techniques Any medical technique which intrudes into the body.

Involution of the uterus The process by which the uterus returns to its normal state after pregnancy.

Jaundice, neonatal A common complaint in newborn babies, caused by inability of the liver to break down successfully an excess of red blood cells. See also *Bilirubin*.

Ketosis The accumulation of lactic acid in various body tissues and fluids, often indicated by acetone in the urine.

Labia The folds (or lips) of skin at the mouth of the vagina.

Lanugo The fine soft body hair of the fetus.

Lasix See *Diuretics*.

Lateral position Transverse lie or horizontal position of a fetus in the uterus (sometimes occurring if the mother has a large pelvis), where the presenting part is either a shoulder or the side of the head.

Laxatives Purgative drugs.

Lay midwives Also known as empirical midwives, lay midwives are not licensed or certified but often attend home births. They have learned through practical experience of "baby catching". In spite of the absence of formal midwifery training some of them are very skilled and may have nursing or medical education.

Leboyer approach See *Gentle birth*.

Let down reflex The flow of milk into the nipple.

Lie The position of the fetus in the uterus.

Ligament A fibrous tissue binding and connecting bones.

Lightening The engagement of the fetus in the pelvis, with its presenting part fitting securely in the pelvic inlet like an egg in an egg cup.

Linea nigra A line of dark skin which appears down the center of the abdomen in some women during pregnancy.

Lithotomy position The standard position for delivery in USA, the mother lying flat on her back, with her legs wide apart and raised, fixed in stirrups.

Lochia Postnatal vaginal discharge of blood.

Longitudinal lie The position of the fetus in the uterus, in which the spines of the fetus and the mother are parallel.

Long L See *Longitudinal lie*.

Low birthweight baby A baby who at birth is below the usual weight at birth of $5\frac{1}{2}$ lb (2.5 kg).

Meconium The first contents of the bowel, present in the fetus before birth and passed during the first days after birth. The presence of meconium in the fluid before delivery is usually taken as a sign of fetal distress.

Miscarriage See *Abortion*.

Molding The shaping of the bones of the baby's skull as it passes through the birth canal.

Mongolism See *Down's syndrome*.

Monilia See *Thrush*.

Monitoring See *Electronic fetal monitoring*.

Monozygotic See *Twins*.

Montgomery's tubercles Small bumps on the areola surrounding the nipple.

Morphine A narcotic opium derivative used as an analgestic.

Morula A stage in the growth of the fertilized egg when it has developed into 32 cells.

Mucus A sticky secretion.

Multigravida A woman in her second or subsequent pregnancy.

Multiple pregnancy The development of two or more babies. See also *Twins*.

Mutation A damaged genetic cell. This can occur naturally or, more commonly, as an effect of outside agents, such as radiation.

Narcotic A drug which induces a state of stupor. See also *Morphine*.

Nasogastric tube A pliable catheter passed into the stomach through the nose.

Nembutal See *Barbiturates*.

Neural tube defects Abnormalities of the central nervous system. See also *Anencephaly; Hydrocephalus; Spina bifida*.

Nicotine A highly poisonous substance present in tobacco. During pregnancy it enters the bloodstream of a woman who smokes, and affects the efficiency of the placenta, usually producing a low birthweight baby.

Nitrous oxide General anesthetic.

Nonstress tests Tests during pregnancy that do not produce fetal stress. See also *Invasive techniques*.

Notochord The cells which form the primitive nervous system.

Nucleus The central part or core of a cell which contains genetic information.

Occipito anterior The position of the baby in the uterus when the back of its head (the crown or occiput) is toward the mother's front (anterior).

Occipito posterior The position of the baby in the uterus when the back of its head is toward the mother's back.

Ovary One of the two female glands, set at the entrance of the fallopian tubes, which regularly produce eggs.

Oviduct See *Fallopian tube.*

Ovulation The production of the ripe egg by the ovary.

Oxygenate To saturate with oxygen.

Oxytocin A hormone secreted by the pituitary gland which stimulates uterine contractions and the milk glands in the breasts to produce milk.

Oxytocin challenge test A way of assessing the condition of the fetus and of the placenta, by which oxytocin is introduced into the mother's bloodstream and the reactions of the fetal heart to uterine contractions are recorded.

Palpation Feeling the parts of the baby through the mother's abdominal wall.

Paracervical Regional anesthesia sometimes used during labor, involving a series of local anesthetic injections around the cervix.

Partogram A chart recording the development of labor and condition of the fetus.

Pelvic floor The muscular structure set within the pelvis which supports the bladder and the uterus.

Pelvis The bones forming a girdle about the hips.

Penthrane A general anesthetic. See also *Anesthetic.*

Pentobarbital See *Barbiturates.*

Perinatal The period from 28 weeks gestation to one week following delivery.

Perineum The area surrounding the vagina and between the vagina and the rectum.

Pessary A vaginal suppository.

Phenothiazine Strong tranquilizers used in the treatment of nausea and vomiting. See also *Tranquilizers.*

Phototherapy Treatment by exposure to light, used in the treatment of jaundice.

Pitocin The synthetic form of oxytocin, used to induce or accelerate labor.

Pituitary gland A gland set just below the brain which, among other functions, secretes various hormones controlling the menstrual cycle. In late pregnancy it produces a hormone which stimulates the milk glands.

Placenta The organ which develops on the inner wall of the uterus and supplies the fetus with all its life supporting requirements and carries waste products to the mother's system.

Placental function tests Tests to assess the condition and efficiency of the placenta. See also *Estriol; Oxytocin challenge test.*

Placental insufficiency An inadequate life support for the fetus, resulting in a baby at special risk.

Placenta previa A condition where the placenta lies over the cervix. It can result in ante-partum hemorrhage. A woman with a complete placenta previa is delivered by Cesarean section.

Polyhydramnios An excess of amniotic fluid in the uterus.

Posterior See *Occipito posterior.*

Postmaturity The state of the fetus in an overdue pregnancy. The skin may be dry and peeling, and the fingernails may need cutting immediately after birth.

Postnatal After the birth.

Postpartum After the delivery.

PP See *Presenting part.*

Preeclampsia An illness in which a woman has high blood pressure, edema, albumin in the urine and often an excessive weight gain as well. See also *Eclampsia.*

Premature See *Preterm.*

''Prepping'' Procedures carried out by midwife to prepare woman for delivery.

Presentation The position of the fetus in the uterus before and during labor.

Presenting part That part of the fetus which is lying directly over the cervix.

Preterm A baby born before the 37th week of pregnancy and weighing less than $5\frac{1}{2}$ lb (2.5 kg).

Primigravida A woman having her first pregnancy.

Progesterone A hormone produced by the corpus luteum and then by the placenta.

Prostaglandins Natural substances, which stimulate the onset of labor contractions. Prostaglandin gel is used to soften the cervix and induce labor.

Psychoprophylaxis A method of preparation for childbirth. Also known as the Lamaze method.

Pubis The bones forming the front of the lower pelvis.

Puerperium The four weeks following delivery.

Pursestring (Shirodkar) suture Stitches passed through and around the cervix, and then drawn tight to support the uterus when the cervix is incompetent.

Pyelitis An infection of the kidneys. It is treated by a course of antibiotics.

Pyridoxine Vitamin B6.

Quickening The first noticeable movements of the fetus.

Rectus muscle The muscles running up the center of the abdomen.

REM Rapid eye movement in sleep, indicating mental activity.

Respiratory depression See *Depression, respiratory.*

Rhesus factor A distinguishing characteristic of the red blood corpuscles. All human beings have either Rhesus positive or Rhesus negative blood. If the mother is Rhesus negative and the fetus Rhesus positive severe complications and Rhesus disease (the destruction of the red corpuscles by antibodies) may occur unless prevented by anti-D gamma globulin.

Rooting The baby's instinctive searching for the nipple.

Rubella (German measles) A mild virus which may cause congenital abnormalities in the fetus if contracted by a woman during the first 12 weeks of pregnancy.

Sacrum The big bone at the base of the spine, forming the back of the pelvis.

Salicylate See *Aspirin.*

Scan (Screen) A way of building up a picture of an object by bouncing high frequency sound waves off it. The sonar or ultrasound scan is used during pregnancy to show the development of the fetus in the uterus. See also *Transducer.*

Senna Derivatives of the cassia plant, components of many laxatives.

Shirodkar See *Pursestring suture.*

Shoulder dystocia See *Dystocia, shoulder.*

Show A vaginal discharge of bloodstained mucus occurring before labor, resulting from the onset of cervical dilatation. Sign of labor.

Small for dates Babies who are born at the right time but for

some reason have not flourished in the uterus. See also *Placental insufficiency.*

Sonargram See *Doppler.*

Sperm (Spermatozoon) The male reproductive cell which fertilizes the egg.

Spina bifida A congenital neural tube defect, in which the fetal spinal cord forms outside the spinal column.

Spinal anesthetic An injection of anesthetic into the spinal cord.

Spontaneous abortion See *Abortion.*

Stanislavsky technique Acting exercises for increasing body awareness and muscle control.

Stasis of milk A reduction in the flow of milk from the milk glands.

Steroids Drugs used in the treatment of skin disorders, asthma, hay fever, rheumatism and arthritis. Because they alter the chemical balance of the metabolism they may cause fetal abnormalities if used extensively.

Stethoscope, fetal A large belled instrument placed against the pregnant woman's abdomen for the fetal heart to be heard.

Stillbirth The delivery of a dead baby after the 28th week of pregnancy.

Stool bulk producers Drugs to treat constipation.

Streptomycin A broad spectrum antibiotic which should not be taken in pregnancy. See also *Antibiotics.*

Stress tests Tests during pregnancy that cause stress to the fetus.

Stretch marks See *Striae.*

Striae Silvery lines that sometimes appear on the skin of the breasts, thighs and abdomen after the skin has been stretched during pregnancy.

Sulpha drugs See *Sulphonamides.*

Sulphonamides Chemicals sometimes used to combat infections. See also *Antibacterials.*

Supplementary feeding Additional bottles given a breastfed baby.

Surfactant A creamy fluid which reduces the surface tension of the lungs so that they do not stick together when deflated. Preterm babies may have breathing difficulties because the surfactant has not developed sufficiently.

Suture The surgical stitching together of a wound or tear.

Systolic pressure The blood pressure built up in the arteries when the heart is beating. It is the upper figure on any record. See also *Diastolic pressure.*

Tachycardia An abnormally fast heart rate in the fetus and newborn baby. This is a rate of above 160 beats per minute.

Telemetry A method of monitoring, using radio waves. See also *Electronic fetal monitoring.*

Teratogenic A general term for drugs which cause physical defects in the embryo.

Term The end of pregnancy: 40 weeks from the LMP.

Termination An artificially induced abortion before the end of the 28th week of pregnancy. Sometimes used as synonym for induction.

Tetracycline A wide spectrum antibiotic which should be avoided during pregnancy, as it can affect the fetal teeth and bones. See also *Antibiotics.*

Thrombosis A blood clot in the heart or blood vessels.

Thrush A yeast infection which can form in the mucous membranes of the mouth or genitals.

Thyroid gland A gland in the throat which produces hormones that control the metabolic rate.

Tochodynamometer A pressure gauge attached by a belt to the mother's abdomen to record contractions.

Touch relaxation A means of releasing muscular tension by resting the hand on tense areas and drawing out the tension from them.

Toxemia See *Preeclampsia* and *Eclampsia*.

Toxic Poisonous.

Toxoplasmosis, congenital Toxoplasmosis is a parasitic disease spread by cat feces. If it crosses the placenta during the first 12 weeks of pregnancy, it can cause blindness in the baby.

Tranquilizers Drugs used to calm a state of anxiety or tension without inducing unconsciousness. Tranquilizers, such as Valium, should be avoided. During labor they can cause fetal respiratory depression. Major tranquilizers (along with antihistamines and hypnotics, which are sometimes used for their tranquilizing properties) should also be avoided during pregnancy. See also *Barbiturates*.

Transducer An instrument which is sensitive to the echoes of very high frequency sound-waves bounced off the developing fetus, and which translates the information to build up an image on a television screen. This form of scan is known as ultrasound. See also *Scan*.

Transition A point between the first and second stages of labor when the cervix has dilated to between 7 and 8 cm.

Trial of labor A situation in which, although a Cesarean section seems necessary, the mother is allowed to go into labor in order to see if a natural delivery is possible.

Trilene See *Anesthetic*.

Twins The simultaneous development of two babies in the uterus, either as a result of the production of two eggs which are fertilized independently by two sperms—dizygotic or fraternal twins—or, more rarely, as a result of one fertilized egg dividing to produce monozygotic or identical twins.

Ultrasound See *Scan; Transducer*.

Umbilical cord The cord connecting the fetus to the placenta.

Undescended testicle A testicle which has failed to drop naturally from the lower abdomen into the scrotum.

Uterine action, incoordinate Irregular uterine contractions.

Uterine inertia Weak and ineffective uterine contractions.

Uterus (Womb) The hollow muscular female organ in which the fertile egg becomes embedded where it develops into the embryo and then the fetus, for the period of gestation.

Vacuum extractor An instrument, used as an alternative to forceps, which adheres to the baby's scalp by suction and, with the help of the mother's bearing down efforts, can be used to pull the baby out of the vagina.

Vagina The canal between the uterus and the external genitals. It receives the penis during intercourse and is the passage through which the baby is delivered.

Vernix A creamy substance which often covers the fetus whilst in the uterus, to protect it from the amniotic fluid.

Vertex presentation (VX) See *Cephalic presentation*.

Vistaril A non barbiturate hypnotic tranquilizer with antihistamine properties.

Vulva The external part of the female reproductive organs, including the labia and clitoris.

XX/XY chromosomes The chromosomes which genetically distinguish the female and male respectively.

Yolk sac The sac which stores the nutrients for the developing fertile egg.

Index

A

Acknowledgments

Dorling Kindersley would like to thank the following for their special assistance: Chris Meehan; David Ashby; Susan Berry; Sue Burt; Giovanni Caselli; Kate Duffield; Helen Dziemidko; Harry Pepper and the staff of City Engraving; Eleanor Enkin; Dr Murray Enkin; Daisy Hayes; Andrew Heritage; Ken Hone; Dr Meeks Joankins; Elaine and Jerry Kingett; Kevin Molloy; Mike Snaith and Phil Baskerville and the staff of MS Filmsetting; Negs Photographic Services; Frederick Ford of Radius; Helen Sampey.

The photograph on page 55 is reproduced courtesy of Cornell Medical Center, New York.

Photographer Camilla Jessel wishes to thank all the parents and parents-to-be who allowed themselves and their children to be photographed for this book—especially those who so generously agreed to share the experience of the birth of their babies.

She is also deeply grateful to all the staff of the Delivery Suite of the West Middlesex Hospital, Isleworth, for their warm cooperation and advice—equally the staff of the Special Care unit, the Antenatal Department and the Hounslow Community Midwife Service.

Artists

David Ashby
Giovanni Caselli
Andrew Farmer
Shian Hartshorn
Terri Lawlor
Miriam Mills
Kevin Molloy
Andrew Popkiewicz
Les Smith